Pushing the Limits with
iOS 5 Programming

Pushing the Limits with
iOS 5 Programming

ADVANCED APPLICATION DEVELOPMENT FOR APPLE iPHONE®, iPAD®, AND iPOD® TOUCH

Rob Napier and Mugunth Kumar

A John Wiley and Sons, Ltd, Publication

Dedication

To Neverwood. Thanks for your patience.
Rob

To my mother who shaped the first twenty years of my life
Mugunth

Publisher's Acknowledgements

Some of the people who helped bring this book to market include the following:

Editorial and Production

VP Consumer and Technology Publishing Director: Michelle Leete
Associate Director–Book Content Management: Martin Tribe
Associate Publisher: Chris Webb
Acquisitions Editor: Chris Katsaropolous
Assistant Editor: Ellie Scott
Development Editor: Tom Dinse
Copy Editor: Maryann Steinhart
Technical Editor: Mithilesh Kumar
Editorial Manager: Jodi Jensen
Senior Project Editor: Sara Shlaer
Editorial Assistant: Leslie Saxman

Marketing

Associate Marketing Director: Louise Breinholt
Marketing Executive: Kate Parrett

Composition Services

Compositor: Wiley Indianapolis Composition Services
Proofreaders: Laura Albert, Lindsay Amones, Melissa D. Buddendeck, Melissa Cossell
Indexer: Potomac Indexing, LLC

About the Authors

Rob Napier is a builder of tree houses, hiker, and proud father. He began developing for the Mac in 2005, and picked up iPhone development when the first SDK was released, working on products such as The Daily, PandoraBoy, and Cisco Mobile. He is a major contributor to Stack Overflow and maintains the *Cocoaphony* blog (cocoaphony.com).

Mugunth Kumar is an independent iOS developer based in Singapore. He graduated in 2009 and holds a Masters degree from Nanyang Technological University, Singapore, majoring in Information Systems. He writes about mobile development, software usability, and iOS-related tutorials on his blog (blog.mugunthkumar.com). Prior to iOS development he worked for Fortune 500 companies GE and Honeywell as a software consultant on Windows and .NET platforms. His core areas of interest include programming methodologies (Object Oriented and Functional), mobile development and usability engineering. If he were not coding, he would probably be found at some exotic place capturing scenic photos of Mother Nature.

About the Technical Editor

Mithilesh Kumar is a software engineer with a passion for user interface design, Internet protocols, and virtual worlds. He likes to prototype and build applications for iOS and Mac OS X platforms. He has extensive experience in developing UI and core components for telephony clients capable of voice, video, instant messaging, presence, and voicemail.

Mithilesh graduated with a Masters degree in Computer Science from Virginia Tech with emphasis on Human-Computer Interaction. While at graduate school, he co-authored several research papers in the area of user interfaces, computer graphics and network protocols.

Authors' Acknowledgements

Rob thanks his family for giving up many evenings that he spent in the basement writing, hacking, and otherwise failing to come upstairs. Mugunth thanks his parents and friends for their support while writing this book. Thanks to Wiley for making this book possible. It went extremely well, particularly due to Sara Shlaer's continual guiding hand. Thanks to Mithilesh Kumar who made sure what we said was true, and Tom Dinse who made sure that it was intelligible. Thanks to Chris Katsaropoulos for first reaching out and getting this project rolling. Thanks to the Apple engineers who answer questions on development forums on all those still-under-NDA issues, and the whole iOS developer community who share so much. And special thanks to Steve Jobs for building toys we could build a career around.

Contents

Introduction

Apple has a history of alternating its releases between user-focus and developer-focus. The good news about iOS 5 is that it's all about the developers. The addition of Automatic Reference Counting (ARC) alone is worth the upgrade for developers. In one move, Apple has eliminated the number one cause of crashes in iOS applications, while making the code easier to write and faster to run. Moving to ARC is the single best thing you can do for your application. It's the most important Objective-C feature since the autorelease pool.

But iOS 5 adds many more features for the developer. From iCloud to automatic data protection, the operating system now takes care of more of the hard problems, letting developers focus on making the best apps.

Most visible to developers is the new Xcode. Some of it is better, some of it is just different, and some of it will make you crazy. It's the new game in town, though, and everyone needs to get used to it. This book will help you figure it out.

If you're ready to take on the newest Apple release and push your application to the limits, this is the book to get you there.

Who This Book Is For

This is not an introductory book. There are many books out there that will teach you Objective-C and take you step by step through Interface Builder. This is not that book. This book assumes that you have a little experience with iOS. Maybe you're self-taught, or maybe you've taken a class. You've hopefully written at least most of an application, even if you haven't submitted it yet. If you're ready to move beyond the basics, to learn the best practices and the secrets that the authors have learned from practical experience writing real applications, then this is the book for you.

This book also is not just a list of recipes. There's plenty of sample code here, but the focus is on learning how to design, code, and maintain great iOS apps. A lot of this book is about *why* rather than just *how*. You'll learn about as much about design patterns and writing reusable code as about syntax and new frameworks.

All the examples use Xcode 4. If you're not comfortable with Xcode 4 yet, don't worry. Chapter 2 is devoted to getting you up to speed.

What This Book Covers

The iOS platforms always move forward, and so does this book. Most of the examples here require iOS 5. All examples use Automatic Reference Counting. Except in a very few places, this book will not cover backward compatibility. If you've been shipping code long enough to need backward compatibility, you probably know how to deal with it. This book is about writing the best-possible apps using the best features available.

This book focuses on the iPhone 4 and iPad 2. Most topics here are applicable to the original iPad, iPod touch, iPhone 3GS, and Apple TV. At the time of writing the iPhone 5 and iPad 3 have not been released, but everything here should apply to them as well. Chapter 12 is devoted to dealing with the differences between the platforms.

How This Book Is Structured

iOS has an extremely rich set of tools, from high-level frameworks like UIKit to very low-level tools like Core Text. Often, there are several ways to achieve a goal. As a developer, how do you pick the right tool for the job?

This book separates the everyday from the special purpose, helping you pick the right solution to each problem. You'll learn why each framework exists, how the frameworks relate to each other, and when to choose one over another. Then you'll learn how to make the most of each framework for solving its type of problem.

There are four parts to this book, moving from the most common tools to the most powerful:

Part I: What's New?

If you're familiar with iOS 4, then this section quickly introduces you to the new features of iOS 5.

- **Chapter 1: The Brand New Stuff** — iOS adds a lot of new features, and here you get a quick overview of what's available.

- **Chapter 2: Getting Comfortable with Xcode 4** — Apple recently redesigned the Xcode interface, and it can take some getting used to. This chapter shows you how to get the most out of it.

Part II: Getting the Most Out of Everyday Tools

As an iOS developer, you've encountered a wide variety of common tools, from notifications to table views to animation layers. But are you using these tools to their full potential? In this part, you learn the best practices in Cocoa development from seasoned developers.

- **Chapter 3: Everyday Objective-C**—If you're ready to move to the next level in Objective-C, this chapter introduces you to the tools experienced developers use every day to improve application design, maintainability, and reusability.

- **Chapter 4: Hold On Loosely: Cocoa Design Patterns**—Cocoa relies on a number of common and consistent design patterns. You learn what they are so you can solve problems the same way Apple does.

- **Chapter 5: Getting Table Views Right**—Table views are perhaps the most complex and commonly used UI element in iOS. They are simple and elegant in design, but confusing to developers who don't understand how they work. You learn how to use them correctly and to solve some special problems like infinite scrolling.

- **Chapter 6: Better Drawing**—Custom drawing is intimidating to many new developers, but it's a key part of building beautiful and fast user interfaces. You'll discover the available drawing options from UIKit to Core Graphics, and how to optimize them to look their best while keeping them fast.

■ **Chapter 7: Layers Like an Onion: Core Animation**—iOS devices have incredible facilities for animation. With a powerful GPU and the highly optimized Core Animation, you can build engaging, exciting, and intuitive interfaces. In this chapter, you go beyond the basics and learn the secrets of animation.

■ **Chapter 8: Tackling Those Pesky Errors**—You try to write perfect code, but sometimes things go wrong. How your application reacts to the unexpected is what separates decent apps from extraordinary apps. You'll learn the common patterns for error handling, how to log, and how to make your code more resilient against the unexpected.

Part III: The Right Tool for the Job

There are tools that are part of nearly every application, and there are tools that you only need from time to time. In this section, you learn about those tools and techniques that are a little more specialized.

■ **Chapter 9: Controlling Multitasking**—Multitasking is an important part of many applications, and you learn how to do multiple things at once while your application is running and when your application is in the background.

■ **Chapter 10: REST for the Weary**—REST-based services are a mainstay of modern applications, and you learn how to best implement them in iOS.

■ **Chapter 11: Batten the Hatches with Security Services**—User security and privacy are paramount today, and you learn how to protect your application and user data from attackers with the keychain, certificates, and encryption.

■ **Chapter 12: Running on Multiple iPlatforms and iDevices**—The iOS landscape gets more complex every year with iPod touch, iPhone, iPad, Apple TV, and a steady stream of new editions. It's not enough just to write once, run everywhere. You need your applications to be their *best* everywhere. You'll learn how to adapt your apps to the hardware and get the most out of every platform.

■ **Chapter 13: Internationalization and Localization**—While you may want to focus on a single market today, there are small things you can do to ease the transition to a global market tomorrow. Save money and headaches later, without interrupting today's development.

■ **Chapter 14: Selling Past the Sale with In App Purchases**—In App Purchases are still an untapped market for many developers. Users like the add-on content, and developers love the extra revenue. You learn the best ways to make this important feature a reality in your application.

Part IV: Pushing the Limits

This section is what this book is all about. You've learned the basics. You've learned the everyday. Now push the limits with the most advanced tools available. You learn the ins and outs of deep iOS.

■ **Chapter 15: Cocoa's Biggest Trick: Key-Value Observing**—Many of Apple's most powerful frameworks rely on KVO for their performance and flexibility. You learn how to leverage the flexibility and speed of KVO, as well as the trick that makes it so transparent.

■ **Chapter 16: Think Different: Blocks and Functional Programming**—Many developers are still absorbing the addition of blocks to Objective-C. They're valuable for interacting with Apple frameworks, but they also open new ways of thinking about your program. Embrace a new style, and maximize its benefits in your next project.

- **Chapter 17: Going Offline**—Network programming is hard, but even harder is providing a seamless offline experience. Learn how to best cache your data and integrate it into your network engine.

- **Chapter 18: Fancy Text Layout**—From UIKit to Core Text, iOS is full of ways to display text. There's no perfect solution for displaying rich text in iOS, so it's important to learn the trade-offs so you can choose the right solution and use it correctly.

- **Chapter 19: Building a (Core) Foundation**—When you want the most powerful frameworks available on iOS, you're going to want the Core frameworks like Core Graphics, Core Animation, and Core Text. All of these rely on Core Foundation. In this chapter you learn how to work Core Foundation data types so you can leverage everything iOS has to offer.

- **Chapter 20: Deep Objective-C**—When you're ready to pull back the curtain on how Objective-C really works, this is the chapter for you. You learn how to use the Objective-C runtime directly to dynamically modify classes and methods. You also learn how Objective-C method calls are dispatched to C function calls, and how you can take control of the system to extend your programs in incredible ways.

You can skip around in this book to focus on the topics you need most. Each chapter stands alone, except for those that require Core Foundation data objects (particularly Core Graphics, Core Animation, and Core Text). Those chapters direct you to Chapter 19, "Building a (Core) Foundation," when you need that information.

What You Need to Use This Book

All examples in this book were developed with Xcode 4.2 on Mac OS X 10.7 and iOS 5. You need an Apple developer account to access most of the tools and documentation, and you need a developer license to run applications on your iOS device. Visit `http://developer.apple.com/programs/ios` to sign up.

Most of the examples in this book will run in the iOS Simulator that comes with Xcode 4.2. You can use the iOS Simulator without an Apple developer license.

There are few differences between Xcode 4.2 on Mac OS X 10.6 and 10.7, so all examples should work under 10.6.

Finding Apple Documentation

Apple provides extensive documentation at its website and within Xcode. The URLs change frequently and are often very long. This book refers to Apple documents by title rather than by URL. To find documents in Xcode, press Cmd-Option-? or click Help → Documentation and API Reference. In the Documentation Organizer, click the Search icon, type in the name of the document, and then select the document from the search results. See Figure 1 for an example of how to search for the *Coding Guidelines for Cocoa*.

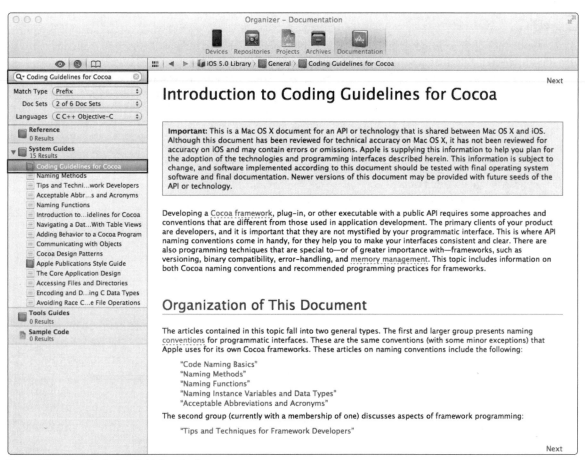

Figure 1 Searching for Coding Guidelines for Cocoa

To find documents at the Apple developer site, visit `developer.apple.com`, click Member Center and log in. Select the iOS Dev Center, and enter the document title in the Search Developer search box.

The online documentation is generally identical to the Xcode documentation. You may receive results for both iOS and Mac. Make sure to choose the iOS version. Many iOS documents are copies of their Mac counterparts, and occasionally include function calls or constants that are not available on iOS. This book guides you about which features are available on iOS.

Source Code

As you work through the examples in this book, you may choose either to type in all the code manually or to use the source code files that accompany the book. All of the source code used in this book is available for download at www.wrox.com/go/ptl/ios5programming. For example, you will find the following sample code online in the Chapter 18 folder, in the SimpleLayout project, and the CoreTextLabel.m file:

CoreTextLabel.m (SimpleLayout)

```
-  (id)initWithFrame:(CGRect)frame {
   if ((self = [super initWithFrame:frame])) {
     CGAffineTransform
     transform = CGAffineTransformMakeScale(1, -1);
     CGAffineTransformTranslate(transform,
                                 0, -self.bounds.size.height);
     self.transform = transform;
     self.backgroundColor = [UIColor whiteColor];
   }
   return self;
 }
```

Some source code snippets shown in the book are not comprehensive and are meant to help you understand the chapter. For those instances, you should refer to the files available on the website for the complete source code.

Part I

What's New?

Chapter 1

The Brand New Stuff

In 2007, the late Steve Jobs took the stage at Macworld and proclaimed that software running on iPhone was at least five years ahead of the competition. Since its initial release, Apple has been iterating the operating system year after year, and has even added two new devices, the iPad and Apple TV, to the list of products capable of running it. As the operating system was customized to run on more devices than just the iPhone, it was rebranded as iOS. Today, it's almost 5 years old, and iOS 5 is easily the biggest update to iOS since the original launch, possibly making the software five years ahead of the competition again.

This book is about programming with iOS 5. Targeting intermediate to advanced iOS developers, this book, unlike most others, covers advanced topics of iOS development. Rather than learning about frameworks and the features available on the iOS SDK, you learn about how to make the best use of those features to help push your apps to the next level. This chapter briefly describes the new features covered in detail in the book and tells you the chapters in which they are discussed.

The History of iOS

The second version, iPhone OS 2, was the first to have a public SDK. From then on, with every release of the operating system, Apple introduced several major features and a lot more minor API changes. This section briefly describes the history of the iOS. The remaining sections in the chapter provide an overview of what's new in iOS 5.

iPhone OS 3 brought Core Data from Mac to iPhone. Other additions include Apple Push Notification Service, External Accessory Kit, In App Purchases through the `StoreKit.framework`, in app email sheets, the `MapKit.framework` that allows developers to embed Google Maps into their apps, read-only access to the iPod library, and keychain data sharing. OS 3.1 added video editor support, a minor update. iPhone OS 3.2 added Core Text and gesture recognizers, file sharing, and PDF generation support, another minor (yet so major) update. OS 3.2 also added a whole new product, iPad, support for developing apps that run on iPad, and universal apps that run on iPad (3.2) and iPhone (3.1.3). 3.2 was iPad only and didn't run on iPhone or iPod touch devices.

iPhone OS 4 (rebranded as iOS 4) introduced much-awaited multitasking support, local notifications, read-only access to calendar (Event Kit framework, `EventKit.framework`), blocks, Grand Central Dispatch (GCD), in app message composer sheets (SMS), and Retina display support. This version was iPhone only and didn't support developing apps for iPad. A minor update, iOS 4.2, unified iPhone and iPad operating systems.

What's New

iOS 5 introduces several important features like iCloud, Automatic Reference Counting (ARC), Storyboards, built-in Twitter framework, and several other minor features. The next few sections introduce you to the key features added to iOS 5 and the chapters in which they are discussed in detail and where I provide guidance about how to push your apps to the next level.

iCloud

iCloud is a new cloud service provided by Apple. iCloud differs from competing similar offerings in that it's more a cloud-based *service* than cloud-based *storage*. Developers have been using third-party services for synchronizing data across multiple devices. Dropbox is the most popular of these services; however, even Dropbox API version 0 (the latest version as of this writing), doesn't support conflict handling, something that's critical for data integrity. While Dropbox has conflict resolution, it's not exposed to developers via their API. iCloud, on the other hand, supports file storage and has conflict resolution built into the iOS 5 SDK.

iCloud also supports storing key-value data on the cloud, which is good enough for apps that need settings and other similar data to be kept in sync.

iCloud is not just a hard disk on the cloud. Think of iCloud as a cloud-based service that just happens to support data storage.

iOS 5 adds several new APIs for adding iCloud support:

- `UIDocument` (very similar to its kin, `NSDocument`, on Mac)
- `UIManagedDocument`, for managing your Core Data storage
- Additions to `NSFileManager` to move and restore files from iCloud

iCloud is covered in detail in Chapter 17.

LLVM 3.0 Compiler

LLVM (Low Level Virtual Machine) is a new compiler project partly funded by Apple. While technically not a part of iOS 5, developers should be equipped with the knowledge of the new features available in LLVM. Improved auto complete and speedier compilation are just a part of LLVM's new features. In Chapter 2 you learn about the features of LLVM and how LLVM augments Xcode 4's features.

Automatic Reference Counting

Another important feature of iOS 5 is *Automatic Reference Counting* (ARC). It is a compiler-level feature provided by the new LLVM compiler. This means that you can use it without increasing the minimum SDK support to iOS 5. ARC can be used in apps targeting iOS 4 onward, and Xcode 4.2 also provides support for migrating your code to use ARC using the Convert to Objective-C ARC tool. With the new LLVM compiler slowly becoming mainstream, ARC will supercede the current retain/release memory management.

> Automatic Reference Counting is *not* like garbage collection offered on Mac OS X from version 10.5 (Leopard). Garbage collection is automatic memory management. This means that developers don't have to write a matching release for every retain statement. The compiler automatically inserts them for you.

ARC adds two new lifetime qualifiers—`strong` and `weak`—and it also imposes new rules, such as that you can no longer invoke release, retain on any object. This applies to custom `dealloc` methods as well. When using ARC, your custom `dealloc` methods should only release resources (files or ports) and not instance variables.

ARC is covered in detail in Chapter 3.

Storyboards—Draw Your Flow

Storyboards is a new way to design your user interface. Prior to iOS 5 you used Interface Builder nib files to define your UI one view controller at a time. With Storyboards, you can define in one file the complete UI flow of your app, including interaction among the different view controllers.

You can use Storyboards to define all view controllers in your app. You don't have to create multiple Storyboards or worry about performance. The Interface Builder build tool automatically splits your storyboard file into parts and loads it individually at runtime without affecting performance.

On iOS 5, storyboards replace `MainWindow.xib` nib file (and possibly every other view controller's nib file). The new project template in Xcode 4.2 helps in creating storyboards. You can also add a storyboard to your old projects and optionally make it the main storyboard by adding an entry to the `Info.plist` file.

> Storyboards, unlike ARC, is an iOS 5-specific feature, and using Storyboards means that you need to raise your minimum supported OS to iOS 5.

You will learn more about storyboards in Chapter 5.

UIKit Customization—Appearance Proxy

Apple (and even Microsoft) has always been against UI customization, or *theming*. Its reasoning is that theming makes it difficult for users to understand the user interface. The Web, on the other hand, has made a huge revolution on this front and this has had an effect on the latest release of iOS as well. Beginning with iOS 5, some native apps like Reminders get some rich customization. With iOS 5, most properties of UIKit elements can be customized. This includes `backgroundColor`, `tintColor`, and a lot more. Customization is supported by a `UIView` subclass if it implements the `UIAppearance` protocol. The protocol also allows customization based on the contained view. For example, you can have a different tint when a custom view of yours is within a navigation bar.

Chapter 5 covers UI customization.

Twitter Framework and Accounts Framework

iOS 5 integrates Twitter experience right into the OS. This means sending a tweet from your app is as easy as sending an email using an in app email sheet. The framework also handles authentication for you, which means you no longer need to do the oAuth/xAuth authentication yourself. Twitter framework on iOS 5 integrates with Accounts framework to provide account authentication. As of this writing, Twitter is the only third-party authentication system supported natively on iOS 5. But, by looking at the decoupled design of Twitter framework and Accounts framework, there is a possibility that additional services might be introduced later on. While there are some advantages of using these frameworks, it's still an iOS 5-specific feature, which means that using it requires you to limit your app to devices running iOS 5 and later. Additionally, when you send out a tweet through iOS, you will not be able to customize the sender (via text). As such, your tweet will be sent as "via iOS." (See Figure 1-1.)

© Twitter 2011

Figure 1-1 Screenshot from Twitter.com showing the "via" text

When you create a new application on Twitter, you can name it so when you tweet using this application's credentials, its name shows up in the "via" text. The built-in `Twitter.framework` on iOS 5 doesn't allow setting this text, so if you are considering using Twitter for increasing your brand's reach, you may have to evaluate branding versus ease of development.

Adding Twitter experience to your app with the new `Twitter.Framework` is as easy as sending an in app email. This differs from an app email in one aspect. Instead of providing a delegate callback, the `TWTweetComposeViewController` of `Twitter.Framework` provides a `completionHandler`. Chapter 16 shows you an example of this in action.

Other New Features

In addition to the "big" features discussed in the preceding sections, iOS 5 also adds several other features, including dedicated support for magazine apps, a native image processing library, AirPlay mirroring support, and new controls added to `UIKit.framework`.

Newsstand Kit

Newspaper or magazine apps can make use of the `NewsstandKit.framework` to deliver digital content. Although it was technically possible to do something similar with iOS 4, iOS 5 introduces several new APIs to enable content for the latest release to be downloaded in the background. Additionally it also enables publishers to provide a cover art image (front cover) for their magazine instead of an icon. Apps developed using this framework appear within the Newsstand app and display the cover art instead of the app icon.

Core Image for Image Processing

Camera apps can use features in Core Image to apply image processing filters. The classes `CIImage` and `CIFilter` add basic image-editing functions like cropping, rotation (affine transform), and color inversion, to advanced features like gamma correction, white point adjustment, false color, sepia toning, temperature and tint correction, and many more that would be present in any entry-level image editor. This feature of iOS 5 will be tremendously useful for camera-enhancement apps that compete with apps like Instagram or Camera+. iPhone camera is already the most popular camera on Flickr. This framework will take it even further.

Core Image for Feature Detection

Core Image has another important element: feature detection. At WWDC 2011, Apple demonstrated a feature of Photo Booth that tracks the location of a face and adorns it with birds circling the head. With Core Image, you can add such features with very little programming effort. The class `CIDetector` has a convenient `featuresInImage:` method that returns a list of `CIFeature` objects detected in the given image.

Core Image is discussed in Chapter 6.

Other Minor Enhancements

iOS 5 adds many other minor enhancements like AirPlay video support, mirroring (which can be disabled by your app if you are showing protected content); better document support; improvements in data protection (Chapter 11); a new control, `UIStepper`; capability to add a password entry field to the UIAlertView just like the AppStore password prompt; a new `UIPageViewController` for creating page curl effects like iBooks; and much more. All these major and minor enhancements together make iOS 5 the biggest enhancement since its inception.

Summary

Adoption rates of iOS have always been way ahead of the competition. A couple of years ago, when iPhone OS 3.0 was launched, adoption rates were partly hindered on iPod touch because the upgrade cost $10. However, Apple soon made it free and adoption rates increased. Similarly, when Apple released iOS 4, the adoption rate was initially slow because of performance issues on older phones such as iPhone 3G and the original iPhone (and equivalent iPod touches). Some features—mainly multitasking—were also not available for older devices. Nevertheless, the latest iOS usually gets adopted on more than 90 percent of devices within the first two months of launch.

With iOS 5, adoption rates should be the fastest ever for the following reasons. First, the update is free for all devices, unlike iPhone OS 3. Second, unlike iOS 4, iOS 5 doesn't make older devices (the iPhone 3GS) run slower. Finally, for end users, cleaner notifications, iTunes wi-fi sync, and iMessage are killer features that should accelerate iOS 5 adoption.

All this means that you should start using every iOS 5 feature as soon as possible to get your app to shine in all its glory. Features like iCloud and UIKit customizations alone should be reason enough to update your apps to iOS 5. That said, the next chapters start you on your iOS 5 journey.

Further Reading

Apple Documentation

The following documents are available in the iOS Developer Library at `developer.apple.com` or through the Xcode Documentation and API Reference.

iCloud

What's New in iOS 5

Twitter Framework

Accounts Framework

Other Resources

How is a file conflict detected using the API - Dropbox forums
`http://forums.dropbox.com/topic.php?id=40492`

Chapter 2

Getting Comfortable with Xcode 4

Apple officially announced Xcode 4 at WWDC 2010 (June 2010), and the beta version was available to attendees. It was in beta for quite a while (around 9 months) and a Gold Master was made available through iOS/Mac developer center in February 2011. Weeks later, in March, Xcode 4 was officially released and developers who subscribe to the iOS or Mac developer programs were able to get it for free. Others were able to buy it from the Mac App Store.

Xcode 4 is a completely rewritten IDE (integrated development environment) replacing Xcode 3. The major features include, but are not limited to, single window editing, navigators, integrated Interface Builder, an integrated Git version control system, and *schemes* (a new way to configure and share build settings in your product). You learn in detail about every major feature in this chapter.

Xcode 4 features are not just skin deep—they come with some huge compiler-level changes as well. The LLVM compiler is the new brain behind Xcode. Apple made LLVM-GCC the default compiler in the original version of Xcode. Beginning with Xcode 4.0 and in the version that is released with iOS 5 (Xcode 4.2), LLVM 3.0 is the default compiler; it uses Clang as its front end. Using Clang as the front end over GCC has several advantages, and several new features of Xcode 4 were added because of this change. Because Apple is moving from GCC to LLVM, you should know how to harness the power of the new compiler to increase your coding and debugging speed, and how to use the IDE to be more productive. The most important feature of the LLVM compiler is better and faster compilation with the Clang front end, which provides better code completion support.

This chapter covers the important features of the IDE, the new features offered by the LLVM compiler, the built-in integrated version control system, schemes (new to Xcode 4), writing readable and commentable project configuration files, and finally, the features of the new Xcode 4 Organizer.

Getting to Know the New User Interface

Xcode 4 features a whole new iTunes-like user interface (UI). The toolbar is gone in favor of iTunes-like Play/Stop buttons. The build setting chooser is gone in favor of the new schemes selector. There's a new LED-like status display similar to iTunes. Developers who are used to Xcode 3 will feel at home once they know where things are, what has been removed, and what has been superseded. You'll welcome the new additions and actually be more productive than ever. This section helps you bridge the gap between Xcode 3 and Xcode 4.

This section covers the six most important changes to Xcode 4. The first important change is the new navigators. There are seven navigators that can be accessed by clicking the buttons highlighted in Figure 2-1. They can also be accessed via the shortcut keys Cmd-1 to Cmd-7.

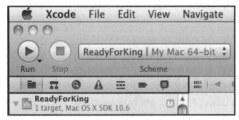

Figure 2-1 The Xcode navigator items

The same navigators can be accessed from the Xcode's View menu item as shown in Figure 2-2.

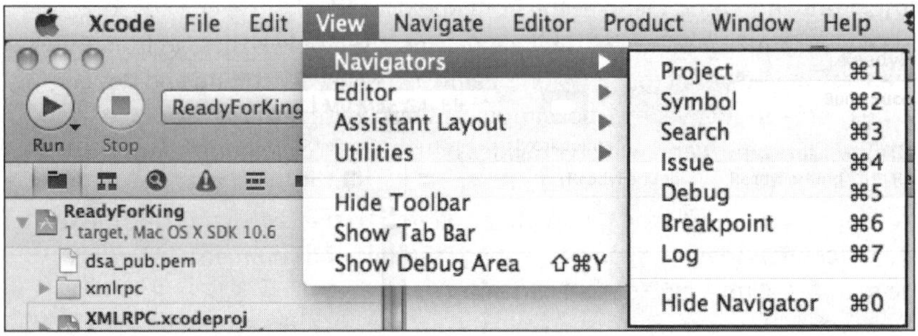

Figure 2-2 Accessing the new navigators from the menu bar

The first view in the Navigators area is the project navigator. Previously, this was the Groups and Files list. From the Groups and Files list you were able to add frameworks and edit the target's properties. With Xcode 4, however, this functionality is moved to the project and build settings editor view. The Xcode 4 workspace pane can now edit more types of files than just Objective-C or property list files, and the project and build settings editor just happens to be one such editor. You can access the build settings editor by selecting the project file from the project navigator. Figure 2-3 shows Xcode 4 project navigator.

Figure 2-3 Xcode project navigator view

The subsequent navigators are Symbol, Search, Issue, Debug, Breakpoint, and Log. You look at them in detail later in this chapter.

Tabbed Editor

The second major change is the new tabbed editor. Unlike its predecessor, Xcode 4 supports opening multiple tabs within the same window. This means that you will spend less time searching for the window that displays your source file. Figure 2-4 shows Xcode 4's tabbed editor in action.

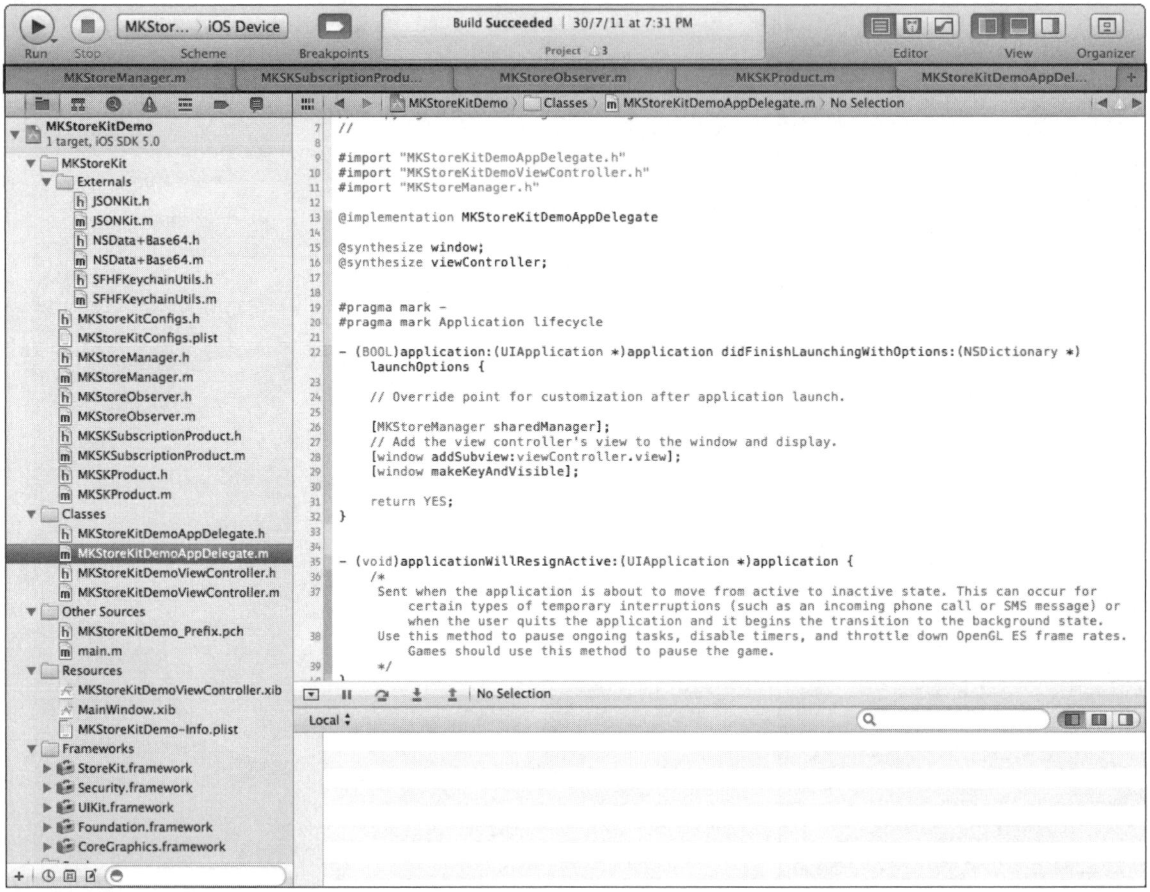

Figure 2-4 Xcode 4 window showing a several opened tabs

The tabbed editor in Xcode 4 behaves differently from tabbed editors in, for example, Eclipse, Visual Studio, or TextMate. Think of Xcode 4's tabs as virtual workspaces instead of just file editors. The navigator pane's file selection and search criteria are preserved when you switch back and forth between tabs. I recommend opening three to four tabs, each showing a related group of files. For example, you can use one tab to show your model classes, use another tab for your view controllers, a third tab for Interface Builder files, and maybe, if you use Core Data, use a fourth tab for showing Core Data-related files. Use tabs to make the workspace suit your thought process or workflow. Going to work on your Core Data files? Switch to the Core Data tab. Going to work on Interface Builder? Switch to the Interface Builder tab.

Changes to Key Bindings

The third major change is to key bindings. Xcode 4 has changed most of its keyboard shortcuts, which means you have to learn those quick shortcut keys again. Three commonly used shortcuts for debugging are changed to F6 (Step over), F7 (Step into), and F8 (Step out). Another commonly used shortcut that has been changed is for switching between header and source code counterparts. Xcode 3 used Cmd-*Opt*-Up Arrow; Xcode 4 uses Cmd-*Ctrl*-Up Arrow. The shortcut for *Build and Run*, which was Cmd-Return, is now Cmd-R.

For a good, comprehensive list of keyboard shortcuts, I recommend Cocoa Samurai's list, available for download at `http://cocoasamurai.blogspot.com/2011/03/xcode-4-keyboard-shortcuts-now.html`, and another by The Pragmatic Studio, available at `http://pragmaticstudio.com/media/Xcode4Shortcuts.pdf`.

Project Settings Editor

The fourth major change is the new project settings editor. In Xcode 3 you normally edit your project settings by Cmd-clicking your target from the Groups and Files list and choosing Edit. This has been completely revamped and moved to the project settings editor. The project settings editor also allows you to edit your build settings and other commonly accessed functions like the `NSZombieEnabled` and `GuardMalloc` options. Furthermore, adding additional frameworks to your product and passing command line arguments are all now a part of this build settings panel of the project settings editor.

Integrated Version Control

The fifth major change is the supported integrated version control system. Xcode 3 supported Subversion (SVN), Perforce, and Concurrent Versions System (CVS) for versioning your source code. Xcode 4 removes support for Perforce and CVS and adds Git. Later in this chapter you learn how to get the best out of your version control system.

Workspaces

The sixth major change is the addition of workspaces to projects. In Xcode 3, the top level of your app is the project. In Xcode 4 you can create a workspace and add multiple projects within it. For example, if you are writing a Mac + iOS app, you can share a wealth of code. Instead of manually copying and pasting code, you can extract the common code into a separate static library project and add it to the workspace. The primary advantage of a workspace is *implicit dependencies*. This means that when you build your Mac app (or iOS app), Xcode 4 automatically detects that it's dependent on your static library project and builds it first, without you explicitly requesting it to do so.

All in One Window

Unlike Xcode 3, Xcode 4 is a single window IDE like Eclipse or Visual Studio. Every file you use in your project can be opened without "switching" to it using Mac's Exposé. With full screen editing in Lion, you will appreciate the single window IDE and find yourself spending less time switching or searching for a window.

The IDE, as you saw earlier in this chapter, consists of a set of navigators, a workspace area, and the utility area. There are seven navigators that replace the functionality of the Groups and Files view.

The workspace area is where you edit your files, which can be either source code or plist or even Interface Builder (IB) files. There are three different kinds of editors: the Standard editor that you use for editing files, the Assistant editor for editing files related to the current file in Standard editor, and a Versions editor that shows the version history of a file.

The Utility area is akin to the Inspector pane found on most other applications. Below the Utility area is the library from where you can drag user interface elements into your IB or code snippets into your source code. Let's take a closer look at the different navigators available in Xcode 4.

Navigating the Navigators

Seven navigator panes are built into Xcode 4. These features were also present in Xcode 3 (in the Groups and Files view), but are presented in a more meaningful way in Xcode 4.

> In Xcode 3, there used to be a single view—the Groups and Files view—where you did pretty much everything. You chose the file to edit, edited project settings, added frameworks, accessed breakpoints and debug logs, and a lot more all from the same view. Xcode 4 groups these actions into seven different navigators.

All navigators have a filter and scope box (shown in Figure 2-5) that can be accessed using Cmd-Opt-J. This shortcut puts the focus on the filter and scope box below the navigator from where you can search for a project file. The keyboard shortcut works for all navigators, so if you are in, say, the symbol navigator, you can use this to quickly filter symbols. The filter box might have additional buttons to restrict the scope, and sometimes (as in the debug navigator) it might be replaced with a UI that looks different but offers the same functionality.

> You can press the shortcut key Cmd-Opt-J to quickly jump to the filter and scope box.

Navigators provide a clear separation of duties on the UI. For example, there is a dedicated navigator for breakpoints, a dedicated navigator for issues, and another for logs. Although it might be difficult to switch to the new, separate navigators, you will appreciate them once you get accustomed to them.

Some features, like the capability to create smart groups, were dropped probably because few people use them. However, if you have a project in Xcode 3 that uses smart groups, opening it in Xcode 4 and saving it doesn't remove them from the project file. So when you open the project again on Xcode 3, you will still see your smart groups.

Project Navigator

The project navigator is equivalent to the Groups and Files view in Xcode 3. As its name suggests, the project navigator helps you locate your source code files, frameworks, and targets. Similar to Xcode 3, the project navigator also serves as a source code control UI. This means that when you add files to the project navigator, they are automatically added to your source control (if you use one) and the project navigator also updates the UI with the files' source control status.

Figure 2-5 Xcode navigator showing the search and scope bar

Symbol Navigator

You can jump to the symbol navigator with the Cmd-2 shortcut. The symbol navigator makes it easy to locate a specific symbol or class in your project. The Clang front end of the LLVM compiler integrates well with Xcode 4 and has made it faster to browse through symbols in the project.

Search Navigator

The search navigator is functionally exactly the same as the Xcode 3's Find and Replace feature. You can access this navigator with the traditional Cmd-Shift-F shortcut or the navigator shortcut Cmd-3.

Issue Navigator

When you build your project, compiler warnings, error messages, or analyzer warnings appear on the issue navigator. The issue navigator on Xcode 4 is clear of build log messages, unlike Xcode 3's equivalent debug view. In Xcode 4, build logs are moved to a separate navigator called the log navigator, which maintains every build log in chronological order. You can access this using the navigator shortcut Cmd-4.

Debug Navigator

The debug panel in Xcode 3, which you access by pressing Cmd-Shift-Y, is equivalent to Xcode 4's debug navigator. You can access the debug navigator in Xcode 4 using the navigator shortcut Cmd-5. The most important addition is the scope slider. Instead of the filter and scope search box present in other navigators, the debug navigator uses a scope slider. Drag the scope slider to customize your scope preference.

Breakpoint Navigator

The sixth navigator is the breakpoint navigator. On Xcode 3, this was managed in a separate window. The nifty addition here is the ability to quickly add a symbolic breakpoint or an exception breakpoint. You can access the breakpoint navigator using the shortcut Cmd-6.

> **A noteworthy feature of the breakpoint navigator is the ability to share your breakpoints with co-workers. From the breakpoint navigator, Cmd-Click the project file and click Share Breakpoints.**

Log Navigator

On Xcode 3, logs can be either configured to either clear themselves for every build or continue to add to the current project log. On Xcode 4, this is no longer the case. With the log navigator, every build gets its own log entry and you can even search for entries in a log that was created several builds ago. You can access the log navigator using the shortcut Cmd-7.

Help from Your Assistant

Xcode 4 has three main editors, and they are akin to multiwindow document editing present in other competing IDEs. The two editors that augment Xcode 4's Standard editor are the Assistant editor and the Versions editor. The best thing about the Assistant editor is that, when you turn in on, it intelligently knows the most relevant file to the file you are currently working with.

For example, when you are editing a Core Data model, turning on Assistant editor opens the corresponding Core Data's model file. Similarly, when you are editing an Interface Builder file, it opens the corresponding header file.

A common action like adding an `IBAction` declaration in your header and coming back to the Interface Builder to connect it can be easily done within the same window using the Assistant editor.

Integrated Interface Builder

Prior to Xcode 4, Interface Builder was a standalone application, and the most common mistake a programmer would make was failing to sync Interface Builder and Xcode properly. For example, forgetting to save an Interface Builder connection could crash your app at runtime. Additionally, the very fact that there are two applications for writing iOS apps confuses developers coming from an Eclipse or Visual Studio background. Those difficulties are in the past because Xcode 4 integrates Interface Builder right into the main IDE, and it's now very easy to sync your user interface with the controller code.

Interface Builder Panels

Interface Builder on Xcode 3 usually has multiple windows floating around. At a bare minimum, you have the main document window, the library panel, the inspector, and the actual user interface view. In Xcode 4, the library and inspector are brought into the utility area. The document window is docked to the left. Figure 2-6 shows a classical Interface Builder file open in Xcode 4.

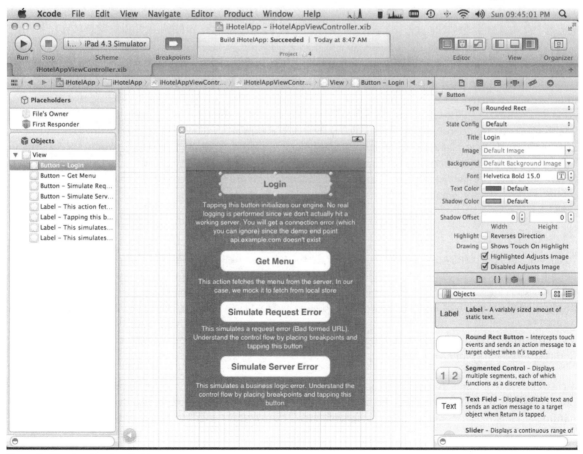

Figure 2-6 Xcode 4 Interface Builder

The left pane now contains the objects in the Interface Builder file. The utility area shows properties for the selected object.

> **When you turn on the Assistant editor, Xcode 4 will automatically open the correct header file for you.**

Generating Code Using Assistant Editor and Integrated Interface Builder

The most important feature that has been added to Xcode 4's integrated Interface Builder is the capability to generate properties (`IBOutlet`) or event handling (`IBAction`) code directly from IB. When the Assistant editor is open, all you have to do is command-click and drag objects to the header file to generate properties, or command-click and drag events from the Utility area to the header to generate `IBActions`. If your drag destination is valid, Xcode shows an insertion marker and adds the code right in. No connections needed. It's all done for you.

LLVM Compiler 3.0: A Tryst with the Brain

Xcode 3 and prior versions were not as "intelligent" compared to competing IDE such as Eclipse or Visual Studio. The main reason for this is that Xcode 3 used GCC as the compiler. While GCC is a good compiler, it doesn't offer much interoperability with the IDE. A compiler normally has a front end that converts source code into an intermediate representation and expands preprocessor macro definitions. It also has a back end that generates code and optimizes it. The GCC compiler is essentially a back-end compiler, which means that when you provide it with source code, it generates compiled binary for it. It was primarily developed for compiling code and not for parsing it. Essentially, this means that Apple has to write its own version of parsers to assist you with debugging. GCC is GPL, so Apple's version of parsers cannot use the same GCC code without changing the Xcode license to GPL. Because Apple's parsers and GCC are from different code base, there were always some discrepancies between what the GCC compiler "thinks" and what Xcode "thinks."

The Clang Front End

To alleviate this problem, Apple is slowly switching to the LLVM compiler. With Xcode 4.2 debuting with iOS 5, the default compiler is LLVM compiler 3.0. Although LLVM is not as "efficient" as GCC in code generation, it's more modular and extensible. LLVM is also more than twice as fast in terms of compile time (thereby increasing your productivity). A number of front ends have been developed for LLVM, and one of these is Clang, which is heavily funded by Apple. (Clang stands for *C language*.) Clang supports incremental compilation, which means that the IDE can actually compile the code as you type and show you near-instantaneous compilation errors. You will find this very useful when you start using Xcode 4.

A clear example of this is that Xcode 3 suggests nearly every symbol indexed after you type `@synthesize`, but Xcode 4 shows suggestions only of the properties in the corresponding header file. Moreover, the modular nature of Clang makes it easy to support code refactoring and features like Edit All in Scope.

I'm a Bug! Fix Me

LLVM's tighter integration with IDE also helps Xcode 4 to offer suggestions about what the developer must do when the compiler encounters an error. This feature is called Fix-it.

Figure 2-7 shows a suggestion to remove the closing square brackets to match the number of opening brackets.

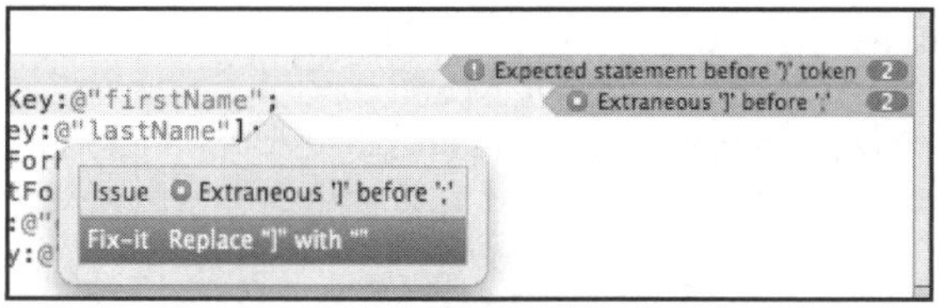

Figure 2-7 Xcode 4 Fix-it in action

Git Your Versions Here

Another interesting feature addition to Xcode 4 is the integrated Git version control system. Git is a distributed version control system written by Linus Torvalds (yes, the same guy behind the Linux kernel) primarily to maintain the Linux kernel repository. The distributed nature, speed, reliability, cheap branching, and the ability to easily do nonlinear software development encouraged more and more users to adopt Git.

Integrated Git Version Control System

Git is primarily a command-line system, much like most other Unix/Linux systems. Don't fret. Xcode 4 has built-in support for Git, and the project navigator even shows the commit statuses of your file. However, the decision to use Git over any other version control system shouldn't be based solely on this. The main reason I advocate using Git for your next iOS app is its cheap branching and its nonlinear development support.

Versions Editor

The Versions editor is the third type of editor available in Xcode 4. (As mentioned previously in this chapter, the other two editor types are the Standard editor and the Assistant editor.) The integrated Versions editor comes in handy when you want to visually analyze differences between two versions of a file. If your project uses Git (or SVN), you can compare a file with a previous revision from its repository. The Versions editor allows you to pick any older version of a file by scrubbing through a timeline resembling the classical Time Machine UI. With OS X Lion, Apple might even consider adding local versions support to Xcode and you would be able to compare local versions of files in addition to the versions in the repository.

Git Best Practices

Apple's AppStore is a walled garden, and if you are an active developer, Apple has probably rejected you at least once. Imagine a product development with, say, ten features. Out of these ten features, you develop four for version 1.0, and another two for version 1.5, and remaining four for version 2.0. You have submitted version 1.0 and are working on the fifth and sixth features. A couple of weeks into development, you get a reply from Apple that your app is rejected. Let's assume that the third feature violates some of Apple's policies and is not allowed in its current state. In a traditional SCM system, you check out the old code, work on the fix, and submit the fix to Apple. You then come back to your code that has the fifth and sixth features added and painstakingly merge these bug fixes to your latest-and-greatest code. While SVN and other source code control systems offer branching, it's quite hard to use and as the size of project grows, branching becomes an expensive operation (both timewise and disk-usagewise). With Git, this kind of merging, branching, and parallel development is very easy mostly because of the way Git stores change sets.

> For a deeper introduction to Git, I recommend reading *Pro Git* or *Version Control With Git*. (See the "Further Reading" section at the end of the chapter for details.) The first book gives you an in-depth understanding about how Git works; the second helps you get started with and make the best use of Git in your project.

I suggest you follow these steps when using Git in your next iOS app:

1. Let your master branch reflect your latest-and-greatest code for the version available on the App Store.
2. For every new version you are working on, create a new branch.
3. For every major feature you implement, create a branch from the version branch.
4. Merge your branch with the master whenever you submit your app to the App Store.
5. Optionally tag your master branch after the app is approved.

When you follow these steps, you can easily fix bugs and issues with a particular version and merge your changes with the latest branch you are working on, all within couple of minutes.

For example, if Apple were to reject your app, all you would need to do is check out the master branch, make your fixes, resubmit to the App Store, check out your current working branch, and merge the changes you made in the master to it. With Git, nonlinear development gets really easy. Try using it. You will not regret it.

Schemes

The most powerful yet most confusing addition to Xcode 4 is schemes. In Xcode 3, there is a build configuration selection combo box, where you specify an active configuration; an active target; an active executable; the active architecture (instruction set); and the target device before running the app. Even the default set of options has an overwhelmingly high combination of selections, and for complicated project settings, choosing the right executable for the right target or device and instruction set becomes challenging. To top it off, Xcode 3 even allows choosing a wrong executable as active for a given target. Schemes have been introduced in Xcode

4 to help developers handle these issues easily. A scheme is a single entity that combines all of the above-mentioned settings. A scheme is a set of instructions for building a product. The product can be (in most cases will be) a collection of targets with its own build configurations. You can also use your existing `xcconfig` files for those targets. You learn about this later in this chapter.

Why Schemes?

The previous method of choosing four different options whenever you want to build something makes it difficult to do it right every time. There are times when you would have built and submitted the debug version of the app to the App Store or tried to debug the release configuration of the app, only to find your breakpoints were not getting hit. With schemes in place, all you have to do is to choose your scheme and every other option is automatically applied. When you are building your product for debugging, you obviously don't want to strip off debug statements. On the other hand, when you are building for the App Store, you almost always want to optimize your build for performance and strip off debug statements. That holds good for Ad Hoc deployments as well. Wait! It doesn't end there. These schemes can also be shared among co-workers by committing into the repository.

Think of Schemes as Implementing Your Intentions

With schemes you can automatically choose the correct configuration for a target by choosing a scheme that matches your *intent*. That is, if your intent is, "I want to debug this product," choose the Run scheme. If your intent is, "I want to submit this product to AppStore/Adhoc distribution," choose the Archive scheme.

With schemes, you select one option based on your intent. All your other settings are applied automatically. With some tweaks, you can customize the settings that are applied when a scheme is created. You will learn this in the next section.

Creating a Scheme

The easiest way to create a scheme is to let Xcode 4 auto-create one for you. When you open a project created on Xcode 3 in Xcode 4, it automatically creates a default scheme. Every scheme has its own unique settings panel that allows you to customize or tweak the default scheme setting. The following list discusses actions in a scheme.

- **Run**—The Run action builds the included targets using the debug build configuration. On the settings panel of this action you can change the debugger you want to use (GDB or LLDB) and the build configuration, the default being Debug. The Run action's settings panel is where you specify command-line arguments, provide default data, or provide mock location data (using GPX files) to your app. You can also enable diagnostics-related arguments like Enabling Zombies or Guard Malloc from here (from Xcode 4.1 onward).

  To take it even further, you can duplicate the scheme and try different debuggers (and/or settings) on each.

- **Test**—The Test action runs your test targets. On the settings panel, you can customize which tests should be executed. Schemes are fully integrated with the OCUnit Objective-C testing framework and tests written will show up on the settings panel. Test failures show up on the Issue and Log navigators instead of the console, which means that navigating to the correct method that caused the test case to fail is now easier.

  By duplicating this scheme, you can create two test schemes: one testing your model classes, and one testing, say, your helper methods.

■ **Profile**—The Profile action builds your target and attaches it to Instruments. When you choose this, Instruments automatically launches and shows you the list of instruments available. You can edit the scheme to always launch the Time Profiler tool or the Leaks tool (or any other) automatically.

You can duplicate the profile scheme so that you have two schemes: one launching Leaks and the other launching Time Profiler.

■ **Analyze**—The Analyze action runs the Clang static analyzer on your code and warns you of potential memory leaks. There isn't much to customize here except the build configuration to use for this scheme.

■ **Archive**—The Archive action is used for making `xcarchive` files (or `ipa` files) used for submitting to the App Store. Archives automatically appear on the Xcode organizer from where you can validate/ submit to the App Store. With a dedicated Archive scheme, you are no longer required to create an Ad Hoc build configuration or an "App Store" build configuration for your product like you do in Xcode 3. These specific distribution configurations differ in most cases from the release configuration only by the signing certificate. Because the signing happens later, you can use the release configuration for archiving your apps. Signing it for submitting to the App Store or for Ad Hoc distribution is done through the Xcode organizer.

Sharing Your Schemes

By default, a scheme created by Xcode 4 is saved to the project bundle under the `xcuserdata` directory. Normally this directory is excluded from repositories, which means schemes generated on your machine stay on your machine. In some cases, you might want to share schemes with co-workers. To do so, go to the Manage scheme options panel and select the Shared checkbox for every scheme you want to share. This is illustrated in Figure 2-8.

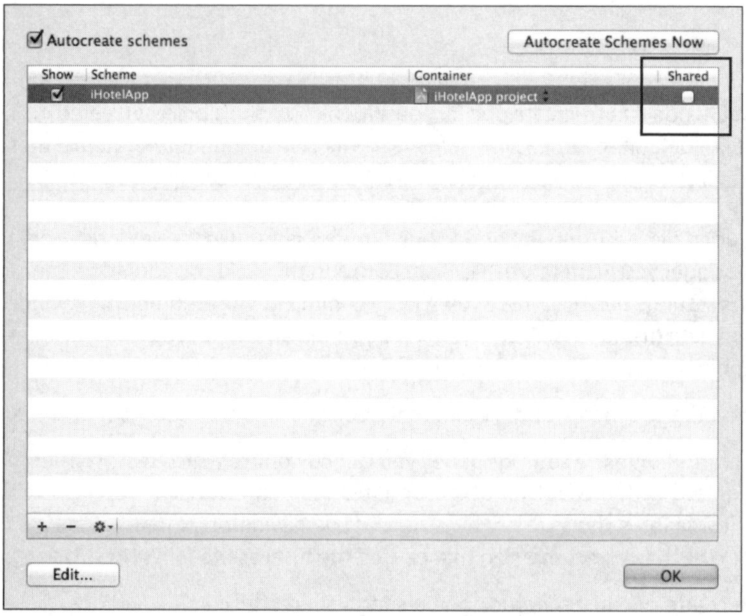

Figure 2-8 Sharing Schemes

When you check the Shared option, your schemes are copied over to the `xcshareddata` directory. By adding this directory to your repository, you can share your custom schemes with co-workers.

Schemes are actually a better way to customize your IDE/Environment than Xcode 3's method of using multiple configurations. Give it a try and you will like it.

Build Configurations You Can Comment

In most projects, you would have depended on Xcode's build settings panel to edit/change your build settings. But this build settings panel has one major drawback. You cannot easily comment on a particular change you made on your project's configuration. Xcode (both 3 and 4) provides an easy way to do this by using `xcconfig` files.

Creating an `xcconfig` File

An `xcconfig` file is a plaintext file that contains build configurations for your target. Start by adding a Debug configuration file to your project. You can choose this from the templates in the new file wizard's Other section. Figure 2-9 illustrates this.

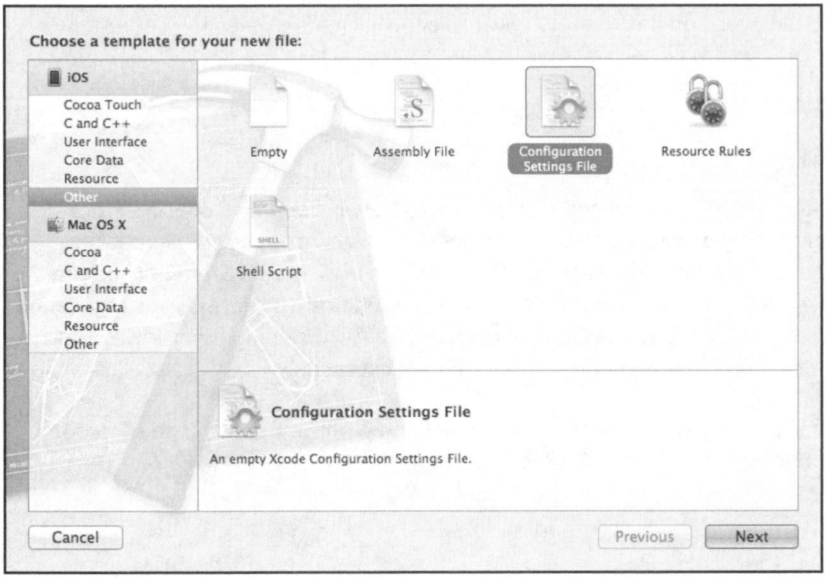

Figure 2-9 Adding a new configuration file

Name the file `debug.xcconfig`. Now open the build settings editor and select Basic and Levels as options. Copy these build settings to the configuration file you just created. You can select a row and use Cmd-C to copy and paste them on the configuration file.

Repeat these steps for the Release configurations in another file called `release.xcconfig`. Once you create this basic configuration, you can set all settings to default in the build settings editor.

Now, you need to tell Xcode to use this build configuration file instead of the specified build settings. To do so, select the project and then, in the project settings editor, choose the project again. In the Info panel, expand the configuration section and choose your config file.

That's it. You have now created a build configuration file that's readable and commentable, which you can share with co-workers through your SCM. Ready to refactor this?

Refactoring the Build Configuration File

When you created the build configuration file, you probably noticed that many identical settings appear on both the debug and release configurations. You can easily avoid duplicating them by creating a `shared.xcconfig` file and copying those settings to it. Once you are done with the `shared.xcconfig` file, remove those entries from the `debug.xcconfig` and `release.xcconfig` files. Now use the `include` statement to add the `shared.xcconfig` entries to both files:

```
#include "shared.xcconfig"
```

This will automatically import all the shared settings into both the configuration files. Now when you run your app, everything should work. You can even add this to every new project you create or even to Xcode's new project templates.

Xcode 4 Organizer

Xcode 4 Organizer is a one-stop shop for anything related to Xcode that's not programming specific. From the Organizer, you can manage project repositories, perform SCM operations, and manage your application archives, provisioning profiles, and devices. Open the Organizer window by pressing Cmd-Shift-2 or clicking the rightmost button on your Xcode 4 toolbar. You will use the Xcode 4 Organizer mostly to access your application archives, submit your apps to the App Store and to manage your devices and provisioning profiles. Xcode 4 also has a new feature called Automatic Device Provisioning, discussed in the next section.

The first tab of Xcode 4 Organizer shows the list of devices and provisioning profiles currently loaded. Xcode 4 provides an easy way to export this list and import it on a new machine. If you ever want to migrate your developer settings to another computer, this is the place you should look for.

Automatic Device Provisioning

From the provisioning profiles list on the Devices tab, you can see a checkbox near the footer called Automatic Device Provisioning. When enabled, Xcode 4 can automatically download and install a developer certificate and a distribution certificate from your iOS developer program portal. Xcode 4 can also create a wild card provisioning profile (with an Implicit App ID) automatically, and that profile can be used for your apps that don't require an Explicit App ID.

Apps with any of the following features—Push Notification, Game Center, iCloud, or In App Purchases—cannot use the implicit App ID and hence cannot depend on Xcode's Automatic Device Provisioning.

Viewing Crash Logs and Console NSLog Statements

The Devices tab shows you a list of devices that have been connected to your development machine at least once. When you expand the device by clicking the disclosure triangle, you will be able to see Device logs and screenshots for that device. When a device is connected, you will see additional entries like Console logs, provisioning profiles installed on the device, and a list of applications provisioned. (This includes apps you run via Xcode or apps that you install via Ad Hoc distribution.)

Viewing Applications' Sandbox Data

With Xcode 4 (beginning with Xcode 4.2), you can view, delete, or add files to an app's sandbox inside a device. This makes debugging on the device easier. To access the device's sandbox, select the connected device from the left pane, choose Applications from the list, and choose the application for which you want to see the sandbox. Delete or add files from here or copy them locally to your computer.

Managing Repositories

Xcode 4 automatically adds the repositories for any project you have opened into the Repositories tab. The repositories section serves as a pretty good alternative for Git (or SVN) GUI access for most purposes.

If you are a "Unix-y" person and prefer to use the command line, I suggest you stay away from any GUI tools, and use them only for viewing diffs. A quick, lightweight tool I recommend is GitX. It has a command line tool to "pipe" Git diff output and shows you a visual diff. My workflow has always been like this:

```
git diff | gitx
```

Accessing Your Application Archives

You can access your application archives from the Xcode 4 Organizer and validate or submit your apps from there. In the previous section, you saw how to archive an application using the archive scheme action. This archive can be accessed from the Archives tab of Xcode 4 Organizer.

Viewing Objective-C and SDK Documentation

Organizer also makes it easy to access the SDK documentation. The Documentation tab of Organizer shows the list of docsets installed. In most cases that would be the latest two iOS SDKs, the latest two Mac OS X SDKs, and the current Xcode library.

Summary

Xcode 4 IDE is a huge improvement over Xcode 3. While it is still not as stable as Xcode 3, you should start using and getting accustomed to it. Some features such as new key-bindings, schemes, and integrated Interface Builder might look different and confusing at first, but as you get used to them you will start appreciating them, especially for the time they save. Apple has already stopped supporting Xcode 3, and new features like storyboarding and ARC migration tools are available only on Xcode 4. It only makes sense to start using the latest-and-greatest IDE as soon as possible.

Further Reading

Apple Documentation

The following documents are available in the iOS Developer Library at `developer.apple.com` or through the Xcode Documentation and API Reference.

Apple Developer: Debugging with Xcode 4

Apple Developer: Orientation to Xcode 4

Apple Developer: Designing User Interfaces with Xcode 4

WWDC Videos

The following session videos are available at `developer.apple.com`.

Session 307: Moving to the Apple LLVM Compiler

Session 316: LLVM Technologies in Depth

WWDC 2011 Session 313: Mastering Schemes with Xcode 4

Blogs

Cocoa Samurai. "Xcode 4 keyboard shortcuts now available!"
`http://cocoasamurai.blogspot.com/2011/03/xcode-4-keyboard-shortcuts-now.html`

The Pragmatic Studio. "Xcode 4 shortcuts"
`http://pragmaticstudio.com/media/Xcode4Shortcuts.pdf`

Pilky.me. "Xcode 4: the super mega awesome review"
`http://pilky.me/view/15`

Napier, Rob. *Cocoaphony: Mac and iPhone, on the brain.* "Building the Build System – Part 1 – Abandoning the Build Panel"
`http://robnapier.net/blog/build-system-1-build-panel-360`

Web Resources

GitX.Mac OS X Git Client
```
http://gitx.frim.nl/
```

Books

Chacon, Scott. *Pro Git* (Apress 2009, ISBN 978-1430218333).
```
http://progit.org/book/
```

Loeliger, Jon. *Version Control With Git: Powerful Tools and Techniques for Collaborative Software Development* (O'Reilly Media 2009, ISBN 978-0596520120)
```
http://oreilly.com/catalog/9780596520137
```

Part II

Getting the Most Out of Everyday Tools

Chapter 3

Everyday Objective-C

This chapter covers many everyday best practices for Cocoa development, along with several underused features that more developers should be familiar with. Chapter 4 delves deeper into broad Cocoa patterns; here you focus on language features.

You begin by learning the critical Cocoa naming conventions that will improve your code's readability. Next you are introduced to one of the most exciting new features of iOS 5: Automatic Reference Counting (ARC). This will change how you develop your applications and dramatically reduce bugs and crashes. Then you learn how to best use properties and accessors to manage data in your objects. Finally, you learn about categories, extensions, and protocols, which are all commonly used throughout Cocoa.

By the end of this chapter, you should be very comfortable with the most important language features of Objective-C and feel confident that you are using the best practices of experienced Cocoa developers.

Naming Conventions

Throughout iOS, naming conventions are extremely important. If you understand how to read them correctly, the names of methods and functions throughout the iOS SDK tell you a great deal about how they are supposed to be called and what they do. Once you're used to the naming conventions, you can often guess what the name of a class or method is, making it much easier to find the documentation for it. This section touches on some of the most important naming convention rules and those that cause problems for developers with experience in other languages.

> The best source of information on Cocoa naming conventions is Apple's *Coding Guidelines for Cocoa*, which is available at `developer.apple.com`.

The first thing to know is that in Cocoa, ease of reading is more important than ease of writing. Code spends much more of its life being read, maintained, and debugged than written. Cocoa naming conventions always favor the reader by striving for clarity over brevity. This is in stark contrast to C, which favors extremely terse naming. Because Objective-C is a dynamic language, the compiler provides far fewer safeguards than a static language like C++. Good naming is a critical part of writing bug-free code.

The most important attribute of a good name is clarity. The names of methods should make it clear what types they accept and return. For instance, this method is extremely confusing:

```
- (void)add;   // Confusing
```

It looks like `add` should take a parameter, but it doesn't. Does it add some default object?

Yes, so names like these are much clearer:

```
- (void)addEmptyRecord;
- (void)addRecord:(Record *)record;
```

Now it's clear that `addRecord:` accepts a `Record`. The type of the object should match the name if there is any chance of confusion. For instance, this is a common mistake:

```
- (void)setURL:(NSString *)URL;   // Incorrect
```

It's incorrect because something called `setURL:` should accept an `NSURL`, not an `NSString`. If you need a string, then you should add some kind of indicator to make this clear:

```
- (void)setURLString:(NSString *)string;
- (void)setURL:(NSURL *)URL;
```

This rule shouldn't be overapplied. It's better to have a property called `name` than `nameString`, as long as there is no `Name` class in your system that might confuse the reader.

Clear naming also means that you should avoid abbreviations in most cases. Use `backgroundColor` rather than `bgcolor`, and `stringValue` rather than `to_str`. There are exceptions to the use of abbreviations, particularly for things that are best known by their abbreviation. For example, `URL` is better than `uniformResourceLocator`. An easy way to determine whether an abbreviation is appropriate is to say the name out loud. You say "source" not "src." But most people say "URL" as either "u-ar-el" or "earl." No one says "uniform resource locator" in speech, so you shouldn't in code. There are a few abbreviations such as `alloc`, `init`, `rect`, and `pboard` that Cocoa uses for historical reasons that are considered acceptable. Apple has generally been moving away from even these abbreviations as it releases new frameworks.

There are several kinds of variables in a program: instance variables, static variables, automatic (stack) variables, and so on. It can be very difficult to understand code if you don't know what kind of variable you're looking at. Naming conventions should make the intent of a variable clear. After coding in many different styles with different teams, my recommendations are the following:

- Prefix static (package-scoped) variables with `s` and nonconstant global variables with `g`. Generally you should avoid nonconstant globals; for example, the following is a static declaration:

  ```
  static MYThing *sSharedInstance;
  ```

- Constants are named differently in Cocoa from the way they are named in Core Foundation. In Core Foundation, constants are prefixed with a `k`. In Cocoa, they are not. File-local (static) constants should generally be prefixed with `k` in my opinion, but there is no hard-and-fast rule here. The following are examples of a file constant and a public constant:

```
static const NSUInteger kMaximumNumberOfRows = 3;
NSString * const MYSomethingHappenedNotification =
                                    @"SomethingHappened";
```

- Method arguments are generally prefixed with an article such as *a*, *an*, or *the*. The last is less common and sometimes suggests a particularly important or unique object. Prefixing your arguments this way helps avoid confusing them with local variables and ivars. It is particularly helpful to avoid modifying them unintentionally.

- Suffix instance variables (ivars) with an underscore or prefix them with m. I avoid prefixing with underscore because Apple reserves the leading underscore, and I've occasionally collided with instance variables in the superclass. Also, key-value coding (KVC) automatically retrieves private instance variables that begin with an underscore. This breaks encapsulation in a way that isn't obvious in the code and provides no warning. To avoid that, I use another naming convention (trailing underscore, based on Google's approach).

- Classes should always begin with a capital letter. Methods and variables should always begin with a lowercase letter. All classes and methods should use camel case—never underscores—to separate words.

> Cocoa and Core Foundation use slightly different naming conventions, but their basic approach is the same. For more information on Core Foundation naming, see Chapter 19.

Cocoa naming is tightly coupled with memory management. With the addition of ARC, this is no longer as critical, but it is important to understand when working on non-ARC code. The naming convention is quite simple, as the following extract from the Memory Management Programming Guide (developer.apple.com) shows:

> *You take ownership of an object if you create it using a method whose name begins with* alloc *or* new *or contains* copy *(for example,* alloc, newObject, *or* mutableCopy*), or if you send it a* retain *message. You are responsible for relinquishing ownership of objects you own using* release *or* autorelease. *Any other time you receive an object, you must not release it.*

Even in ARC code, you should be aware of this naming convention and avoid using alloc, new, copy, retain, and release to mean anything other than their traditional meanings.

Automatic Reference Counting

One of the most powerful additions to iOS 5 is ARC. ARC greatly reduces the most common programmer error in Cocoa development: mismatching retain and release. ARC does not eliminate retain and release, it just makes them a compiler problem rather than a developer problem most of the time. In the vast majority of cases this is a major win, but it's important to understand that retain and release are still going on. ARC is not the same thing as garbage collection. Consider the following code, which assigns a value to an ivar:

```
@property (strong, nonatomic) NSString *title;
...
@synthesize title = title_;
...
title_ = [NSString stringWithFormat:@"Title"];
```

Without ARC, `title_` is underretained in the preceding code. The `NSString` assigned to it is autoreleased, so it will disappear at the end of the run loop, and the next time someone accesses `title_`, the program will crash. This kind of error is incredibly common and can be very difficult to debug. Moreover, if `title_` had a previous value, then that old value has been leaked because it wasn't released.

Using ARC, the compiler automatically inserts extra code to create the equivalent of this:

```
id oldTitle = title_;
title_ = [NSString stringWithFormat:@"Title"];
[title_ retain];
[oldTitle release];
```

The calls to `release` and `retain` still happen, so there is a small overhead, and there may be a call to `dealloc` during the `release`. But generally this makes the code behave the way the programmer intended it to without creating an extra garbage collection step. Memory is reclaimed faster than with garbage collection, and decisions are made at compile time rather than at runtime, which generally improves overall performance. As with other compiler optimizations, the compiler is free to optimize memory management in various ways that would be impractical for the programmer to do by hand. ARC-generated memory management is often dramatically faster than the equivalent hand-coded memory management.·

But this is not garbage collection. In particular, it cannot handle reference (retain) loops the way Snow Leopard garbage collection can. For example, the object graph in Figure 3-1 shows a retain loop between Object A and Object B:

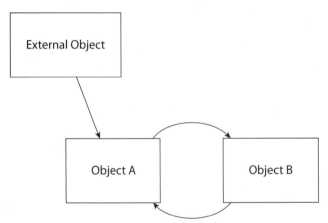

Figure 3-1 A retain loop

If the link from "External Object" to "Object A" is broken, then under Snow Leopard garbage collection both Object A and Object B will be destroyed because they are orphaned from the program. Under ARC, Object A and Object B will not be destroyed because each still has a retain count greater than zero. So in iOS, you need to keep track of your strong relationships to avoid reference loops.

Property relationships have two main forms: `strong` and `weak`, which map to the former `retain` and `assign`. As long as there is a strong reference to an object, it will continue to exist. This is nearly identical to `shared_ptr` in C++, except that the code to manage the reference counts is injected by the compiler rather than determined at runtime with operator overloads.

Objective-C has always had the problem of reference loops, but they really don't come up that often in practice. Anywhere you would have used an `assign` property in the past, use a `weak` property under ARC and you should be fine. Most reference loops are caused by delegates, and a `delegate` property should almost always be `weak`. Weak references have the advantage of automatically being set to `nil` when the referenced object is destroyed. This is a significant improvement over `assign` properties, which can point to freed memory.

> Prior to ARC, the default storage class for synthesized properties was `assign`. Under ARC, there is no default storage class for synthesized properties. You must provide one in the `@property` line.

There are two major changes when switching to ARC for most code:

- Don't use `retain`, `release`, or `autorelease`. You can just delete these. ARC should do the right thing.

- If your `dealloc` only releases ivars, you don't need `dealloc`. This will be done automatically for you, and you can't call `release` in any case. If you still need `dealloc` to do other things (remove KVO observations, for instance), don't call `[super dealloc]`. This last change is surprising, but the compiler will give you errors if you forget.

As noted previously, ARC is not garbage collection. It is a compiler feature that injects calls to `retain` and `release` at appropriate places in the code. This means that it is fully interoperable with existing, manual memory management code, as long as all the code uses the correct naming conventions. For example, if you call a method named `copySomething`, ARC will expect the result of that method to have a +1 retain count. If needed, it will insert a balancing `release`. It doesn't matter to ARC whether that +1 retain count was created by ARC code inside of `copySomething`, or manual memory management inside of `copySomething`.

This breaks if you violate Cocoa's naming conventions. For instance, if you have a method that returns the copyright notice as an autoreleased string, and call the method `copyRight`, then how ARC behaves depends on whether the calling and called code are both compiled with ARC.

ARC looks at the name `copyRight`, sees that it begins with `copy`, and so assumes that it returns a +1 retain count object. If `copyRight` is compiled with ARC, and the calling code is compiled with ARC, everything will still work. ARC will inject an extra retain in `copyRight` because of its name, and it will inject an extra release in the calling code. It may be a little less efficient, but the code will neither crash nor leak.

If, however, the calling code is compiled with ARC, but `copyRight` is not, then the calling code will inject an extra release, and the code will crash. If the calling code is not compiled with ARC, but `copyRight` is, then ARC will inject an extra retain, and the code will leak.

The best solution to this problem is to follow Cocoa's naming conventions. In this example, you could name this method `copyright` and avoid the problem entirely. ARC determines the memory management rules based on whole camel case words in the method.

If renaming an incorrect method is impossible, you can add the attribute `NS_RETURNS_RETAINED` or `NS_RETURNS_NOT_RETAINED` to your method declaration to tell the compiler which memory management rule to use. These are defined in `NSObjCRuntime.h`.

ARC introduces four restrictions on your code so that it can properly add retain and release calls for you:

- **No calls to** `retain`, `release`, **or** `autorelease`. This is usually the easiest rule. Just delete them. It also means that you cannot override these methods, but you should almost never do that anyway. If you were overriding these methods to implement the Singleton pattern, see Chapter 4 for information about how to properly implement this pattern without overriding these methods.

- **No object pointers in C structs.** This seldom comes up, but if you have been storing an object in a C struct, you either need to store it in an object, or you need to cast it to `void*` (see the next rule for more information on casting to `void*`). C structs can be destroyed at any time by calling `free`, and this interferes with automatically tracking objects that are stored in them.

- **No casting between** `id` **and** `void*` **without a bridging cast.** This mostly impacts Core Foundation code. See Chapter 19 for full details on bridging casts and how to use them with ARC.

- **No** `NSAutoreleasePool`. Rather than creating your own autorelease pools by hand, just wrap any code you want to have its own pool in a `@autoreleasepool{}` block. If you had special code to control when you drained your pool, it is almost certainly unnecessary. `@autoreleasepool` is up to 20× faster than `NSAutoreleasePool`.

Most code will have no problem with these rules. There is a new tool in Xcode under the `Edit>Refactor` menu called `Convert to Objective-C ARC....` It will do the majority of the work for you.

ARC is perhaps the greatest advancement in Objective-C since the autorelease pool. If at all possible, you should convert your code to ARC. If you can't convert everything, convert as much as you can. It is faster, less buggy, and easier to write than manual memory management. Switch to ARC today.

Properties

Objective-C 2.0 introduced several interesting changes. A key improvement was nonfragile ivars. This allows classes to add ivars without recompiling their subclasses. This feature mostly affects framework developers like Apple rather than application developers, but it has some useful side effects. The most popular is synthesized properties.

What few people realize is that synthesized properties can generate their own ivar. For example:

MyClass.h

```
@interface MyClass : NSObject
@property (copy) NSString *string;
@end
```

MyClass.m

```
@implementation MyClass
@synthesize string=string_;
@end
```

The ivar `string_` is automatically generated, even though it is not listed in the header. Even more interesting, you could put the property declaration in a private extension or the `@implementation` block making a fully private property. (You cannot synthesize an ivar for a property defined in a category. See "Categories and Extensions" later in this chapter for more information on the differences.)

In your code, I encourage you either to declare all of your ivars in the interface or to synthesize all of your ivars. Don't have some declared in the interface and some not declared in the interface.

My recommendation is to switch entirely to properties and fully synthesized ivars. Put your public properties in the header, and your private properties in an extension in the .m file. So a full example might look like this:

MyClass.h

```
@interface MyClass : NSObject
@property (readwrite, weak) id delegate;
@property (readonly, strong) NSString *readonlyString;
@end
```

MyClass.m

```
@interface MyClass () // Private methods
@property (readwrite, strong) NSString *readonlyString;
@property (readwrite, strong) NSString *privateString;
@end

@implementation MyClass
@synthesize delegate=delegate_;
@synthesize readonlyString=readonlyString_;
@synthesize privateString=privateString_;
@end
```

Note how `readonlyString` is redefined in the class extension to be `readwrite`. This allows you to create a private setter.

Property Attributes

While we're discussing properties, you should also consider the attributes you apply to your properties. Let's consider each category in turn.

- **Atomicity** — `nonatomic`. There is no `atomic` attribute. Anything not declared `nonatomic` is atomic. This is an easy attribute to misunderstand. Its purpose is to make setting and getting the property thread safe. That does not mean that the underlying object is thread safe. For instance, if you declare an `NSMutableArray` property called `stuff` to be atomic, then `self.stuff` is thread safe and `self.stuff=otherStuff` is thread safe. But accessing the array with `objectAtIndex:` is not thread safe. You will need additional locking to handle that. The `atomic` attribute is implemented similar to this:

```
[_propertyLock lock];
id result = [[value retain] autorelease];
[_propertyLock unlock];
return result;
```

The pattern of `retain/autorelease` ensures that the object will not be destroyed until the caller's autorelease pool drains. This protects the caller from other threads releasing the object in the middle of access. Managing the lock and calling `retain` and `autorelease` can be expensive (though atomic properties are much cheaper with ARC). If you will never access this property from another thread, or if you need more elaborate locking anyway, then this kind of atomicity is wasteful. It turns out that this is the case most of the time, and you usually want to use `nonatomic`. In the fairly small number of cases where this kind of atomicity is useful, there unfortunately is no way to call it out because there is no `atomic` attribute. It's helpful to add a comment in these cases to make it clear that you're making the property atomic on purpose.

> ARC provides significant performance benefits to atomic properties, and best practices regarding `nonatomic` **may change in the near future.**

- **Writability** — `readwrite`, `readonly`. These should be fairly self-explanatory. If a property is `readonly`, then only a getter will be available. If it is `readwrite`, then both a setter and getter will be available. There is no `writeonly` attribute.

- **Setter Semantics** — `weak`, `strong`, `copy`. These should be fairly obvious, but there are some things to consider. First, you often should use `copy` for immutable classes such as `NSString` and `NSArray`. It is possible that there is a mutable subclass of your property's class. For instance, if you have an `NSString` property, you might be passed an `NSMutableString`. If that happens, and you only hold a reference to the value (`strong`), your property might change behind your back as the caller mutates it. That often isn't what you want, and so you will note that most `NSString` properties use the `copy` semantic. This is also usually true for collections like `NSArray`. Copying immutable classes is generally very cheap because it can almost always be implemented with `retain`.

Property Best Practices

Properties should represent the state of the object. Getters should have no externally visible side effects (they may have internal side effects such as caching, but those should be invisible to callers). Generally they should be efficient to call and certainly should not block.

Private Ivars

While I prefer properties for everything, some people prefer ivars, especially for private variables. In iOS 5, you can declare ivars in the `@implementation` block like this:

```
@implementation Something{
   NSString *name;
}
```

This syntax moves the private ivar out of the public header, which is good for encapsulation, and keeps the public header easier to read. ARC automatically retains and releases ivars, just like other variables. The default storage class is strong, but you can create weak ivars as shown here:

```
@implementation Something{
   __weak NSString *name;
}
```

Accessors

Avoid accessing ivars directly. Use accessors instead. There are a few exceptions that I discuss in a moment, but first I discuss why you should use accessors.

Prior to ARC, one of the most common iOS bugs was failure to use accessors. Developers would fail to retain and release their ivars correctly, and the program would leak or crash. Because ARC automatically manages retains and releases, some developers may believe that this rule is no longer important, but there are other reasons to use accessors.

- **Key-value observing:** Perhaps the most critical reason to use accessors is that properties can be observed. If you do not use accessors, you need to make calls to `willChangeValueForKey:` and `didChangeValueForKey:` every time you modify a property. Using the accessor will automatically call these when they are needed.

- **Side effects:** You or one of your subclasses may include side effects in the setter. There may be notifications posted or events registered with `NSUndoManager`. You shouldn't bypass these unless it's necessary. Similarly, you or a subclass may add caching to the getter that direct ivar access will bypass.

- **Locking:** If you introduce locking to a property in order to manage multithreaded code, direct ivar access will break this and likely crash your program.

- **Consistency:** One could argue that you should just use accessors when you know you need them for one of the preceding reasons, but this makes the code very hard to maintain. It is better that every direct ivar access be suspicious and explained rather than having to constantly remember which ivars require accessors and which do not. This makes the code much easier to audit, review, and maintain. Accessors, particularly synthesized accessors, are highly optimized in Objective-C, and they are worth the overhead.

That said, there are a few places where you should not use accessors:

- **Inside of accessors:** Obviously you cannot use an accessor within itself. Generally you should also not use the get accessor inside of the setter either (this can create infinite loops in some patterns). An accessor may speak to its own ivar.

- **Dealloc:** ARC greatly reduces the need for `dealloc`, but it still comes up sometimes. It is best not to call external objects inside of `dealloc`. The object may be in an inconsistent state, and it is likely confusing to the observer to receive several notifications that properties are changing when what is really meant is that the entire object is being destroyed.

- **Initialization:** Similar to `dealloc`, the object may be in an inconsistent state during initialization and you generally shouldn't fire notifications or have other side effects during this time. This is also a common place to initialize readonly variables like an `NSMutableArray`. This avoids declaring a property `readwrite` just so you can initialize it.

Accessors are highly optimized in Objective-C and provide important features for maintainability and flexibility. As a general rule, you should refer to all properties, even your own, using their accessors.

Categories and Extensions

Categories allow you to add methods to an existing class at runtime. Any class, even Cocoa classes provided by Apple, can be extended with categories, and those new methods will be available to all instance of the class. This approach was inherited from Smalltalk and is somewhat similar to extension methods in C#.

Categories were designed to break up large classes into more manageable pieces, hence the name. If you look at large Foundation classes, you will find that sometimes they are broken into several pieces. For instance, `NSArray` includes the `NSExtendedArray`, `NSArrayCreation`, and `NSDeprecated` categories defined in `NSArray.h`, plus the `NSArrayPathExtensions` category defined in `NSPathUtilities.h`. Most of these are split up to make it simpler to implement in multiple files, but some categories, like the `UIStringDrawing` category on `NSString`, exist specifically to allow different code to be loaded at runtime. On Mac, AppKit loads the `NSStringDrawing` category. On iOS, UIKit loads the `UIStringDrawing` category. This provides a more elegant way to split up the code than `#ifdef`. On each platform, you simply compile the appropriate implementation (`.m`) files, and the functionality becomes available.

Prior to Objective-C 2.0, `@protocol` definitions could not include optional methods. Developers used categories as "informal protocols." The complier knows the methods defined in a category, but it will not generate a warning if the methods are not implemented. This made all the protocol's methods optional. I discuss this further in "Formal and Informal Protocols" later in this chapter, but for iOS I do not recommend this use of categories. Formal protocols now support optional methods directly.

Because the compiler will not check that you have implemented methods in the category, using categories solely to break up large classes has trade-offs. An implementation file that's getting overly large is often an indication that you need to refactor your class to make it more focused rather than define categories to split it up. But if your class is correctly scoped, you may find splitting up the code with categories is convenient. On the other hand, using categories can scatter the methods into different files, which can be confusing, so use your best judgment.

Declaration of a category is straightforward. It looks like a class interface declaration with the name of the category in parentheses:

```
@interface NSMutableString (Capitalize)
- (void)capitalize;
@end
```

`Capitalize` is the name of the category, but it isn't used for anything. Note that there are no ivars declared here. Categories cannot declare ivars, nor can they synthesize properties (which is the same thing). You'll see how to add category data later in this chapter.

The `Capitalize` category does not require that `capitalize` actually be implemented anywhere. If it isn't and a caller attempts to invoke it, it will raise an exception. The compiler gives you no protection here. If you do implement it, then *by convention* it looks like this:

```
@implementation NSMutableString (Capitalize)
- (void)capitalize {
  [self setString:[self capitalizedString]];
}
@end
```

I say "by convention" because there is no requirement that this be defined in a category implementation or that the category implementation have the same name as the category interface. However, if you provide an `@implementation` block named `Capitalize`, then it must implement all the methods from the `@interface` block named `Capitalize`. Adding the parentheses and category name after the class name allows you to continue adding methods in another compile unit (`.m` file). You can implement your category methods in the main `implementation` block, in a named category `implementation` block for the class, or not implement them at all.

Technically a category can override methods, but that's dangerous and not recommended. If two categories implement the same method, then it is undefined which one is used. If a class is later split into categories for maintenance reasons, your override could become undefined behavior, which is a maddening kind of bug to track down. Moreover, using this feature can make the code hard to understand. Category overrides also provide no way to call the original method. I recommend against using categories to override existing methods, except for debugging. Even for debugging, I prefer swizzling, which is covered in Chapter 20.

A very good use of categories is to provide utility methods to existing classes. When doing this, I recommend naming the header and implementation files using the name of the original class plus the name of the extension. For example, you might create a simple `MyExtensions` category on `NSDate`:

NSDate+MYExtensions.h

```
@interface NSDate (MYExtensions)
- (NSTimeInterval)timeIntervalUntilNow;
@end
```

NSDate+MYExtensions.m

```
@implementation NSDate (MYExtensions)
- (NSTimeInterval)timeIntervalUntilNow {
  return [self timeIntervalSinceNow];
}
@end
```

If you have only a few utility methods, it is convenient to put them together into a single category with a name like `MYExtensions` (or whatever prefix you use for your code). This makes it easy to drop your favorite extensions into each project. Of course, this is also code bloat, so be careful about how much you throw into a "utility" category. Objective-C can't do dead-code stripping as effectively as C or C++.

If you have a large group of related methods, particularly a collection that might not always be useful, it's a good idea to break those into their own category. Look at `UIStringDrawing.h` in UIKit for a good example of this.

+load

Categories are attached to classes at runtime. It's possible that the library that defines the category is dynamically loaded, so categories can be added quite late. (While you can't write your own dynamic libraries in iOS, the system frameworks are dynamically loaded and include categories.) Objective-C provides a hook called `+load` that you can run when the category is first attached. Like `+initialize`, you can use this to implement category-specific setup such as initializing static variables. You can't safely use `+initialize` in a category because the class may implement this already. If multiple categories implemented `+initialize`, it would be undefined which one would run.

Hopefully you're ready to ask the obvious question: "If categories can't use `+initialize` because they might collide with other categories, what if multiple categories implement `+load`?" This turns out to be one of the few really magical parts of the Objective-C runtime. The `+load` method is special-cased in the runtime so that every category may implement it and all the implementations will run. There are no guarantees on order, and you shouldn't try to call `+load` by hand.

`+load` is called regardless of whether the category is statically or dynamically loaded. It is called when the category is added to the runtime, which often is at program launch, before `main`, but could be much later.

Classes can have their own +load method (not defined in a category) and those will be called when the classes are added to the runtime. This is seldom useful unless you're dynamically adding classes.

You don't need to protect against being run multiple times in +load the way you do with +initialize. The +load message is only sent to classes that actually implement it, so you won't accidentally get calls from your subclasses the way you can in +initialize. Every +load will be called exactly once. You shouldn't call [super load].

Category Data using Associative References

While categories can't create new ivars, they can do the next best thing: They can create associative references. Associative references allow you to attach key-value data to arbitrary objects.

Consider the case of a Person class. You'd like to use a category to add a new property called emailAddress. Maybe you use Person in other programs, and sometimes it makes sense to have an email address and sometimes it doesn't, so a category can be a good solution to avoid the overhead when you don't need it. Or maybe you don't own the Person class, and the maintainers won't add the property for you. In any case, how do you attack this problem? First, just for reference, take a look at the Person class:

```
@interface Person : NSObject
@property (readwrite, copy) NSString *name;
@end

@implementation Person
@synthesize name=name_;
@end
```

Now you can add a new property, emailAddress, in a category using an associative reference:

```
#import <objc/runtime.h>
@interface Person (EmailAddress)
@property (readwrite, copy) NSString *emailAddress;
@end

@implementation Person (EmailAddress)

static char emailAddressKey;

- (NSString *)emailAddress {
  return objc_getAssociatedObject(self, &emailAddressKey);
}

- (void)setEmailAddress:(NSString *)emailAddress {
  objc_setAssociatedObject(self, &emailAddressKey,
                           emailAddress,
                           OBJC_ASSOCIATION_COPY);
}
@end
```

Note that associative references are based on the key's memory address, not its value. It does not matter what is stored in `emailAddressKey`; it only needs to have a unique address. That's why it's common to use an unassigned `static char` as the key.

Associative references have good memory management, correctly handling copy, assign, or retain semantics according to the parameter passed to `objc_setAssociatedObject`. They are correctly released when the related object is deallocated.

Associative references are a great way of attaching a relevant object to an alert panel or control. For example, you can attach a "represented object" to an alert panel, as shown in the following code. This code is available in the sample code for this chapter.

ViewController.m (AssocRef)

```
id interestingObject = ...;
UIAlertView *alert = [[UIAlertView alloc]
                       initWithTitle:@"Alert" message:nil
                       delegate:self
                       cancelButtonTitle:@"OK"
                       otherButtonTitles:nil];
objc_setAssociatedObject(alert, &kRepresentedObject,
                         interestingObject,
                         OBJC_ASSOCIATION_RETAIN_NONATOMIC);
[alert show];
```

Now, when the alert panel is dismissed, you can figure out why you cared:

```
- (void)alertView:(UIAlertView *)alertView
clickedButtonAtIndex:(NSInteger)buttonIndex {
  UIButton *sender = objc_getAssociatedObject(alertView,
                                              &kRepresentedObject);
  self.buttonLabel.text = [[sender titleLabel] text];
}
```

Many programs handle this with an ivar in the caller like `currentAlertObject`, but associative references are much cleaner and simpler. For those familiar with Mac development, this is similar to `representedObject`, but more flexible.

One limitation of associative references (or any other approach to adding data via a category), is that it doesn't integrate with `encodeWithCoder:`, so they're difficult to serialize via a category.

Category Data using the Flyweight Pattern

If you're sharing code with pre-10.6 Mac OS X, then associative references aren't an option and you'll need to use the older approach: the Flyweight pattern. Rather than store the data inside the object, you store it outside the object and keep track of some key to find it. In this case, each `Person` instance must have a unique `identifier`, as shown in this code:

Person.h (Flyweight)

```objc
@interface Person : NSObject
@property (readonly, copy) NSString *identifier;
@property (readwrite, copy) NSString *name;
- (Person *)initWithIdentifier:(NSString *)anIdentifier;
@end
```

Person.m (Flyweight)

```objc
@implementation Person
@synthesize identifier=identifier_;
@synthesize name=name_;

- (Person *)initWithIdentifier:(NSString *)anIdentifier {
  if ((self = [super init])) {
    identifier_ = [anIdentifier copy];
  }
  return self;
}
@end
```

Now you create a static NSMutableDictionary to keep track of your emailAddress data:

Person+EmailAddress.h (Flyweight)

```objc
@interface Person (EmailAddress)
@property (readwrite, copy) NSString *emailAddress;
@end
```

Person+EmailAddress.m (Flyweight)

```objc
@implementation Person (EmailAddress)

static NSMutableDictionary *sEmailAddressForIdentifier = nil;

+ (void)load {
  sEmailAddressForIdentifier =
    [[NSMutableDictionary alloc] init];
}

- (NSString *)emailAddress {
  return [sEmailAddressForIdentifier
          objectForKey:[self identifier]];
}

- (void)setEmailAddress:(NSString *)anAddress {
  [sEmailAddressForIdentifier setObject:[anAddress copy]
                                 forKey:[self identifier]];
}
@end
```

You can now set an email address for a `Person` object just as you would set a name, as shown here:

main.m (Flyweight)

```
...
Person *person = [[Person alloc] initWithIdentifier:@"someone"];
person.name = @"A Name";
person.emailAddress = @"myaddress@example.org";
...
```

There are some problems with this approach. There's no good way to release memory, unless you can somehow track when `Person` objects are destroyed. But for a wide variety of problems, this approach works pretty well in cases where associative references aren't an option.

Class Extensions

Objective-C 2.0 adds a useful twist on categories, called *class extensions*. These are declared exactly like categories, except the name of the category is empty:

```
@interface MYObject ()
- (void)doSomething;
@end
```

Class extensions are a great way to declare private methods inside of your `.m` file. The difference between a category and an extension is that methods declared by an extension are exactly the same as methods declared in the main interface. The compiler will make sure you implement them all, and they will be added to the class at compile time rather than runtime as categories are. You can even declare synthesized properties in extensions.

Formal and Informal Protocols

Protocols are an important part of Objective-C, and in Objective-C 2.0 formal protocols have become common. In Objective-C 1.0, there was no `@optional` tag for protocol methods, so all methods were mandatory. It is rare that this is useful. Often you want some or all of the protocol to be optional. Because this wasn't possible in Objective-C 1.0, developers commonly used "informal protocols" and sometimes you'll still come across these.

An informal protocol is a category on `NSObject`. Categories tell the compiler that a method exists, but do not require that the method be implemented. This technique allowed developers to document the interface and prevent compiler warnings, while indicating that any child of `NSObject` could implement the methods. This isn't a great approach to defining an interface, but in Objective-C 1.0, it was the best there was.

With Objective-C 2.0, formal protocols can declare optional methods, and many informal protocols on Mac are migrating to formal protocols. Luckily, iOS has always used Objective-C 2.0, so formal protocols are the norm.

Most developers are familiar with how to declare that a class implements a formal protocol. You simply include the protocols in angle brackets after the superclass:

```
@interface MyAppDelegate : NSObject <UIApplicationDelegate,
                                     UITableViewDatasource>
```

Declaring a protocol is similarly easy:

```
@protocol UITableViewDataSource <NSObject>

@required
- (NSInteger)tableView:(UITableView *)tableView
 numberOfRowsInSection:(NSInteger)section;
- (UITableViewCell *)tableView:(UITableView *)tableView
        cellForRowAtIndexPath:(NSIndexPath *)indexPath;

@optional
- (NSInteger)numberOfSectionsInTableView:(UITableView *)tv;
- (NSString *)tableView:(UITableView *)tableView
titleForHeaderInSection:(NSInteger)section;
...
```

There are some important points to note in this example. First, protocols can inherit just like classes. The UITableViewDataSource protocol inherits from the <NSObject> protocol. Your protocols should almost always inherit from <NSObject>, just as your classes inherit from NSObject.

> NSObject **is split into both a class and a protocol. This is primarily to support** NSProxy, **which inherits from the protocol, but not the class.**

For delegate protocols, the delegating object is always the first parameter. This is important because it allows a single delegate to manage multiple delegating objects. For instance, one controller could be the delegate for multiple UIAlertView instances. Note the slight difference in naming convention when there are parameters other than the delegating object. If there are no other parameters, the class name comes last (numberOfSectionsInTableView:). If there are other parameters, the class name comes first as its own parameter (tableView:numberOfRowsInSection:).

Once you've created your protocol, you will often need a property to hold it. The typical type for this property is id<Protocol>:

```
@property(nonatomic, weak) id<MyDelegate> delegate;
```

This means "any object that conforms to the MyDelegate protocol." It is possible to declare both a specific class and a protocol, and it's possible to declare multiple protocols in the type:

```
@property(nonatomic, weak) MyClass* <MyDelegate,
                           UITableViewDelegate> delegate;
```

This indicates that `delegate` must be a subclass of `MyClass` and must conform to both the `<MyDelegate>` and `<UITableViewDelegate>` protocols.

Protocols are an excellent alternative to subclassing in many cases. A single object can conform to multiple protocols without suffering the problems of multiple inheritance (as found in C++). If you are considering an abstract class, a protocol is often the better choice. Protocols are extremely common in well-designed Cocoa applications.

Summary

Much of good Objective-C is "by convention" rather than enforced by the compiler. This chapter covers several of the important techniques you'll use every day to get your programs to the next level. Conforming to Cocoa's naming conventions will greatly improve the reliability and maintainability of your code, and give you key-value coding and observing for free. Correct use of properties will make memory management easy, especially since the addition of ARC. And good use of categories and protocols will keep your code easy to understand and extend.

Further Reading

Apple Documentation

The following document is available in the iOS Developer Library at `developer.apple.com` or through the Xcode Documentation and API Reference.

Coding Guidelines for Cocoa

Other Resources

Gallagher, Matt, "Method names in Objective-C," *Cocoa With Love*.

`cocoawithlove.com/2009/06/method-names-in-objective-c.html`

Stevenson, Scott, "Cocoa Style for Objective-C," *CocoaDevCentral*.
`cocoadevcentral.com/articles/000082.php`

## Chapter 4

Hold On Loosely: Cocoa Design Patterns

If you're like most iOS developers, Objective-C is not your first language. You probably have a background in other object-oriented languages like Java, C++, or C#. You may have done development in C. None of these languages really prepare you for how to think in Objective-C.

In the beginning there was Simula, and Simula had two children: C++ from Bell Labs and Smalltalk from Xerox PARC. From C++ sprung Java, which tried to make things easier. Microsoft wrote Java.NET and called it C#. Today, most developers are trained in this branch of Simula. Its patterns include generic programming, static typing, customization through subclassing, method calling, and strong object ownership.

Objective-C and Cocoa come from the Smalltalk fork. NeXT developed a framework called NeXTSTEP. It was written in Objective-C and implemented many of Smalltalk's patterns. When Apple brought NeXTSTEP to the Mac, it renamed it Cocoa, although the NS prefix remains to this day. Cocoa has very different patterns, and this is what sometimes gives new developers trouble. Common Cocoa patterns include protocols, dynamic typing, customization through delegation, message passing, and shared object ownership.

I'm not going to give a computer science history lesson here, but it's important to understand that Objective-C is not Java and it's not C++. It's really Smalltalk. Because few developers learn Smalltalk, most need to adjust their thinking to get the most out of Objective-C.

In this chapter I use the terms Objective-C and Cocoa interchangeably. Technically, Objective-C is a language and Cocoa is a collection of frameworks implemented in Objective-C. In principle you could use Objective-C without Cocoa, but in practice this is never done. In the following sections you learn the major Cocoa design patterns and how best to apply them in your programs.

The pattern names used in this chapter come from the book *Design Patterns* (Addison-Wesley Professional 1994. ISBN: 978-0201633610) by Eric Gamma, Richard Helm, Ralph Johnson, and John Vlissides—sometimes called "The Gang of Four." Apple maps its patterns to the *Design Pattern* names in the chapter "Cocoa Design Patterns" of the *Cocoa Fundamentals Guide* (see the "Further Reading" section at the end of this chapter).

Understanding Model-View-Controller

The most important pattern in Smalltalk and Cocoa is called *model-view-controller (MVC)*. This is an approach to assigning responsibilities within a program. *Model* classes are responsible for representing information. *View* classes are responsible for interfacing with the user. *Controller* classes are responsible for coordinating between models and views.

There are subtle differences between how Smalltalk and Cocoa implement MVC. This chapter discusses only how Cocoa uses MVC.

Using Model Classes

A good model class encapsulates a piece of data in a presentation-independent way. A classic example of a good model class is `Person`. A `Person` might have a name, an address, a birthdate, and an image. The `Person` class, or related model classes, would encapsulate storing and retrieving related information from a data source, but would have no display or editing features. The same `Person` class should be easily reusable on an iPhone, iPad, Mac, or a command-line program. Model classes should reference only other model classes. They should never reference views or controllers. A model class might have a delegate that happens to be a controller, but it should implement this using a protocol so that it does not need to reference the specific controller class.

Model class names are generally simple nouns like `Person`, `Dog`, and `Record`. You often include a two- or three-letter prefix to identify them as your code and prevent collisions, such as `RNPerson`.

Model classes can be mutable or immutable. An *immutable* class cannot change once it is created. `NSString` is a good example of this. A *mutable* class like `NSMutableString` can change after it is created. In this context, "change" refers only to changes that are visible outside the object. It doesn't matter if internal data structures like caches change.

There are many advantages to immutable objects. They can save time and memory. Immutable objects can implement `copy` by calling `retain`. Because it's impossible for the object to change, you don't have to make a real copy. Immutable objects are inherently thread safe without locking, which makes them much faster and safer to access in multithreaded code. Because everything is configured at initialization time, it is much easier to ensure the object is always in a consistent state. You should use immutable model classes unless there is a reason to make them mutable.

Model classes are often the most testable and reusable classes in the system. Designing them well is one of the best ways to improve the overall quality of your code. Historically, Apple sample code has not included well-designed model classes. This confuses new developers who believed that controllers (or worse, views) are supposed to hold data. More recent sample code from Apple has improved, and the example project `TheElements` includes good examples of model classes. Look at `AtomicElement` and `PeriodicElements`. (See the "Further Reading" section at the end of this chapter.)

Using View Classes

View classes are responsible for interfacing with the user. They present information and accept user events. (This is the biggest deviation from Smalltalk MVC, where controller classes are responsible for user events.) View classes should not reference controller classes. As with model classes, view classes may have a delegate that happens to be a controller, but they shouldn't reference the controller class directly. They also shouldn't reference other views, except their immediate superview and subviews. Views may reference model classes, but generally only the specific model object that they are displaying. For instance a `PersonView` object might display a single `Person` object. It is easier to reuse view objects that do not reference custom model objects. For instance, a `UITableViewCell` is highly reusable because it displays only strings and images. There is sometimes a trade-off between reusability and ease-of-use in view objects, and finding the right balance is an important part of your architecture. In my experience, specialized views that handle a specific model class are often very useful for application writers. Framework writers, such as the UIKit team, need to emphasize reusability.

Model-specific view class names often append `View` to the model class, such as `PersonView` or `RecordView`. You should do this only if the view is a subclass of `UIView`. Some kinds of view classes have special names. Reusable views are generally called *cells* such as `UITableViewCell` on iOS or `NSCell` on Mac. Lightweight, hardware-optimized view classes are generally called *layers* such as `CALayer` or `CGLayer`. Whether or not they are subclasses of `UIView` or `NSView`, they are still MVC view classes.

Views are responsible for accepting events from users, but not for processing them. When a user touches a view, the view may respond by alerting a delegate that it has been touched, but it should not perform logic or modify other views. For example, pressing a Delete button should simply tell a delegate that the Delete button has been pressed. It should not tell the model classes to delete the data, nor tell the table view to remove the data from the screen. Those functions are the responsibility of a controller.

Using Controller Classes

Between the models and the views lie the controllers, which implement most of the application-specific logic. Most controllers coordinate between model classes and view classes. For example `UITableViewController` coordinates between the data model and the `UITableView`.

Some controllers coordinate between model objects or between view objects. These sometimes have names ending in `Manager` such as `CALayoutManager` and `CTFontManager`. It is common for managers to be singletons.

Controllers are often the least-reusable parts of a program, which is why it is so critical not to allow view and model classes to reference them directly. Even controllers should avoid referencing other controllers directly. In this context, "directly" means referring to specific classes. It is fine to refer to protocols that are implemented by a controller. For instance, `UITableView` references `<UITableViewDelegate>`, but should not reference `MyTableViewController`.

A common mistake is to allow many objects to reference the application delegate directly. For example, you may want to access a global object. A common, but incorrect, solution is to add this global object as a property on the application delegate, and access it as shown here:

```
// Do not do this
MyAppDelegate *appDelegate =
   (MyAppDelegate*)[[UIApplication sharedApplication] delegate];
Something *something = [appDelegate something];
// Do not do this
```

It is very difficult to reuse code that uses this pattern. It relies on `MyAppDelegate`, which is hard to move to other programs that have their own application delegate. The better way to access global objects is the Singleton pattern, discussed later in this chapter.

The model-view-controller pattern is very effective at improving code reuse. Applying it properly to your programs helps them fit into the Cocoa framework and simplify development.

Understanding Delegates and Data Sources

A *delegate* is a helper object that manages the behavior of another object. For example, `UITableView` needs to know how tall each row should be. `UITableView` has a `rowHeight` property, but this isn't sufficient for all problems. What if the first row should be taller than the other rows? Apple might have added a `firstRowHeight` property for that case. Then it might have added `lastRowHeight` and `evenRowHeight` properties. `UITableView` would become much more complicated, and still would be limited to uses that Apple had specifically designed for.

Instead `UITableView` takes a delegate, which can be any object class that conforms to the `<UITableViewDelegate>` protocol. Every time `UITableView` is ready to draw a row, it asks its delegate how tall that row should be. This allows you to implement arbitrary logic for row height. It could be based on the data in that row, or a user configuration option, or any other criteria that is appropriate for your application. Delegation makes customization extremely flexible.

Some objects have a special kind of delegate called a *data source*. `UITableView` has a data source protocol called `<UITableViewDataSource>`. Generally a delegate is responsible for appearance and behavior, while a data source is responsible for the data to be displayed. Splitting the responsibilities this way can be useful in some cases, but most of the time the delegate and the data source are the same object. This object is generally the controller. For instance, `UITableViewController` conforms to both `<UITableViewDelegate>` and `<UITableViewDataSource>`.

As a general rule, objects do not retain their delegates. If you create a class with a `delegate` property, it should almost always be declared `weak`. In most cases, an object's delegate is also its controller, and the controller almost always retains the original object. If the object retained its delegate, you would have a retain loop and would leak memory. There are exceptions to this rule. For example, `NSURLConnection` retains its delegate, but only while the connection is loading. After that `NSURLConnection` releases its delegate, avoiding a permanent retain loop.

Delegates are often observers (see "Working with the Observer Pattern" later in this chapter). It is common for objects to have delegate methods that parallel their notifications. For example, `UIApplication` sends its delegate `applicationWillTerminate:`. It also posts the notification `UIApplicationWill TerminateNotification`.

Configuring your objects using delegation is a form of the Strategy pattern. The Strategy pattern encapsulates an algorithm, and allows you to change how an object behaves by attaching different strategy (algorithm) objects. A delegate is a kind of Strategy object that encapsulates the algorithms determining the behavior of another object. For instance, a table view's delegate implements an algorithm that determines how high the table view's rows should be. Delegation reduces the need for subclassing by moving customization logic into helper objects. This improves reusability and can simplify your code by moving complex customization logic out of the main program flow. Before adding configuration properties to your classes, consider adding a delegate instead.

Working with the Command Pattern

The Command pattern encapsulates a request as an object. Rather than calling a method directly, you package the method call into an object and dispatch it, possibly at a later time. This can provide significant flexibility and allows requests to be queued, redirected, logged, and serialized. It also supports undoing operations by storing the inverse of the commands. Cocoa implements the Command pattern using target-action and `NSInvocation`. In this section you will learn how to use `NSInvocation` to create more complex dispatch objects such as trampolines.

Using Target-Action

The simplest form of the Command pattern in Cocoa is called *target-action*. This isn't a full implementation of the Command pattern because it doesn't encapsulate the request into a separate object, but it allows similar flexibility.

`UIControl` is an excellent example of target-action. You configure a `UIControl` by calling `addTarget:action:forControlEvents:`. This establishes a *target*, which is the object to send a message, an *action*, which is the message to send, and a set of events that will trigger the message. The action selector must conform to a particular signature. In the case of `UIControl`, the signature must be in one of the following forms:

```
- (void)action;
- (void)action:(id)sender;
- (void)action:(id)sender forEvent:(UIEvent *)event;
```

`UIControl` can then dispatch its `action` like this:

```
[target performSelector:action
            withObject:self
            withObject:event];
```

Because of how Objective-C message passing works, this use of `performSelector:...` works whether `action` takes one, two, or no parameters. (See Chapter 20 for details of how Objective-C message passing is implemented.)

Target-action is very common in Objective-C. Controls, timers, toolbars, gesture recognizers, `IBAction`, notifications, and other parts of Cocoa rely on this pattern.

Target-action is similar to delegation. The main difference is that in target-action the selector is configurable, while in delegation the selector is defined by a protocol. It is easier for a single object to be the target of several `NSTimer` objects than it is to be the delegate of several `UITableView` objects. To listen to multiple `NSTimer` objects, you only need to configure them with different actions:

```
[NSTimer scheduledTimerWithTimeInterval:1 target:self
              selector:@selector(firstTimerFired:) ...];
[NSTimer scheduledTimerWithTimeInterval:1 target:self
              selector:@selector(secondTimerFired:) ...];
```

To listen to multiple table views, you need to check which table view sent the request:

```
- (NSInteger)numberOfSectionsInTableView:(UITableView*)tv {
  if (tv == self.tableView1) {
    return [self.dataset1 count];
  }
  else if (tv == self.tableView2) {
    return [self.dataset2 count];
  }
  else {
    NSAssert(NO, @"Bad tv: %@", tv);
    return 0;
  }
}
```

Each delegate method must include this `if` logic, which can become very cumbersome. For this reason, multiple instances of a class generally do not share the same delegate.

On the other hand, delegation allows you to verify at compile time that the required methods are implemented. The compiler cannot verify that the target of an `NSTimer` implements a given action.

> While the compiler cannot determine if a target implements a given action, you can check for simple typos by turning on the Undeclared Selector warning (GCC_WARN_UNDECLARED_SELECTOR, `-Wundeclared-selector`). This generates a warning if an `@selector(...)` expression references an unknown selector.

As a general rule, if your object will send only one message to its target object, use target-action. If it will send multiple messages, use delegation.

Using Method Signatures and Invocations

`NSInvocation` is a traditional implementation of the Command pattern. It bundles a target, a selector, a method signature, and all the parameters into an object that can be stored and invoked at a later time. When the invocation is invoked, it will send the message and the Objective-C runtime will find the correct method implementation to execute.

A *method implementation* (`IMP`) is a function pointer to a C function with the following signature:

```
id function(id self, SEL _cmd, ...)
```

Every method implementation takes two parameters, `self` and `_cmd`. The first parameter is the `self` pointer that you are familiar with. The second parameter, `_cmd`, is the selector that was sent to this object. This is a reserved symbol in the language and is accessed exactly like `self`. For more details on how to work with method implementations, see Chapter 20.

> While the `IMP` typedef suggests that every Objective-C method returns an `id`, obviously there are many Objective-C methods that return other types such as integers or floating-point numbers, and many Objective-C methods return nothing at all. The actual return type is defined by the message signature, discussed below, not the `IMP` typedef.

`NSInvocation` includes a target and a selector. As discussed in the section "Using Target-Action," a target is the object to send the message to, and the selector is the message to send. A selector is roughly the name of a method. I say "roughly" because selectors don't have to map exactly to methods. A selector is just a name, like `initWithBytes:length:encoding:`. A selector isn't bound to any particular class or any particular return value or parameter types. It isn't even specifically a class or instance selector. You can think of a selector as a string. So `-[NSString length]` and `-[NSData length]` have the same selector, even though they map to different methods' implementations.

`NSInvocation` also includes a method signature (`NSMethodSignature`). This encapsulates the return type and the parameter types of a method. An `NSMethodSignature` does not include the name of a method, only the return value and the parameters. Here is how you can create one by hand:

```
NSMethodSignature *sig =
        [NSMethodSignature signatureWithObjCTypes:"@@:*"];
```

This is the signature for `-[NSString initWithUTF8String:]`. The first character (@) indicates that the return value is an `id`. To the message passing system, all Objective-C objects are the same. It can't tell the difference between an `NSString` and an `NSArray`. The next two characters (@:) indicate that this method takes an `id` and a `SEL`. As discussed above, every Objective-C method takes these as its first two parameters. They're implicitly passed as `self` and `_cmd`. Finally, the last character (*) indicates that the first "real" parameter is a character string (`char*`).

> If you do work with type encoding directly, you can use `@encode(type)` to get the string that represents that type rather than hard-coding letter. For example, `@encode(id)` is the string "@".

You should seldom call `signatureWithObjCTypes:`. I only do it here to show it's possible to build a method signature by hand. The way you generally get a method signature is to ask a class or instance for it. Before you do that, you need to consider whether the method is an instance method or a class method. The method `-init` is an instance method and is marked with a leading hyphen (-). The method `+alloc` is a class method and is marked with a leading plus (+). You can request instance method signatures from instances and class method signatures from classes using `methodSignatureForSelector:`. If you want the instance method signature from a class, you use `instanceMethodSignatureForSelector:`. The following example demonstrates this for `+alloc` and `-init`.

```
SEL initSEL = @selector(init);
SEL allocSEL = @selector(alloc);
NSMethodSignature *initSig, *allocSig;

// Instance method signature from instance
initSig = [@"String" methodSignatureForSelector:initSEL];

// Instance method signature from class
initSig = [NSString
            instanceMethodSignatureForSelector:initSEL];

// Class method signature from class
allocSig = [NSString
            methodSignatureForSelector:allocSEL];
```

If you compare `initSig` and `allocSig`, you will discover that they are the same. They each take no additional parameters (besides `self` and `_cmd`) and return an `id`. This is all that matters to the message signature.

Now that you have a selector and a signature, you can combine them with a target and parameter values to construct an `NSInvocation`. An `NSInvocation` bundles everything needed to pass a message. Here is how you create an invocation of the message `[set addObject:stuff]` and invoke it:

```
NSMutableSet *set = [NSMutableSet set];
NSString *stuff = @"Stuff";
SEL selector = @selector(addObject:);
NSMethodSignature *sig =
            [set methodSignatureForSelector:selector];

NSInvocation *invocation =
        [NSInvocation invocationWithMethodSignature:sig];
[invocation setTarget:set];
[invocation setSelector:selector];
// Place the first argument at index 2.
[invocation setArgument:&stuff atIndex:2];
[invocation invoke];
```

Note that the first argument is placed at index 2. As discussed above, index 0 is the target (`self`) and index 1 is the selector (`_cmd`). `NSInvocation` sets these automatically. Also note that you must pass a pointer to the argument, not the argument itself.

Invocations are extremely flexible, but they're not fast. Creating an invocation is hundreds of times slower than passing a message. Invoking an invocation is cheap, however, and invocations can be reused. They can be dispatched to different targets using `invokeWithTarget:` or `setTarget:`. You can also change their parameters between uses. Much of the cost of creating an invocation is in `methodSignatureForSelector:`, so caching this result can significantly improve performance.

Invocations do not retain their object arguments by default, nor do they make a copy of C string arguments. To store the invocation for later use, you should call `retainArguments` on it. This retains all object arguments and copies all C string arguments. When the invocation is released, it releases the objects and frees its copies of the C strings. Invocations do not provide any handling for pointers other than Objective-C objects and C strings. If you're passing raw pointers to an invocation, you're responsible for managing the memory yourself.

> If you use an invocation to create an `NSTimer`, such as by using `timerWithTimeInterval:invocation:repeats:`, the timer automatically calls `retainArguments` on the invocation.

Invocations are a key part of the Objective-C message dispatching system. This integration with the message dispatching system makes them central to creating trampolines and undo management.

Using Trampolines

A *trampoline* "bounces" a message from one object to another. This allows a proxy object to move messages to another thread, cache results, coalesce duplicate messages, or any other intermediary processing you'd like. Trampolines generally use `forwardInvocation:` to handle arbitrary messages. If an object does not respond to a selector, before Objective-C throws an error it creates an `NSInvocation` and passes it to the object's `forwardInvocation:`. You can use this to forward the message in any way that you'd like. For full details, see Chapter 20.

In this example, you create a trampoline called `RNObserverManager`. Any message sent to the trampoline will be forwarded to registered observers that respond to that selector. This provides functionality similar to `NSNotification`, but is easier to use and faster if there are many observers.

Here is the public interface for `RNObserverManager`:

RNObserverManager.h (ObserverTrampoline)

```
#import <objc/runtime.h>
@interface RNObserverManager: NSObject

- (id)initWithProtocol:(Protocol *)protocol
            observers:(NSSet *)observers;
- (void)addObserver:(id)observer;
- (void)removeObserver:(id)observer;

@end
```

You initialize this trampoline with a protocol and an initial set of observers. You can then add or remove observers. Any method defined in the protocol will be forwarded to all the current observers if they implement it.

Here is the skeleton implementation for `RNObserverManager`, without the trampoline piece. Everything should be fairly obvious.

RNObserverManager.m (ObserverTrampoline)

```objc
@interface RNObserverManager ()
@property (nonatomic, readonly, strong)
                                    NSMutableSet *observers;
@property (nonatomic, readonly, strong) Protocol *protocol;
@end

@implementation RNObserverManager
@synthesize observers = observers_;
@synthesize protocol = protocol_;

- (id)initWithProtocol:(Protocol *)protocol
            observers:(NSSet *)observers {
  if ((self = [super init])) {
    protocol_ = protocol;
    observers_ = [NSMutableSet setWithSet:observers];
  }
  return self;
}

- (void)addObserver:(id)observer {
  NSAssert([observer conformsToProtocol:self.protocol],
          @"Observer must conform to protocol.");
  [self.observers addObject:observer];
}

- (void)removeObserver:(id)observer {
  [self.observers removeObject:observer];
}
@end
```

Now you override `methodSignatureForSelector:`. The Objective-C message dispatcher uses this method to construct an `NSInvocation` for unknown selectors. You override it to return method signatures for methods defined in `protocol`, using `protocol_getMethodDescription`. You need to get the method signature from the protocol rather than from the observers because the method may be optional, and the observers might not implement it.

```objc
- (NSMethodSignature *)methodSignatureForSelector:(SEL)sel
{
  // Check the trampoline itself
  NSMethodSignature *
  result = [super methodSignatureForSelector:sel];
  if (result) {
    return result;
  }

  // Look for a required method
  struct objc_method_description desc =
          protocol_getMethodDescription(self.protocol,
                                        sel, YES, YES);
  if (desc.name == NULL) {
    // Couldn't find it. Maybe it's optional
```

```
      desc = protocol_getMethodDescription(self.protocol,
                                            sel, NO, YES);
   }

   if (desc.name == NULL) {
      // Couldn't find it. Raise NSInvalidArgumentException
      [self doesNotRecognizeSelector: sel];
      return nil;
   }

   return [NSMethodSignature
                      signatureWithObjCTypes:desc.types];
}
```

Finally, you override `forwardInvocation:` to forward the invocation to the observers that respond to the selector:

```
- (void)forwardInvocation:(NSInvocation *)invocation {
   SEL selector = [invocation selector];
   for (id responder in self.observers) {
      if ([responder respondsToSelector:selector]) {
         [invocation setTarget:responder];
         [invocation invoke];
      }
   }
}
```

To use this trampoline, you create an instance, set the observers, and then send messages to it as the following code shows. Variables that hold a trampoline should generally be of type `id` so that you can send any message to it without generating a compiler warning.

```
@protocol MyProtocol <NSObject>
- (void)doSomething;
@end

...

id observerManager = [[RNObserverManager alloc]
                  initWithProtocol:@protocol(MyProtocol)
                            observers:observers];

[observerManager doSomething];
```

This behaves similarly to posting a notification. You can use this technique to solve a variety of problems. For example, you can create a proxy trampoline that forwards all messages to the main thread as shown here:

RNMainThreadTrampoline.h (ObserverTrampoline)

```
@interface RNMainThreadTrampoline : NSObject
@property (nonatomic, readwrite, strong) id target;
- (id)initWithTarget:(id)aTarget;
@end
```

RNMainThreadTrampoline.m (ObserverTrampoline)

```objc
@implementation RNMainThreadTrampoline
@synthesize target = target_;

- (id)initWithTarget:(id)aTarget {
  if ((self = [super init])) {
    target_ = aTarget;
  }
  return self;
}

- (NSMethodSignature *)methodSignatureForSelector:(SEL)sel
{
  return [self.target methodSignatureForSelector:sel];
}

- (void)forwardInvocation:(NSInvocation *)invocation {
  [invocation setTarget:self.target];
  [invocation retainArguments];
  [invocation performSelectorOnMainThread:@selector(invoke)
                               withObject:nil
                            waitUntilDone:NO];
}

@end
```

`forwardInvocation:` can transparently coalesce duplicate messages, add logging, forward messages to other machines, and perform a wide variety of other functions. See Chapter 20 for more discussion, including how to couple with `NSProxy`.

Using Undo

The Command pattern is central to undo management. By storing Command objects (`NSInvocation`) in a stack, you can provide arbitrary undo and redo functionality.

Before performing an action that the user should be able to undo, you pass its inverse to `NSUndoManager`. A convenient way to do this is with `prepareWithInvocationTarget:`. For example:

```objc
- (void)setString:(NSString *)aString {
  // Make sure there is really a change
  if (! [aString isEqualToString:string_]) {
    // Send the undo action to the trampoline
    [[self.undoManager prepareWithInvocationTarget:self]
      setString:string_];

    // Perform the action
    string_ = aString;
  }
}
```

When you call `prepareWithInvocationTarget:`, the undo manager returns a trampoline that you can send arbitrary messages to. These are converted into `NSInvocation` objects and stored on a stack. When the user wants to undo an operation, the undo manager just invokes the last command on the stack.

The Command pattern is used throughout Cocoa and is a useful tool for your architectures. It helps separate request dispatching from the requests themselves, improving code reusability and flexibility.

Working with the Observer Pattern

The Observer pattern allows an object to notify many observers of changes in its state, without requiring that the observed object have special knowledge of the observers. The Observer pattern comes in many forms in Cocoa, including `NSNotification`, delegate observations, and key-value observing (KVO). It encourages weak coupling between objects, which makes components more reusable and robust.

Delegate observations are discussed in "Understanding Delegates and Data Sources" earlier in this chapter. KVO is discussed fully in Chapter 15. The rest of this section focuses on `NSNotification`.

Most Cocoa developers have encountered `NSNotificationCenter`. It provides loose coupling by allowing one object to register to be notified of events defined by string names. This can be simpler to implement and understand than KVO. Here's an example of how to use it well.

Poster.h

```
// Define a string constant for the notification
extern NSString * const PosterDidSomethingNotification;
```

Poster.m

```
        NSString * const PosterDidSomethingNotification =
                        @"PosterDidSomethingNotification";

    . . .

        // Include the poster as the object in the notification
        [[NSNotificationCenter defaultCenter]
          postNotificationName:PosterDidSomethingNotification
    object:self];
```

Observer.m

```
// Import Poster.h to get the string constant
#import "Poster.h"

. . .

    // Register to receive a notification
    [[NSNotificationCenter defaultCenter] addObserver:self
      selector:@selector(posterDidSomething:)
```

```
        name:PosterDidSomethingNotification object:nil];

...

- (void) posterDidSomething:(NSNotification *)note {
  // Handle the notification here
}

- (void)dealloc {
  // Always remove your observations
  [[NSNotificationCenter defaultCenter]
    removeObserver:self];
  [super dealloc];
}
```

Notice the name `PosterDidSomethingNotification`. It begins with the class of the poster, which should always be the class of the `object`. It then follows a "will" or "did" pattern. This is very similar to delegate methods and that's intentional. The ending `Notification` is traditional for notification names to distinguish them from other string constants like keys or paths.

This example uses a string constant for the notification name. This is critical for avoiding typos. Notification string constants do not traditionally begin with a `k` as some constants do. I recommend the value of the string constant match the name of the string constant as shown in this example. This makes obvious which constant is being used when you see the value in debug logs.

The placement of `const` is important when declaring string constants. This declaration is correct:

```
extern NSString * const RNFooDidCompleteNotification;
```

This declaration is incorrect:

```
extern const NSString * RNFooDidCompleteNotification;
```

The former is a constant pointer to an immutable string. The latter is a changeable pointer to an immutable string. `NSString` is always immutable because it is an immutable class. So `NSString * const` is useful. `const NSString *` is useless. This is easier to remember if you read the declaration from right to left: "`const` pointer to `NSString`."

As I mentioned earlier, the beginning of the notification name should always be the class of `object`. In this case that is `Poster`. This is almost always `self` (the object posting the notification). For consistency, the notification should always include an `object`, even if it is a singleton.

The observer should consider carefully whether to observe a specific object or `nil` (all notifications with a given name, regardless of the value of `object`). Observing a specific object can be cleaner and ensures that the observer won't receive notifications from instances that it is unaware of. A class that has a single instance today may have additional instances tomorrow.

If you observe a specific instance, it should generally be something you `retain` in an ivar. Observing something does not `retain` it, and the object you are observing could deallocate. That won't cause a crash; you just won't receive notifications from that object anymore. But it's sloppy and likely indicates a flaw in your design. It also uses unneeded slots in the notification table, which is bad for performance.

While observing an object that deallocates won't cause a crash, notifying a deallocated observer will. This is why you should always call `removeObserver:` in your `dealloc` if any part of your object calls `addObserver:....` Make a habit of this. It's one of the most common and preventable causes of crashes in code that uses notifications.

Calling `addObserver:selector:name:object:` multiple times with the same parameters causes you to receive multiple callbacks. This is almost never what you want. Generally it is easiest to start observing notifications in `init` and stop in `dealloc`. But what if you want to watch notifications from one of your properties, and that property can change? This example shows how to write `setPoster:` so that it properly adds and removes observations for a `poster` property:

```
- (void)setPoster:(Poster *)aPoster {
  NSNotificationCenter *nc =
                  [NSNotificationCenter defaultCenter];

  if (poster_ != nil) {
    // Remove all observations for the old value
    [nc removeObserver:self name:nil object:poster_];
  }

  poster_ = aPoster;

  if (poster_ != nil) {
    // Add the new observation
    [nc addObserver:self
          selector:@selector(anEventDidHappen:)
              name:PosterDidSomethingNotification
            object:poster_];
  }
}
```

The checks for `nil` are very important here. Passing `nil` as the `object` or the `name` means "any object" or "any notification."

While observing specific instances is cleaner and protects you against surprises when new objects are added to the system, there are reasons to avoid it. First, you may not really care which object is posting the notification. The object may not actually exist when you want to start observing notifications it might post, or the object instance may change over time.

There are also performance considerations when observing notifications. Every time a notification is posted, `NSNotificationCenter` has to search through the list of all registered observers to determine which observers to notify. The time required to search this list is proportional to the total number of observations registered in the `NSNotificationCenter`. When the total number of observations in the program reaches a few hundred, the time to search this list can become noticeable on an iPhone, particularly older models. The time required to call `removeObserver:` is similarly proportional to the total number of observations. This can cause serious performance problems if you have a large number of observations and post many notifications or remove observers often.

What if you want to observe a notification from a large number of objects, but not necessarily every object that might post that notification? For instance, you might be interested in changes to music tracks, but only the tracks in your current playlist. You could observe every track, but that can be very expensive. A better technique is to observe `nil` and check in the callback whether you were actually interested, as shown here:

```
// Observe all objects, whether in your tracklist or not
[[NSNotificationCenter defaultCenter]
   addObserver:self selector:@selector(trackDidChange:)
   name:TrackDidChangeNotification object:nil];

...

- (void)trackDidChange:(NSNotification *)note {
   // Verify that you cared about this track
   if ([self.tracks containsObject:[note object]]) {
      ...
   }
}
```

This reduces the number of observations, but adds an extra check during the callback. It depends on the situation whether this is faster or slower, but it is generally better than creating hundreds of observations.

Posting notifications is synchronous. This trips up many developers who expect the notification to execute on another thread or otherwise run asynchronously. When you call `postNotification:`, observers are notified one at a time before returning. The order of notification is not guaranteed.

Notifications are a critical part of many Cocoa programs. You just need to keep the preceding issues in mind, and they'll be a very useful part of your architecture.

Working with the Singleton Pattern

The Singleton pattern is in many ways just a global variable. It provides a global way to access a specific object. The Singleton pattern is common throughout Cocoa. In most cases you can identify it by a class method that begins with `shared`, such as `+sharedAccelerometer`, `+sharedApplication`, and `+sharedURLCache`. Some singleton access methods have other prefixes, such as `+[NSNotificationCenter defaultCenter]` and `+[NSUserDefaults standardUserDefaults]`. These are generally older classes inherited from NeXTSTEP. Most new frameworks use the `shared` prefix followed by their class name (without its namespace prefix).

The Singleton pattern is one of the most misused patterns in Cocoa because of some unfortunate sample code published by Apple. In the *Cocoa Fundamentals Guide*, Apple includes an implementation of the Singleton pattern that overrides the major memory management methods, `allocWithZone:`, `copyWithZone:`, `retain`, retainCount, release, and autorelease. Using Apple's example, multiple calls to [[Singleton alloc] init] return the same object. This is almost never needed or appropriate. Apple's explanation to this code indicates that it is only useful in cases where it is mandatory that there only be one instance of the class. That is seldom the case. Most of the time, it is only convenient that there be one instance of the class that is easily accessible. Many classes, such as NSNotificationCenter, work perfectly well if multiple instances exist. Unfortunately, many developers do not carefully read the explanation, and incorrectly copy this example.

Sometimes a strict singleton is appropriate. For example, if a class manages a unique shared resource, it may be impossible to have more than one instance. In this case it is often better to treat the creation of multiple instances as a programming error with NSAssert rather than transparently returning a shared instance. You will see how to implement this kind of assertion later in this section.

If you are creating a transparently strict singleton, make sure that it is an implementation detail and not something the caller must know. For instance, the class should be immutable. If the caller has requested distinct instances using +alloc, then it is very confusing if changes to one modify the other.

In the vast majority of cases, you should use a shared singleton rather than a strict singleton. A shared singleton is just a specific instance that is easy to fetch with a class method. It is generally stored in a static variable. There are many ways to do this, but my recommendation is this pattern, using +initialize:

```
static Singleton *sSingleton;

@implementation Singleton

+ (void)initialize {
  NSAssert(self == [Singleton class],
         @"Singleton is not designed to be subclassed.");
  sSingleton = [Singleton new];
}

+ (Singleton *)sharedSingleton {
  return sSingleton;
}
@end
```

This approach is easy to write, fast, and thread safe. Other approaches achieve thread safety by adding an @synchronize in +sharedSingleton, but this adds a significant performance penalty every time +sharedSingleton is called. +initialize is automatically called exactly once per class, so it is inherently thread safe.

It is possible to subclass Singleton, but it's seldom necessary so I prefer to forbid it rather than include the extra complexity needed to allow it. In most cases, the best way to customize a singleton is using the Strategy pattern described in "Understanding Delegates and Data Sources" earlier in this chapter. Rather than subclassing, put the changeable logic into a separate object and assign it to the singleton as a delegate. You can provide a default delegate object if the caller doesn't provide one. This is a rare case where the object (the singleton) should retain its delegate. A major advantage of this approach is that replacing the delegate immediately changes the singleton's behavior for all users of the singleton, even if they've stored the singleton in their own ivars.

Most of the problems with subclassing are eliminated if you can determine the correct subclass in `+initialize`. For example, you might make a compile-time decision like this:

```
+ (void)initialize {
   if (self == [Singleton class]) {
#if DEBUG
      sSingleton = [SingletonDebug new];
#else
      sSingleton = [SingletonRelease new];
#endif
   }
}
```

You could make similar runtime decisions such as checking the version of iOS or whether you are on an iPhone or iPad. In those cases, there's no problem with subclassing `Singleton` because it can only be set once.

If you really need to change the singleton instance at runtime, you can provide a `+setSharedSingleton:` method:

```
+ (void)initialize {
   if (self == [Singleton class]) {
      sSingleton = [Singleton new];
   }
}

+ (Singleton *)sharedSingleton {
   return sSingleton;
}

+ (void)setSharedSingleton:(Singleton *)aSingleton {
   sSingleton = aSingleton;
}
```

The problem with this approach is that other objects may already have pointers to the previous object when you call `setSharedSingleton:`. The preceding code is also not fully thread safe.

While a shared singleton is usually the best approach, sometimes you do require a strict singleton. For example, you may have a singleton that manages the connection to the server, and the server protocol may forbid multiple simultaneous connections from the same device. As a general rule, you should first try to redesign the protocol so that it doesn't have this restriction, but there are cases where this is impractical and a strictly enforced singleton is the best approach.

In most cases the best way to implement this is as a shared singleton, but treat calls to `init` as a programming error with `NSAssert` as shown here:

```
- (id)init {
   // Forbid calls to -init or +new
   NSAssert(NO, @"Cannot create instance of Singleton");

   // You can return nil or [self initSingleton] here,
```

```
    // depending on how you prefer to fail.
    return nil;
  }

  // Real init method
  - (id)initSingleton {
    self = [super init];
    if ((self = [super init])) {
      // Init code
    }
    return self;
  }

  + (void)initialize {
    NSAssert(self == [Singleton class],
         @"Singleton is not designed to be subclassed.");
    sSingleton = [[Singleton alloc] initSingleton];
  }
```

The advantage of this approach is that it prevents callers from believing they are creating multiple instances when that is forbidden. Frameworks should avoid silently fixing programming errors. This just makes bugs hard to track down.

As discussed in "Understanding Model-View-Controller," developers often use the application delegate to store global variables like this:

```
  // Do not do this
  MyAppDelegate *appDelegate =
      (MyAppDelegate*)[[UIApplication sharedApplication] delegate];
  Something *something = [appDelegate something];
  // Do not do this
```

In almost all cases, this would be better implemented with a `Something` singleton like the following:

```
  Something *something = [Something sharedSomething];
```

This way, when you copy the `Something` class to another project, it's self-contained. You don't have to extract bits of the application delegate along with it. If the application delegate is storing configuration information, it's best to move that into `NSUserDefaults` or a singleton `Configuration` object.

The Singleton pattern is one of the most common patterns in well-designed Cocoa applications. Don't overuse it. If an object is only used in a few places, just pass it to the objects that need it. But for objects that have applicationwide scope, it is a very good way to maintain loose coupling and improve code reusability.

Summary

This chapter explored the most pervasive patterns in Cocoa, particularly Strategy, Observer, Command, and Singleton. You learned how several patterns combine to facilitate Cocoa's central architecture: model-view-controller. Cocoa uses design patterns focused on loose coupling and code reusability. Understanding these patterns will help you anticipate how Apple frameworks are structured and improve your code's integration with iOS. The patterns Apple uses in iOS are well established and have been studied and refined for years throughout industry and academia. Correctly applying these patterns will improve the quality and reusability of your own programs.

Further Reading

Apple Documentation

The following documents are available in the iOS Developer Library at `developer.apple.com` or through the Xcode Documentation and API Reference.

"Cocoa Design Patterns," *Cocoa Fundamentals Guide*. This entire document is valuable to understanding Cocoa, but the section "Cocoa Design Patterns" focuses on how Cocoa applies the well-established software patterns.

The Elements (Sample Code). Historically, Apple sample code has not demonstrated good design or coding practices. The focus has typically been to show how a specific feature works, and the sample code typically ignores Apple's recommendations and common best practice. Apple appears to have changed its approach to sample code, and some recent examples are well designed and written. *The Elements* is a good example that developers can use to model their own projects.

Notification Programming Guide. Explains the Observer pattern implemented with NSNotification.

Undo Architecture. Explains how to use NSUndoManager using the Command pattern.

Other Resources

Gamma, Erich *et al. Design Patterns: Elements of Reusable Object-Oriented Software*. (Addison-Wesley Professional, 1994. ISBN: 978-0201633610) This book is a collection of well-known design patterns, explained in practical terms with code examples in C++ and Smalltalk. It should be part of every developer's library. Erich Gamma and his co-authors did not invent these patterns and *Design Patterns* is not an exhaustive list of all patterns. This book attempts to catalog patterns that the authors found in common use among developers, and provide a framework by which developers can apply known solutions to their unique problems.

AgentM, "Elegant Delegation," *Borkware Rants*. AgentM provides a somewhat different `MDelegateManager` class than my `RNObserverManager`. It was designed for Objective-C 1.0, so it does not rely on @protocol, but is still worth studying.
`borkware.com/rants/agentm/elegant-delegation`

Burbeck, Steve. "Applications Programming in Smalltalk-80™: How to use Model-View-Controller (MVC)." (1987, 1992). This is the definitive paper defining the MVC pattern in Smalltalk. NeXTSTEP (and later Cocoa) modified the pattern somewhat, but the Smalltalk approach is still the foundation of MVC.
`st-www.cs.illinois.edu/users/smarch/st-docs/mvc.html`

## Chapter 5

Getting Table Views Right

Table views are arguably the most ubiquitous and often used control on the iOS platform. Most of the quality apps on the App Store use table views, and not just for showing a hierarchical list of data. They are also used for complex structured, scrollable views. Table views are used as cheap substitute for creating vertically scrollable views even if the content they display is not a list of data. For example, in the built-in contacts app, the contacts list is a UITableView but so is the view for adding a new contact. Additionally, new interaction patterns have been introduced by third-party application developers, and have been quite commonly used on other apps as well.

iOS has been around for four years, so this chapter assumes that you are well versed with concepts like UITableViewDelegate and UITableViewDataSource.

> If you are not familiar with UITableViewDelegates and UITableViewDataSource, read Chapter 8 in *Beginning iPhone Development: Exploring the iPhone SDK* by Dave Mark and Jeff Lamarche (Apress 2009, ISBN 978-1430216261) before finishing this chapter.

This chapter focuses on the advanced aspects of table views and shows you how to create complex (yet common) UIs like Pull-To-Refresh and infinite scrolling lists. It also briefly explains how to use table view row animations to create accordions or options drawers (a UI that shows available toolbar elements just below the table view cell that is acted upon) and several other interesting UI paradigms.

After exploring new user interaction paradigms, you learn about the best practices that you should adopt to write cleaner UITableViewController code (code that is easy to modify later).

The second part of the chapter shows you how to create and use storyboards and introduces you to the new UIAppearance protocol, a new feature in iOS 5. You also learn how to add storyboards to your existing iOS app without completely rewriting them. With that, let's get started.

UITableView Class Hierarchy

A UITableView is a subclass of UIScrollView that allows users to scroll through a list of UITableViewCells, which are a subclass of UIView.

UITableView and UIScrollView share several things in common. For a heavily customized view that is not a list of data, you can directly use a UIScrollView and populate it with UIView or UIControl subclasses, but there are certain advantages to using a UITableView in this case. First, it's always advisable to use a higher-level abstraction whenever possible. Second, there are several subtle functionalities that a `UITableView` takes care of automatically. One of them is the ability to dequeue and reuse `UITableViewCells` easily, which improves performance and reduces memory consumption. Another is its elegant and easy way to populate content through its data source and receive feedback on actions through the delegate. If you use a custom `UIScrollView`, you have to do these two by yourself. While it's not difficult to do this, you probably will not get any added advantage by doing it yourself.

Understanding Table Views

A `UITableView` is normally used in conjunction with several other classes like `UITableViewController`, `UITableViewDelegate`, `UITableViewDataSource`, and `UITableViewCell`. This section briefly discusses the functionalities of each of these classes.

UITableViewController

A `UITableViewController` is a subclass of a `UIViewController` that performs some additional functions related to table view loading. If you are initializing a `UITableViewController` from a nib file, it loads the archived table view. If not, it creates a unconfigured table view. In both cases, you can access the table view using the `tableView` property of the `UITableViewController`.

Additionally, a `UITableViewController` reloads the table and clears cell selection, as it is about to appear for the first time (`viewWillAppear`). It then, in `viewDidAppear`, flashes the scroll indicators to indicate that the view is scrollable. You can override these methods and provide custom implementations as well.

The `UITableViewController` also handles the delegates and data source for your table. For table views created without a nib file, the delegate and data source becomes the table view controller. For table views created with a nib file, the delegate and data source is set from that file.

My recommendation is to use a separate `UITableViewController` for every table view you use within your view. Using multiple `UITableViewControllers` makes it easy to understand (and modify) the code later in the project's lifecycle. You learn how to use multiple `UITableViewControllers` within a single view/nib file later in this chapter.

UITableViewCell

`UITableViewCell` is a subclass of `UIView` that adds certain properties and functionalities to a `UIView` that are useful when used in a `UITableView`. Instead of you manually adding custom elements, a `UITableViewCell` adds often-used elements like a `textLabel`, `detailedTextLabel`, and an `imageView` that are exposed using properties. You specify the kind of cell you need by choosing a `UITableViewCellStyle`. The second most important property provided by a `UITableViewCell` is the capability to maintain distinct `selected` and `highlighted` states.

In most cases, you will be using a custom subclass of a `UITableViewCell` in your app. The next section discusses the different ways of creating a `UITableViewCell` and the pros and cons of using it.

Speed Up Your Tables

You might already know how to create a custom table view cell that scrolls butter-smooth like Tweetie (Twitter for iPhone). Loren Brichter has open-sourced his custom table view cell and explained in his blog how to do it (see the "Further Reading" section)." In this section, you develop a table view and populate it with cells created using different techniques, including Loren's, and you learn to analyze performance using Instruments. When you finish this section, you will understand *why* Loren's method makes your table view scroll smoothly. You also learn *how* to troubleshoot and find performance bottlenecks if your table views aren't scrolling as fast as they should. Once you know the "how" behind a technique, you can apply that techniques elsewhere.

A Word on Performance and Interface Builder

Whenever you talk about performance, the first thing you hear from most iOS developers is, "Don't use Interface Builder." Using Interface Builder (IB) to build interfaces is quite a controversial topic in the iOS developer community. Veteran Mac developers, or those who have switched from developing native Windows apps (using VB or C#), understand what IB does and why should it be used. Some web developers, on the other hand, often correlate IB to web-authoring tools and thus assume that IB slows down the app and degrades performance. My advice is that you should never pay attention to any advice about improving the performance of your app without measuring it. Tools like Instruments can help you with performance measurement; later in this chapter you learn how to use them.

Keep in mind that IB is not a code generator. It is an editor that generates XML-based archives of your view. In most cases, nib files do not lower the performance compared to an equivalently coded UI. (I illustrate this later in this chapter.) Additionally, using a nib file helps you isolate your "view" to a separate file, which keeps your controller free of view-related code (especially in your `viewDidLoad` method). That's a cleaner way to implement and adhere to the MVC design pattern.

To Use or Not to Use Interface Builder?

Having said that, the only place where I recommend using coded UI over IB is for high-performance `UITableViewCells`. The iOS rendering mechanism slows down when your `UITableViewCell` has many subviews. As of this writing, based on informal testing, only the latest, dual-core A5-powered iPad 2 gives acceptable scrolling performance for a fairly customized `UITableViewCell` (probably because of the super-fast graphics processor). By "acceptable scrolling performance," I mean getting at least 60 frames per second when scrolling the table. You learn how to measure this later in this chapter. The old iPhone 3G was slowest at 25 fps; other devices fall somewhere between 60 and 25 fps.

The performance hit when using a table view cell isn't caused by unarchiving nib files, but by rendering multiple subviews. Hence, a coded UI doesn't mean moving your `addSubView:` methods to the `initWithStyle:reuseIdentifier` method, but rather overriding the `drawRect` method and directly drawing your content instead of using subviews. Avoiding subviews (especially subviews that have transparency and blends with other views behind), improves performance.

In the next section you first write a table view with a thousand rows and measure the scrolling performance using Instruments. You also learn how to use Instruments to identify areas with alpha blended layers that are time-consuming to render. You gradually improve the performance by avoiding subviews and measuring performance in each step.

To complete the example, you need to have an iOS device provisioned for development, as some of these things cannot be done on the iOS Simulator.

UITableView with Subviews in a Custom UITableViewCell

Create a view-based iPhone application with Xcode and call it TableViewPerformance. You can leave storyboards, but enable ARC. You can download this code from the `Chapter 5/TableViewPerformance` folder on the book's website. Open `TableViewPerformanceViewController.xib` and drag a `UITableView` to it. You will populate this `UITableView` with three different types of cells.

Add a `UITableViewCell` subclass and call it CustomCell and create an IB file for it. Add a title label, a subtitle label, a time label, and a thumbnail image to it. Your IB file should look like Figure 5-1.

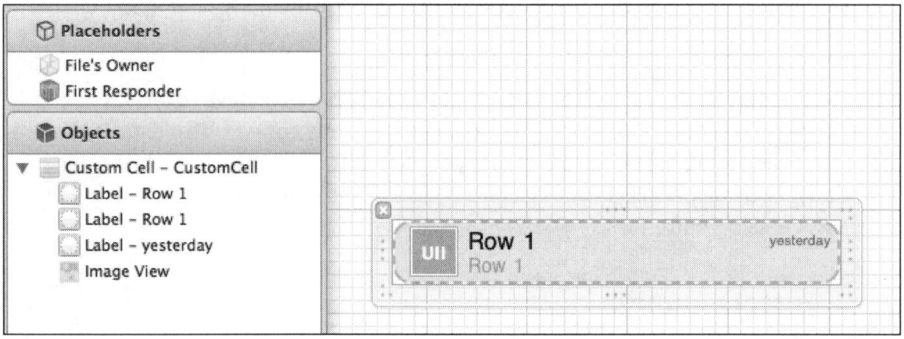

Figure 5-1 Custom cell nib

Now open `TableViewPerformanceViewController.m` and add the following code for the TableViewDataSource.

```
- (NSInteger)numberOfSectionsInTableView:(UITableView *)tableView {
return 1;
}

- (NSInteger)tableView:(UITableView *)tableView
            numberOfRowsInSection:(NSInteger)section {
return 1000;
}

// table with with normal XIB based cells
```

```
- (UITableViewCell *)tableView:(UITableView *)tableView
          cellForRowAtIndexPath:(NSIndexPath *)indexPath {
   static NSString *CellIdentifier = @"CustomCell";

   CustomCell *cell = (CustomCell*)[tableView
dequeueReusableCellWithIdentifier: CellIdentifier];
   if (cell == nil) {
   NSArray *nib = [[NSBundle mainBundle
loadNibNamed:@"CustomCell" owner:self options:nil];
   cell = (CustomCell*)[nib objectAtIndex:0];
   }

   cell.titleLabel.text = [NSString stringWithFormat:@"Row %d",
   indexPath.row];
   cell.subTitleLabel.text = [NSString stringWithFormat:@"Row %d",
   indexPath.row];
   cell.timeTitleLabel.text = @"yesterday";
   cell.imageView.image = [UIImage imageNamed:@"ios5"];
   cell.selectionStyle = UITableViewCellSelectionStyleNone;
   return cell;
}
```

Nothing fancy here. What you have done is to set some arbitrary values to the cells. Now profile this app in Instruments. Click and hold the Play button and choose Profile to profile the app. Choose the Core Animation trace template as shown in Figure 5-2.

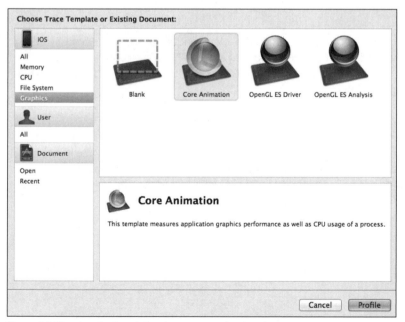

Figure 5-2 Choosing the Core Animation trace template from Instruments

Expand the debug options panel in Instruments by clicking View → Detail in Instruments. (This should be selected and showing up by default). Select the Color Blended Layers checkbox.

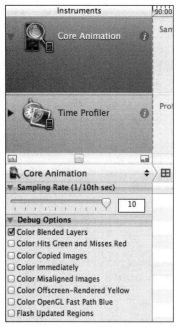

Figure 5-3 Select Color Blended Layers

The app should be running on your device. Because you turned on Color Blended Layers, your iPhone screen should look similar to Figure 5-4. Now scroll your table view and look at the frames per second measurement on Instruments. Depending on your debug device's processor and GPU speed, this might vary. I got somewhere around 38-45 fps on the iPhone 4 running a beta of iOS 5.

With Color Blended Layers, iOS shows transparent layers in red and opaque layers in green. In Figure 5-4, most of the areas around the labels in the custom cell are transparent and blended. These transparent layers have a computational cost to render. The system has to blend the layer with the layer below it to compute its color and then draw it. The rendering speed can be drastically improved by avoiding this. You see a couple of techniques to do that in the next section. When you implement them, you will find that the fps measurements improve as well.

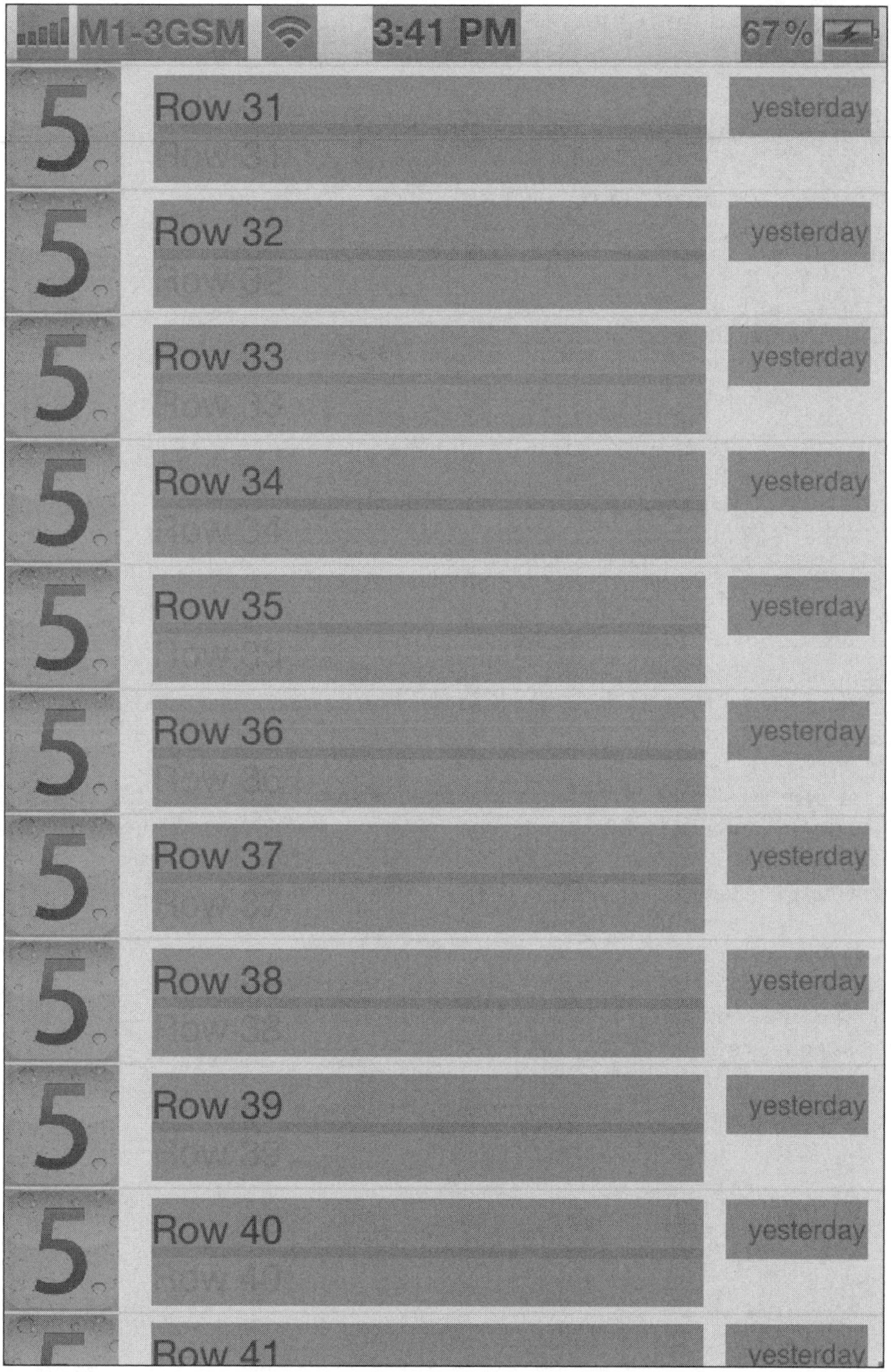

Figure 5-4 iOS device screen using custom cells

UITableView with a Default UITableViewCell

Replace the code in `cellForRowAtIndexPath:` in the controller file with this:

```
- (UITableViewCell *)tableView:(UITableView *)tableView
 cellForRowAtIndexPath:(NSIndexPath *)indexPath {

    static NSString *CellIdentifier = @"Cell";
    UITableViewCell *cell = [tableView
dequeueReusableCellWithIdentifier:CellIdentifier];
    if (cell == nil) {
        cell = [[[UITableViewCell alloc]
initWithStyle:UITableViewCellStyleSubtitle
reuseIdentifier:CellIdentifier] autorelease];

    }
cell.textLabel.text = [NSString stringWithFormat:
@"Row %d", indexPath.row];
    cell.detailTextLabel.text = [NSString stringWithFormat:
@"Row %d", indexPath.row];
    cell.imageView.image = [UIImage imageNamed:@"ios5"];
    return cell;
}
```

Instead of using your custom cell in this code, you use the framework's built-in `UITableViewCell` with `UITableViewCellStyleSubtitle`. Now profile the app again. When you turn on Color Blended Layers, your iPhone screen should look like Figure 5-5.

Observe that the transparent layers are all gone except for a few near the images. When you scroll the list, you find that the performance is slightly better and feels smoother than how it was previously. Observe that the fps measurement hits 60. When you hit 60 fps, you can technically stop improving the scrolling performance, but in this case, only the latest iPhone 4 was able to reach 60 fps while scrolling. The iPhone 3G and 3GS were much slower.

Moreover, with built-in cells you are limited to just four styles, and in any normal case, that just might not be enough. In the next method you use a custom cell that uses CoreGraphics methods to draw the image and text directly on the cell without using subviews.

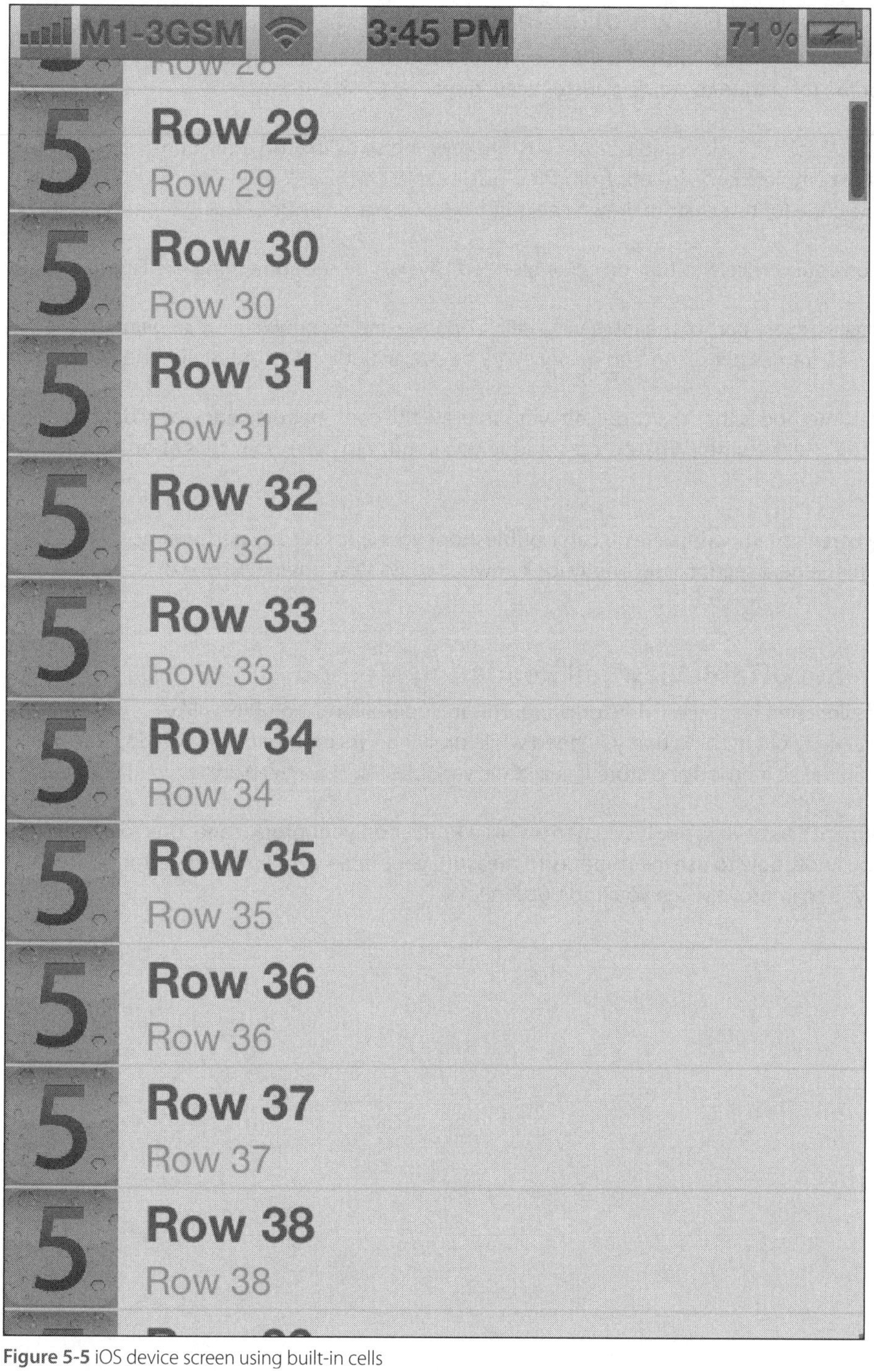

Figure 5-5 iOS device screen using built-in cells

UITableView with a Custom Drawn UITableViewCell

Loren Brichter of Tweetie (now known as Twitter for iPhone) wrote about butter-smooth scrolling in Tweetie. In this example, you use Loren's technique to create a custom cell for your `UITableView`.

Create a custom `UITableViewCell` class and do your custom drawing so as to render the content similar to the nib file. You can get the complete code for this from the `Chapter 5/TableViewPerformance` folder on the book's website. The code for this custom drawn cell is in file `CustomDrawnCell.m`.

When you run this code on your device and turn on Color Blended Layers, you see something like Figure 5-6.

With your custom drawn cells, every part of the table view cell is opaque and your table view scrolling is fast and smooth. I was getting 60 frames per second on nearly every device, including the oldest, iPhone 3G.

The only problem with this method is that the code you write to draw the content gets annoyingly difficult to read (although it's not difficult to write). Whatever technique you use, try to make your cells as opaque as possible.

Now that you know why Loren's method is fast, you can troubleshoot your apps for any performance bottlenecks quite easily. In the next section, you briefly look at what could slow down `UITableViewCell` rendering.

Things to Avoid in the UITableViewCell Rendering Method

You should always avoid allocating resources while drawing. This includes allocating objects like `NSDateFormatter`, `UIFont`, or anything that you need while drawing. I recommend that you do your allocation in a class-level initialize method and store it in a static variable. Use it for every instance of your cell.

If you still find the performance to be low, use Instruments's Time Profiler on your project and look for bottlenecks. Now that you know how to use Instruments to measure your table view scrolling performance, it should be quite easy for you to improve when you find bottlenecks.

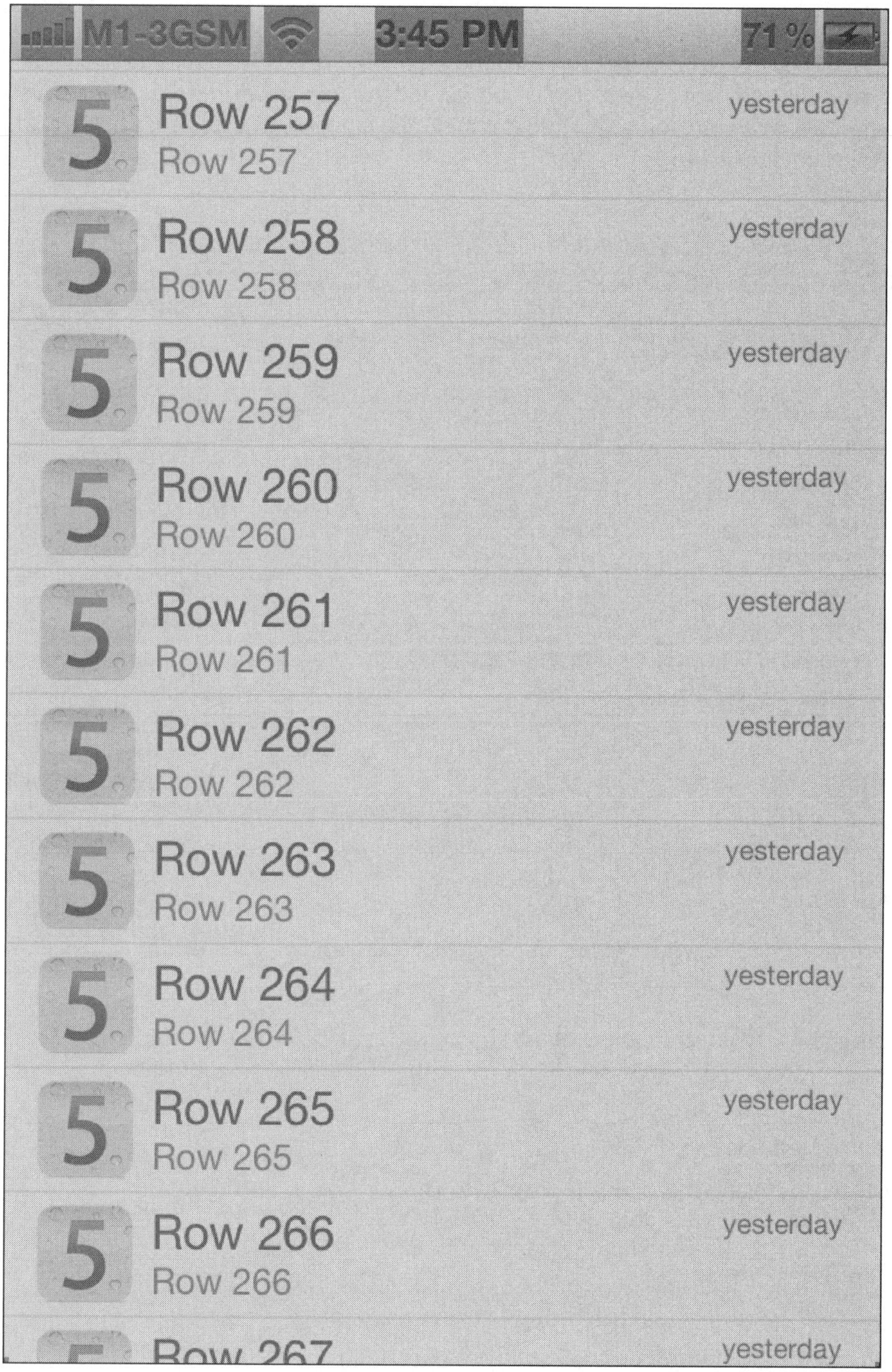

Figure 5-6 iOS device screen using custom drawn cells

Custom Nonrepeating Cells

Table views are used not just for showing a list of data but also for complex and structured scrollable layouts. If your table view structure has a nonrepeating pattern of cells, you can add the custom cell into the same nib file as the table view and connect `IBOutlets`. Figure 5-7 illustrates this. This way, you can just return a pointer to this `IBOutlet` in `cellForRowAtIndexPath:`.

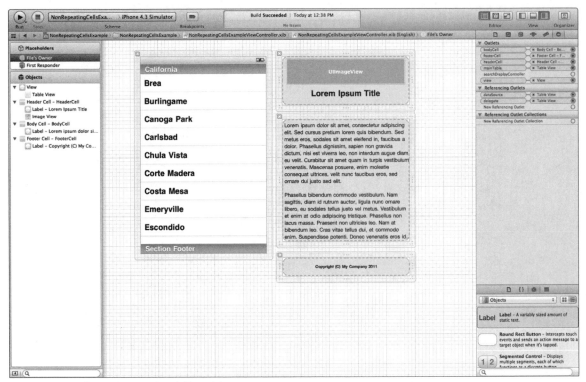

Figure 5-7 The different objects in the nib file and their connections

The following code snippet shows how to return these objects from the `UITableViewDataSource` methods.

UITableViewDataSource Methods

```
-(CGFloat) tableView:(UITableView*) tableView
heightForRowAtIndexPath:(NSIndexPath *)indexPath {

    switch (indexPath.row) {

        case 0:
            return self.headerCell.frame.size.height;
            break;
        case 1:
            return self.bodyCell.frame.size.height;
            break;
```

```
            case 2:
                return self.footerCell.frame.size.height;
                break;

            default:
                return 0;
                break;
        }
    }

    - (UITableViewCell *)tableView:(UITableView *)tableView
      cellForRowAtIndexPath:(NSIndexPath *)indexPath {

        switch (indexPath.row) {

            case 0:
                return self.headerCell;
                break;
            case 1:
                return self.bodyCell;
                break;
            case 2:
                return self.footerCell;
                break;

            default:
                return nil;
                break;
        }
    }
```

You can get the code from the `Chapter 5/NonRepeatingCellsExample` folder on the books' website. Note that `UIKit` objects don't conform to `NSCopying` or `NSMutableCopying` protocols and hence cannot be copied or cloned. That means that if you need two body cells—say one in row 1 and another in row 2—you have to load them from their nib files every time you need them. But fret not; the nib file-loading methods are optimized for performance and once loaded, nibs are cached.

> You can use a similar technique as in the previous example for creating custom table view headers and footers. Just create custom table header/footer views within the same nib file and drag them to the `UITableView` in IB. Your view gets added as a header or footer depending on where you dropped it.

Advanced Table Views

So far you've seen some of the basic, often-used implementations of table views. Now you're ready to look at some advanced implementations of table views, beginning with Pull-to-Refresh.

Pull-To-Refresh

In this section you write a `PullToRefreshTableView` class based on enormego's excellent open source implementation (see "Further Reading" section). This class isolates most of the Pull-To-Refresh code into a super class. Later on, when you need to add a Pull-to-Refresh feature to your table view, all you need to do is inherit your view controller from `PullToRefreshTableViewController` instead of `UIViewController` and override methods to perform the actual refresh.

Sounds object-oriented, right? Let's delve into the code. First, download the files from the book's website, in the Chapter 5 \ `PullToRefreshTableViewExample folder`.

Create a view-based project and add these files:

`EGORefreshTableHeaderView.h`

`EGORefreshTableHeaderView.m`

`PullToRefreshViewController.h`

`PullToRefreshViewController.m`

`RefreshArrow.png`

`RefreshArrow@2x.png`

The `PullToRefreshTableViewController` is a subclass of `UIViewController` that abstracts the mechanics behind the Pull-To-Refresh. It handles the `UIScrollView` delegates and adds the `EGORefreshHeaderView` to the top of your `UITableView` when it is pulled beyond a certain threshold. It also remembers the last refreshed state. By default this is stored in a key that uses your subclass name and a suffix string. In case this is not enough and you have multiple instances of the same class displaying different data, you can customize the key in which the last refreshed date is remembered. The key is stored in a property called `keyNameForDataStore`.

To implement Pull-To-Refresh in your code, inherit your view controller from `PullToRefreshViewController` and override the `doRefresh` method to perform the actual refresh. Once the refresh is done, set the loading state to `NO`. It's as simple as that. The `PullToRefreshViewController` also needs you to link your target with `QuartzCore.Framework`.

When you inherit your view controller from `PullToRefreshViewController`, you will see a `tableView` in the IBOutlet list in IB. Connect this `tableView` to the table in your nib file.

Now in the controller, override the `doRefresh` method and perform your network call (or any time-consuming refresh operation). Once the refresh operation is complete, set the loading state to `NO`.

Following is the sample code snippet for your view controller:

Sample doRefresh Implementation

```
-(void) doRefresh  {

// Do your time consuming operation here.
```

```
// The performSelector shown below is for your illustration
    [self performSelector:@selector(loadingComplete)
    withObject:nil afterDelay:2];
}
-(void) loadingComplete  {

    self.loading = NO;
// the loading property is exposed by
PullToRefreshViewController. When you set this to NO,
it restores the tableview back to its normal position.
}
```

Enormego did an excellent job of writing the mechanics behind Pull-to-Refresh. This takes it to the next level by abstracting the logic out and providing a super-easy way to implement it in any of your view controllers with under five lines of code. Along similar lines, let's now look at another commonly used technique: infinite scrolling.

Infinite Scrolling

Infinite scrolling is normally used in Twitter clients or any app that displays chronologically ordered data. Data for which the number of items are unknown or is immensely large, (unlike a contacts list), is the right candidate for infinite scrolling.

For this example, you extend the same `PullToRefreshTableViewExample` sample code, and add methods for implementing the infinite scrolling mechanics. The class adds a section to the end of your table view that shows a single "Loading" cell. For this, you add a couple properties called `numberOfSections` and `endReached` to the class `PullToRefreshTableView`.

```
@property (nonatomic) NSInteger numberOfSections;

@property (nonatomic) BOOL endReached;
```

You then add a method, `loadMore`, that will be called when the user reaches the end of the current page in the table view. The super class implementation for this will be empty and you will leave that for the subclasses to implement. For the complete code, get it from the book's website `Chapter 5/ InfiniteScrollingExample` folder. Do *not* implement the `numberOfSectionsInTableView:` in your subclass. The super class (`PullToRefreshViewController`) does this automatically for you. Instead, set the number of sections using the super class property `numberOfSections`. The parent class adds an additional section to the end of your table to show the loading cell.

You should override the method `loadMore` defined in the super class and provide implementation for loading more content. When your server returns no content, you can set the `endReached` property to `YES`. This prevents the loading cell from being shown again. The following sample code snippet explains this.

Sample loadMore Implementation

```
-(void) incrementPageCount  {
    self.pageCount ++;
    if(self.pageCount == 5) self.endReached = YES;
    [self.tableView reloadData];
```

```
}
-(void) loadMore  {
    [self performSelector:@selector(incrementPageCount) withObject:nil
afterDelay:2]; // simulate a network operation
}
```

The super class adds a loading section as the last section of the table view, and your table view data source methods will be called for sections you are not aware of. You should forward these calls to the super class of the `tableView:numberOfRowsInSection:` method and `tableView:cellForRowAtIndexPath:` for sections greater than your section count. In other words, let the super class handle sections greater that the `numberOfSections` for you. This implementation shows the `loadingCell`.

The following code snippet explains this.

Sample TableView Data Source

```
- (NSInteger)tableView:(UITableView *)tableView numberOfRowsInSection:(NSInteger)section {
    // Return the number of rows in the section.
    if(section == self.numberOfSections)  {
        return [super tableView:tableView numberOfRowsInSection:section];
    }
    return 20 * self.pageCount; // we are assuming 20 rows per page
}

- (UITableViewCell *)tableView:(UITableView *)tableView
 cellForRowAtIndexPath:(NSIndexPath *)indexPath {

    if(indexPath.section == self.numberOfSections)  {
        return [super tableView:tableView
 cellForRowAtIndexPath:indexPath];
    }
    static NSString *CellIdentifier = @"Cell";

    UITableViewCell *cell =
[tableView dequeueReusableCellWithIdentifier:CellIdentifier];
    if (cell == nil) {
        cell = [[[UITableViewCell alloc]
 initWithStyle:UITableViewCellStyleSubtitle
 reuseIdentifier:CellIdentifier] autorelease];
    }

cell.textLabel.text = [NSString stringWithFormat:
@"Row %d", indexPath.row];
    cell.detailTextLabel.text = [NSString stringWithFormat:
@"Row %d", indexPath.row];

    cell.imageView.image = [UIImage imageNamed:@"ios5"];
    cell.selectionStyle = UITableViewCellSelectionStyleNone;
    return cell;
}
```

That completes it. With very few changes, you have added infinite scrolling support to the Pull-To-Refresh example code. Implementing infinite scrolling in your apps should be a lot easier with this code.

Inline Editing and Keyboard

Form-filling is a common UI pattern found on both web and mobile environments. On iOS, forms are usually developed using `UITableView` with each cell representing one data entry field. It is also possible to use a `UIScrollView`, but I recommend against that for the reasons stated in the first few sections of this chapter.

The most important point to remember here is to show data entry fields above the keyboard when the keyboard is shown. To do so, you need to dynamically adjust your table views.

When your table view contains data entry fields like a `UITextField` or a `UITextView`, and the table view is long enough to cover the screen, you will have a problem accessing data entry fields that are hidden by the keyboard. The easiest—and recommended—way to overcome this problem is to use a `UITableViewController` for your form. Otherwise, if you use a `UIViewController` and a `UITableView` as its subview, you must explicitly code for scrolling your UI so that elements that might get hidden by the keyboard stay visible.

> You can scroll your UI's frame by observing the `UIKeyBoardDidShowNotification` and `UIKeyBoardDidHideNotification`. The notification posts an object (`NSDictionary`) containing information pertaining to the size of the keyboard, the animation duration, and the animation curve.

Also note that, as the table view is scrolled, your cells are recycled and reused. Any data entered is lost when the cell is recycled, so you should copy the entered data from the UI to your model classes (or `NSString`) immediately after the entry is made. Implementing this is quite easy. One way is to set the delegate of your `UITextField` to the table view controller and handle `textFieldDidEndEditing`. But a good design practice is to let the table cell handle the delegate and notify its super class. (You learn more about such best practices throughout this chapter.) The super class should save the data to the corresponding model object and prepopulate the table view cell with values from the model when it's created or dequeued in `cellForRowAtIndexPath`.

The following code segment shows you how to do this.

Saving and Restoring Data from UITextField Inside a Custom UITableViewCell

```
cell.inputText.text = [self.data objectAtIndex:indexPath.row];
    cell.onTextEntered = ^(NSString* enteredString) {

        [self.data insertObject:enteredString
    atIndex:indexPath.row];
    };
```

This code assumes that the cell handles `IBAction` and `textFieldDidEndEditing` and passes the `enteredString` value to the table view controller using a block. The data entered is stored in a member variable (`data`), and is restored on the line above. Two lines and that's it. You can use delegates as well, but blocks are cleaner and result in much less code. You learn more about blocks in Chapter 16.

Animating a UITableView

You have now seen some practical implementations of `UITableView`. Next, you take it to the next level by learning how to make the best use of the animations provided by it. The `UIKit` framework provides some default animation styles for animating rows in a `UITableView`. These animations play a very important role in giving subtle hints to the user about what is happening behind the scenes.

A good example of this is the phone app on your iPhone. When you toggle between all calls and missed calls, the complete list animates to show or hide the relevant data. Similarly, on the settings app, when you turn on Airplane mode, the Carrier row hides because it's no longer relevant. But if these actions happen without animations, users will be confused about what is happening. One thing that sets iOS apart from its competitor is that it is easy to create a compelling user experience that blends well with the OS. In this case, implementing these animations is very easy with `UITableView`. Using methods in `UITableView`, you can animate a row insertion, row deletion, or row updates with fewer than ten lines of code.

The most important thing to remember here is that prior to your table updates, you should update your models. Failure to do so will result in an `NSInteralInconsistencyException` (crash). In other words, if you are displaying a list of items, inserting a new row in the table view should be done after updating the model.

Remember, if you have to perform a batch of animated updates on `UITableView`, you can sandwich them between calls to `beginUpdates` and `endUpdates`. iOS automatically computes the changes and performs the correct animation sequence for you. The following are the commonly used methods for performing animated updates to a `UITableView`:

```
insertRowsAtIndexPaths:withRowAnimation:

deleteRowsAtIndexPaths:withRowAnimation:

reloadRowsAtIndexPaths:withRowAnimation:
```

In the following list, the first parameter is the array of index paths you need to add and the second is the animation style that should be used. The animation style can be one of the following values (the last item in this list is new in iOS 5):

```
UITableViewRowAnimationFade, UITableViewRowAnimationNone

UITableViewRowAnimationRight, UITableViewRowAnimationLeft

UITableViewRowAnimationTop, UITableViewRowAnimationBottom

UITableViewRowAnimationMiddle

UITableViewRowAnimationAutomatic
```

On iOS 5, you can use a new style, `UITableViewRowAnimationAutomatic`, and the system automatically chooses the correct animation for you. iOS 5 also introduces two new methods to move a complete section from one location to another. This is helpful in case you want to visually show movement of a complete section.

The following are methods for moving rows and/or sections in a `UITableView`:

```
moveSection: toSection:

moveRowAtIndexPath: toIndexPath:
```

Partially Reloading Tables

You can use the `reloadRowsAtIndexPaths:withRowAnimation:` method to partially reload a table view. For example, if you get a push notification that data currently displayed on the table view should be updated, you can reload just that single row in a `UITableView`. I recommend using the `UITableViewRowAnimationFade` or `UITableViewRowAnimationNone` style on iOS 4 and earlier, and `UITableViewRowAnimationAutomatic` on iOS 5 for this.

Practical Implementations of Table View Animations

With the built-in `UITableView` animations you can easily implement custom controls like accordion or show and hide drawers that expose additional controls. The next sections provide some ideas for implementing them. Custom controls like these can be implemented in multiple ways. So instead of focusing on code, you learn the process behind building them.

Implementing an Accordion List

Accordion is a control that is often found on content-rich websites to categorize navigational links. It contains a list of sections and subitems under each section. Sections can be opened to reveal the items within and can be closed or collapsed to hide them. On iOS, accordions are often used to model a single-level hierarchical navigation menu. The *USA Today* app's pictures tab is an example of this. Let's dissect the view and analyze how a control like that could be created.

From the UI, it appears that the section headers are tappable and every section has either one row or zero rows based on whether it is in an expanded state or not. This means you need a custom section view that tells the parent controller (your table view controller) that it was tapped.

For this example, design a custom `UIView` that has one big tappable button. You will use this view as the custom section view for your table. Override the `tableView:viewForHeaderInSection:` method, create your `UIView`, and return it. These views should notify (via a delegate or handler) the table view of the button-tapped event back to the table view. On this handler, the table view controller should do two things. First, it should update the models and secondly the table view. For updating models, you can save the tapped section's index as the currently expanded index. Once this is done, you can refresh the table view. This can be done in two ways, either by firing `reloadData` to the table view or by calculating the changes and calling the necessary `addRowsAtIndexPaths:withRowAnimation:` and `deleteRowsAtIndexPaths:with RowAnimation:` methods. The reload data method refreshes the entire table and users will not know what happened behind the scenes. For getting the accordionlike UI effect, you should call `deleteRowsAtIndex Paths:withRowAnimation:` for the old section (currently expanded row) and `addRowsAtIndexPaths :withRowAnimation:` for the tapped section. Because you are doing two operations on the table view and you don't want the table to update itself for every operation, you should sandwich them between the methods `beginUpdates` and `endUpdates`.

The most complicated part here is to match the changes to the model and the UI synchronously. When your model doesn't exactly reflect your UI, your code will crash with an `NSInternalInconsitencyException`.

Animating rows on iOS 4 and before must be done manually. For rows that are deleted, use `UITable ViewRowAnimationTop`**; for rows inserted, use** `UITableViewRowAnimationBottom`**. For rows that are updated, use** `UITableViewRowAnimationFade` **or** `UITableViewRow AnimationNone`**. On iOS 5, you can use** `UITableViewRowAnimationAutomatic` **and the framework automatically chooses the right animation for you.**

Implementing a Drawer

Implementing a drawerlike UI is done similarly to implementing an accordion list. A drawer is a unique row in the table view that, instead of showing data, shows tools to manipulate the data. The Twitter client TweetBot (and many other apps) uses this to show context-sensitive menu options for a table view row.

Implementing a drawer is slightly easier (programmatically) than implementing an accordion. Create a custom `UITableViewCell` for your drawer in your table view nib file and connect it to an `IBOutlet`. Next, maintain an `NSIndexPath` pointer that will store the currently tapped row and update this when a row is selected (`TableView:didSelectRowAtIndexPath:`). Insert a new row below the selected row and remove the previously added drawer (if any) using `insertRowsAtIndexPaths:withRowAnimation:` methods.

Now comes the tricky part. Your data source methods (`numberOfRowsInSection`) should return one additional row if your stored index path is not `nil`. Your `cellForRowAtIndexPath` should return the pointer to the drawer cell (remember that `IBOutlet` connection you made) for `indexPath` that is one row higher than the saved `indexPath`. Play around with these methods and you should get it. Implementation is mathematically complicated, but programmatically easy.

Using Gesture Recognizers in Table View Cells

Swipe gestures like the swipe-to-delete or swipe-to-reveal options on Twitter for iPhone are another interesting type of interaction pattern. With gesture recognizers introduced in iOS 3.2, you can attach a swipe gesture recognizer (`UISwipeGestureRecognizer`) to your table cells' `contentView`. Attaching a long press gesture recognizer (`UILongPressGestureRecognizer`) can help in showing a context-sensitive menu (using a `UIActionSheet`) for a given table view cell element.

Table views can be customized pretty easily to create a wealth of new UI elements and interaction patterns like the two commonly used patterns covered earlier in this chapter. In most cases, the UI boils down to techniques explained in the previous sections.

With that, let's proceed to the next section where you learn about writing cleaner and leaner code that is easier to manage, read, and understand.

Table View Best Practices: Writing Clean Code with Lean Controllers

If you have been doing iOS development for quite a while, you know that your controller's `cellForRow AtIndexPath:` can easily get messy and unmanageable as your project evolves. When you use the model-view-controller paradigm in your software project (not just iOS), strive to make your controller as lean as possible. Keeping the controller lean is arguably the easiest way to keep your code readable and manageable. The next section discusses briefly how to refactor your code adhering to these ideas.

Data Binding Guidelines

When you are writing a table view controller subclass, the bulk of your code is written in the `UITableView Delegate` and `UITableViewDataSource` methods. Focusing on how to write these methods clearly solves the problem. The `cellForRowAtIndexPath` method often contains code that sets values for every individual UI element of the cell. The best way to set the values for individual UI elements in the cell is to move this code elsewhere. Now, where should it be moved? That depends on the kind of custom cell you are using. Based on your app's functionality, your table views need to be bound with associated data.

This technique, often called *data binding,* is a bit underrepresented on iOS, at least when compared to Mac. The best way to bind data is to pass your data model object to the custom table view cell and let it bind the data. Let's classify table view cells into three types based on how you would normally associate data with them.

The first type is a subclass of `UITableViewCell` and is a custom cell designed to display a specific kind of data, which in most cases is closely tied to the specifics of the app. An example for a RSS Reader app would be a "`FeedCell`" that displays a feed.

The second type is designed and developed in a generic way similar to Apple's `UITableViewCell` implementation. You create your cells by specifying a style and these cells can be used in other classes or projects for displaying many different types of data models. For example, you could create generic cells like `MyTableViewSwitchCell` for displaying a title text and an on/off `UISwitch` or `MyTableViewInputCell` for displaying a title text and a `UITextField` for data entry.

The third type of cell is a native `UITableViewCell` provided by the `UIKit` framework. In any of these three cases, as far as possible, try to move the data binding code to the cell itself.

The first case is straightforward. Write a method within the `FeedCell` that accepts your model object as a parameter and set the individual UI elements to the values in the Feed model object. That is, move your data binding code to the `FeedCell`, the subclass of `UITableViewCell`. For example, in the case of a RSS Reader app, the `FeedCell` should have a public method that looks similar to this:

Bind Method in Your FeedCell

```
-(void) bind:(Feed*) feedToBeDisplayed {
self.titleLabel.text = feedToBeDisplayed.text;
self.timeStampLabel.text = feedToBeDisplayed.modifiedDateString;
...
}
```

Instead of writing this code in the view controller's data source method, `cellForRowAtIndexPath:`, it's moved to the `UITableViewCell` subclass. This means that if the format of the cell needs to be changed at a later stage, like adding an author name field to your Feed model object and FeedCell, you can do it in one place.

When you use the system default `UITableViewCell` for displaying your data, I recommend adding this bind method to a category class on `UITableViewCell`.

If you have multiple models using the same `UITableViewCell`, consider creating multiple category classes, one for each model; for example, create `UITableViewCell+Feed.h/m` for displaying feeds and say, `UITableViewCell+Subscription.h/m` for displaying subscriptions on the same cell. Be careful when naming the bind method. When a category contains a duplicated method name, it overrides the previously defined method and there is no defined order in which this overriding happens. I recommend naming them `bind<ModelClassName>`, which is readable and understandable. For example, the names `bindFeed:(Feed*)` and `bindSubscription:(Subscription*)` follow this convention.

The third case is when you have a generic custom table cell like the `MyTableViewSwitchCell`. In this case, too, you can apply the previous technique. Add category methods on your generic custom table view cell.

More often than not, you would be reusing the same `FeedCell` in multiple tables and in multiple view controllers. Moving the data binding code out of the table view controller (or any generic view controller) will reduce the clutter on the controllers and make it easy to maintain your code.

Multiple UITableViewControllers Inside a Single UIViewController

The next often-seen UI is multiple table views within a same `UIViewController`. Figure 5-8 shows a project with multiple table views within a single `UIViewController`.

Spaghetti code starts creeping in when both the table's data source and delegate are set to the file's owner—the parent `UIViewController`. The second stage of "spaghettiness" creeps in when you add `UISearchDisplayController` to both these tables. Now your `cellForRowAtIndexPath:` method will look similar to this:

Sample cellForRowAtIndexPath

```
-(UITableViewCell *)tableView:(UITableView *)tableView
   cellForRowAtIndexPath:(NSIndexPath *)indexPath {
  if(tableView == self.firstTable)   {
    //return first table's cell
  else if(tableView == self.secondTable) {
    //return second table's cell
}
```

```
  else if(tableView ==
    self.firstSearchDisplayController.searchTableView) {
        //return first table's search cell
}
  else if(tableView ==
    self.secondSearchDisplayController.searchTableView) {
        //return second table's search cell
  }
}
```

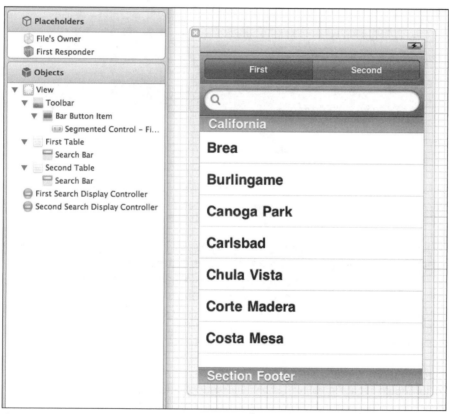

Figure 5-8 Interface Builder showing a project with multiple UITableViews within a single view

Obviously, there should be a better way, right? As it happens, there is. Instead of setting the delegate and data source to the file's owner, create custom UITableViewController subclasses for each table and set the delegate and data source to its own controller. This is illustrated in Figure 5-9.

Create custom subclasses called FirstTableViewController and SecondTableViewController and move the cellForRowAtIndexPath methods in the file's owner to these two classes. You will reduce the number of if statements used by half. You can do something similar to this to isolate the search display controller's delegate as well if the code for it gets long and unmanageable. You might end up creating more files and more classes, but that's just fine.

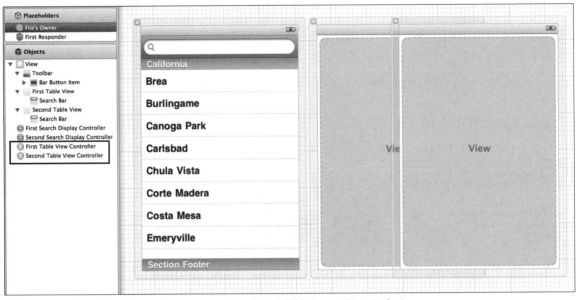

Figure 5-9 Interface Builder showing a better way to add multiple UITableViews within a single view

The first rule of thumb for refactoring is to revisit your code to check whether the `if` statements you are using are truly for a logical branching and not for class-based switching.

The second rule is to check if you are using an `if` condition to branch code for different kinds of tables, like in the `cellForRowAtIndexPath:` method. As I showed you previously, code like this should be refactored and solved elegantly using object-oriented techniques. Every class-based switching like this can be solved in an object-oriented way. This refactoring technique holds good for any language, not just Objective-C.

Adhering to these two refactoring techniques should reduce much of the code in your controller class. Remember that your controller should act as a mediator among your models and UI elements defined at that level and not at the subclass level. In other words, a view controller can set the property of a UI element defined in its scope but not that of a UI element that is inside a subclass. For example:

```
self.textLabel.text = NSLocalizedString(@"Hello", @"")
```

is okay, but

```
self.customView.textLabel.text = NSLocalizedString(@"Hello", @"")
```

should be avoided. The recommended way is to move this code into the `customView's` class. Apply these techniques and start writing cleaner and leaner controllers.

Let's now move on to storyboards, a new, powerful concept that will help you write even less code. This is something new to iOS 5 and requires your app's minimum deployment OS version to be 5.0.

Storyboards

Prior to iOS 5, interface elements and views were created using IB and saved in nib files. Storyboards are a new way to create them, and in addition to creating interface elements, you can now specify the navigation (called *segues*) between those interfaces when you use storyboards. This was something you could not do previously without writing code. You can think of storyboards as a graph of all your view controllers connected by segues that dictate the transition between them.

The benefits of storyboards don't stop there. They also make it easy for developers to create static table views without a data source. How many times have you wanted to create a table view that's not bound to a real data source? (For example, a table that shows a list of options instead of data.) A common-use case for this is your app's settings page. Storyboards also help co-developers and/or clients understand the complete workflow of the app.

Let's get started with storyboards and discuss how to do things that you do with nib files using storyboards, like communicating between controllers. Later on, you learn how to create a static table view without a data source and finally, the most interesting aspect of Storyboards, which is writing your own custom transition animations.

Getting Started with Storyboards

You can use storyboards for new projects or add them to an existing project that doesn't have a storyboard yet. For existing projects you can add storyboards just like how you add a new file to a project. You learn more about how to instantiate view controllers in this storyboard later in this chapter.

For new projects, storyboards can be created in Xcode 4.2 by using the new project template and selecting the Use Storyboard option as shown in Figure 5-10. This is selected by default for you.

When you create a new project using storyboards, the `info.plist` key of your app contains a key called `UIMainStoryboardFile`. This key supersedes `NSMainNibFile` that was used prior to iOS 5. You can continue to use `NSMainNibFile` if your app's main window is loaded from a nib file instead of a storyboard. However, you can't use both `UIMainStoryboardFile` and `NSMainNibFile` in the same app. `UIMainStoryboardFile` takes precedence and your nib file specified in `NSMainNibFile` never gets loaded.

> Your application can store the complete storyboard in one file and IB automatically builds it into separate files optimized for loading. In short, you don't have to be worried about loading time or performance when using Storyboards.

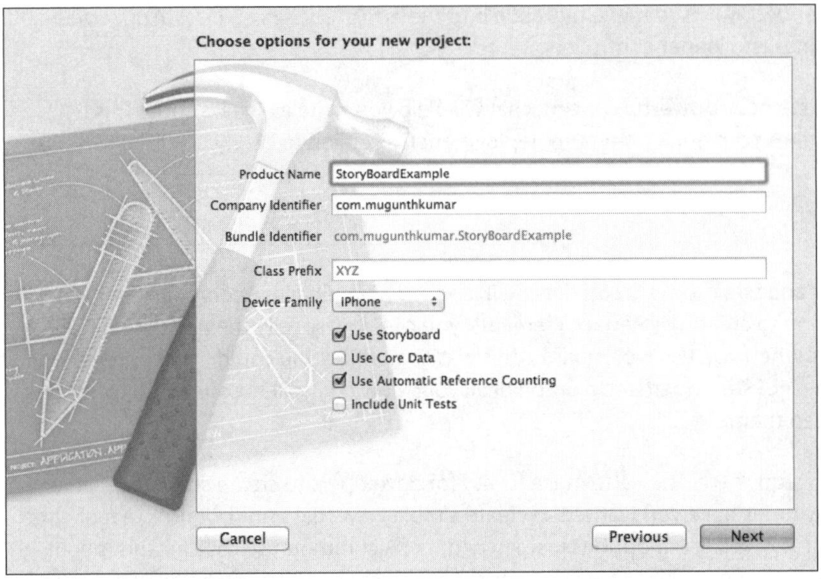

Figure 5-10 New Project Template in Xcode 4.2 showing the Use Storyboard option

Instantiating a Storyboard

When your `UIMainStoryboardFile` is set, the compiler automatically generates code for instantiating it and loads it as your application's startup window. If you are adding storyboards in an existing app, you should be doing this programmatically. The methods for instantiating view controllers within a storyboard are defined in the `UIStoryboard` class.

When you want to display a view controller specified in your storyboard, you load the storyboard using this method:

```
+ storyboardWithName:bundle:
```

Loading View Controllers within a Storyboard

Loading view controllers within a storyboard is very similar to the nib loading method, and with the `UIStoryboard` object, you can instantiate view controllers using the following method:

```
– instantiateInitialViewController
```

```
– instantiateViewControllerWithIdentifier:
```

Segues

Segues are transitions defined in your storyboard file. UIKit provides two default transition styles, Push and Modal. They behave similar to the `pushViewController:animated:` and `presentModalViewController:animated:` methods you use in iOS 4. In addition to this, you can create custom segues and create new kinds of transitions between view controllers. You look at this later in this chapter.

You create segues by connecting certain events on view controllers with other view controllers on your storyboard file. You can drag from a button to a view controller, from a gesture recognizer object to a view controller, and so on. IB creates a segue between them, and you can select the segue and use the inspector panel to modify the transition styles.

The inspector panel also allows you to set a custom class if you select a custom transition style. You can think of a segue as something that connects an action with a transition. Actions that can trigger segues can be button tap events, row selection events on static table views, a recognized gesture, or even audio events. The compiler automatically generates the necessary code to perform a segue when the event to which you connected the segue occurs.

When a segue is about to be performed, a `prepareForSegue:sender:` method is invoked on the source view controller and an object of type `UIStoryboardSegue` is passed to it. You can override this method to pass data to the destination view controller. The next section explains how to do this.

> When a view controller performs multiple segues, the same `prepareForSegue:sender:` method gets called for every segue. To identify the performed segue, you should use the segue identifier to check if the performed segue is the intended one and pass data accordingly. As a defensive programming practice, I would advise you to perform this check even if the view controller performs only one segue. This would ensure that later on, when you add a new segue, your app will continue to run without crashing.

Passing Data

Now that storyboards automatically handle view navigation, how will you be passing data to the new view? In iOS 4, you instantiate a view controller, get a pointer to it, fill in the initial data, and pass it to `presentViewController:animated:` or `pushViewController:animated:`.

On iOS 5, when you use Storyboards, instantiating view controllers and presenting them to the user are done automatically for you. You are given a chance to fill in data by overriding the `prepareForSegue:sender:` method. By overriding this method, you can get the pointer to the destination view controller and set the initial values there.

The framework calls the same methods that you used before like `viewDidLoad`, `initWithCoder:` or `NSObject`'s `awakeFromNib` method, and this means that you can continue writing your view controller's initialization code as you would do on iOS 4.

Returning Data

With Storyboards, there is no change in how you communicate data back to the parent view controller. Data created/entered by the user on modal forms that you present can be retuned to the parent via delegates or blocks. The only difference is that on your parent view controller, you have to set the delegate in the `prepareForSegue:sender:` method to `self`.

Instantiating Other View Controllers

On iOS 5, UIViewController has a `storyboard` property that retains a pointer to the storyboard object (`UIStoryBoard`) from which it was instantiated. This is `nil` when your view controller was created manually or from a nib file. With this back reference, you can instantiate other view controllers defined in your storyboard from any other view controller. You do this by identifying the view controller by its identifier. The following method on `UIStoryBoard` allows you to do this:

```
- instantiateViewControllerWithIdentifier:
```

This means that you can still have view controllers on your storyboard that are not connected with any other view controllers through segues and yet they can be initialized and used.

Performing Segues Manually

While Storyboards can automatically trigger segues based on actions, there might be cases when you need to perform segues programmatically. You might use this is to handle actions that cannot be handled by the storyboard file. To perform a segue, you call the `performSegueWithIdentifier:sender:` method of the view controller. When you perform segues manually, you can pass the caller and the context objects in the sender parameter. This will be sent to the `prepareForSegue:sender:` method later.

Building Table Views with Storyboard

One of the important advantages of Storyboards is the capability to create static tables from IB. With Storyboards, you can build two types of table views: a static table that doesn't need a special class for providing a data source, and a table view containing a prototype cell (similar to custom table view cells in iOS 4) that binds data from a model.

Static Tables

You can create static tables in your storyboard by dragging a table, selecting it, and from the inspector, choosing Static Cells.This is shown in Figure 5-11.

Static cells are great for creating settings pages (or pages whose content doesn't come from a Core Data model or a web service or any such data source) like Apple's own Settings app.

> Static cells can be created only for table views that are from a `UITableViewController`. **You cannot create static cell for table views that are added as a subview of a** `UIViewController` **view.**

Prototype Cells

Prototype cells are similar to custom table view cells, but instead of creating this on separate nib files and loading them in the data source method, `cellForRowAtIndexPath:`, you create them in IB on your storyboard and just set the data on your data source methods.

All prototype cells should be identified using a custom identifier. This is to ensure proper functioning of the table view cell queuing methods.

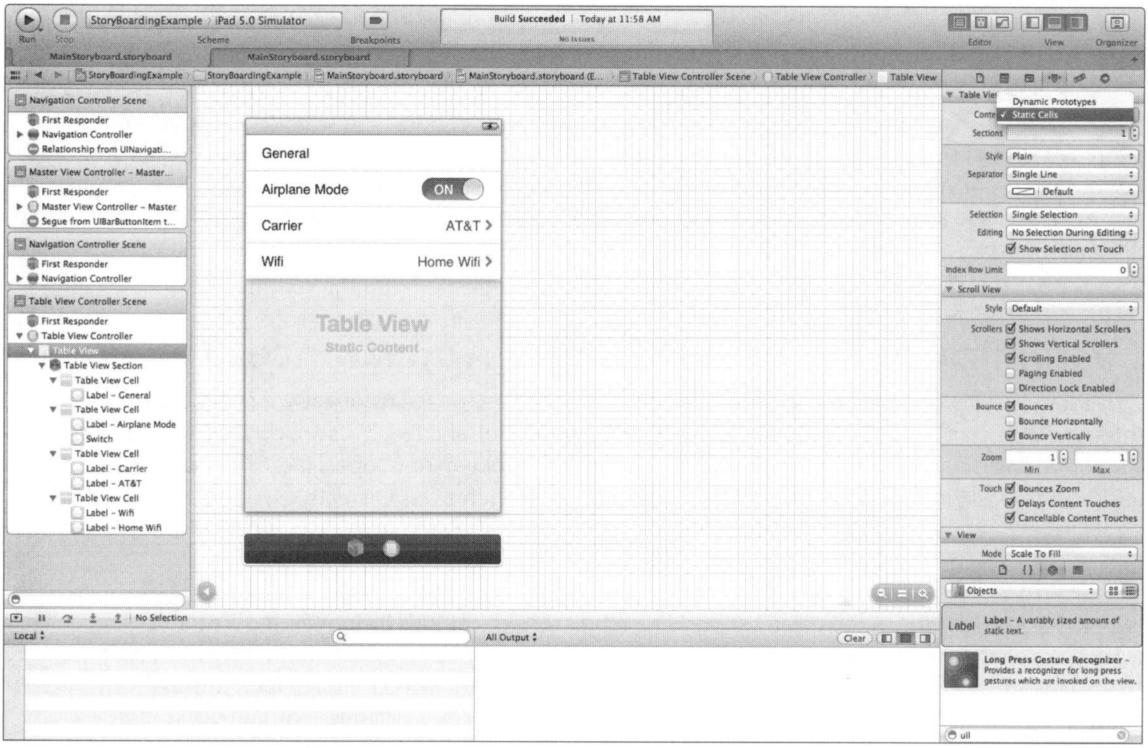

Figure 5-11 A storyboard illustrating static table view creation

Custom Transitions

Another advantage of Storyboards is that it is now easy to create custom transition effects for your view controllers.

When segues are performed, the compiler generates necessary code to present or push the destination controller based on the transition style you set on your storyboard. You learned that there are two types of transition styles, Push and Modal, supported natively by iOS. There is also a third type (Custom) and when you choose this, you can provide your own subclass of `UIStoryboardSegue` that handles your custom transition effects.

Create a subclass of `UIStoryBoardSegue` and override the `perform` method. In the `perform` method, access the pointer to the source view controller's main view's layer and do your custom transition animation (using Core Animation). Once the animation is complete, push or present your destination view controller (you can get a pointer to this from the segue object). It's as simple as that.

Another Advantage

When you use storyboards, it becomes easy for co-developers (and/or clients) to understand the app's flow. Instead of going through multiple nib files and cross-referencing the instantiation code for understanding the flow, co-developers can open the storyboard file and see the complete flow. This alone should be a compelling reason to use them.

A Disadvantage

The only drawback I can think of is that storyboards are iOS 5 only. Writing code to selectively use storyboards for iOS 5 devices and falling back to normal nib files for iOS 4 devices is too cumbersome and not worth the effort. When you use storyboards, raise your target's deployment target to iOS 5. If your app were an iPad-only app, I would recommend using iOS 5 because most iPad users will already be on that because iOS 5 doesn't alienate iPad 1 and all new features of iOS 5 are available on both iPad 1 and 2. But otherwise, on iPhone apps or universal apps, my recommendation is to wait until you can avoid using iOS 4 completely.

Customizing Your Views Using UIAppearance Protocol

This last section covers a small, important addition to iOS 5: a method to customize your view appearance through Apple's native classes. Prior to iOS 5, customizing the look and feel of native controls was not natively supported and was often difficult for developers. A common problem developers face is to change the appearance of all instances of a control. The proper way of doing this was to create the complete control from scratch. But because that was time-consuming, some developers resorted to overriding or swizzling methods like `drawRect:`.

With iOS 5, Apple has provided default support for most `UIKit` controls by formalizing customization using a couple protocols—namely `UIAppearance` and `UIAppearanceContainer`. Any UI control that adheres to the `UIAppearance` protocol can be customized to have a different look and feel. Want more? The `UIAppearance` protocol even allows you to specify a different look and feel based on where the control is contained. That is, you can specify the appearance of a control (say the `tintColor` of a `UIBarButtonItem` for example) to be different when it is contained within a specific view (`UINavigationBar` or `UIPopoverViewController`). You do this by getting an appearance proxy object for the control's class and using that to customize the appearance. Let's look at an example.

To customize the tint color of a bar button throughout your application, you set the `tintColor` to the `UIBarButtonItem`'s appearance proxy like this:

```
[[UIBarButtonItem appearance] setTintColor:[UIColor redColor]];
```

Note that the `setTintColor` method existed in iOS 4, in `UIBarButtonItem`. But it was applicable only to a particular instance of the control. With the appearance proxy object, you are now able to customize the appearance of any object created using the said class.

On similar lines, you can also customize the appearance of a control depending on the contained view, by using the following method:

```
[[UIBarButtonItem appearanceWhenContainedIn:[UINavigationBar class], nil]
setTintColor:[UIColor redColor]];
```

The first parameter is a `nil` terminated list of all container classes like `UINavigatorBar`, `UIPopOverController` that adheres to the `UIAppearanceContainer` protocol.

Starting with iOS 5, most UI elements have added support to `UIAppearance` protocol. Additionally, controls like the `UISwitch`.in iOS 5 allow you to easily to change the color of the "on" gradient to the designer's choice.

While Apple was against UI customization in the beginning (on both Mac and iOS), it is slowly changing, and you could see Apple's own native apps (like the new Reminders app) having customized user interfaces. With `UIAppearance` protocol you should be able to achieve the same with far less code.

Summary

By customizing the UI appearance and writing unique custom controls, you can take your app to the next level. To help you do so, this chapter discussed some of the advanced table view concepts, including measuring and improving the performance of your table view scrolling using Instruments, creating custom controls like accordion, and drawers using table views. You then learned about some important refactoring techniques to keep your controller code cleaner. After that you learned about Storyboards and how to integrate them within your existing apps. Finally, you learned about the UI customization protocol introduced in iOS 5.

Further Reading

Apple Documentation

The following documents are available in the iOS Developer Library at `developer.apple.com` or through the Xcode Documentation and API Reference.

What's New in iOS 5—Apple Developer

TableView Programming Guide iOS Developer Documentation

TableViewSuite—iOS Developer Library

UIViewController Programming Guide: iOS Developer Documentation (Storyboards)

WWDC Videos

The following session video is available at `developer.apple.com`.

Session 309 - Introducing Interface Builder Storyboarding WWDC 2011

Other Resources

Fast scrolling in Tweetie with UITableView
`http://blog.atebits.com/2008/12/fast-scrolling-in-tweetie-with-uitableview/`

Enormego's Pull-To-Refresh – Github
`https://github.com/enormego/EGOTableViewPullRefresh`

Chapter 6

Better Drawing

Your users expect a beautiful, engaging, and intuitive interface. It is up to you to deliver. No matter how powerful your features, if your interface seems "clunky," you're going to have a hard time making the sale. This is about more than just pretty colors and flashy animations. A truly beautiful and elegant user interface is a key part of a user-centric application. Keeping your focus on delighting your user is the key to building exceptional applications.

One of the tools you need to create an exceptional user interface is custom drawing. In this chapter you will learn the mechanics of drawing in iOS, with focus on flexibility and performance. This chapter will not cover iOS UI design. For information on how to design iOS interfaces, you should start with Apple's *iOS Human Interface Guidelines* and *iOS Application Programming Guide*, available in the iOS Developer Documentation.

In this chapter, you will learn about the several drawing systems in iOS, with a focus on UIKit and Core Graphics. By the end of this chapter, you will have a strong grasp of the UIKit drawing cycle, drawing coordinate systems, graphic contexts, paths, and transforms. You will know how to optimize your drawing speed through correct view configuration, caching, pixel alignment, and use of layers. You will be able to avoid bloating your application bundle with avoidable prerendered graphics.

With the right tools, you can achieve your goal of a beautiful, engaging, and intuitive interface, while maintaining high performance, low memory usage, and small application size.

iOS's Many Drawing Systems

iOS has several major drawing systems: UIKit, Core Graphics (Quartz), Core Animation, Core Image, and OpenGL ES. Each is useful for a different kind of problem.

- **UIKit**—This is the highest-level interface, and the only interface in Objective-C. It provides easy access to layout, compositing, drawing, fonts, images, animation, and more. You can recognize UIKit elements by the prefix `UI`, such as `UIView` and `UIBezierPath`. UIKit also extends `NSString` to simplify drawing text with methods like `drawInRect:withFont:`.

- **Core Graphics (also called Quartz 2D)**—The primary drawing system underlying UIKit, this is what you use most frequently to draw custom views. Core Graphics is highly integrated with `UIView` and other parts of UIKit. Core Graphics data structures and functions can be identified by the prefix `CG`.

- **Core Animation**—This provides powerful two- and three-dimensional animation services. It is also highly integrated into `UIView`. Chapter 7 covers Core Animation in detail.

- **Core Image**—A Mac technology first available in iOS 5, Core Image provides very fast image filtering such as cropping, sharpening, warping, and just about any other transformation you can imagine. The basics of Core Image are covered in Chapter 1.

- **OpenGL ES**—Most useful for writing high-performance games—particularly 3D games—Open GL ES is a subset of the OpenGL drawing language. For other applications on iOS, Core Animation is generally a better choice. OpenGL ES is portable between most platforms. A discussion of OpenGL ES is beyond the scope of this book, but there are many good books available on the subject.

UIKit and the View Drawing Cycle

When you change the frame or visibility of a view, draw a line, or change the color of an object, the change is not immediately displayed on the screen. This sometimes confuses developers who incorrectly write code like this:

```
progressView.hidden = NO; // This line does nothing
[self doSomethingTimeConsuming];
progressView.hidden = YES;
```

It's important to understand that the first line (`progressView.hidden = NO`) does absolutely nothing useful. This code does not cause the progress view to be displayed while the time-consuming operation is in progress. No matter how long this method runs, you will never see the view displayed. Figure 6-1 shows what actually happens in the drawing loop.

All drawing occurs on the main thread, so as long as your code is running on the main thread, nothing can be drawn. That is one of the reasons you should never execute a long-running operation on the main thread. Not only does it prevent drawing updates but it also prevents event handling (such as responding to touches). As long as your code is running on the main thread, your application is effectively "hung" to the user. This isn't noticeable as long as you make sure that your main thread routines return quickly.

You may now be thinking, "Well, I'll just run my drawing commands on a background thread." You can't do that because UIKit isn't thread-safe. Any attempt to modify a view on a background thread leads to undefined behavior, including drawing corruption and crashes. (See the section "Caching and Background Drawing" later in the chapter for more information on how you can draw in the background.)

This behavior is not a problem to be overcome. The consolidation of drawing events is one part of iOS's capability to render complex drawings on limited hardware. As you see throughout this chapter, much of UIKit is dedicated to avoiding unnecessary drawing, and this consolidation is one of the first steps.

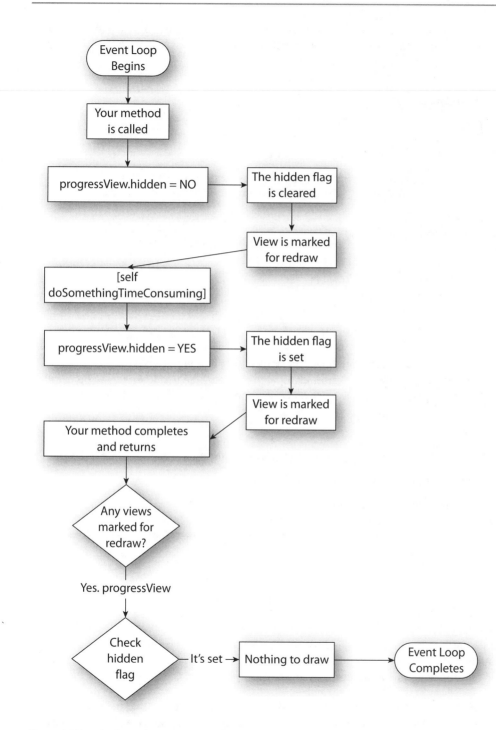

Figure 6-1 How the Cocoa drawing cycle consolidates changes

So how do you start and stop an activity indicator for a long-running operation? You use dispatch or operation queues to put your expensive work in the background, while making all of your UIKit calls on the main thread, as shown in the following code.

ViewController.m (TimeConsuming)

```
- (IBAction)doSomething:(id)sender {
  [sender setEnabled:NO];
  [self.activity startAnimating];

  dispatch_queue_t bgQueue = dispatch_get_global_queue(
                   DISPATCH_QUEUE_PRIORITY_DEFAULT, 0);

  dispatch_async(bgQueue, ^{
    [self somethingTimeConsuming];

    dispatch_async(dispatch_get_main_queue(), ^{
      [self.activity stopAnimating];
      [sender setEnabled:YES];
    });
  });
}
```

When the `IBAction` is called, you start animating the activity indicator. You then put a call to `somethingTimeConsuming` on the default background dispatch queue. When that finishes, you put a call to `stopAnimating` on the main dispatch queue. Dispatch and operation queues are covered in Chapter 9.

To summarize

- iOS consolidates all drawing requests during the run loop, and draws them all at once.

- You must not block the main thread to do complex processing.

- You must not draw into the main view graphics context except on the main thread. You should check each UIKit method to ensure it does not have a main thread requirement. Some UIKit methods can be used on background threads as long as you are not drawing into the main view context. See "CGLayer" later in this chapter for examples.

View Drawing versus View Layout

`UIView` separates the layout ("rearranging") of subviews from drawing (or "display"). This is important for maximizing performance because layout is generally cheaper than drawing. Layout is cheap because `UIView` caches drawing operations onto GPU-optimized bitmaps. These bitmaps can be moved around, shown, hidden, rotated, and otherwise transformed and composited very inexpensively using the GPU.

When you call `setNeedsDisplay` on a view, it is marked "dirty" and will be redrawn during the next drawing cycle. You should not call it unless the content of the view has really changed. Most UIKit views automatically manage redrawing when their data is changed, so you generally don't need to call it except on custom views.

When a view's subviews need to be rearranged because of an orientation change or scrolling, UIKit calls `setNeedsLayout`. This, in turn, calls `layoutSubviews` on the affected views. By overriding `layoutSubviews`, you can make your application much smoother during rotation and scrolling events. You can rearrange your subviews' frames without necessarily having to redraw them, and you can hide or show views based on orientation. You can also call `setNeedsLayout` if your data changes in ways that only need layout updates rather than drawing.

Custom View Drawing

Views can provide their content by including subviews, including layers, or implementing `drawRect:`. Typically if you implement `drawRect:`, you don't mix this with layers or subviews, although it's legal and sometimes useful to do so. Most custom drawing is done with UIKit or Core Graphics, although OpenGL ES has become easier to integrate when needed.

2D drawing generally breaks down into several operations:

- Lines
- Paths (filled or outlined shapes)
- Text
- Images
- Gradients

2D drawing does not include manipulation of individual pixels because that is destination dependent. You can achieve this with a bitmap context, but not directly with UIKit or Core Graphics functions.

Both UIKit and Core Graphics use a "painter" drawing model. This means that each command is drawn in sequence, overlaying previous drawings. Order is very important in this model, and you must draw back to front.

Drawing with UIKit

In the "old days" before iPad, most custom drawing had to be done with Core Graphics because there was no way to draw arbitrary shapes with UIKit. In iPhoneOS 3.2, Apple added `UIBezierPath` and made it much easier to draw entirely in Objective-C. UIKit still lacks support for lines, gradients, shading, and some advanced features like controlling anti-aliasing and precise color management. Even so, UIKit is now a very convenient way to manage the most common custom drawing needs.

The simplest way to draw rectangles is with `UIRectFrame` or `UIRectFill`, as shown in the following code.

```
- (void)drawRect:(CGRect)rect {
  [[UIColor redColor] setFill];
  UIRectFill(CGRectMake(10, 10, 100, 100));
}
```

Notice how you first set the pen color using `-[UIColor setFill]`. Drawing is done into a graphics context provided by the system before calling `drawRect:`. That context includes a lot of information including stroke color, fill color, text color, font, transform, and more. At any given time, there is just one stroke pen and one fill pen, and their colors are used to draw everything. The "Managing Graphics Contexts" section later in this chapter covers how to save and restore contexts, but for now just note that drawing commands are orderdependent, and that includes commands that change the pens.

> The graphics context provided to `drawRect:` is specifically a view graphics context. There are other types of graphics contexts, including PDF and bitmap contexts. All of them use the same drawing techniques, but a view graphics context is optimized for drawing onto the screen. This distinction will be important when I discuss `CGLayer`.

Paths

UIKit includes much more powerful drawing commands than its rectangle functions. It can draw arbitrary curves and lines using `UIBezierPath`. A Bézier curve is a mathematical way of expressing a line or curve using a small number of control points. Most of the time, you don't need to worry about the math because `UIBezierPath` has simple methods to handle the most common paths: lines, arcs, rectangles (optionally rounded), and ovals. With these, you can quickly draw most shapes needed for UI elements. The following code is an example of a simple shape scaled to fill the view, as shown in Figure 6-2. You draw this several ways in the upcoming examples.

FlowerView.m (Paths)

```
-  (void)drawRect:(CGRect)rect {
   CGSize size = self.bounds.size;
   CGFloat margin = 10;
   CGFloat radius = rint(MIN(size.height - margin,
                             size.width - margin) / 4);

   CGFloat xOffset, yOffset;
   CGFloat offset = rint((size.height - size.width) / 2);
   if (offset > 0) {
     xOffset = rint(margin / 2);
     yOffset = offset;
   }
   else {
     xOffset = -offset;
     yOffset = rint(margin / 2);
   }

   [[UIColor redColor] setFill];
   UIBezierPath *path = [UIBezierPath bezierPath];
   [path addArcWithCenter:CGPointMake(radius * 2 + xOffset,
                                      radius + yOffset)
```

```
                radius:radius
             startAngle:-M_PI
               endAngle:0
              clockwise:YES];
    [path addArcWithCenter:CGPointMake(radius * 3 + xOffset,
                                       radius * 2 + yOffset)
                    radius:radius
                startAngle:-M_PI_2
                  endAngle:M_PI_2
                 clockwise:YES];
    [path addArcWithCenter:CGPointMake(radius * 2 + xOffset,
                                       radius * 3 + yOffset)
                    radius:radius
                startAngle:0
                  endAngle:M_PI
                 clockwise:YES];
    [path addArcWithCenter:CGPointMake(radius + xOffset,
                                       radius * 2 + yOffset)
                    radius:radius
                startAngle:M_PI_2
                  endAngle:-M_PI_2
                 clockwise:YES];
    [path closePath];
    [path fill];
}
```

This creates a path made up of a series of arcs and fills it with red. Creating a path does not cause anything to be drawn. A UIBezierPath is just a sequence of curves, like an NSString is a sequence of characters. Only when you call fill is the curve drawn into the current context.

Note the use of the M_PI (π) and M_PI_2 ($\pi/2$) constants. Arcs are described in radians, so π and fractions of π are important. math.h defines many such constants that you should use rather than recomputing them. Arcs measure their angles clockwise, with 0 radians pointing to the right, $\pi/2$ radians pointing down, π (or -π) radians pointing left, and $-\pi/2$ radians pointing up. You can use $3\pi/2$ for up if you prefer, but I find -M_PI_2 easier to visualize than 3*M_PI_2. If radians give you a headache, you can make a function out of it:

```
CGFloat RadiansFromDegrees(CGFloat d) {
    return d * M_PI / 180;
}
```

Generally I recommend just getting used to radians rather than doing so much math, but if you need unusual angles, it can be easier to work in degrees.

When calculating radius and offset, you use rint (round to closest integer) to ensure that you're point aligned (and therefore pixel aligned). That helps improve drawing performance and avoids blurry edges. Most of the time that's what you want, but in cases where an arc meets a line, it can lead to off-by-one drawing errors. Usually the best approach is to move the line so that all the values are integers, as discussed in the following section.

Figure 6-2 Output of FlowerView

Understanding Coordinates

There are subtle interactions between coordinates, points, and pixels that can lead to poor drawing performance and blurry lines and text. Consider the following code:

```
CGContextSetLineWidth(context, 3.);

// Draw 3pt horizontal line from {10,100} to {200,100}
CGContextMoveToPoint(context, 10., 100.);
CGContextAddLineToPoint(context, 200., 100.);
CGContextStrokePath(context);
```

```
// Draw 3pt horizontal line from {10,105.5} to {200,105.5}
CGContextMoveToPoint(context, 10., 105.5);
CGContextAddLineToPoint(context, 200., 105.5);
CGContextStrokePath(context);
```

Figure 6-3 shows the output of this program on a non-Retina display, scaled to make the differences more obvious.

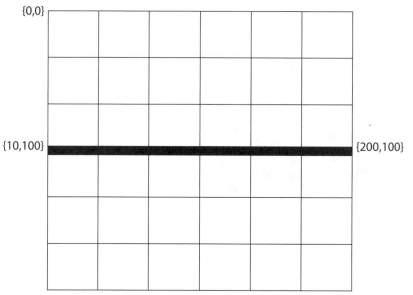

Figure 6-3: Comparison of line from {10,100} and line from {10,105.5}

The line from {10, 100} to {200, 100} is much more blurry than the line from {10, 105.5} to {200, 105.5}. The reason is because of how iOS interprets coordinates.

When you construct a CGPath, you work in so-called *geometric coordinates*. These are the same kind of coordinates that mathematicians use, representing the zero-dimensional point at the intersection of two grid lines. It is impossible to draw a geometric point or a geometric line because they are infinitely small and thin. When iOS draws, it has to translate these geometric objects into *pixel coordinates*. These are two-dimensional boxes that can be set to a specific color. A pixel is the smallest unit of display area that the device can control.

Figure 6-4 shows the geometric line from {10, 100} to {200, 100}.

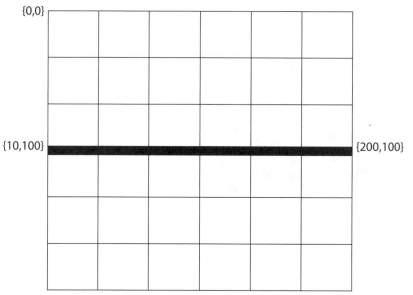

Figure 6-4 Geometric line from {10, 100} to {200, 100}

When you call CGContextStrokePath, iOS centers the line along the path. Ideally, the line would be 3 pixels wide, from $y = 98.5$ to $y = 101.5$, as shown in Figure 6-5.

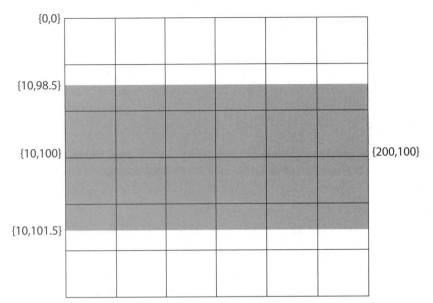

Figure 6-5 Ideal three-pixel line

This line is impossible to draw, however. Each pixel must be a single color, and the pixels at the top and bottom of the line include two colors. Half is the stroke color, and half is the background color. iOS solves this problem by averaging the two. This is the same technique used in anti-aliasing. This is shown in Figure 6-6.

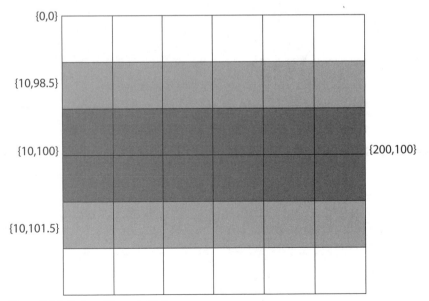

Figure 6-6 Anti-aliased three-pixel line

On the screen, this line will look slightly blurry. The solution to this problem is to move horizontal and vertical lines to the half-point so that when iOS centers the line, the edges fall along pixel boundaries, or to make your line an even width.

You can also encounter this problem with nonintegral line-widths, or if your coordinates aren't integers or half-integers. Any situation that forces iOS to draw fractional pixels will cause blurriness.

Fill is not the same as stroke. A stroke line is centered on the path, but fill colors all the pixels up to the path. If you fill the rectangle from {10,100} to {200,103}, then each pixel is filled correctly, as shown in Figure 6-7.

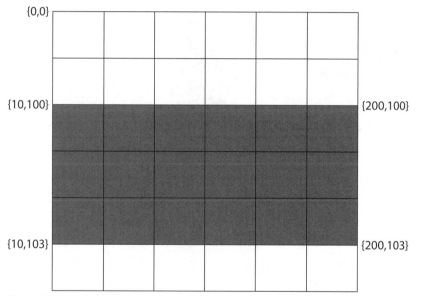

Figure 6-7 Filling the rectangle from {10,100} to {200,103}

The discussion so far has equated points with pixels. On a Retina display, these are not equivalent. The iPhone 4 has four pixels per point and a scale factor of two. That subtly changes things, but generally for the better. Because all the coordinates used in Core Graphics and UIKit are expressed in points, all integral line widths are effectively an even number of pixels. For example, if you request a 1-point stroke width, this is the same as a 2-pixel stroke width. To draw that line, iOS needs to fill one pixel on each side of the path. That's an integral number of pixels, so there's no anti-aliasing. You can still encounter blurriness if you use coordinates that are neither integers nor half-integers.

Offsetting by a half-point is unnecessary on a Retina display, but it doesn't hurt. As long as you intend to support iPhone 3GS or iPad 2, you need to apply a half-point offset for drawing horizontal and vertical lines.

All of this only applies to horizontal and vertical lines. Sloping or curved lines should be anti-aliased so that they're not jagged, so there's generally no reason to offset them.

Resizing and contentMode

Returning to `FlowerView` from the section "Paths" earlier in this chapter, if you rotate the device as shown in Figure 6-8, you'll see that the view is distorted, even though you have code that adjusts for the size of the view.

Figure 6-8 Rotated FlowerView

iOS optimizes drawing by taking a snapshot of the view and adjusting it for the new frame. The `drawRect:` method isn't called. The property `contentMode` determines how the view is adjusted. The default, `UIViewContentModeScaleToFill`, scales the image to fill the new view size, changing the aspect ratio if needed. That's why the shape is distorted.

There are a lot of ways to automatically adjust the view. You can move it around without resizing it, or you can scale it in various ways that preserve or modify the aspect ratio. The key is to make sure that any mode you use exactly matches the results of your `drawRect:` in the new orientation. Otherwise, your view will "jump" the next time you redraw. This usually works as long as your `drawRect:` doesn't consider its `bounds` during drawing. In `FlowerView`, you use the `bounds` to determine the size of your shape, so it's hard to get automatic adjustments to work correctly.

Use the automatic modes if you can because they can improve performance. When you can't, ask the system to call `drawRect:` when the frame changes by using `UIViewContentModeRedraw`, as shown in the following code.

```
- (void)awakeFromNib {
    self.contentMode = UIViewContentModeRedraw;
}
```

Transforms

iOS platforms have access to a very nice GPU that can do matrix operations very quickly. If you can convert your drawing calculations into matrix operations, then you can leverage the GPU and get excellent performance. Transforms are just such a matrix operation.

iOS has two kinds of transforms: affine and 3D. `UIView` handles only affine transforms, so that's all I discuss right now. An affine transform is a way of expressing rotation, scaling, shear, and translation (shifting) as a matrix. These transforms are shown in Figure 6-9.

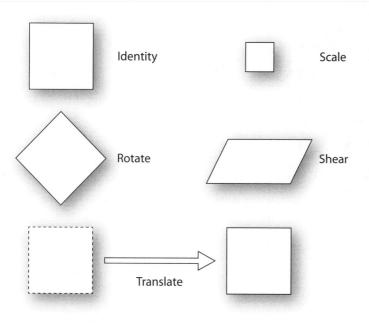

Identity

Scale

Rotate

Shear

Translate

Figure 6-9 Affine transforms

A single transform combines any number of these operations into a 3x3 matrix. iOS has functions to support rotation, scaling, and translation. If you want shear, you'll have to write the matrix yourself. (You can also use `CGAffineTransformMakeShear` from Jeff LaMarche; see "Further Reading" at the end of the chapter.)

Transforms can dramatically simplify and speed up your code. Often it is much easier and faster to draw in a simple coordinate space around the origin and then to scale, rotate, and translate your drawing to where you want it. For instance, `FlowerView` includes a lot of code like this:

```
CGPointMake(radius * 2 + xOffset, radius + yOffset)
```

That's a lot of typing, a lot of math, and a lot of things to keep straight in your head. What if instead you just draw it in a 41×4 box as shown in Figure 6-10?

Now all the interesting points fall on nice, easy coordinates like {0,1} and {1,0}. The following code shows how to draw using this transform. Compare the highlighted sections with the `FlowerView` code earlier in this chapter.

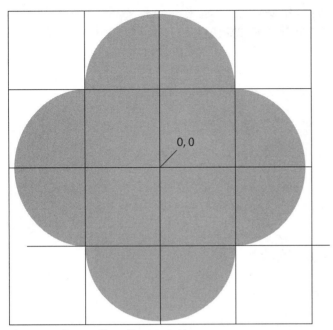

Figure 6-10 Drawing FlowerView in a 4×4 box

FlowerTransformView.m (Transforms)

```
static inline CGAffineTransform
CGAffineTransformMakeScaleTranslate(CGFloat sx, CGFloat sy,
                                    CGFloat dx, CGFloat dy)
{
  return CGAffineTransformMake(sx, 0.f, 0.f, sy, dx, dy);
}

- (void)drawRect:(CGRect)rect {
  CGSize size = self.bounds.size;
  CGFloat margin = 10;

  [[UIColor redColor] set];
  UIBezierPath *path = [UIBezierPath bezierPath];
  [path addArcWithCenter:CGPointMake(0, -1)
                  radius:1
              startAngle:-M_PI
                endAngle:0
               clockwise:YES];
  [path addArcWithCenter:CGPointMake(1, 0)
                  radius:1
              startAngle:-M_PI_2
                endAngle:M_PI_2
               clockwise:YES];
  [path addArcWithCenter:CGPointMake(0, 1)
                  radius:1
              startAngle:0
                endAngle:M_PI
```

```
                     clockwise:YES];
    [path addArcWithCenter:CGPointMake(-1, 0)
                   radius:1
              startAngle:M_PI_2
                endAngle:-M_PI_2
               clockwise:YES];
    [path closePath];

    CGFloat scale = floor((MIN(size.height, size.width)
                          - margin) / 4);

    CGAffineTransform transform;
    transform = CGAffineTransformMakeScaleTranslate(scale,
                                          scale,
                                   size.width/2,
                                  size.height/2);
    [path applyTransform:transform];
    [path fill];
}
```

When you're done constructing your path, you compute a transform to move it into your view's coordinate space. You scale it by the size you want divided by the size it currently is (4), and you translate it to the center of the view. The utility function CGAffineTransformMakeScaleTranslate isn't just for speed (although it is faster). It's easier to get the transform correct this way. If you try to build up the transform one step at a time, each step affects later steps. Scaling and then translating is not the same as translating and then scaling. If you build the matrix all at once, you don't have to worry about that.

This technique can be used to draw complicated shapes at unusual angles. For instance, to draw an arrow pointing to the upper right, it's generally easier to draw it pointing to the right and then rotate it.

You have a choice between transforming the path using applyTransform: and transforming the whole view by setting the transform property. Which is best depends on the situation, but I usually prefer to transform the path rather than the view when practical. Modifying the view's transform makes the results of frame and bounds more difficult to interpret, so I avoid it when I can. As you see in the following section, you can also transform the current context, which sometimes is the best approach.

Drawing with Core Graphics

Core Graphics, sometimes called Quartz 2D or just Quartz, is the main drawing system in iOS. It provides destination-independent drawing, so you can use the same commands to draw to the screen, layer, bitmap, PDF, or printer. Anything starting with CG is part of Core Graphics. Figure 6-11 and the following code provide an example of a simple scrolling graph.

GraphView.h (Graph)

```
@interface GraphView : UIView
@property (nonatomic, readonly, strong)
                                NSMutableArray *values;
@property (nonatomic, readonly, strong) NSTimer *timer;
@end
```

Figure 6-11 Simple scrolling graph

GraphView.m (Graph)

```
#import "GraphView.h"

@implementation GraphView
@synthesize values=values_;
@synthesize timer=timer_;

const double kXScale = 5.0;
const double kYScale = 100.0;

- (void)awakeFromNib {
  values_ = [NSMutableArray array];
```

```objc
    timer_ = [NSTimer scheduledTimerWithTimeInterval:0.25
                                              target:self
                           selector:@selector(updateValues:)
                                            userInfo:nil
                                             repeats:YES];
}

- (void)updateValues:(NSTimer *)timer {
  double nextValue = sin(CFAbsoluteTimeGetCurrent())
                       + ((double)rand()/(double)RAND_MAX);
  [self.values addObject:
                     [NSNumber numberWithDouble:nextValue]];
  NSUInteger maxValues =
                  floorl(self.bounds.size.width / kXScale);

  if ([self.values count] > maxValues) {
    [self.values removeObjectsInRange:
     NSMakeRange(0, [self.values count] - maxValues)];
  }

  [self setNeedsDisplay];
}

- (void)dealloc {
  [timer_ invalidate];
}

- (void)drawRect:(CGRect)rect {
  if ([self.values count] == 0) {
    return;
  }

  CGContextRef ctx = UIGraphicsGetCurrentContext();
  CGContextSetStrokeColorWithColor(ctx,
                             [[UIColor redColor] CGColor]);
  CGContextSetLineJoin(ctx, kCGLineJoinRound);
  CGContextSetLineWidth(ctx, 5);

  CGFloat yOffset = self.bounds.size.height / 2;

  double y = [[self.values objectAtIndex:0] doubleValue];
  CGContextMoveToPoint(ctx, 0, y * kYScale + yOffset);

  for (NSUInteger x = 1; x < [self.values count]; ++x) {
    y = [[self.values objectAtIndex:x] doubleValue];
    CGContextAddLineToPoint(ctx, x * kXScale,
                            y * kYScale + yOffset);
  }

  CGContextStrokePath(ctx);
}

@end
```

Every second, this code adds a new number to the end of the data and removes an old number from the beginning. Then it marks the view as dirty with `setNeedsDisplay`. The drawing code gets the current context, sets various advanced line drawing options not available with `UIBezierPath`, and moves to the first point. For each number, it adds a line to that point in the graph and finally strokes the path.

Note that the "current path" is an attribute of the `CGContext`, not a separate object. Instead, you could use a `CGPath` as shown in the following code.

GraphView.m (Graph)

```
- (void)drawRect:(CGRect)rect {
  if ([self.values count] == 0) {
    return;
  }

  CGContextRef ctx = UIGraphicsGetCurrentContext();
  CGContextSetStrokeColorWithColor(ctx,
                              [[UIColor redColor] CGColor]);
  CGContextSetLineJoin(ctx, kCGLineJoinRound);
  CGContextSetLineWidth(ctx, 5);

  CGMutablePathRef path = CGPathCreateMutable();

  CGFloat yOffset = self.bounds.size.height / 2;
  CGAffineTransform transform =
  CGAffineTransformMakeScaleTranslate(kXScale, kYScale,
                                    0, yOffset);

  double y = [[self.values objectAtIndex:0] doubleValue];
  CGPathMoveToPoint(path, &transform, 0, y);

  for (NSUInteger x = 1; x < [self.values count]; ++x) {
    y = [[self.values objectAtIndex:x] doubleValue];
    CGPathAddLineToPoint(path, &transform, x, y);
  }

  CGContextAddPath(ctx, path);
  CGPathRelease(path);
  CGContextStrokePath(ctx);
}
```

Using a `CGPath` this way allows you to simplify your math with a transform. You can't apply a scaling transform to the view or the context because that would distort the line.

> **Core Graphics uses the Core Foundation memory management rules. Core Foundation objects require manual retain and release, even under ARC. Note the use of** `CGPathRelease`**. For full details, see Chapter 19.**

You may be tempted to cache the CGPath here so that you don't have to compute it every time. That's a good instinct, but in this case it wouldn't help. iOS already avoids calling drawRect: except when the view is dirty, which only happens when the data changes. When the data changes, you need to calculate a new path. Caching the old path in this case would just complicate the code and waste memory.

Mixing UIKit and Core Graphics

Within drawRec:, UIKit and Core Graphics can generally intermix without issue, but outside of drawRect: you may find that things drawn with Core Graphics appear upside down. UIKit uses an upper-left origin (ULO) coordinate system, while Core Graphics uses a lower-left origin (LLO) system by default. As long as you use the context returned by UIGraphicsGetCurrentContext inside of drawRect:, everything is fine because this context is already flipped. But if you create your own context using functions like CGBitmapContextCreate, it'll be LLO. You can either do your math backward or you can flip the context:

```
CGContextTranslateCTM(ctx, 0.0f, height);
CGContextScaleCTM(ctx, 1.0f, -1.0f);
```

This moves (translates) the height of the context, and then flips it using a negative scale. When going from UIKit to Core Graphics, the transform is reversed:

```
CGContextScaleCTM(ctx, 1.0f, -1.0f);
CGContextTranslateCTM(ctx, 0.0f, -height);
```

First flip it, and then translate it.

Managing Graphics Contexts

Before calling drawRect:, the drawing system creates a graphics context. (CGContext). A context includes a lot of information such as a pen color, text color, current font, transform, and more. Sometimes you may want to modify the context and then put it back the way you found it. For instance, you may have a function to draw a specific shape with a specific color. There is only one stroke pen, so when you change the color, this would change things for your caller. To avoid side effects, you can push and pop the context using CGContextSaveGState and CGContextRestoreGState.

Do not confuse this with the similar-sounding UIGraphicsPushContext and UIGraphicsPopContext. They do not do the same thing. CGContextSaveGState remembers the current state of a context. UIGraphicsPushContext changes the current context. Here's an example of CGContextSaveGState.

```
[[UIColor redColor] setStroke];
CGContextSaveGState(UIGraphicsGetCurrentContext());
[[UIColor blackColor] setStroke];
CGContextRestoreGState(UIGraphicsGetCurrentContext());
UIRectFill(CGRectMake(10, 10, 100, 100)); // Red
```

This code sets the stroke pen color to red and saves off the context. It then changes the pen color to black and restores the context. When you draw, the pen is red again.

The following code illustrates a common error.

```
[[UIColor redColor] setStroke];
// Next line is nonsense
UIGraphicsPushContext(UIGraphicsGetCurrentContext());
[[UIColor blackColor] setStroke];
UIGraphicsPopContext();
UIRectFill(CGRectMake(10, 10, 100, 100)); // Black
```

In this case, you set the pen color to red and then switch context to the current context, which does nothing useful. You then change the pen color to black, and pop the context back to the original (which effectively does nothing). You now will draw a black rectangle, which is almost certainly not what was meant.

The purpose of UIGraphicsPushContext is not to save the current *state* of the context (pen color, line width, etc.), but to switch contexts entirely. Say you are in the middle of drawing something into the current view context, and now want to draw something completely different into a bitmap context. If you want to use UIKit to do any of your drawing, you'd want to save off the current UIKit context, including all the drawing that had been done, and switch to a completely new drawing context. That's what UIGraphicsPushContext does. When you finish creating your bitmap, you pop the stack and get your old context back. That's what UIGraphicsPopContext does. This only matters in cases where you want to draw into the new bitmap context with UIKit. As long as you use Core Graphics functions, you don't need to push or pop contexts because Core Graphics functions take the context as a parameter.

This is a pretty useful and common operation. It's so common that Apple has made a shortcut for it called UIGraphicsBeginImageContext. It takes care of pushing the old context, allocating memory for a new context, creating the new context, flipping the coordinate system, and making it the current context. Most of the time, that's just what you want.

Here's an example of how to create an image and return it using UIGraphicsBeginImageContext. The result is shown in Figure 6-12.

MYView.m (Drawing)

```
- (UIImage *)reverseImageForText:(NSString *)text {
  const size_t kImageWidth = 200;
  const size_t kImageHeight = 200;
  CGImageRef textImage = NULL;
  UIFont *font = [UIFont boldSystemFontOfSize:17.0];

  UIGraphicsBeginImageContext(CGSizeMake(kImageWidth,
                                         kImageHeight));

  [[UIColor redColor] set];
  [text drawInRect:CGRectMake(0, 0,
                              kImageWidth, kImageHeight)
        withFont:font];

  textImage =
      UIGraphicsGetImageFromCurrentImageContext().CGImage;
```

```
    UIGraphicsEndImageContext();

    return [UIImage imageWithCGImage:textImage
                              scale:1.0
                        orientation:UIImageOrientationUpMirrored];

}
```

Figure 6-12 Text drawn with reverseImageForText:

Optimizing UIView Drawing

`UIView` and its subclasses are highly optimized, and when possible you should use them rather than custom drawing. For instance, `UIImageView` is faster and uses less memory than anything you're likely to put together in an afternoon with Core Graphics. The following sections cover a few things to keep in mind when using `UIView` to keep it drawing as well as it can.

Avoid Drawing

The fastest drawing is the drawing you never do. iOS goes to great lengths to avoid calling `drawRect:`. It caches an image of your view and moves, rotates, and scales it without any intervention from you. Using an appropriate `contentMode` lets the system adjust your view during rotation or resizing without calling `drawRect:`. The most common cause for `drawRect:` running is when you call `setNeedsDisplay`. Avoid calling `setNeedsDisplay` unnecessarily. Remember, though, `setNeedsDisplay` just schedules the view to be redrawn. Calling `setNeedsDisplay` many times in a single event loop is no more expensive, practically, than calling it once, so don't coalesce your calls. iOS is already doing that for you.

Those familiar with Mac development may be familiar with partial view drawing using `setNeedsDisplay InRect:`. iOS does not perform partial view drawing, and `setNeedsDisplayInRect:` is the same as `setNeedsDisplay`. The entire view will be redrawn. If you want to partially redraw of a view, you should use `CALayer` (discussed in Chapter 7) or use subviews.

Caching and Background Drawing

If you need to do a lot of calculations during your drawing, cache the results when you can. At the lowest level, you can cache the raw data you need rather than asking for it from your delegate every time. Beyond that, you can cache static elements like `CGFont` or `CGGradient` objects so that you only generate them once. Fonts and gradients are useful to cache this way because they are often reused. Finally, you can cache the entire result of a complex drawing operation. Often the best place to cache such a result is in a `CGLayer`, which is discussed later in the section "CGLayer." Alternatively, you can cache the result in a bitmap, generally using `UIGraphicsBeginImageContext` as discussed in "Managing Graphics Contexts" earlier in this chapter.

Much of this caching or precalculation can be done in the background. You may have heard that you must always draw on the main thread, but this isn't completely true. There are several UIKit functions that must only be called on the main thread, such as `UIGraphicsBeginImageContext`, but you are free to create a `CGBitmapContext` object on any thread using `CGBitmapCreateContext` and draw into it. Since iOS 4, you can use UIKit drawing methods like `drawAtPoint:` on background threads as long as you draw into your own `CGContext` and not the main view graphics context (the one returned by `UIGraphicsGetCurrentContext`). You should only access a given `CGContext` on one thread, however.

Custom Drawing Versus Prerendering

There are two major approaches to managing complex drawing. You can draw everything programmatically with `CGPath` and `CGGradient`, or you can prerender everything in a graphics program like Adobe Photoshop and display it as an image. If you have an art department and plan to have extremely complex visual elements, then Photoshop is often the only way to go.

There are a lot of disadvantages to prerendering, however. First, it introduces resolution dependence. You may need to manage 1-scale and 2-scale versions of your images and possibly different images for iPad and iPhone. This complicates workflow and bloats your product. It can make minor changes difficult and lock you into precise element sizes and colors if every change requires a round trip to the artist. Many artists are still unfamiliar with how to draw stretchable images and how to best provide images to be composited for iOS.

Apple originally encouraged developers to prerender because early iPhones couldn't compute gradients fast enough. Since the iPhone 3GS, this has been less of an issue, and each generation makes custom drawing more attractive.

Today, I recommend custom drawing when you can do it in a reasonable amount of code. This is usually the case for small elements like buttons. When you do use prerendered artwork, I suggest that you keep the art files fairly "flat" and composit in code. For instance, you may use an image for a button's background, but handle the rounding and shadows in code. That way, as you want to make minor tweaks, you don't have to rerender the background.

Pixel Alignment and Blurry Text

One of the most common causes of subtle drawing problems is pixel misalignment. If you ask Core Graphics to draw at a point that is not aligned with a pixel, it performs anti-aliasing, as discussed in "Understanding Coordinates" earlier in this chapter. This means it draws part of the information on one pixel and part on another, giving the illusion that the line is between the two. This illusion makes things smoother, but that also makes them fuzzy. Anti-aliasing also takes processing time, so it slows down drawing. When possible, you want to make sure that your drawing is pixel aligned to avoid this.

Prior to the Retina display, pixel aligned meant integer coordinates. As of iOS 4, coordinates are in points, not pixels. There are two pixels to the point on the current Retina display, so half-points (1.5, 2.5) are also pixel aligned. In the future, there might be four or more pixels to the point, and it could be different from device to device. Even so, unless you need pixel accuracy, it is easiest to just make sure you use integer coordinates for your frames.

Generally it is the frame origin that matters for pixel alignment. This causes an unfortunate problem for the `center` property. If you set the center to an integral coordinate, your origin may be misaligned. This is particularly noticeable with text, especially with `UILabel`. Figure 6-13 demonstrates this problem. It is subtle, and may be difficult to see in print, so you can also demonstrate it with the program `BlurryText` available with the online files for this chapter.

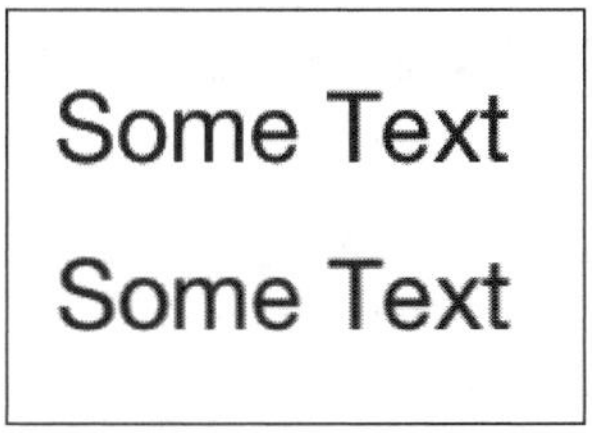

Figure 6-13 Text that is pixel aligned (top) and unaligned (bottom)

There are two solutions. First, odd font sizes (13 rather than 12 for instance) will typically align correctly. If you make a habit of using odd font sizes, you can often avoid the problem. To be certain to avoid the problem, you need to make sure that the frame is integral either by using `setFrame:` instead of `setCenter:`, or by using a `UIView` category like `setAlignedCenter::`

```
- (void)setAlignedCenter:(CGPoint)center {
  self.center = center;
  self.frame = CGRectIntegral(self.frame);
}
```

Because this effectively sets the frame twice, it is not the fastest solution, but it is very easy and fast enough for most problems. `CGRectIntegral()` returns the smallest integral rectangle that encloses the given rectangle.

As pre-Retina displays phase out, this will be less of an issue as long as you set `center` to integer coordinates. For now, though, it is still a concern.

Alpha, Opaque, Hidden

Views have three properties that appear related, but are actually orthogonal: `alpha`, `opaque`, and `hidden`.

The `alpha` property determines how much information a view contributes to the pixels within its frame. So an `alpha` of 1 means that all of the view's information is used to color the pixel. An `alpha` of 0 means that none of the view's information is used to color the pixel. Remember, nothing is really transparent on an iPhone screen. If you set the entire screen to transparent pixels, the user isn't going to see the circuit board or the ground. In the end, it's just a matter of what color to draw the pixel. So as you raise and lower the `alpha`, you're changing how much this view contributes to the pixel versus views "below" it.

Marking a view `opaque` or not does not actually make its content more or less transparent. `Opaque` is a promise that the drawing system can use for optimization. When you mark a view as `opaque`, you're promising the drawing system that you will draw every pixel in your rectangle with fully opaque colors. That allows the drawing system to ignore views below yours and that can improve performance, particularly when applying transforms. You should mark your views `opaque` whenever possible, especially views that scroll like `UITableViewCell`. However, if there are any partially transparent pixels in your view, or if you don't draw every pixel in your rectangle, setting `opaque` can have unpredictable results. Setting a nontransparent `backgroundColor` ensures that all pixels are drawn.

Closely related to `opaque` is `clearsContextBeforeDrawing`. This is `YES` by default, and sets the context to transparent black before calling `drawRect:`. This avoids any garbage data in the view. It's a pretty fast operation, but if you're going to draw every pixel anyway, you can get a small benefit by setting it to `NO`.

Finally, `hidden` indicates that the view should not be drawn at all and is generally equivalent to an `alpha` of 0. The `hidden` property cannot be animated, so it's common to hide views by animating `alpha` to 0.

Hidden and transparent views do not receive touch events. The meaning of transparent is not well defined in the documentation, but through experimentation I've found that it is an `alpha` less than 0.1. You should not rely on this particular value, but the point is that "nearly transparent" is generally treated as transparent. You cannot create a "transparent overlay" to catch touch events by setting the `alpha` very low.

You can make a view transparent and still receive touch events by setting its `alpha` to 1, `opaque` to `NO`, and `backgroundColor` to `nil` or `[UIColor clearColor]`. A view with a transparent background is still considered visible for the purposes of hit detection.

CGLayer

CGLayer is a very effective way to cache things you draw often. This should not be confused with CALayer, which is a more powerful and complicated layer object from Core Animation. CGLayer is a Core Graphics layer that is optimized, often hardware optimized, for drawing into CGContext.

There are several kinds of CGContext. The most common is a view graphics context, designed to draw to the screen, which is returned by UIGraphicsCurrentContext. Contexts are also used for bitmaps and printing, however. Each of these has different attributes, including maximum resolution, color details, and available hardware acceleration.

At its simplest, a CGLayer is similar to a CGBitmapContext. You can draw into it, save it off, and use it to draw the result into a CGContext later. The difference is that you can optimize CGLayer for use with a particular kind of graphics context. If a CGLayer is destined for a view graphics context, it can cache its data directly on the GPU, which can significantly improve performance. CGBitmapContext can't do this because it doesn't know that you plan to draw it on the screen.

The following example demonstrates caching a CGLayer. In this case it's cached in a static variable the first time the view is drawn. You can then "stamp" the CGLayer repeatedly while rotating the context. You use UIGraphicsPushContext so that you can use UIKit to draw the text into the layer context, and UIGraphicsPopContext to return to the normal context. This could be done with CGContextShowTextAtPoint instead, but UIKit makes it very easy to draw an NSString. Figure 6-14 shows the ouput.

LayerView.m (Layer)

```
@implementation LayerView

- (void)drawRect:(CGRect)rect {
  static CGLayerRef sTextLayer = NULL;

  CGContextRef ctx = UIGraphicsGetCurrentContext();

  if (sTextLayer == NULL) {
    CGRect textBounds = CGRectMake(0, 0, 200, 100);
    sTextLayer = CGLayerCreateWithContext(ctx,
                                          textBounds.size,
                                          NULL);

    CGContextRef textCtx = CGLayerGetContext(sTextLayer);
    CGContextSetRGBFillColor (textCtx, 1.0, 0.0, 0.0, 1);
    UIGraphicsPushContext(textCtx);
    UIFont *font = [UIFont systemFontOfSize:13.0];
    [@"Pushing The Limits" drawInRect:textBounds
                            withFont:font];
    UIGraphicsPopContext();
  }

  CGContextTranslateCTM(ctx, self.bounds.size.width / 2,
```

```
                            self.bounds.size.height / 2);

    for (NSUInteger i = 0; i < 10; ++i) {
      CGContextRotateCTM(ctx, 2 * M_PI / 10);
      CGContextDrawLayerAtPoint(ctx,
                                CGPointZero,
                                sTextLayer);
    }
}

@end
```

Figure 6-14 Output of LayerView

Summary

iOS has a rich collection of drawing tools. This chapter focused on Core Graphics and its Objective-C descendant, UIKit. By now you should have a good understanding of how systems interact and how to optimize your iOS drawing.

Chapter 7 discusses Core Animation, which puts your interface in motion. Also covered is `CALayer`, a powerful addition to `UIView` and `CGLayer`, and an important tool for your drawing toolbox even if you're not animating.

iOS 5 brings Core Image to iOS for tweaking pictures. That is discussed briefly in Chapter 1. iOS also has ever-growing support for OpenGL ES for drawing advanced 3D graphics and textures. OpenGL ES is a book-length subject of its own, so it isn't tackled here, but you can get a good introduction in Apple's "OpenGL ES Programming Guide for iOS" (see the "Further Reading" section).

Further Reading

Apple Documentation

The following documents are available in the iOS Developer Library at `developer.apple.com` or through the Xcode Documentation and API Reference.

Drawing and Printing Guide for iOS

iOS Human Interface Guidelines

iOS Application Programming Guide

OpenGL ES Programming Guide for iOS

Quartz 2D Programming Guide

Technical Q&A QA1708: Improving Image Drawing Performance on iOS

View Programming Guide for iOS

Other Resources

LaMarche, Jeff, *iPhone Development*. Jeff has several articles that provide a lot of insight into using `CGAffineTransform`.
`iphonedevelopment.blogspot.com/search/label/CGAffineTransform`.

Chapter 7

Layers Like an Onion: Core Animation

The iPhone has made animation central to the mobile experience. Views slide in and out, applications zoom into place, pages fly into the bookmark list. Apple has made animation not just a beautiful part of the experience, but a better way to let the user know what's happening and what to expect. When views slide into place from right to left, it is natural to press the left-pointing button to go back to where you were. When you create a bookmark and it flies to the toolbar, it's more obvious where you should look to get back to that bookmark. These subtle cues are a critical part of making your user interface intuitive as well as engaging. To facilitate all this animation, iOS devices include a powerful GPU and frameworks that let you harness that GPU easily.

In this chapter you discover the two main animation systems of iOS: view animations and the Core Animation framework. You learn how to draw with Core Animation layers and how to move layers around in two and three dimensions. Common decorations like rounded corners, colored borders, and shadows are trivial with CALayer, and you learn to apply them quickly and easily. You learn how to create custom automatic animations, including animating your own properties. Finally, Core Animation is all about performance, so you learn how to manage layers in multithreaded applications.

This chapter focuses on animations for view-based programming. These frameworks are ideal for most iOS applications except games. Game development is outside the scope of this book, and is usually best served by built-in frameworks like OpenGL ES or third-party frameworks like Cocos2D. For more information on OpenGL ES, see the *OpenGL ES for iOS* portal at developer.apple.com. For more information on Cocos2D, see cocos2d-iphone.org.

View Animations

UIView provides rich animation functionality that is very easy to use and well optimized. Most common animations can be handled with +animateWithDuration:animations: and related methods. You can use UIView to animate frame, bounds, center, transform, alpha, backgroundColor, and contentStretch. Most of the time you'll animate frame, center, transform, and alpha.

It's likely that you are familiar with basic view animations, so I'll just touch on the high points in this section and then move on to more advanced layer-based drawing and animation.

Let's start with a very simple animation of a ball that falls when you tap the view. CircleView just draws a circle in its frame. The following code creates the animation shown in Figure 7-1.

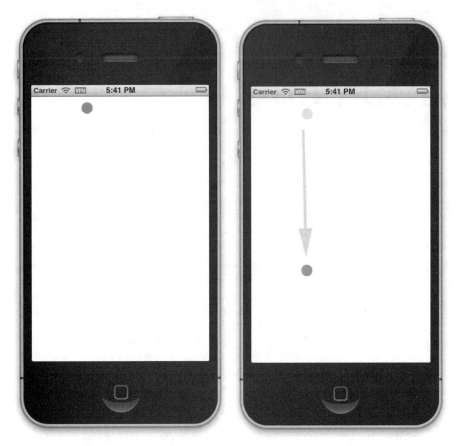

Figure 7-1 CircleView animation

ViewAnimationViewController.m (ViewAnimation)

```
#import "ViewAnimationViewController.h"
#import "CircleView.h"

@implementation ViewAnimationViewController
@synthesize circleView = circleView_;

- (void)viewDidLoad {
  [super viewDidLoad];
  self.circleView = [[CircleView alloc] initWithFrame:
                  CGRectMake(0, 0, 20, 20)];
  self.circleView.center = CGPointMake(100, 20);
  [[self view] addSubview:self.circleView];

  UITapGestureRecognizer *g;
  g = [[UITapGestureRecognizer alloc]
      initWithTarget:self
      action:@selector(dropAnimate)];
  [[self view] addGestureRecognizer:g];
```

```
}

- (void)viewDidUnload {
  [super viewDidUnload];
  self.circleView = nil;
}

- (void)dropAnimate {
  [UIView animateWithDuration:3 animations:^{
    self.circleView.center = CGPointMake(100, 300);
  }];
}
@end
```

This is the simplest kind of view-based animation, and it can handle most common problems, particularly animating size, location, and opacity. It's also common to animate `transform` to scale, rotate, or translate the view over time. Less commonly, you can animate `backgroundColor` and `contentStretch`. Animating the background color is particularly useful in HUD-style interfaces to move between mostly transparent and mostly opaque backgrounds. This can be more effective than just animating the overall `alpha`.

Chaining animations is also straightforward, as shown in the following code.

```
- (void)dropAnimate {
  [UIView
   animateWithDuration:3 animations:^{
     self.circleView.center = CGPointMake(100, 300);
   }
   completion:^(BOOL finished){
     [UIView animateWithDuration:1 animations:^{
       self.circleView.center = CGPointMake(250, 300);
     }
     ];
   }];
}
```

Now the ball will drop and the move to the right. But there's a subtle problem with this code. If you tap the screen while the animation is in progress, the ball will jump to the lower left and then animate to the right. That's probably not what you want. The issue is that every time you tap the view, this code runs. If an animation is in progress, then it's canceled and the `completion` block runs with `finished==NO`. You look at how to handle that next.

Managing User Interaction

The problem mentioned in the previous section is caused by a user experience mistake: allowing the user to send new commands while you're animating the last command. Sometimes that's what you want, but in this case it isn't. Anytime you create an animation in response to user input, you need to consider this issue.

When you animate a view, by default it automatically stops responding to user interaction. So while the ball is dropping, tapping it won't generate any events. In this example, however, tapping the main view causes the animation. There are two solutions. First, you can change your user interface so that tapping the ball causes the animation:

```
[self.circleView addGestureRecognizer:g];
```

The other solution is to ignore taps while the ball is animating. The following code shows how to disable the `UIGestureRecognizer` in the gesture recognizer callback , and then enable it when the animation completes.

```
- (void)dropAnimate:(UIGestureRecognizer *)recognizer {
  [UIView
    animateWithDuration:3 animations:^{
      recognizer.enabled = NO;
      self.circleView.center = CGPointMake(100, 300);
  }
  completion:^(BOOL finished){
    [UIView
      animateWithDuration:1 animations:^{
        self.circleView.center = CGPointMake(250, 300);
    }
    completion:^(BOOL finished){
      recognizer.enabled = YES;
    }
    ];
  }];
```

This technique is nice because it minimizes side effects to the rest of the view, but you might want to prevent all user interaction for the view while the animation runs. In that case you would replace `recognizer.enabled` with `self.view.userInteractionEnabled`.

Drawing with Layers

View animations are powerful, and you should rely on them whenever you can, especially for basic layout animation. They also provide a small number of stock transitions that you can read about in the Animations section of the *View Programming Guide for iOS* available at `developer.apple.com`. If you have basic needs, these are great tools.

But you're here to go beyond the basic needs, and view animations have a lot of limitations. Their basic unit of animation is `UIView`, which is a pretty heavyweight object, so you need to be careful about how many of them you use. `UIView` also doesn't support three-dimensional layout, except for basic z-ordering, so it can't create anything like Cover Flow. To move your UI to the next level, you need to learn to use Core Animation.

Core Animation provides a variety of tools, several of which are useful even if you don't intend to animate anything. The most basic and important part of Core Animation is `CALayer`. This section explains how to draw with `CALayer` without animations. You explore animating later in the chapter.

> Don't confuse `CALayer` from Core Animation with `CGLayer` from Core Graphics. Both are layers, but they have dramatically different purposes. See Chapter 6 for more information on `CGLayer`. In this chapter, when I refer to a layer, I mean `CALayer`.

In many ways, CALayer is very much like UIView. It has a location, size, transform, and content. You can override a draw method to draw custom content, usually with Core Graphics. There is a layer hierarchy exactly like the view hierarchy. You might ask, why even have separate objects?

The most important answer is that UIView is a fairly heavyweight object that manages drawing and event handling, particularly touch events. CALayer is all about drawing. In fact, UIView relies on a CALayer to manage its drawing, which allows the two to work very well together.

Every UIView has a CALayer to do its drawing. And every CALayer can have sublayers, just like every UIView can have subviews. Figure 7-2 shows the hierarchy.

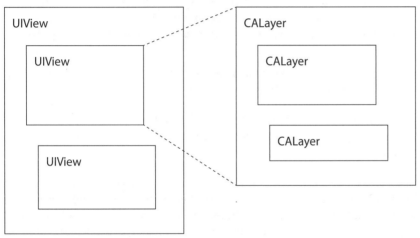

Figure 7-2 View and layer hierarchies

Layers draw whatever is in its contents property, which is a CGImage (see the note at the end of this section). It's your job to set this somehow, and there are various ways of doing that. The simplest approach is to assign it directly, as shown here, and discussed more fully in "Setting Contents Directly" later in this section.

```
UIImage *image = ...;
CALayer *layer = ...;
layer.contents = (__bridge id)[image CGImage];
```

If you do not set the contents property directly, then Core Animation will go through the following methods to create it.

1. [CALayer setNeedsDisplay]—Your code needs to call this. It marks the layer as dirty, requesting that contents be updated using the following steps. Unless setNeedsDisplay is called, the contents property is never updated, even if it's nil.

2. [CALayer displayIfNeeded]—The drawing system automatically calls this as needed. If the layer has been marked dirty by a call to setNeedsDisplay, then the drawing system will continue with the following steps.

3. [CALayer display]—This is called by displayIfNeeded when appropriate. You shouldn't call it directly. The default implementation calls the delegate method displayLayer: if the delegate

implements it. If not, `display` calls `drawInContext:`. You can override `display` in a subclass to set `contents` directly.

4. `[delegate displayLayer:]`—The default `[CALayer display]` calls this if the delegate implements it. Its job is to set `contents`. If this method is implemented, even if it does nothing, then no further custom drawing code will be run.

5. `[CALayer drawInContext:]`—The default `display` method creates a view graphics context and passes it to `drawInContext:`. This is similar to `[UIView drawRect:]`, but no UIKit context is set up for you automatically. To draw with UIKit, you need to call `UIGraphicsPushContext()` to make the passed context the current context. Otherwise, just use the passed context to draw with Core Graphics. The default `display` method takes the resulting context, creates a `CGImage` (see note below) and assigns it to `contents`. The default `[CALayer drawInContext:]` calls `[delegate drawLayer:inContext:]` if it's implemented. Otherwise it does nothing. Note that you may call this directly. See the section "Drawing in Your Own Context" later in this section for information on why you would call this directly.

6. `[delegate drawLayer:inContext:]`—If implemented, the default `drawInContext:` calls this to update the context so that `display` can create a `CGImage`.

As you can see, there are several ways to set the contents of a layer. You can set it directly with `setContent:`, you can implement `display` or `displayLayer:`, or you can implement `drawInContext:` or `drawLayer:inContext:`. In the rest of this section I discuss each approach.

The drawing system almost never automatically updates `contents` in the way that `UIView` is often automatically refreshed. For instance, `UIView` draws itself the first time it's put on screen. `CALayer` does not. Marking a `UIView` as dirty with `setNeedsDisplay` automatically redraws all the subviews as well. Marking a `CALayer` as dirty with `setNeedsDisplay` does not impact sublayers. The thing to remember is that the default behavior of a `UIView` is to draw when it thinks you need it. The default behavior of a `CALayer` is to never draw unless you explicitly ask for it. `CALayer` is a much lower-level object, and it is optimized to not waste time doing anything that wasn't explicitly asked for.

> The `contents` **property is usually a** `CGImage`**, but this is not always the case. If you use custom drawing, then Core Animation will use a private class,** `CABackingStorage`**, for** `contents`**. You can set** `contents` **to either a** `CGImage` **or the** `contents` **of another layer.**

Setting Contents Directly

Providing a content image (shown in the following code) is the easiest solution if you already have an image handy.

LayersViewController.m (Layers)

```
#import <QuartzCore/QuartzCore.h>
...
  UIImage *image = [UIImage imageNamed:@"pushing.png"];
  self.view.layer.contents = (__bridge id)[image CGImage];
```

> You must always import `QuartzCore.h` and link with `QuartzCore.framework` to use Core Animation. This is an easy thing to forget.

The cast to `__bridge id` is needed because `contents` is defined as an `id`, but actually expects a `CGImageRef`. To make this work with ARC, a cast is required. (This may be resolved in a later version of iOS.) A common error is to pass a `UIImage` here instead of a `CGImageRef`. You won't get a compiler error or runtime warning. Your view will just be blank.

By default, the contents are scaled to fill the view, even if that distorts the image. As with `contentMode` and `contentStretch` in `UIView`, `CALayer` can be configured to scale its image in different ways using `contentsCenter` and `contentsGravity`.

Implementing Display

The job of `display` or `displayLayer:` is to set `contents` to a correct `CGImage`. You can do this any way you'd like. The default implementation creates an `CGContext`, passes it to `drawInContext:`, turns the result into a `CGImage`, and assigns it to `contents`. The most common reason to override this is if your layer has several states, and you have an image for each. Buttons often work this way. You can create those images by loading them from your bundle, drawing them with Core Graphics, or any other way you'd like.

Whether to subclass `CALayer` or use a delegate is really a matter of taste and convenience. `UIView` has a layer and it must be that layer's delegate. In my experience it's dangerous to make a `UIView` the delegate for any of the sublayers. This can create infinite recursion when the `UIView` tries to copy its sublayers in certain operations such as transitions. So you can implement `displayLayer:` in `UIView` to manage its layer, or you can have some other object be the delegate for sublayers.

Having `UIView` implement `displayLayer:` seldom makes sense in my opinion. If your view content is basically several images, it's usually a better idea to use a `UIImageView` or a `UIButton` rather than a custom `UIView` with hand-loaded layer content. `UIImageView` is highly optimized for displaying images. `UIButton` is very good at switching images based on state, and includes a lot of good user interface mechanics that are a pain to reproduce. Don't try to reinvent UIKit in Core Animation. UIKit likely does it better than you will.

What can make more sense is to make your `UIViewController` the delegate for the layers, particularly if you aren't subclassing `UIView`. This avoids extra objects and subclasses if your needs are pretty simple. Just don't let your `UIViewController` get overcomplicated.

Custom Drawing

As with `UIView`, you can provide completely custom drawing with `CALayer`. Typically you'll draw with Core Graphics, but using `UIGraphicsPushContext`, you can also draw with UIKit.

> See Chapter 6 for information on how to draw with Core Graphics and UIKit.

Using `drawInContext:` is just another way of setting `contents`. It's called by `display`, which is called only when the layer is explicitly marked dirty with `setNeedsDisplay`. The advantage of this over setting `contents` directly is that `display` automatically creates a `CGContext` appropriate for the layer. In particular, the coordinate system is flipped for you. (See Chapter 6 for a discussion of Core Graphics and flipped coordinate systems.) The following code shows how to implement the delegate method `drawLayer:inContext:` to draw the string "Pushing The Limits" at the top of the layer using UIKit. Because Core Animation does not set a UIKit graphics context, you need to call `UIGraphicsPushContext` before calling UIKit methods, and `UIGraphicsPopContext` before returning.

DelegateView.m (Layers)

```
@implementation DelegateView

- (id)initWithFrame:(CGRect)frame {
    self = [super initWithFrame:frame];
    if (self) {
        [self.layer setNeedsDisplay];
    }
    return self;
}

- (void)drawLayer:(CALayer *)layer inContext:(CGContextRef)ctx {
    UIGraphicsPushContext(ctx);
    [[UIColor whiteColor] set];
    UIRectFill(layer.bounds);
    [[UIColor blackColor] set];
    UIFont *font = [UIFont systemFontOfSize:48.0];
    [@"Pushing The Limits" drawInRect:[layer bounds]
                            withFont:font
                       lineBreakMode:UILineBreakModeWordWrap
                           alignment:UITextAlignmentCenter];
    UIGraphicsPopContext();
}

@end
```

Note the call to `setNeedsDisplay` in `initWithFrame:`. As discussed earlier, layers do not automatically draw themselves when put on screen. You need to mark them as dirty with `setNeedsDisplay`.

You may also notice the hand-drawing of the background rather than using the `backgroundColor` property. This is intentional. Once you engage in custom drawing with `drawLayer:inContext:`, most automatic layer settings like `backgroundColor` and `cornerRadius` are ignored. Your job in `drawLayer:inContext:` is to draw everything needed for the layer. There isn't helpful compositing going on for you like in `UIView`. If you want layer effects like rounded corners together with custom drawing, then put the custom drawing onto a sublayer, and round the corners on the superlayer.

Drawing in Your Own Context

Unlike `[UIView drawRect:]`, it is completely legal to call `[CALayer drawInContext:]` yourself. You just need to generate a context and pass it in. This is nice for capturing the contents of a layer onto a bitmap or

PDF so you can save it or print it. This is mostly useful if you want to composite this layer with something else because if all you want is a bitmap, you could just use `contents`.

`drawInContext:` only draws the current layer, not any of its sublayers. If you want to draw the layer and its sublayers, use `renderInContext:`. That also captures the current state of the layer if it's animating. It use the current state of the render tree that Core Animation maintains internally, so it doesn't call `drawInContext:`.

Moving Things Around

Now that you can draw in a layer, let's look into how to use those layers to create powerful animations.

Layers naturally animate. In fact, you need to do a small amount of work to prevent them from animating. Consider this example:

LayerAnimationViewController.m (LayerAnimation)

```
- (void)viewDidLoad {
  [super viewDidLoad];
  CALayer *squareLayer = [CALayer layer];
  squareLayer.backgroundColor = [[UIColor redColor] CGColor];
  squareLayer.frame = CGRectMake(100, 100, 20, 20);
  [self.view.layer addSublayer:squareLayer];

  UIView *squareView = [UIView new];
  squareView.backgroundColor = [UIColor blueColor];
  squareView.frame = CGRectMake(200, 100, 20, 20);
  [self.view addSubview:squareView];

  [self.view addGestureRecognizer:
   [[UITapGestureRecognizer alloc]
     initWithTarget:self
     action:@selector(drop:)]];
}

- (void)drop:(UIGestureRecognizer *)recognizer {
  NSArray *layers = self.view.layer.sublayers;
  CALayer *layer = [layers objectAtIndex:0];
  [layer setPosition:CGPointMake(200, 250)];

  NSArray *views = self.view.subviews;
  UIView *view = [views objectAtIndex:0];
  [view setCenter:CGPointMake(100, 250)];
}
```

This draws a small red sublayer and a small blue subview. When the view is tapped, both are moved. The view jumps immediately to the new location. The layer animates over a quarter second. It's fast, but it's not instantaneous like the view.

`CALayer` implicitly animates all properties that support animation. You can prevent this by disabling actions:

```
[CATransaction setDisableActions:YES];
```

I discuss actions further in the "Auto-animate with Actions" section later in this chapter.

> `disableActions` **is a very poorly named property. Because it begins with a verb, you would expect it to have a side effect (disabling actions) rather than returning the current value of the property. It should be** `actionsDisabled` **(or** `actionsEnabled` **to be parallel with** `userInteractionEnabled`**). Apple may remedy this eventually, as it has with other misnamed properties. In the meantime, make sure to call** `setDisableActions:` **when you mean to change it. You won't get a warning or error if you call** `[CATransaction disableActions]` **in a void context.**

Implicit Animations

You now know all the basics of animation. Just set layer properties and your layers animate in the default way. But what if you don't like the defaults? For instance, you may want to change the duration of the animation. First, you need to understand transactions.

Most of the time when you change several layer properties, you want them all to animate together. You also don't want to waste the renderer's time calculating animations for one property change if the next property change affects it. For instance, `opacity` and `backgroundColor` are interrelated properties. Both affect the final displayed pixel color, so you want to know about both animations when working out the intermediate values.

Core Animation bundles property changes into atomic transactions (`CATransaction`). An implicit `CATransaction` is created for you the first time you modify a layer on a thread that includes a run loop. (If that last sentence piqued your interest, see the "Core Animation and Threads" section later in this chapter.) During the run loop, all layer changes are collected, and when the run loop completes, all the changes are committed to the layer tree.

To modify the animation properties, you need to make changes to the current transaction. The following changes the duration of the current transaction to 5 seconds rather than the default quarter-second.

```
[CATransaction setAnimationDuration:2.0];
```

You can also set a completion block to run after the current transaction finishes animating using `[CATransaction setCompletionBlock:]`. You can use this to chain animations together, among other things.

While the run loop creates a transaction for you automatically, you can also create your own explicit transactions using `[CATransaction begin]` and `[CATransaction commit]`. These allow you to assign different durations to different parts of the animation, or to disable animations for only a part of the event loop.

> **See the "Auto-animate with Actions" section of this chapter for more information on how implicit animations are implemented and how you can extend them.**

Explicit Animations

Implicit animations are powerful and convenient, but sometimes you want more control. That's where CAAnimation comes in. With CAAnimation, you can manage repeating animations, precisely control timing and pacing, and employ layer transitions. Implicit animations are implemented using CAAnimation, so everything you can do with an implicit animation can be done explicitly as well.

The most basic animation is a CABasicAnimation. It interpolates a property over a range using a timing function, as shown in the following code.

```
CABasicAnimation *anim = [CABasicAnimation
                            animationWithKeyPath:@"opacity"];
anim.fromValue = [NSNumber numberWithDouble:1.0];
anim.toValue = [NSNumber numberWithDouble:0.0];
anim.autoreverses = YES;
anim.repeatCount = INFINITY;
anim.duration = 2.0;
[layer addAnimation:anim forKey:@"anim"];
```

This pulses the layer forever, animating the opacity from one to zero and back over 2 seconds. When you want to stop the animation, remove it:

```
[layer removeAnimationForKey:@"anim"];
```

An animation has a key, a fromValue, a toValue, a timingFunction, a duration, and some other configuration options. The way it works is to make several copies of the layer, send setValue:forKey: messages to the copies and then display. It captures the generated contents and displays them.

If you have custom properties in your layer, you may notice that they're not set correctly during animation. This is because the layer is copied. You must override initWithLayer: to copy your custom properties if you want them to be available during an animation. I discuss this later in the "Animating Custom Properties" section of this chapter.

CABasicAnimations are basic, as the name implies. They're easy to set up and use, but they're not very flexible. If you want more control over the animation, you can move to CAKeyframeAnimation. The major difference is that instead of giving a fromValue and toValue, you now can give a path or a sequence of points to animate through, along with individual timing for each segment. The *Animation Types and Timing Programming Guide* on developer.apple.com provides excellent examples. They're not technically difficult to set up. Most of the work is on the creative side to find just the right path and timing.

Model and Presentation

A common problem in animations is the dreaded "jump back." The mistake looks like this:

```
CABasicAnimation *fade;
fade = [CABasicAnimation animationWithKeyPath:@"opacity"];
fade.duration = 1;
fade.fromValue = [NSNumber numberWithDouble:1.0];
fade.toValue = [NSNumber numberWithDouble:0.0];
[circleLayer addAnimation:fade forKey:@"fade"];
```

This fades the circle out over 1 second, just as expected, and then suddenly the circle reappears. To understand why this happens, you need to be aware of the difference between the model layer and the presentation layer.

The *model layer* is defined by the properties of the "real" CALayer object. Nothing in the preceding code modifies any property of circleLayer itself. Instead, CAAnimation makes copies of circleLayer and modifies those. These become the *presentation layer*. They represent roughly what is shown on the screen. There is technically another layer called the *render layer* that really represents what's on the screen, but it's internal to Core Animation and you very seldom encounter it.

So what happens in the preceding code? CAAnimation modifies the presentation layer, which is drawn to the screen, and when it completes, all its changes are thrown away and the model layer is used to determine the new state. The model layer hasn't changed, so you snap back to where you started. The solution to this is to set the model layer, as shown here:

```
circleLayer.opacity = 0;
CABasicAnimation *fade;
fade = [CABasicAnimation animationWithKeyPath:@"opacity"];
. . .
[circleLayer addAnimation:fade forKey:@"fade"];
```

Sometimes this works fine, but sometimes the implicit animation in setOpacity: fights with the explicit animation from animationWithKeyPath:. The best solution to that is to turn off implicit animations if you're doing explicit animations:

```
[CATransaction begin];
[CATransaction setDisableActions:YES];
circleLayer.opacity = 0;
CABasicAnimation *fade;
fade = [CABasicAnimation animationWithKeyPath:@"opacity"];
. . .
[circleLayer addAnimation:fade forKey:@"fade"];
[CATransaction commit];
```

Sometimes you see people recommend setting removedOnCompletion to NO and fillMode to kCAFillModeBoth. This is not a good solution. It essentially makes the animation go on forever, which means the model layer is never updated. If you ask for the property's value, you continue to see the model value, not what you see on the screen. If you try to implicitly animate the property afterward, it won't work correctly because the CAAnimation is still running. If you ever remove the animation by replacing it with another with the same name, calling removeAnimationForKey: or removeAllAnimations, the old value snaps back. On top of all of that, it wastes memory.

All of this becomes a bit of a pain, so you may like the following category on CALayer that wraps it all together and lets you set the duration and delay. Most of the time I still prefer implicit animation, but this can make explicit animation a bit simpler.

CALayer+RNAnimation.m (LayerAnimation)

```objc
@implementation CALayer (RNAnimations)

- (void)setValue:(id)value
        forKeyPath:(NSString *)keyPath
          duration:(CFTimeInterval)duration
             delay:(CFTimeInterval)delay {
  [CATransaction begin];
  [CATransaction setDisableActions:YES];
  [self setValue:value forKeyPath:keyPath];
  CABasicAnimation *anim;
  anim = [CABasicAnimation animationWithKeyPath:keyPath];
  anim.duration = duration;
  anim.beginTime = CACurrentMediaTime() + delay;
  anim.fillMode = kCAFillModeBoth;
  anim.fromValue = [[self presentationLayer] valueForKey:keyPath];
  anim.toValue = value;
  [self addAnimation:anim forKey:keyPath];
  [CATransaction commit];
}

@end
```

A Few Words on Timings

As in the universe at large, in Core Animation, time is relative. A second does not always have to be a second. Just like coordinates, time can be scaled.

CAAnimation conforms to the CAMediaTiming protocol, and you can set the speed property to scale its timing. Because of this, when considering timings between layers, you need to convert them, just like you need to convert points that occur in different views or layers.

```objc
localPoint = [self convertPoint:remotePoint fromLayer:otherLayer];
localTime = [self convertTime:remotetime fromLayer:otherLayer];
```

This isn't very common, but it comes up when you're trying to coordinate animations. You might ask another layer for a particular animation and when that animation will end so that you can start your animation.

```objc
CAAnimation *otherAnim = [layer animationForKey:@"anim"];
CFTimeInterval finish = otherAnim.beginTime + otherAnim.duration;
myAnim.beginTime = [self convertTime:finish fromLayer:layer];
```

Setting beginTime like this is a nice way to chain animations, even if you hard-code the time rather than ask the other layer. To reference "now," just use CACurrentMediaTime().

This raises another issue, however. What value should your property have between now and when the animation begins? You would assume that it would be the fromValue, but that isn't how it works. It's the current model value because the animation hasn't begun. Typically this is the toValue.

```
[CATransaction begin];
[CATransaction setDisableActions:YES];
anim = [CABasicAnimation animationWithKeyPath:@"opacity"];
anim.fromValue = [NSNumber numberWithDouble:1.0];
anim.toValue = [NSNumber numberWithDouble:0.5];
anim.duration = 5.0;
anim.beginTime = CACurrentMediaTime() + 3.0;
[layer addAnimation:anim forKey:@"fade"];
layer.opacity = 0.5;
[CATransaction commit];
```

This animation does nothing for 3 seconds. During that time, the default property animation is used to fade `opacity` from 1.0 to 0.5. Then the animation begins, setting the opacity to its `fromValue` and interpolating to its `toValue`. So the layer begins with `opacity` of 1.0, fades to 0.5 over a quarter-second, then 3 seconds, and later jumps back to 1.0 and fades again to 0.5 over 5 seconds. This almost certainly isn't what you want.

You can resolve this using `fillMode`. The default is `kCAFillModeRemoved`, which means that the animation has no influence on the values before or after its execution. This can be changed to "clamp" values before or after the animation by setting the fill mode to `kCAFillModeBackwards`, `kCAFillModeForwards`, or `kCAFillModeBoth`. Figure 7-3 illustrates this.

In most cases, you want to set this to `kCAFillModeBackwards` or `kCAFillModeBoth`.

Into the Third Dimension

Chapter 6 discussed how to use `CAAffineTransform` to make `UIView` drawing much more efficient. This technique limits you to two-dimensional transformations: translate, rotate, scale, and skew. With layers, however, you can apply three-dimensional transformations by adding perspective. This is often called 2.5D rather than 3D because it doesn't make layers into truly three-dimensional objects in the way that OpenGL ES does. But it does allow you to give the illusion of three-dimensional movement.

You rotate layers around an anchor point. By default, the anchor point is in the center of the layer, designated {0.5, 0.5}. It can be moved anywhere within the layer, making it convenient to rotate around an edge or corner. The anchor point is described in terms of a unit square rather than in points. So the lower-right corner is {1.0, 1.0}, no matter how large or small the layer is.

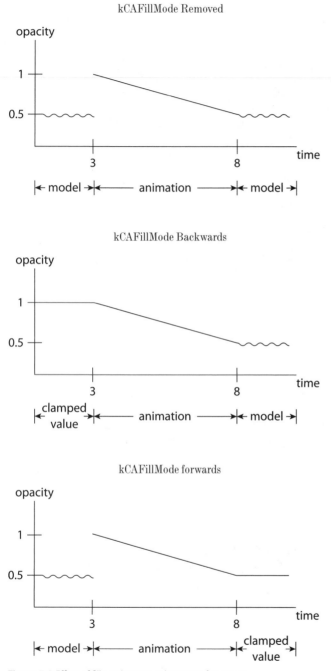

Figure 7-3 Effect of fill modes on media timing functions

Here's a simple example of a three-dimensional box.

BoxViewController.h (Box)

```objc
@interface BoxViewController : UIViewController
@property (nonatomic, readwrite, strong) CALayer *topLayer;
@property (nonatomic, readwrite, strong) CALayer *bottomLayer;
@property (nonatomic, readwrite, strong) CALayer *leftLayer;
@property (nonatomic, readwrite, strong) CALayer *rightLayer;
@property (nonatomic, readwrite, strong) CALayer *frontLayer;
@property (nonatomic, readwrite, strong) CALayer *backLayer;
@end
```

BoxViewController.m (Box)

```objc
@implementation BoxViewController
@synthesize topLayer=topLayer_;
@synthesize bottomLayer=bottomLayer_;
@synthesize leftLayer=leftLayer_;
@synthesize rightLayer=rightLayer_;
@synthesize frontLayer=frontLayer_;
@synthesize backLayer=backLayer_;

const CGFloat kSize = 100.;
const CGFloat kPanScale = 1./100.;


- (CALayer *)layerWithColor:(UIColor *)color transform:(CATransform3D)
transform {
  CALayer *layer = [CALayer layer];
  layer.backgroundColor = [color CGColor];
  layer.bounds = CGRectMake(0, 0, kSize, kSize);
  layer.position = self.view.center;
  layer.transform = transform;
  [self.view.layer addSublayer:layer];
  return layer;
}

static CATransform3D MakePerspetiveTransform() {
  CATransform3D perspective = CATransform3DIdentity;
  perspective.m34 = -1./2000.;
  return perspective;
}

- (void)viewDidLoad {
  CATransform3D transform;

  [super viewDidLoad];
  transform = CATransform3DMakeTranslation(0, -kSize/2, 0);
  transform = CATransform3DRotate(transform, M_PI_2, 1.0, 0, 0);
  self.topLayer = [self layerWithColor:[UIColor redColor]
                             transform:transform];
```

```
    transform = CATransform3DMakeTranslation(0, kSize/2, 0);
    transform = CATransform3DRotate(transform, M_PI_2, 1.0, 0, 0);
    self.bottomLayer = [self layerWithColor:[UIColor greenColor]
                              transform:transform];

    transform = CATransform3DMakeTranslation(kSize/2, 0, 0);
    transform = CATransform3DRotate(transform, M_PI_2, 0, 1, 0);
    self.rightLayer = [self layerWithColor:[UIColor blueColor]
                              transform:transform];

    transform = CATransform3DMakeTranslation(-kSize/2, 0, 0);
    transform = CATransform3DRotate(transform, M_PI_2, 0, 1, 0);
    self.leftLayer = [self layerWithColor:[UIColor cyanColor]
                              transform:transform];

    transform = CATransform3DMakeTranslation(0, 0, -kSize/2);
    transform = CATransform3DRotate(transform, M_PI_2, 0, 0, 0);
    self.backLayer = [self layerWithColor:[UIColor yellowColor]
                              transform:transform];

    transform = CATransform3DMakeTranslation(0, 0, kSize/2);
    transform = CATransform3DRotate(transform, M_PI_2, 0, 0, 0);
    self.frontLayer = [self layerWithColor:[UIColor magentaColor]
                              transform:transform];

    self.view.layer.sublayerTransform = MakePerspetiveTransform();

    UIGestureRecognizer *g = [[UIPanGestureRecognizer alloc]
                              initWithTarget:self
                              action:@selector(pan:)];
    [self.view addGestureRecognizer:g];
}

- (void)pan:(UIPanGestureRecognizer *)recognizer {
    CGPoint translation = [recognizer translationInView:self.view];
    CATransform3D transform = MakePerspetiveTransform();
    transform = CATransform3DRotate(transform,
                                    kPanScale * translation.x,
                                    0, 1, 0);
    transform = CATransform3DRotate(transform,
                                    -kPanScale * translation.y,
                                    1, 0, 0);
    self.view.layer.sublayerTransform = transform;
}
@end
```

This shows how to build a simple box and rotate it based on panning. All the layers are created with `layerWithColor:transform:`. Notice that all the layers have the same `position`. They only appear to be in the shape of a box through transforms that translate and rotate them.

You apply a perspective `sublayerTransform` (a transform applied to all sublayers, but not the layer itself). I won't go into the math here, but the `m34` position of the 3D transform matrix should be set to `-1/EYE_DISTANCE`. For most cases, 2000 units works well, but you can adjust this to "zoom the camera."

You could also build this box by setting `position` and `zPosition` rather than translating, as shown in the following code. This may be more intuitive for some developers.

BoxTransformViewController.m (BoxTransform)

```
- (CALayer *)layerAtX:(CGFloat)x y:(CGFloat)y z:(CGFloat)z
                  color:(UIColor *)color
              transform:(CATransform3D)transform {
  CALayer *layer = [CALayer layer];
  layer.backgroundColor = [color CGColor];
  layer.bounds = CGRectMake(0, 0, kSize, kSize);
  layer.position = CGPointMake(x, y);
  layer.zPosition = z;
  layer.transform = transform;
  [self.contentLayer addSublayer:layer];
  return layer;
}

- (void)viewDidLoad {
  [super viewDidLoad];
  CATransformLayer *contentLayer = [CATransformLayer layer];
  contentLayer.frame = self.view.layer.bounds;
  CGSize size = contentLayer.bounds.size;
  contentLayer.transform =
    CATransform3DMakeTranslation(size.width/2, size.height/2, 0);
  [self.view.layer addSublayer:contentLayer];

  self.contentLayer = contentLayer;

  self.topLayer = [self layerAtX:0 y:-kSize/2 z:0
                           color:[UIColor redColor]
                       transform:MakeSideRotation(1, 0, 0)];
  ...
}

- (void)pan:(UIPanGestureRecognizer *)recognizer {
  CGPoint translation = [recognizer translationInView:self.view];
  CATransform3D transform = CATransform3DIdentity;
  transform = CATransform3DRotate(transform,
                                  kPanScale * translation.x,
                                  0, 1, 0);
  transform = CATransform3DRotate(transform,
                                  -kPanScale * translation.y,
                                  1, 0, 0);
  self.view.layer.sublayerTransform = transform;
}
```

You now need to insert a `CATransformLayer` to work with. If you just use a `CALayer`, then `zPosition` is only used for calculating layer order. It's not used to determine location in space. This makes the box look completely flat. `CATransformLayer` supports full use of `zPosition`, without requiring you to apply a perspective transform.

Decorating Your Layers

A major advantage of `CALayer` over `UIView`, even if you're only working in 2D, is the automatic border effects that `CALayer` provides. For instance, `CALayer` can automatically give you rounded corners, a colored border, and a drop shadow. All of these can be animated, which can provide some nice visual effects. For instance, you can adjust the position and shadow to give the illusion of clicking as the user presses and releases a layer. The following code will create the layer shown in Figure 7-4.

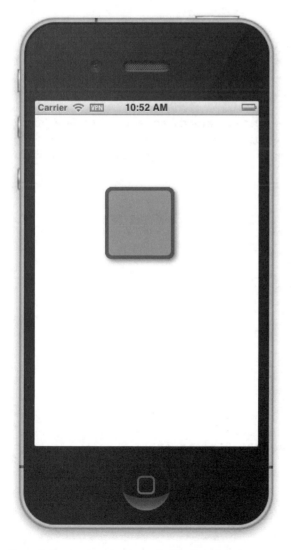

Figure 7-4 Layer with colored, rounded border and shadow.

DecorationViewController.m (Decoration)

```
CALayer *layer = [CALayer layer];
layer.frame = CGRectMake(100, 100, 100, 100);
layer.cornerRadius = 10;
layer.backgroundColor = [[UIColor redColor] CGColor];
layer.borderColor = [[UIColor blueColor] CGColor];
layer.borderWidth = 5;
layer.shadowOpacity = 0.5;
layer.shadowOffset = CGSizeMake(3.0, 3.0);
[self.view.layer addSublayer:layer];
```

Auto-animate with Actions

Most of the time, implicit animations do what you want, but there are times you'd like to configure them. You can turn off all implicit animations using `CATransaction`, but that only applies to the current transaction (generally the current run loop). To modify how an implicit animation behaves, and especially if you want it to always behave that way for this layer, you need to configure the layer's actions. This allows you to configure your animations when you create the layer rather than applying an explicit animation every time you change a property.

Layer actions are fired in response to various changes on the layer, such as adding or removing the layer from the hierarchy or modifying a property. When you modify the `position` property, for instance, the default action is to animate it over a quarter second. In the following examples, `CircleLayer` is a layer that draws a red circle in its center with the given `radius`.

ActionsViewController.m (Actions)

```
CircleLayer *circleLayer = [CircleLayer new];
circleLayer.radius = 20;
circleLayer.frame = self.view.bounds;
[self.view.layer addSublayer:circleLayer];
...
[circleLayer setPosition:CGPointMake(100, 100)];
```

Let's modify this so that changes in position always animate over 2 seconds:

```
CircleLayer *circleLayer = [CircleLayer new];
circleLayer.radius = 20;
circleLayer.frame = self.view.bounds;
[self.view.layer addSublayer:circleLayer];

CABasicAnimation *anim = [CABasicAnimation
                   animationWithKeyPath:@"position"];
anim.duration = 2;
NSMutableDictionary *actions = [NSMutableDictionary
                         dictionaryWithDictionary:
                         [circleLayer actions]];
[actions setObject:anim forKey:@"position"];
circleLayer.actions = actions;
...
[circleLayer setPosition:CGPointMake(100, 100)];
```

Setting the action to [NSNull null] disables implicit animations for that property. A dictionary cannot hold nil, so you need to use the NSNull class.

There are some special actions for when the layer is added to the layer tree (kCAOnOrderIn) and when it's removed (kCAOnOrderOut). For example, you can make a group animation of growing and fade-in like this:

```
CABasicAnimation *fadeAnim = [CABasicAnimation
                                animationWithKeyPath:@"opacity"];
fadeAnim.fromValue = [NSNumber numberWithDouble:0.4];
fadeAnim.toValue = [NSNumber numberWithDouble:1.0];

CABasicAnimation *growAnim = [CABasicAnimation
                                animationWithKeyPath:
                                @"transform.scale"];
growAnim.fromValue = [NSNumber numberWithDouble:0.8];
growAnim.toValue = [NSNumber numberWithDouble:1.0];

CAAnimationGroup *groupAnim = [CAAnimationGroup animation];
groupAnim.animations = [NSArray arrayWithObjects:fadeAnim,
                        growAnim, nil];

[actions setObject:groupAnim forKey:kCAOnOrderIn];
```

Actions are also important when dealing with transitions (kCATransition) when one layer is replaced with another. This is commonly used with a CATransition (a special type of CAAnimation). You can apply a CATransition as the action for the contents property to create special effects like slide show whenever the contents change. By default, the fade transition is used.

Animating Custom Properties

Core Animation implicitly animates several layer properties, but what about custom properties on CALayer subclasses? For instance, in the CircleLayer, you have a radius property. By default, radius is not animated, but contents is (using a fade CATransition). So changing the radius causes your current circle to cross-fade with your new circle. This probably isn't what you want. You want radius to animate just like position. There are a few steps to make this work correctly, as shown in the following example.

CircleLayer.m (Actions)

```
@implementation CircleLayer
@dynamic radius;

- (id)init {
    self = [super init];
    if (self) {
        [self setNeedsDisplay];
    }

    return self;
}
```

```objc
- (id)initWithLayer:(id)layer {
    self = [super initWithLayer:layer];
    [self setRadius:[layer radius]];
    return self;
}

- (void)drawInContext:(CGContextRef)ctx {
    CGContextSetFillColorWithColor(ctx,
                                   [[UIColor redColor] CGColor]);
    CGFloat radius = self.radius;
    CGRect rect;
    rect.size = CGSizeMake(radius, radius);
    rect.origin.x = (self.bounds.size.width - radius) / 2;
    rect.origin.y = (self.bounds.size.height - radius) / 2;
    CGContextAddEllipseInRect(ctx, rect);
    CGContextFillPath(ctx);
}

+ (BOOL)needsDisplayForKey:(NSString *)key {
    if ([key isEqualToString:@"radius"]) {
        return YES;
    }
    return [super needsDisplayForKey:key];
}

- (id < CAAction >)actionForKey:(NSString *)key {
    if ([self presentationLayer] != nil) {
        if ([key isEqualToString:@"radius"]) {
            CABasicAnimation *anim = [CABasicAnimation
                                      animationWithKeyPath:@"radius"];
            anim.fromValue = [[self presentationLayer]
                              valueForKey:@"radius"];
            return anim;
        }
    }

    return [super actionForKey:key];
}

@end
```

I'll start with a reminder of the basics. You call `setNeedsDisplay` in `init` so that your custom `drawInContext:` is called the first time you're added to the layer tree. You implement `initWithLayer:` so that you copy your custom property to the presentation layer. You override `needsDisplayForKey:` so that whenever `radius` is modified, you automatically redraw.

Now you come to your actions. You implement `actionForKey:` to return an animation with a `fromValue` of the currently displayed (`presentationLayer`) radius. This means that you'll animate smoothly if the animation is changed midflight.

> It is critical to note that you implemented the `radius` **property using** `@dynamic` **here, not** `@synthesize`. `CALayer` **automatically generates accessors for its properties at runtime, and those accessors have important logic. It is vital that you not override it by either implementing your own accessors or using** `@synthesize` **to do so.**

Core Animation and Threads

It's worth noting that Core Animation is very tolerant of threading. You can generally modify `CALayer` properties on any thread, unlike `UIView` properties. `drawInContext:` may be called from any thread (although a given `CGContext` should be modified on only one thread at a time). Changes to `CALayer` properties are batched into transactions using `CATransaction`. This happens automatically if you have a run loop. If you don't have a run loop, you need to call `[CATransaction flush]` periodically. If at all possible, though, you should perform Core Animation actions on a thread with a run loop to improve performance.

Summary

Core Animation is one of the most important frameworks in iOS. It puts a fairly easy-to-use API in front of an incredibly powerful engine. There are still a few rough edges to it, however, and sometimes things need to be "just so" to make it work correctly (for example, implementing your properties with `@dynamic` rather than `@synthesize`). When it doesn't work correctly, it can be challenging to debug, so having a good understanding of how it works is crucial. Hopefully this chapter has made you confident enough with the architecture and the documentation to dive in and make some really beautiful apps.

Further Reading

Apple Documentation

The following documents are available in the iOS Developer Library at `developer.apple.com` or through the Xcode Documentation and API Reference.

   Animation Types and Timing Programming Guide

   Core Animation Programming Guide

Other Resources

   Dzhumerov, Milen, "Core Animation's 3D Model," *Code Juggler*. An excellent overview of the math behind the perspective transform, including the magic -1/2000.
   `http://milen.me/technical/core-animation-3d-model/`

   Gallagher, Matt, "Parametric acceleration curves in Core Animation," *Cocoa With Love*. Explains how to implement timing curves that cannot be implemented with `CAMediaTimingFunction`, such as damped ringing and exponential decay.
   `cocoawithlove.com/2008/09/parametric-acceleration-curves-in-core.html`

Chapter 8

Tackling Those Pesky Errors

Error management can be one of the most frustrating parts of development. It's hard enough getting everything to work when things go well, but to build really great apps you need to manage things gracefully when they go wrong. Cocoa provides some tools to make the job easier.

In this chapter you learn the major patterns that Cocoa uses to handle errors that you should use in your own projects. You also learn the major error-handling tools, including assertions, exceptions, and NSError objects. Because your program may crash in the field, you learn how to get those crash reports from your users, and how to log effectively and efficiently.

Error Handling Patterns

There are several useful approaches to handling errors. The first and most obvious is to crash. This isn't a great solution, but don't discount it too quickly. I've seen a lot of very elaborate code around handling extremely unlikely errors, or errors you won't be able to recover from anyway. The most common of these is failure to allocate memory. Consider the following code:

```
NSString *string = [NSString stringWithFormat:@"%d", 1];
NSArray *array = [NSArray arrayWithObject:string];
```

It is conceivable (not really, but let's pretend) that stringWithFormat: might fail because Foundation isn't able to allocate memory. In that case it returns nil, and the call to arrayWithObject: throws an exception for trying to insert nil into an array, and your app probably crashes. You could (and in C you often would) include a check here to make sure that doesn't happen. Don't do that. It needlessly complicates the code, and there's nothing you're going to be able to do anyway. If you can't allocate small amounts of memory, the OS is very likely about to shut you down anyway. Besides, it's almost impossible to write error-handling code in Objective-C that does not itself allocate memory. Accept that in this impossible case you may crash, and keep the code simple.

The next, closely related error-handling approach is NSAssert. This raises an NSInternalInconsisten cyException, which by default crashes your program. Particularly during development, this is a very good thing. It "fails fast," which means the failure tends to happen close to the bug. One of the worst things I see in code is something like this:

```
- (void)doSomething:(NSUInteger)index {
  if (index > self.maxIndex) {
    return;
  }
  ...
}
```

Clearly passing an out-of-range index is a programming error. This code swallows that error, turning it into a no-op. That is incredibly difficult to debug. Note how NSArray handles this situation. If you pass an index out of range it raises an exception very similar to NSAssert. It's the caller's job to pass good values. The worst thing NSArray could do is to silently ignore bad values. It's better to crash. I'll discuss assertions more in the following two sections, "Assertions" and "Exceptions," including how to manage development and release builds, and how to make these a bit more graceful.

The lesson here is that crashing is not the worst-possible outcome. Data corruption is generally the worst-possible outcome, and if getting into a deeply unknown state could corrupt user data, it's definitely better to crash.

Expected errors should be handled gracefully and should never crash. The common pattern for managing expected errors is to return an NSError object by reference. I'll discuss this in "Errors and NSError" later in this chapter.

There is a major difference between expected and unexpected errors. In iOS, failure to allocate small amounts of memory is an unexpected error. It should never happen in normal operation. You should have received a memory warning and been terminated long before you got to that state. You can generally ignore truly unexpected errors and let them crash you. On the other hand, running out of disk space is a rare but expected error. It can easily happen if the user has requested that iTunes fill the device with music. You need to recover gracefully when you cannot write a file.

In the middle are programming errors. These should generally be handled with assertions.

Assertions

Assertions are an important defense against programming errors. An assertion requires that something must be true at a certain point in the program. If it is not true, then the program is in an undefined state and should not proceed. Consider the following example of NSAssert:

```
NSAssert(x == 4, @"x must be four");
```

NSAssert tests a condition, and if it returns NO, raises an exception. This is processed by the current exception handler, which by default calls abort and crashes the program. If you are familiar with Mac development, you may be used to exceptions terminating only the current run loop, but iOS calls abort by default, which terminates the program no matter what thread it runs on.

> Technically abort **sends the process a** SIGABRT, **which can be caught by a signal handler. Generally I do not recommend catching** SIGABRT. **See "Catching and Reporting Crashes" later in this chapter for information about how to handle crashes.**

You can disable NSAssert by setting NS_BLOCK_ASSERTIONS. There are differing opinions on whether NSAssert should be disabled in release code. It really comes down to this: When your program is in an illegal state, would you rather it stop running, or would you prefer that it run in a possibly random way? Different people come to different conclusions here. My opinion is that it's generally better to disable assertions in release code. I've seen too many cases where the programming error would have only caused a minor problem, but the assertion causes a crash. Xcode 4 templates automatically disable assertions when you build for the Release configuration.

That said, while I like removing assertions in the Release configuration, I don't like ignoring them. They're exactly the kind of "this should never happen" error condition that you'd want to find in your logs. Setting NS_BLOCK_ ASSERTIONS completely eliminates them from the code. My solution is to wrap assertions so that they log in all cases. The following code assumes you have an RNLogBug function that logs to your log file. It's mapped to NSLog as an example. Generally I don't like to use #define, but it's necessary here, because __FILE__ and __LINE__ need to be evaluated at the point of the original caller.

This also defines RNCAssert as a wrapper around NSCAssert and a helper function called RNAbstract. NSCAssert is required when using assertions within C functions, rather than Objective-C methods.

RNAssert.h

```
#import <Foundation/Foundation.h>

#define RNLogBug NSLog // Use DDLogError if you're using Lumberjack

// RNAssert and RNCAssert work exactly like NSAssert and NSCAssert
// except they log, even in release mode

#define RNAssert(condition, desc, ...) \
  if (!(condition)) { \
    RNLogBug((desc), ## __VA_ARGS__); \
    NSAssert((condition), (desc), ## __VA_ARGS__); \
  }

#define RNCAssert(condition, desc) \
  if (!(condition)) { \
    RNLogBug((desc), ## __VA_ARGS__); \
    NSCAssert((condition), (desc), ## __VA_ARGS__); \
  }
```

Assertions often precede code that would crash if the assertion were not valid. For example (assuming you're using RNAssert to log even in the Release configuration):

```
RNAssert(foo != nil, @"foo must not be nil");
[array addObject:foo];
```

The problem with this is that in the field, even with assertions turned off, this still crashes. What was the point of turning off assertions if you're going to crash anyway in many cases? That leads to code like this:

```
RNAssert(foo != nil, @"foo must not be nil");
if (foo != nil) {
  [array addObject:foo];
}
```

That's a little better, using `RNAssert` so that you log, but you've got duplicated code. This raises more opportunities for bugs if the assertion and conditional don't match. Instead, I recommend this pattern when you want an assertion:

```
if (foo != nil) {
  [array addObject:foo];
}
else {
  RNAssert(NO, @"foo must not be nil");
}
```

This ensures that the assertion always matches the conditional. Sometimes assertions are overkill, but this is a good pattern in cases where you want one. I almost always recommend an assertion as the default case of a `switch` statement, however.

```
switch (foo) {
  case kFooOptionOne:
    ...
    break;
  case kFooOptionTwo:
    ...
    break;
  default:
    RNAssert1(NO, @"Unexpected value for foo: %d", foo):
    break;
}
```

This way, if you add a new enumeration item, it will help you catch any `switch` blocks that you failed to update.

Exceptions

Exceptions are not a normal way of handling errors in Objective-C. From *Exception Programming Topics* (`developer.apple.com`):

> *The Cocoa frameworks are generally not exception-safe. The general pattern is that exceptions are reserved for programmer error only, and the program catching such an exception should quit soon afterwards.*

In short, exceptions are not for handling recoverable errors in Objective-C. Exceptions are for handling those things that should never happen and which should terminate the program. This is similar to `NSAssert`, and in fact `NSAssert` is implemented as an exception.

Objective-C has language-level support for exceptions using directives such as `@throw` and `@catch`, but you generally should not use these. There is seldom a good reason to catch exceptions except at the top level of your program, which is done for you with the global exception handler. If you want to raise an exception to indicate a programming error, it's best to use `NSAssert` to raise an `NSInternalInconsistencyExce ption`, or create and raise your own `NSException` object. You can build these by hand, but I recommend `+raise:format:` for simplicity.

```
[NSException raise:NSRangeException
            format:@"Index (%d) out of range (%d...%d)",
            index, min, max];
```

There seldom is much reason to do this. In almost all cases, it would be just as clear and useful to use `NSAssert`. Because you generally shouldn't catch exceptions directly, the difference between `NSInternal InconsistencyException` and `NSRangeException` is rarely useful.

Automatic Reference Counting is not exception safe by default in Objective-C. You should expect significant memory leaks from exceptions. In principle ARC is exception safe in Objective-C++, but `@autoreleasepool` blocks are still not released, which can lead to leaks on background threads. Making ARC exception safe incurs performance penalties, which is one of many reasons to avoid significant use of Objective-C++. The clang flag `-fobjc-arc-exceptions` controls this.

Catching and Reporting Crashes

iTunes Connect is supposed to provide crash reports, but it has a lot of limitations. Apple makes a single blanket request to the user for permission to upload crash reports. Many users decline. Reports are updated only once a day. iTunes Connect only supports applications deployed on the App Store, so you need a different system during development and internal betas. In short, if iTunes Connect works for you, great, but often it doesn't.

The best replacement I've found is Quincy Kit (`quincykit.net`). It's easy to integrate into an existing project, and it uploads reports to your own web server after asking user permission. Currently it does not handle uploading logs to go along with the crash report.

Quincy Kit is built on top of PLCrashReporter from Plausible Labs. PLCrashReporter handles the complex problem of capturing crash information. Quincy Kit provides a friendly front end for uploading that information. If you need more flexibility, you might consider writing your own version of Quincy Kit. It's handy and nice, but not all that complicated. You probably should not try to rewrite PLCrashReporter. While a program is in the middle of crashing, it can be in a bizarre and unknown state. Properly handling all of the subtle issues that go with that is not simple, and Landon Fuller has been working on PLCrashReporter for years. Even something as simple as allocating or freeing memory can deadlock the system and rapidly drain the battery. That's why Quincy Kit uploads the crash files when the program restarts rather than during the crash. You should do as little work as possible during the crash event.

When you get your crash reports, depending on how your image was built, they may have symbols or they may not. Xcode generally does a good job of automatically symbolicating the reports (replacing addresses with method names) in Organizer as long as you keep the `.dSYM` file for every binary you ship. Xcode uses Spotlight to find these files, so make sure they're available in a place that Spotlight can search.

Errors and NSError

There is a major difference between a user or environment error, and a programming error. Programming errors should be handled with exceptions in debug mode, and with logging in release mode. If data corruption is possible, programming errors should also raise exceptions in release mode. Failure to allocate small amounts of memory should be treated as a programming error in iOS because it shouldn't be possible and almost certainly indicates a programming error.

User errors or environment errors (network failures, disk full, etc.) should never raise exceptions. They should return errors, generally using an NSError object. NSFileManager is a good example of an object that uses NSError extensively.

```
- (BOOL)copyItemAtPath:(NSString *)srcPath
                toPath:(NSString *)dstPath
                 error:(NSError **)error
```

This method copies a file or directory from one location to another. Obviously that might fail for a variety of reasons. If it does, the method returns NO and updates an NSError object that the caller passes by reference (pointer to a pointer), as shown in this example.

```
NSError *error;
if (! [fileManager copyItemAtPath:srcPath
                           toPath:toPath
                            error:&error]) {
  [self handleError:error];
}
```

This pattern is convenient because the return value is consistent with the success of the operation. If the method instead returned an NSError, then nil would indicate success. This would be confusing and error prone.

Internally the method might look something like this:

```
- (BOOL)copyItemAtPath:(NSString *)srcPath
                toPath:(NSString *)dstPath
                 error:(NSError **)error {

  BOOL success = ...;
  if (! success) {
    if (error != NULL) {
      *error = [NSError errorWithDomain:...];
    }
  }
  return success;
}
```

Note how this checks that error (a pointer to a pointer) is non-NULL before dereferencing it. This allows callers to pass NULL to indicate that they do not care about the error details. They might still check the return value to determine the overall success or failure of the operation.

NSError encapsulates information about an error in a consistent package that is easy to pass around. It can obviously be passed within a program, but because it conforms to NSCoding, it's easy to write to disk or over a network. It can even encapsulate error recovery mechanisms using the NSErrorRecoveryAttempting protocol.

Errors are primarily defined by their domain and a code. The code is an integer, and the domain is a string that allows you to identify the meaning of that integer. For instance, in NSPOSIXErrorDomain the error code 4 indicates that a system call was interrupted (EINTR), but in NSCocoaErrorDomain the error code 4 indicates that a file was not found (NSFileNoSuchFileError). Without a domain, the caller would have to guess how to interpret the error code. You are encouraged to create your own domains for your own errors. You should generally use a Uniform Type Indicator (UTI) for this, such as `com.example.MyApp.ErrorDomain`.

`NSError` includes a user info dictionary that can contain any information you like. There are several pre-defined keys for this dictionary such as `NSLocalizedDescriptionKey`, `NSUnderlyingErrorKey`, and `NSRecoveryAttempterErrorKey`. You're free to create new keys to provide domain-specific information. Several domains already do this, such as `NSStringEncodingErrorKey` for passing the relevant string encoding or `NSURLErrorKey` passing an URL.

Error Localization

Where to localize errors is always a tricky subject. Low-level frameworks tend to present errors in very user-unfriendly ways. Errors like "Interrupted system call (4)" are generally not useful to the user. Translating such an error message into French and Spanish doesn't help anything. It just wastes money and confuses users in more languages. Localizing these kinds of error messages actually makes things more difficult to debug because logs may be sent to you reporting errors in a language you can't read.

> **This last point bears emphasizing. You should never localize a string that you do not intend to display to a user.**

Because errors often need to be logged in the developer's language, I recommend against using `NSLocalizedDescriptionKey` and its relatives in most cases for `NSError`. Instead, localize only at the point of displaying the error. You can keep localized strings for various error codes using a localized string table with the same name as your error domain with `.strings` appended. For instance, for the error domain `com.example.MyApp.ErrorDomain`, you would have a localized strings file named `com.example.MyApp.ErrorDomain.strings`. In that file, just map the error code to the localized value:

```
"1" = "File not found."
```

Then, to read the file, just use `NSBundle`:

```
NSString *key = [NSString stringWithFormat:@"%d", [error code]];
NSString *localizedMessage = [[NSBundle mainBundle]
                          localizedStringForKey:key
                                          value:nil
                                          table:[error domain]];
```

Error Recovery Attempter

An error recovery attempter is a way to encode error recovery options into the `NSError` object. If the error is passed through several layers, this lets the UI communicate back to the original subsystem to let it attempt to recover. The error recovery system encapsulates localized options, some description text (called the "suggestion"), and an object to inform of the selected option. This object should conform to the `NSRecoveryAttempting` informal protocol.

iOS provides no UI integration for error recovery, but it's not hard to roll your own. Here's an example singleton that will manage a `UIActionSheet` based on the error-recovery options.

RNErrorManager.h (ErrorRecovery)

```objc
@interface RNErrorManager : NSObject <UIActionSheetDelegate>
+ (RNErrorManager *)sharedManager;
- (UIActionSheet *)actionSheetForError:(NSError *)error;
@end
```

RNErrorManager.m (ErrorRecovery)

```objc
#import "RNErrorManager.h"

static const char kRNErrorKey;

static RNErrorManager *sSharedManager;

@implementation RNErrorManager

+ (void)initialize {
  sSharedManager = [[RNErrorManager alloc] init];
}

+ (RNErrorManager *)sharedManager {
  return sSharedManager;
}

- (UIActionSheet *)actionSheetForError:(NSError *)error {
  UIActionSheet *sheet = [[UIActionSheet alloc] init];

  sheet.title = [error localizedRecoverySuggestion];
  sheet.delegate = self;
  for (NSString *option in [error localizedRecoveryOptions]) {
    [sheet addButtonWithTitle:option];
  }

  objc_setAssociatedObject(sheet, &kRNErrorKey, error,
                           OBJC_ASSOCIATION_RETAIN_NONATOMIC);
  return sheet;
}

- (void)actionSheet:(UIActionSheet *)actionSheet
clickedButtonAtIndex:(NSInteger)buttonIndex {

  NSError *error = objc_getAssociatedObject(actionSheet,
                                            &kRNErrorKey);

  id attempter = [error recoveryAttempter];

  if ([attempter respondsToSelector:
       @selector(attemptRecoveryFromError:optionIndex:)]) {
    [[error recoveryAttempter] attemptRecoveryFromError:error
```

```
                                        optionIndex:buttonIndex];
  }
  else {
    NSAssert(NO,
                @"Recovery attempter does not implement protocol.");
  }
}

@end
```

In `actionSheetForError:`, this generates a `UIActionSheet`, sets itself as the delegate, and uses `objc_setAssociatedObject` to attach the original `NSError` to the sheet. That way when you are called back, you can figure out the relevant error. When the button is clicked, you fetch the error using `objc_getAssociatedObject` and call the delegate method on the recovery attempter.

The calling code might look like this:

ErrorRecoveryViewController.m (ErrorRecovery)

```
NSArray *options = [NSArray arrayWithObjects:
                        NSLocalizedString(@"Run away",
                                @"OPTION: Avoid error by leaving."),
                        NSLocalizedString(@"Hide",
                                @"OPTION: Avoid error by hiding."),
                        NSLocalizedString(@"Fix",
                                @"OPTION: Fix error"),
                        nil];

NSMutableDictionary *userInfo = [NSMutableDictionary dictionary];

[userInfo setObject:self forKey:NSRecoveryAttempterErrorKey];

[userInfo setObject:options
            forKey:NSLocalizedRecoveryOptionsErrorKey];

[userInfo setObject:NSLocalizedString(@"What do you want to do?",
                            @"Request decision.")
            forKey:NSLocalizedRecoverySuggestionErrorKey];

NSError *error = [NSError errorWithDomain:RNAppErrorDomain
                            code:kRNAppBadThingError
                        userInfo:userInfo];

UIActionSheet *sheet = [[RNErrorManager sharedManager]
                        actionSheetForError:error];
[sheet showInView:self.view];
```

Because you can display `UIActionSheet` many different ways, it's convenient to have `RNErrorManager` return the sheet rather than present the sheet itself. If your application only presents these in one way, then it's easy to move the `showIn...:` call to `RNErrorManager`.

Finally, you actually respond to the user's choice in the original caller. This nicely separates error recovery logic from error presentation, allowing you to provide a consistent error UI throughout your application.

ErrorRecoveryViewController.m (ErrorRecovery)

```objc
- (void)attemptRecoveryFromError:(NSError *)error
                     optionIndex:(NSUInteger)recoveryOptionIndex {

    switch (recoveryOptionIndex) {
      case kRecoveryOptionRunAway:
        NSLog(@"Run Away!");
        break;
      case kRecoveryOptionHide:
        NSLog(@"Hide!");
        break;
      case kRecoveryOptionFix:
        NSLog(@"OK, fix it....");
        break;
      default:
        NSAssert(NO, @"Unknown recovery option: %d",
                recoveryOptionIndex);
        break;
    }
}
```

Logs

Logging is a critical part of debugging. It's also very hard to get right. You want to log the right things and you want to log in the right way. Let's start with logging in the right way.

Foundation provides a single logging call: NSLog. The only advantage NSLog has is that it's convenient. It is inflexible and incredibly slow. Worst of all, it logs to the console, which is never appropriate in released code. NSLog should never appear in production code.

Some people deal with this issue simply:

```
#ifdef DEBUG
#define MYLog NSLog
#else
#define MYLog
#end
```

That's fine for pulling out NSLog, but now you have no logs at all, which is not ideal. What you need is a logging engine that adapts to both development and release. Here are some of the things to consider in your logging engine:

- It should log to console in debug mode and to a file in release mode. If you don't log to console in debug mode, you won't see logging output in Xcode. Ideally it should be able to log to both at the same time.

- It should include logging levels (error, warning, info, verbose).

- It should make sure that logging to disabled logging levels is cheap.

- It should not block the calling thread while it writes to a file or the console.

- It must support log aging to avoid filling the hard disk.

- It should be very easy to call, generally using a C syntax with varargs rather than an Objective-C syntax. The NSLog interface is very easy to use, and you want something that looks basically like that. You definitely don't want simple logging statements to require multiple lines of code.

My current recommendation for iOS logging is Lumberjack from Robbie Hanson of Deusty Designs. See "Further Reading" at the end of this chapter for the link. In general, it requires only a few extra lines of code to configure, and a simple substitution of NSLog calls to DDLog... calls to implement.

This still leaves the question of what to log. If you log too little, you won't have the information you need to debug issues. If you log too much, you'll overwhelm even the best system, hurt performance, and age your logs so quickly that you probably still won't have the information you need. Middle ground is very application specific, but there are some general rules.

When adding a logging statement, ask yourself what you would ever do with it. Are you just relogging something that is already covered by another log statement? This is particularly important if you're logging data rather than just "I'm in this method now."

Avoid calculating complex data if you might not log it. Consider the following code:

```
NSString *expensiveValue = [self expensiveCall];
DDLogVerbose(@"expensiveValue=%@", expensiveValue);
```

If you never use expensiveValue in the upcoming code and verbose logging isn't turned on, you've wasted time calculating it. Lumberjack is written in such a way that this stays cheap:

```
DDLogVerbose(@"expensiveValue=%@", [self expensiveCall]);
```

This translates to

```
do {
  if(ddLogLevel && LOG_FLAG_VERBOSE)
    [DDLog log:...
            format:@"expensiveValue=%@", [self expensiveCall]];
} while(0);
```

In this case, expensiveCall is not executed unless needed. The log level is checked twice (once in the macro and once in [DDLog log:...]), but this is a very cheap operation compared to expensiveCall. If you build your own logging engine, this is a good technique to emulate.

A similar logging trick is to make sure you need to log before entering a loop. In Lumberjack it's done this way:

```
if (LOG_VERBOSE) {
  for (id object in list) {
    DDLogVerbose(@"object=%@", object);
  }
}
```

The point of this is to avoid repeatedly calculating whether to log and to avoid calculating the log string. That's even more important if complex work needs to be done to generate the log.

Most of the time, verbose logging is turned off so even if `DDLogVerbose` checks the level again, the above code is cheaper in most cases, and avoids creating a string for `object`. When verbose logging is turned on the extra `LOG_VERBOSE` check is trivial compared to the rest of the loop.

Logging Sensitive Information

Logging opens up serious privacy concerns. Many applications process information that should never go into a log. Obviously you should not log passwords or credit card numbers, but this is sometimes trickier than it sounds. What if sensitive information is sent over a network and you log the packets? You may need to filter your logs before writing them to avoid this.

Don't ask your customers to "just trust you" with their sensitive information. Not only does it put the customer at risk, but the more of their information in your possession, the more legal issues you have to consider. Few things eat up profits as quickly as consulting lawyers.

Regularly audit your logs to make sure you're not logging sensitive information. After running your program at the maximum logging level, search the logs for your password and any other sensitive information. If you have automated tests, this generally can be added fairly easily.

Encrypting your logs does nothing to help this situation. The problem is that the users send their logs to you, and you have the decryption key. If you feel you need to encrypt your logs, you're probably logging something you shouldn't be.

During development, it is occasionally important to see the real data in the logs. I spent quite some time tracking down a bug where we were dropping the last character of the password. Had we logged the password, this would have been much easier to discover. If you need this kind of functionality, just make sure it doesn't stay in place in production code.

Getting Your Logs

Logs aren't very useful if you can't get to them. Don't forget to include some way to get the logs from the user. If you have a network protocol, you could upload them. Otherwise you can use `MFMailComposeViewController` to send them as an attachment. Keep in mind the potential size of your logs. You often will want to compress them first. I've had good luck using Minizip for this (see "Further Reading"). There are some wrappers for Minizip such as Objective-Zip and ZipArchive, but I'm not particularly impressed with them.

Be sure to ask permission before sending logs. Not only are there privacy concerns, but sending logs can use a lot of bandwidth and battery. Generally you should only need to send logs in response to a problem report.

Summary

Error handling is one of the trickiest parts of any environment. It's much easier to manage things when they go right than when they go wrong. In this chapter you've seen how to best handle things when they go wrong. There's nothing that will make this an easy process, but you should have the tools to make it a manageable one.

Further Reading

Apple Documentation

The following documents are available in the iOS Developer Library at `developer.apple.com` or through the Xcode Documentation and API Reference.

Exception Programming Topics

Error Handling Programming Guide

TN2151: Understanding and Analyzing iPhone OS Application Crash Reports

Other Resources

Clang documentation, "Automatic Reference Counting." This is the official documentation on how ARC and exceptions interact.
`clang.llvm.org/docs/AutomaticReferenceCounting.html#misc.exceptions`

Lumberjack. Mac and iOS logger. code.
`code.google.com/p/cocoalumberjack/`

Olsson, Fredrik, "Exceptions and Errors on iOS," *Jayway Team Blog*. A good discussion of programmer versus user errors and how to deal with exceptions versus other kinds of errors.
`blog.jayway.com/2010/10/13/exceptions-and-errors-on-ios`

Quincy Kit. A nice crash-catcher for iOS.
`quincykit.net`

Volant, Gilles. *zLib and Minizip*. The standard for ZIP file handling. Don't let the "win" and "Dll" fool you. This is highly portable. `www.winimage.com/zLibDll/minizip.html`

Part III

The Right Tool for the Job

Chapter 9
Controlling Multitasking

There are two broad meanings of "multitasking" in iOS. First, it refers to running multiple applications at the same time by allowing one or more applications to run "in the background." Second, it refers to when a single application runs multiple operations simultaneously. Both are important parts of many iOS applications, and this chapter discusses both.

You learn the best practices for multitasking and discover the major iOS frameworks for multitasking: run loops, threads, operations, and Grand Central Dispatch (GCD). If you are familiar with thread-based multitasking from other platforms, you learn how to reduce your reliance on explicit threads and make the best use of iOS's frameworks that avoid threads or handle threading automatically. Perhaps most importantly, you learn how to give your users the illusion of multitasking without wasting system resources.

In this chapter, I assume that you understand the basics of running tasks in the background, and that you are familiar with `beginBackgroundTaskWithExpirationHandler:`, registering an app as location aware, and similar backgrounding issues. If you need information about the fundamental technologies, see "Executing Code in the Background" in the *iOS Application Programming Guide*.

Similarly, this chapter assumes that you have at least a passing familiarity with operation queues and Grand Central Dispatch, though you may never have used them in real code. If you have never heard of them, you should skim the *Concurrency Programming Guide* before continuing.

The sample code for this chapter can be found in the projects `SimpleGCD`, `SimpleOperation`, and `SimpleThread`.

Best Practices for Backgrounding: With Great Power Comes Great Responsibility

In iPhoneOS 3, only one third-party application could run at a time. When the user left your application, it was terminated. This ensured that third-party background applications couldn't waste resources like memory or battery. Apple wanted to make certain that the iPhone didn't suffer the same performance and stability problems of earlier mobile platforms, most pointedly Windows Mobile.

Starting with iOS 4, Apple began to permit third-party applications to run in the background, but only in limited ways. This continued Apple's focus on not allowing third-party applications to destabilize the platform or waste resources. It can be very frustrating, but the policy has generally met its goal. iOS remains focused on the user, not the developer.

Your application should give the illusion that it's always running, even though it isn't. Although your application may be terminated without warning any time it is suspended, it should give the impression that nothing has changed when it launches again. This means that you should avoid displaying a splash screen during loading, and you should save sufficient state when you enter the background to resume seamlessly if terminated. `NSUserDefaults` is a good place to stash small amounts of data during `applicationWillResignActive:`. Larger data structures need to be written to files, usually in `~/Library/Caches`.

Reducing your app's memory footprint is important when going into the background, but so is minimizing the time required to resume. If throwing away your cached information makes resuming from the background as expensive as launching from scratch, there wasn't any point to suspending. Be thoughtful about what you throw away and how long it will take you to re-create it. Everything you do drains the battery, so always look to avoid wasteful processing, even if it doesn't visibly delay your app.

When your application is suspended, it does not receive memory warnings. If its memory footprint is very large, your application is likely to be terminated when there is memory pressure, and you won't have an opportunity to do anything about it. `NSCache` and `NSPurgeableData` are invaluable in addressing this issue. `NSPurgeableData` is an `NSData` object that you can flag as currently in use or currently purgeable. If you store it in an `NSCache` object, and mark it as purgeable with `endContentAccess`, the OS saves it until there is memory pressure. At that point, it discards that data, even if your app is suspended at the time. This saves you the cost of throwing away this object and re-creating it every time the user leaves your app briefly, while ensuring that it can be thrown away if needed.

A lot of framework data is automatically managed for you when your app goes into the background. The data for images loaded with `imageNamed:` are discarded automatically and reread from disk when needed again. Views automatically throw away their backing stores (their bitmap cache). You should expect your `drawRect:` methods to be called when you resume. There is a major exception to this rule. `UIImageView` does not discard its data and this can be quite large. If you have a large image shown in a `UIImageView`, you should generally remove it before going into the background. However, decompressing images can be very expensive, so you shouldn't throw them away too often. There is no one right answer. You need to profile your application.

In Instruments, the VM Tracker is useful for determining how much memory you're using while in the background. It's part of the Allocations template. First create a "memory pressure" app that displays a massive image. Then run your program with the VM Tracker. Note the amount of memory you're using. Press the Home button and note the amount of memory you're using now. This is what you're releasing when you go into the background. Now launch the memory pressure app. Note how much memory you release. Ideally, your background usage should be less than your normal usage without being so low that you delay resuming. Your usage under memory pressure should be as low as possible.

In Instruments, you will see two kinds of memory: dirty memory and resident memory. *Dirty memory* is the memory that iOS can't automatically reclaim when you go into the background. *Resident memory* is your total current memory utilization. Both are important for different reasons. Minimizing dirty memory reduces the likelihood that you will be terminated in the background. Reducing it should be your primary focus. Your application should consume as little resources as possible when it is not the foreground application. `NSCache` and `NSPurgeableData` are excellent tools for reducing dirty memory. Resident memory is your entire memory footprint. Minimizing this helps prevent low memory warnings while you're in the foreground.

> In the Instruments VM Tracker, you may see references to "Memory Tag 70." That's memory for decompressed images and is primarily caused by `UIImage`.

Memory is important, but it's not the only resource. Avoid excessive network activity, disk access, or anything else that will waste battery life. Generally you should complete any user-initiated download using `beginBackgroundTaskWithExpirationHandler:`. Users don't want to have to sit and stare at your application while their data downloads; they want to go play a game. However, you should abort or pause any downloads that weren't requested by the user, provided that you can resume them later.

Some actions are forbidden while in the background. The most significant is OpenGL calls. You must stop updating OpenGL views when you go into the background. A subtle issue here is application termination. The application is allowed to run for a brief time after `applicationWillTerminate:` is called. During that time, the application is "in the background" and must not make OpenGL calls. If it does, it's killed immediately, which could prevent it from finishing other application-termination logic.

> Make sure to shut down your OpenGL updates when the application is terminating as well as when going into the background. `GLKViewController` **automatically handles all of this for you, which is the controller used by the OpenGL Game template in Xcode.**

Running in the background creates new challenges for developers, but users expect this key feature. Just make sure to keep the user as your top priority, test heavily, and watch your resource utilization. Your application should delight, even when it's not on screen.

Understanding Run Loops

Every iOS program is driven by a `do/while` loop that blocks waiting for an event, and then dispatches that event to interested listeners, and repeats until something tells it to stop. The object that handles this is called a run loop (`NSRunLoop`).

You almost never need to understand the internals of a run loop. There are mach ports and message ports and `CFRunLoopSourceRef` types, and a variety of other arcana. These are incredibly rare in normal programs, even in very complex programs. What's important to understand is that the run loop is just a big `do/while` loop, running on one thread, pulling events off of various queues and dispatching them to listeners one at a time on that same thread. This is the heart of an iOS program.

When your `applicationWillResignActive:` method, `IBAction`, or any other entry point to your program is called, it's because an event fired somewhere that traced its way to a delegate call that you implemented. The system is waiting for you to return so it can continue. While your code is running on the main thread, scroll views can't scroll, buttons can't highlight, timers can't fire. The entire UI is hanging, waiting for you to finish. Keep that in mind when you're writing your code.

This doesn't mean everything is on the main run loop. Each thread has its own run loop. Animations generally run on background threads, as does much of `NSURLConnection` network handling. But the heart of the system runs on a single, shared run loop.

> While each thread has a run loop, this doesn't mean that each thread processes its run loop. Run loops only execute their `do/while` loop in response to commands like `runUntilDate:` as discussed in the section "Threading" below. The call to `UIApplicationMain` in `main.m` of almost every project runs the main run loop.

`NSTimer` relies on the run loop to dispatch messages. When you schedule an `NSTimer`, it asks the current run loop to dispatch a selector at a certain time. Each time the run loop iterates, it checks what time it is and fires any timers that have expired. Delay-action methods like `performSelector:withObject:afterDelay:` are implemented by scheduling a timer.

Most of the time all of this happens behind the scenes and you don't need to worry about the run loop. `UIApplicationMain` sets up the main thread's run loop for you, and keeps it running until the program terminates. But what about other threads? The next section covers those.

Threading

Blocking the main thread hangs your program, so that's not acceptable. But some operations take a long time to run. When that happens, you may need to spin off new threads. This is not as common as it may appear. You can write quite complex programs without explicitly creating any additional threads. The frameworks create and manage threads for you in most cases, completely transparently. But sometimes you need to explicitly create your own worker threads. In this section you learn how to do this by hand, and in the later sections you learn better abstractions for handling threads.

Cocoa offers a useful thread abstraction called `NSThread`. While operation queues and Grand Central Dispatch are becoming the preferred way to handle threading, it's very helpful to understand how `NSThread` works by itself, and how to integrate it with a run loop. For this example, you create an application that updates a simple counter on the screen. This could easily be done with an `NSTimer`, but pretend the operation is too expensive to do on the main thread. The source code for this example is in the `SimpleThread` project.

First, create an abstract `NSThread` class called `CounterThread`. This will simplify showing various techniques.

CounterThread.h (SimpleThread)

```
@protocol CounterThreadDelegate <NSObject>
@property (assign) NSUInteger count;
@end

@interface CounterThread : NSThread
@property (strong) id<CounterThreadDelegate> delegate;
@property (assign) BOOL shouldRun;
```

```
- (CounterThread *)initWithDelegate:(id)delegate;
- (void)stop;

// Methods for our subclasses
- (void)processThread;
- (void)updateDelegate;
@end
```

CounterThread.m (SimpleThread)

```objc
@implementation CounterThread
@synthesize delegate=delegate_;
@synthesize shouldRun=shouldRun_;

- (CounterThread *)initWithDelegate:(id)delegate {
  if ((self = [super init])) {
    self.delegate = delegate;
  }
  return self;
}

- (void)stop {
  self.shouldRun = NO;
}

- (void)processThread {
  NSAssert(NO, @"Abstract method. Must be overridden");
}

- (void)updateDelegate {
  // Whatever interesting work we want to do.
  // This call is made on a background thread, so make sure
  // it's threadsafe
  self.delegate.count = self.delegate.count + 1;
}

- (void)main {
  @autoreleasepool {
    self.shouldRun = YES;
    while (self.shouldRun) {
      @autoreleasepool {
        [self processThread];
      }
    }
  }
}
@end
```

The main routine is run when the thread starts. When the main routine ends, the thread will terminate. Releasing an NSThead object does not terminate the thread. The main routine must finish and return. It is possible to call cancel on a thread, but you should avoid this. It leaves memory in an unknown state.

Each thread is responsible for managing its own autorelease pool. The first `@autoreleasepool` takes care of any autoreleased objects that might be generated before reaching the loop. In this code, there aren't any such objects, so there's no real need for this extra pool, but it's a good habit to create one at the top of the thread just as `main.m` does for the main thread. With ARC (Automatic Reference Counting), the compiler optimizes it out if it isn't really needed.

The `@autoreleasepool` in the loop is important. The pool isn't drained until you reach the end of the `@autoreleasepool` block, so without a block inside the loop, autoreleased objects may be retained until the thread terminates.

The `updateDelegate` method does whatever interesting work you want to do. It has to be thread-safe, however. In this example, the delegate's `count` accessors looks like this:

STViewController.m (SimpleThread)

```
// Thread-safe
- (NSUInteger)count {
  return count_;
}

// Thread-safe
- (void)setCount:(NSUInteger)count {
  @synchronized(self) {
    count_ = count;
    NSString *string = [NSString stringWithFormat:@"%d", count];
    [self.label performSelectorOnMainThread:@selector(setText:)
                               withObject:string
                            waitUntilDone:NO];
  }
}
```

The `@synchronized` makes sure that the calls to `setText:` are made in order, not to ensure reading and writing the ivar are atomic. The `count` getter doesn't require an `@synchronized` because there is no point at which reading the scalar is unsafe. Because `setText:` modifies a UIKit object, it has to run on the main thread. That's why you need to call it with `performSelectorOnMainThread:withObject:waitUntilDone:`.

`CounterThread` is an abstract class. In the following examples, concrete subclasses override `processThread` to demonstrate different approaches. There are two critical features of `processThread`:

- It needs to block for some period of time. If it immediately returns, it *busy-waits*. That means it very rapidly checks `shouldRun` over and over. This puts a dramatic load on the CPU, quickly drains the battery, and causes the device to heat up.

- It needs to return periodically. If it blocks indefinitely, the thread cannot check `shouldRun` very often, and the thread may not terminate when it needs to. This can lead to leaking threads, which cause your process's thread count to grow over time. There are a limited number of threads in the system, so this can eventually crash your program. Threads also use memory and other kernel resources, so they need to be terminated at appropriate times.

It is generally better to block too long than to check `shouldRun` too often as long as you are not rapidly generating and destroying threads (which you shouldn't do anyway). An appropriate timeout is often between 1 and 10 seconds.

The simplest concrete implementation of `CounterThread` is `SimpleCounterThread`:

```
@implementation SimpleCounterThread
- (void)processThread {
    [NSThread sleepForTimeInterval:1];
    [self updateDelegate];
}
```

This just sleeps for 1 second and updates the delegate. Then `main` checks `shouldRun` and executes `processThread` again if appropriate. This kind of thread is useful for many operations, but it has a problem. What if you created an `NSTimer` inside `updateDelegate`? It would never execute. That's because this thread is not processing its run loop, and it's the run loop that is responsible for checking the current time and dispatching any timers that have expired. Every thread has a run loop, but something needs to process it (sometimes called "pumping the run loop"). `RunLoopThread` is a subclass of `CounterThread` that demonstrates how to do this by calling `runUntilDate:`.

RunLoopThread.m (SimpleThread)

```
- (void)processThread {
    if (! self.timer) {
        self.timer = [NSTimer
                        scheduledTimerWithTimeInterval:1
                        target:self
                        selector:@selector(updateDelegate)
                        userInfo:nil
                        repeats:YES];
    }

    NSRunLoop *runLoop = [NSRunLoop currentRunLoop];
    [runLoop runUntilDate:[NSDate dateWithTimeIntervalSinceNow:1]];
}
```

Using this approach, the thread behaves very much like the main run loop. The call to `runUntilDate:` will block for no more than 1 second, allowing `processThread` to return and the calling `main` function to check whether the thread should terminate. Using `performSelector:onThread:withObject:waitUntilDone:`, you can now run arbitrary methods on this thread.

I recommend against using `performSelectorInBackground:withObject:` in most cases. This method automatically generates a thread for you, but gives you no access to the thread once it's been created. This makes it easy to accidentally leak threads. The most common mistake is to call `performSelectorInBackground:withObject:` in methods like `viewDidLoad` that can be called more than once. Because you have no ivar holding the thread object, you can't easily determine that there is already a thread running for this operation.

You should generally create a thread object and assign it to a property to keep track of it. In your setter for that property, check whether a thread is already assigned. If it is, that's either a programming error and you should use NSAssert, or it's acceptable and you should terminate the old thread before creating the new one. If you just call performSelectorInBackground:..., you can quickly generate enough threads to crash your program and even cause the device to become unresponsive for a while.

For simple threading needs, NSThread can be a good fit. It makes it easy to create producer-consumer queues, particularly when coupled with @synchronize. It is especially good for architectures that require a small number of long-lived threads. For more complex problems, iOS provides more powerful tools such as operations and dispatch queues that are discussed in the next sections.

Developing Operation-Centric Multitasking

With the many things expected from modern applications, Apple has begun encouraging developers to move toward a more operation-centric rather than thread-centric architecture for multitasking. An operation is an encapsulated unit of work, often expressed in the form of an Objective-C block. Blocks are more fully covered in Chapter 16.

In this example, you create the same timer program as before, but using NSOperation. To simplify creation, you use NSBlockOperation. Again, the actual work is trivial (sleep a second and update a counter), but the same approach works for much more time-consuming operations. The bolded statements are discussed in more detail following the code.

ViewController.m (SimpleOperation)

```objc
- (void)addNextOperation {
  __block typeof(self) myself = self;
  NSOperation *op = [NSBlockOperation blockOperationWithBlock:^{
    [NSThread sleepForTimeInterval:1];
    myself.count = myself.count + 1;
  }];
  op.completionBlock = ^{[myself addNextOperation];};

  [self.queue addOperation:op];
}

- (void)viewDidLoad {
  [super viewDidLoad];
  self.queue = [[NSOperationQueue alloc] init];
  self.count = 0;
  [self addNextOperation];
}

// Thread-safe
- (void)setCount:(NSUInteger)count {
  count_ = count;
  __block typeof(self) myself = self;
  [[NSOperationQueue mainQueue] addOperationWithBlock:^{
    myself.label.text = [NSString stringWithFormat:@"%d", count];
  }];
}
```

```
// Thread-safe
- (NSUInteger)count {
  return count_;
}

- (void)viewDidUnload {
  self.queue.suspended = YES;
  self.queue = nil;
  [self setLabel:nil];
  [super viewDidUnload];
}
```

In `addNextOperation` and `setCount:` you create a strange variable called `myself`. If you reference an object inside of a block, the block automatically retains that object. If you reference `self`, a retain loop is created because `self` retains `queue`, which retains the block. This is such a common retain loop that the compiler gives you a warning if you do this accidentally. The extra variable `myself` breaks this loop because it is marked as `__block` scope, which means it's shared with the block, but not retained by the block. The `typeof` shorthand just makes it easier to paste this extra line when needed.

In `addNextOperation`, you use a completion block to schedule another operation. The completion block is useful for handling all kinds of cleanup. This is somewhat contrived because you normally would schedule all the operations at once, but this is a useful way to add delays with operations.

Note that the `count` accessors again need to be thread-safe because operations may access them from any thread. Rather than using `performSelectorOnMainThread:...`, this example uses the `mainQueue`, which is an `NSOperationQueue` that runs on the main thread.

Operations have some overhead compared to Grand Central Dispatch, which is discussed in the next section. Generally you shouldn't generate huge numbers of very small operations. For example, you should not generate a separate operation for every pixel in a bitmap. Instead, you would create an operation for every row, or perhaps several rows. iOS devices currently do not have many cores, so there is only so much parallel work that they can do. Operations are also not fully as integrated into GCD queues on iOS as they are in OS X. This is likely to improve, however, and you should expect `NSOperation` to grow as the preferred multitasking API in Cocoa.

Multitasking with Grand Central Dispatch

Grand Central Dispatch is at the heart of multitasking in iOS. It is used throughout the system layer for nearly everything. With iOS 5, GCD has added powerful I/O handling routines that make it even more potent.

Much of GCD is very similar to `NSOperation`. In this example, you implement the same timer as in the earlier sections. Notice how the GCD calls almost exactly match the `NSOperation` calls. The changes are bolded.

ViewController.m (SimpleGCD)

```
- (void)addNextOperation {
  __block typeof(self) myself = self;
  double delayInSeconds = 1.0;
  dispatch_time_t popTime = dispatch_time(DISPATCH_TIME_NOW,
```

```
                                         delayInSeconds * NSEC_PER_SEC);
  dispatch_after(popTime, self.queue, ^(void){
    myself.count = myself.count + 1;
    [self addNextOperation];
  });
}

- (void)viewDidLoad {
  [super viewDidLoad];
  self.queue = dispatch_queue_create("net.robnapier.SimpleGCD.VC",
                                     DISPATCH_QUEUE_CONCURRENT);
  self.count = 0;
  [self addNextOperation];
}

- (void)viewDidUnload {
  dispatch_suspend(self.queue);
  dispatch_release(self.queue);
  self.queue = nil;
  [self setLabel:nil];
  [super viewDidUnload];
}

...

- (void)setCount:(NSUInteger)count {
  count_ = count;
  __block typeof(self) myself = self;
  dispatch_async(dispatch_get_main_queue(), ^{
    myself.label.text = [NSString stringWithFormat:@"%d", count];
  });
}
```

One small change from NSOperation is that GCD offers dispatch_after, allowing you to schedule the next operation rather than sleeping. The time is in nanoseconds, which can lead to some confusion because nearly every time interval in iOS is in seconds. Luckily, Xcode automatically provides a conversion snippet if you type dispatch_after and press Enter. Using nanoseconds is optimized for the hardware, not the programmer. Passing the time in seconds would require floating point math, which is more expensive and less precise. GCD is a very low-level framework and does not waste many cycles on programmer convenience.

Creating Synchronization Points with Dispatch Barriers

GCD offers a rich system of serial and concurrent queues. With some thought, you can use these to create many things other than simple thread management. For instance, GCD queues can be used to solve many common locking problems at a fraction of the overhead.

A *dispatch barrier* creates a synchronization point within a concurrent queue. While it is running, no other block on the queue is allowed to run, even if there are other cores available. If that sounds like an exclusive (write) lock, it is. Nonbarrier blocks can be thought of as shared (read) locks. As long as all access to the resource is performed through the queue, this provides very cheap synchronization.

For comparison, you could manage multithreaded access with `@synchronize`, which takes an exclusive lock on its parameter, as shown in the following code.

```
- (id)objectAtIndex:(NSUInteger)index {
  @synchronized(self) {
    return [self.array objectAtIndex:index];
  }
}

- (void)insertObject:(id)obj atIndex:(NSUInteger)index {
  @synchronized(self) {
    [self.array insertObject:obj atIndex:index];
  }
}
```

This is simple to use, but very expensive even when there is little contention. There are many other approaches. Most are either complicated and fast, or simple and slow. GCD barriers offer a nice trade-off.

```
- (id)objectAtIndex:(NSUInteger)index {
  __block id obj;
  dispatch_sync(self.concurrentQueue, ^{
    obj = [self.array objectAtIndex:index];
  });
  return obj;
}

- (void)insertObject:(id)obj atIndex:(NSUInteger)index {
  dispatch_barrier_async(self.concurrentQueue, ^{
    [self.array insertObject:obj atIndex:index];
  });
}
```

All that is required is a `concurrentQueue` property, created by calling `dispatch_queue_create` with the `DISPATCH_QUEUE_CONCURRENT` option. In the reader (`objectAtIndex:`), you use `dispatch_sync` to wait for it to complete. Creating and dispatching blocks in GCD has very little overhead, so this is much faster than using a mutex. The queue can process as many reads in parallel as it has cores available. In the writer, you use `dispatch_barrier_async` to ensure exclusive access to the queue while writing. By making the call asynchronous, the writer returns quickly, but any future reads on the same thread are guaranteed to return the value the writer set. GCD queues are FIFO, so any requests on the queue before the write are completed first, the write runs alone, and only then are requests that were placed on the queue after the write processed. This prevents writer starvation, and ensures that immediately reading after a write always yields the correct result.

Queue Targets and Priority

Queues are hierarchical in GCD. Only the global system queues are actually scheduled to run. You can access these queues with `dispatch_get_global_queue` and a priority constant, `DISPATCH_QUEUE_PRIORITY_HIGH, ..._DEFAULT, ..._LOW,` or `..._BACKGROUND`. The `BACKGROUND` queue was added in iOS 5 and is the lowest-possible priority. All of these queues are concurrent. GCD schedules as many blocks as there are threads available from the `HIGH` queue. When the `HIGH` queue is empty, it moves on to the `DEFAULT` queue, and so on. The system creates and destroys threads as needed, based on the number of cores available and system load.

When you create your own queue, it is attached to one of these global queues (its *target*). By default, it is attached to the DEFAULT queue. When a block reaches the front of your queue, the block is effectively moved to the end of its target queue. When it reaches the front of the global queue, it's executed. You can change the target queue with `dispatch_set_target_queue`.

Once a block is added to a queue, it runs in the order it was added. There is no way to cancel it, and there is no way to change its order relative to other blocks on the queue. But what if you want a high-priority block to "skip to the head of the line?" As shown in the following code, create two queues, a high priority queue and a low priority queue, and make the high priority queue the target of the low priority queue.

```
dispatch_queue_t
low = dispatch_queue_create("low", DISPATCH_QUEUE_SERIAL);

dispatch_queue_t
high = dispatch_queue_create("high", DISPATCH_QUEUE_SERIAL);

dispatch_set_target_queue(low, high);
```

Dispatching to the low priority queue is normal:

```
dispatch_async(low, ^{ /* Low priority block */ });
```

To dispatch to the high priority queue, suspend the low queue and resume it after the high priority block finishes:

```
dispatch_suspend(low);
dispatch_async(high, ^{
  /* High priority block */
  dispatch_resume(low);
});
```

Suspending a queue prevents scheduling any blocks that were initially put on that queue, as well as any queues that target the suspended queue. It won't stop currently executing blocks, but even if the low priority block is next in line for the CPU, it won't be scheduled until `dispatch_resume` is called.

You need to balance `dispatch_suspend` and `dispatch_resume` exactly like `retain` and `release`. If the queue is suspended multiple times, it requires an equal number of resumes.

New in iOS 5

iOS 5 adds several GCD features that are particularly useful for high-performance operations. These are mostly applicable to the operating system itself, and generally you should rely on the OS to handle these things for you. This chapter won't go into them deeply, but it's useful to know they're available. You should expect these technologies to become more central in later versions of iOS.

Queue-Specific Data

Much like associative references discussed in Chapter 3, queue-specific data allows you to attach a piece of data directly to a queue. This can sometimes be a useful and extremely fast way to pass information in and out of a queue. This is combined with *dispatch data*, discussed in the next section, to allow extremely high-performance data passing that reduces memory copying and allocation/deallocation churn.

Like associative references, queue-specific data uses a unique address as its key, rather than a string or other identifier. This is usually achieved by passing the address of a `static char`. Unlike associative references, queue-specific data does not know how to retain and release. You have to pass it a destructor function that it calls when the value is replaced. For memory you've allocated with `malloc`, this is `free`. It's difficult to use this with Objective-C objects under ARC, but Core Foundation objects are a bit easier to use, as demonstrated here. In this example, `value` is released automatically when the queue is destroyed or if another value is set for kMyKey.

```
static char kMyKey;
CFStringRef *value = CFStringCreate...;
dispatch_queue_set_specific(queue,
                            &kMyKey,
                            (void*)value,
                            (dispatch_function_t)CFRelease);
...

dispatch_sync(queue, ^{
  CFStringRef *string = dispatch_get_specific(&kMyKey);
  ...
});
```

One nice thing about queue-specific data is that they respect queue hierarchies. So if the current queue doesn't have the given key assigned, `dispatch_queue_get_specific` automatically checks the target queue, then that queue's target queue, and on up the chain.

Dispatch Data

Dispatch data is the foundation of one of the most powerful low-level performance advances in iOS 5, and you will likely never need to use it directly. Dispatch data are blocks of noncontiguous, immutable memory buffers that can be very quickly joined and split up between blocks with minimal copying. Buffers can also be incrementally released as they are processed, improving memory usage.

This is an incredibly robust system, and is the basis for a feature called *dispatch I/O*, which promises significant I/O performance improvements on multicore iOS devices, and particularly on the Mac. However, in most cases, you will get most of the benefit for free by using the higher-level abstractions without taking on the complexity of using dispatch I/O directly. My recommendation is to leave this technology alone while it finishes maturing and Apple works out the best patterns for using it. You may want to start looking at it now if your application needs to process very large amounts of data very quickly, and you've found that memory allocation or disk access are your major bottlenecks. These types of problems are very common for the OS, but less common at the application layer. See the "Further Reading" section for links to more information.

Summary

The future of iOS development is multitasking. Apps will need to do more operations in parallel to leverage multicore hardware and provide the best experience for users. Traditional threading techniques are still useful, but operation queues and Grand Central Dispatch are more effective and promise greater performance with less contention and less locking. Learning to manage your internal multitasking, and behaving appropriately when multitasking with other applications, is a foundational part of today's iOS development.

Further Reading

Apple Documentation

The following documents are available in the iOS Developer Library at `developer.apple.com` or through the Xcode Documentation and API Reference.

iOS Application Programming Guide, "Executing Code in the Background"

File System Programming Guide. "Techniques for Reading and Writing Files." The section "Processing a File Using GCD" includes example code explaining dispatch I/O channels.

Threading Programming Guide

WWDC Sessions

The following session videos are available at `developer.apple.com`.

WWDC 2011, "Session 320: Adopting Multitasking in Your App"

WWDC 2011, "Session 210: Mastering Grand Central Dispatch"

Other Resources

Ash, Mike. *NSBlog*. Mike Ash is one of the most prolific writers on low-level threading issues out there. While some of this is now dated, many of his blog posts are still required reading.
`http://mikeash.com/pyblog/`

- Friday Q&A 2010-01-01: NSRunLoop Internals
- Friday Q&A 2009-07-10: Type Specifiers in C, Part 3
- Friday Q&A 2010-07-02: Background Timers
- Friday Q&A 2010-12-03: Accessors, Memory Management, and Thread Safety

CocoaDev, "LockingAPIs." CocoaDev collects much of the accumulated wisdom of the Cocoa developer community. The Locking APIs page includes links and discussion of the available technologies and tradeoffs.
`http://www.cocoadev.com/index.pl?LockingAPIs`

Chapter 10

REST for the Weary

Most iOS applications have to communicate with a remote web server in one way or another at some point. Some apps can run and be useful without a network connection, and web server communication might be short-lived (or even optional) for the application. Apps that fall into this category are those that sync data with a remote server when a connection is present, such as to-do lists.

Another set of apps needs nearly continuous network connectivity to provide any meaningful value to the user. These are typically apps that act as a mobile client for a web service. Twitter clients, foursquare, Gowalla, and most apps you write fall into this category. This chapter presents some techniques for writing apps the right way for consuming a web service. Caching data offline or synchronizing data with a remote server is discussed in Chapter 17.

It's 2011, and a quick search for Twitter in Apple's App Store turns up nearly 650 iPad apps and more than 3,000 iPhone apps. Today, if you want to create the next Twitter client, you don't have to know anything about web services or the Twitter REST API. There are more than a dozen implementations of the Twitter API in Objective-C. The same is true for most public services like Facebook's Graph API and Dropbox. Hence, rather than explaining how to build your next Twitter client, this chapter provides some insights and best practices for designing your next iPhone app that consumes a generic, simple, and hypothetical web service. The ideas and techniques presented here are generic enough to be applied easily on any of the projects you might undertake. If you have been an iPhone developer for at least a year, you might already have implemented a project like this, where your customer sends you a REST documentation of his server APIs. You would have been introduced to the server developer and probably had some control over negotiating the output format and error handling stuff. In most cases, both the client and the server code would have been developed in tandem.

In addition to discussing the REST implementation on iOS, this chapter provides some guidelines for the server that will help you achieve the following goals:

▓ Improve the code quality

▓ Reduce development time

▓ Improve code readability and maintainability

▓ Increase the perceived performance of the app

The Worldwide Web Consortium has identified two major classes of web services. (W3C Web Services Architecture 2004): RESTful services that manipulate XML representation of web resources using a uniform set of stateless operations, and arbitrary services that might expose any operation. SOAP and WSDL fall under the second category. Web services used in 2011 are mostly RESTful, including but not limited to Twitter APIs, foursquare, and Dropbox. This chapter focuses on consuming a RESTful service in your application.

The REST Philosophy

The three most important features of a RESTful server that an iOS developer should know about are its statelessness, uniform resource identification, and cacheability.

A RESTful server is always stateless. This means every API is treated as a new request and no client context is remembered on the server. Clients do maintain the state of the server, which includes but is not limited to caching responses and login access tokens.

Resource identification on a RESTful server is done through URLs. For example, instead of accepting a resource ID as a parameter, a REST server accepts it as a part of the URL. For example, `http://example.com/resource?id=1234` becomes `http://example.com/resources/1234`.

This method of resource identification, along with the fact that a RESTful server doesn't maintain the state of the client, allows clients to cache responses based on the URL, just as a browser caches web pages.

Response from a RESTful server is usually sent in a uniform, agreed-upon format, usually to decouple the client/server interface. The client iOS app communicates with a RESTful server through this agreed-upon data exchange format. As of today, the most commonly used formats are XML and JSON. The next section discusses the differences among the formats and the ways you can parse them in your app.

Choosing Your Data Exchange Format

Web services traditionally support two major kinds of data exchange format: JSON (JavaScript Object Notation) and XML (eXtensible Markup Language). Microsoft pioneered XML as the default data exchange format for its SOAP services, while JSON became an open standard described in RFC 4627. While there are debates over which is superior, as an iOS developer you should be able to handle both kinds of data format on your app.

There are several parsers available for both XML and JSON for Objective-C. The following sections discuss some of the most commonly used toolkits.

Parsing XML on iOS

XML parsing can be done using two kinds of parsers, a DOM parser or a SAX parser. A SAX parser is a sequential parser and returns parsed data on a callback as it steps through the XML document. Most SAX parsers work by taking in a URL as a parameter and giving you data as it becomes available. For example, the `NSXMLParser` foundation class has a method called `initWithContentsOfURL:`.

```
(id)initWithContentsOfURL:(NSURL *)url;
```

You essentially initialize a parser object with the URL and the `NSXMLParser` does the rest. Parsed data becomes available through callback via delegate methods defined in `NSXMLParserDelegate`. The most commonly handled methods are

```
parserDidStartDocument:

parserDidEndDocument:
```

```
parser:didStartElement:namespaceURI:

qualifiedName:attributes:

parser:didEndElement:namespaceURI:qualifiedName:

parser:foundCharacters:
```

Because the parser uses delegation to return data, you need a subclass of NSXMLParser for every object you are handling. This tends to make your code base a bit more verbose compared to a DOM parser.

A DOM parser, on the other hand, loads the complete XML before it starts parsing. The advantage of using a DOM parser is its capability to access data at random using XPath queries and there is no delegation like in the SAX model. The most commonly used methods in NSXMLDocument are

```
(id)initWithContentsOfURL:(NSURL *)url options:(NSUInteger)mask
error:(NSError **)error

initWithData:options:error:

initWithXMLString:options:error:
```

Once you initialize the NSXMLDocument you can access the contents using NSXMLNode and NSXMLElement methods like

```
nodesForXPath:error:
```

Using a DOM parser makes your code cleaner and easier to read. While this comes at the expense of execution time for handling web service requests, the effect is minor because DOM parsers become slower only for documents larger than a megabyte or so. A web service response generally is less than that. Any performance gain you get is negligible compared to the time of the network operation. These performance gains make a lot of sense when you are parsing XML from your resource bundle.

To learn more about XML performance, download and test the XML Performance app published by Apple (see the "Further Reading" section at the end of this chapter).

Parsing JSON on iOS

The second data exchange format is JSON, which is much more commonly used than XML. While Apple has a JSON processing framework, it was a private API in iOS 4 and Snow Leopard and was not available for general use. However, there are many other alternatives to choose from. The most commonly used frameworks by far are SBJson, TouchJSON, YAJL, and JSONKit. (See the "Further Reading" section for the links to download these frameworks.) Almost all frameworks have category extensions on NSString, NSArray, and NSDictionary to convert to and from JSON. The code samples in this chapter use JSONKit. With iOS 5, Apple introduced NSJSONSerialization that can be used for parsing if your app is iOS 5 only. You learn about NSJSONSerialization later in this chapter.

JSONKit has convenience category extensions for NSString, NSArray, and NSDictionary. To convert a JSON response from your web service into a foundation class object (either a NSArray or a NSDictionary), use the extension method on NSString, as in the following sample code fragment.

```
NSMutableDictionary *responseDict = [responseString
mutableObjectFromJSONString];
```

Similarly, converting your Foundation objects into JSON strings is also straightforward. The following code explains how to serialize a Foundation object (`NSDictionary` in this case) to a JSON string for sending it to the server as a post data.

```
NSMutableDictionary *postDict = [NSMutableDictionary dictionary];
[postDict setObject:@"theAccessToken" forKey:@"access_token"];
[postDict setObject:@"abcde12345" forKey:@"emp_id"];
// … fill in other parameters
NSString *jsonString = [postDict JSONString];
```

The category methods `mutableObjectFromJSONString` and `JSONString` defined in the JSONKit come in very handy when processing JSON on iOS. In most cases, these are the only two methods you will ever need while handling JSON. Note that the other frameworks, namely SBJson, TouchJSON, and YAJL, have equivalent implementations. In short, whatever library you use, JSON processing is almost always much simpler than XML.

NSJSONSerializer

In iOS 5, Apple introduced its own JSON parsing and serializing framework, called `NSJSONSerialization`. Apple's classes are fast compared to other frameworks, but you should use this framework only if you are willing to support only iOS 5. `NSJSONSerialization` also lacks the capability to serialize custom objects, something JSONKit can do. JSONKit has a couple of convenient methods that accomplish this: `serialize UnsupportedClassesUsingDelegate:selector:error:` and `serializeUnsupportedClasses UsingBlock:error:`.

If your JSON parsing needs unsupported class handling, you will not be able to use `NSJSONSerialization`.

> When you are choosing a library for your app, you might have to do some performance evaluation.
> (You can compare the frameworks using the open source test project json-benchmarks on Github.
> See the "Further Reading" section for the link to this tool.) Because all five (SBJson, TouchJSON, YAJL,
> JSONKit, and NSJSONSerialization) are actively developed, every library is equally good and there
> is no one best library as of this date. Keep a close eye on them and be ready to swap frameworks
> if one seems superior to another. Usually, swapping a JSON library shouldn't require monumental
> refactoring since in most cases it involves changing the class category extension methods.

XML Versus JSON

Source code fragments in this chapter are based on using JSON. You will learn how to design your classes to make it easy to add XML support without affecting the rest of the code base. In every case, JSON processing on iOS is an order of magnitude easier than XML. So if your server supports both XML and JSON formats, choosing JSON is a wise decision. If your server code is not yet developed, start by supporting JSON initially.

Designing the Data Exchange Format

It's essential to keep in mind that we are talking about data exchange between client and server. The most common mistake iOS developers make is to think of JSON as some arbitrary data sent by the server in response to an API call. While that's true to some extent, a quick look at what happens on the server will give you a better picture of what JSON actually is.

Internally, every server is coded using some object-oriented programming language. Whether it's Java, Scala, Ruby, or C# (even PHP and Python support objects to some extent), any data you need on your iOS app will likely be an object on the server as well. Whether the object is an ORM (object relational mapping)-mapped entity or a business object is of little importance. Let's call them model objects and these objects are serialized to JSON only at the transport level. Most object-oriented languages provide interfaces to serialize objects and developers usually harness this to convert their objects to JSON. This means the JSON you see on the response is just a different representation of the objects (or object list) on the server.

Keep this concept in mind while writing your code, and you will probably create model objects for every equivalent server model object. When you do that, you need not worry about changes affecting your code later. Refactoring will be far easier.

Rather than thinking in terms of JSON strings, it makes more sense to think in terms of objects. Design and develop your code such that you always reconstruct model objects for every object on the server. When the reconstructed objects on your iOS app match 100 percent with the objects on the server, the goal of data exchange is attained and your app will be error free.

In short, think of JSON as a data exchange format instead of a language with a bunch of syntax. Consider documenting the data exchange contracts on an object basis rather than as primitive data types. These objects in turn become the model objects for your app. You see this in detail a little later in this chapter, and you look at how to convert JSON dictionaries into models by using Objective-C's key-value coding/observing (KVC/KVO) mechanism.

Model Versioning

In the past, at least from the late 1990s or early 2000s until the first iPhone was launched in 2007, most client/server development happened in tandem with a web-based interface. Native clients were not commonly used. The client app running on the web browser is always deployed together with the server. As such, it wasn't really necessary to handle versioning in your models. However, on iOS, deploying the client requires that the app be physically installed on your user's device. This could take days or months, so you should also handle situations when the server is accessed with an older client. How many older versions of the client you want to support depends on your business goals. As an iOS developer, you should probably build support for catering to those business needs. Using class clusters on your iOS app is one way to do that. You learn more about this shortly.

A Hypothetical Web Service

From here on, as we delve deeper into the topic for each chapter, we describe a hypothetical app concept and develop the iOS code for it. As an iOS developer you probably do mostly projects that talk to an arbitrary web service instead of a known, publicly available service like Twitter or Facebook or Flickr. Second, nearly every such popular service has an open source implementation for iOS.

Assume that you are in charge of developing an iPhone app for a restaurant. The restaurant uses iPads to take orders. Orders can be placed directly with waiters who enter it into their iPads. Customers can also directly place orders using the kiosks (a dedicated iPad running your app) on their tables. Here's a brief description of the top-level functionalities of the app:

1. Customer orders are sent to the remote servers based on the customers' table numbers, whereas waiters pick a table number along with every order they send through their own login accounts. So it's clear that there are two kinds of login/authentication mechanisms. One is the traditional username/password-based type, and the other is based on customer table numbers. In all cases the server will exchange an access token for a given authentication information. The important point is that you should develop one code base that caters to both types of login. After logging in, every web service requires you to send an access token with every subsequent call you make.

   ▪ This requirement translates to the `/loginwaiter` and `/logintable` web service endpoints.

   ▪ Both these endpoints returns an access token. In the iOS client implementation you will learn how to "remember" this access token and send it along with every request.

2. Customers should be able to see the menu, along with the details of every menu item including the photos/videos of the food and ratings left by other customers.

   ▪ This requirement translates to a web service `/menuitems` endpoint and a `/menuitem/<itemid>` that returns a JSON object that will be modeled as a `MenuItem` object.

   ▪ In the iOS implementation you will learn how to map the JSON keys to your model object with as little code as possible by making use of Objective-C's most powerful technique, key-value coding (KVC).

3. Customers should be able to submit reviews of an item.

   ▪ This requirement translates to a web service endpoint `/menuitem/<itemid>/review`.

   ▪ In these cases, some iOS apps show a floating heads-up display (commonly known as HUD) that prevents users from doing any operation until the review is posted. This is clearly bad from a user experience point. You will see how to post reviews in the background without showing a modal HUD.

While there are other requirements for this app, these three cover the most commonly used patterns when talking to a web service.

Important Reminders

Keep these essential points in mind as you build your app:

▪ **Never make a synchronous network call**—Even if they are on a background thread, synchronous calls do not report progress. Another reason is that to cancel a synchronous request running on a background thread, you have to kill the thread, which is again not a good idea. Additionally, you will not be able to control the number of network calls in your app. This is very critical to the performance of your app. You learn about this later in this chapter.

■ **Avoid using runloop-based threading directly for network operations (unless your project is small and has just a couple of API calls)**—Running your own threads has some caveats, as explained above.

■ **Use** NSOperationQueue **or GCD-based threading instead**—NSOperationQueue helps with controlling the queue length and the number of concurrent network operations. Later in this chapter you learn the benefits of using a NSOperationQueue.

Let's start designing the iOS app's web service architecture.

RESTEngine Architecture (iHotelApp Sample Code)

iOS apps traditionally use model-view-controller (MVC) as the primary design pattern. When you are developing a REST client in your app, you should isolate the REST calls to their own class. The stateless nature of REST and its cachable nature can be best applied when it's written in its own class. Moreover, it also provides a layer of isolation (which is also good for unit testing), and helps in keeping your controller code cleaner. Now let's get started with choosing a network management framework.

NSURLConnection versus Third-Party Frameworks

Apple provides classes in CFNetwork.framework, such as NSURLConnection, for making asynchronous requests. However, for developing RESTful services, you need to customize those classes by subclassing them. Rather than reinvent what's already available for the development of web services, I recommend using ASIHTTPRequest (see the entry for Copsey, ASIHTTPRequest Documentation 2011 in the "Further Reading" section at the end of this chapter). ASIHTTPRequest encapsulates many often-used features like basic or digest authentication, form posts, and uploading or downloading files. Another important feature it provides is an NSOperationQueue encapsulation, which you can use to queue network requests.

My advice is generally to refrain from using third-party code when you're developing for iOS. However, there are some components and frameworks that are worth using. My advice here is to avoid third-party code that is heavily interdependent. ASIHTTPRequest is a nice wrapper that doesn't bloat your code base while providing very powerful features. You can add just the necessary classes from the framework into your app (as opposed to other libraries where you have to link your app against the complete library). In our case, rather than reinvent what's already available, for the development of web services I recommend using ASIHTTPRequest. ASIHTTPRequest encapsulates many often-used features like basic or digest authentication, message formats for form posts, and uploading or downloading files. More importantly, it provides an NSOperationQueue encapsulation, which you can use to queue network requests and control the number of concurrent operations.

The code sample provided in the download files for this chapter uses ASIHTTPRequest. You can find the code for this in the Chapter 10 folder (iHotelApp) on the book's website.

Note that the code download for this chapter is quite vast. The chapter provides important code snippets, and you should look at the corresponding files. Open the project in Xcode to better understand the code and the architecture.

The RESTEngine mocks calls to the API by reading them out of sample JSON files because the API is not set up. This shouldn't affect the architecture of the code.

Creating the RESTEngine

The RESTEngine is the heart of the iHotelApp. This class encapsulates every call to the web service standalone class, which handles your network calls. Data should be passed from RESTEngine to view controllers only as Model objects instead of JSON or NSDictionary objects. (The process of creating model classes is discussed in the next section.) Now what should happen when there is a back end-related error? Communicating errors from RESTEngine to the view controller will be covered in the subsequent section. The following are the first two important steps that need to be done.

1. Create a RESTEngine and add it to your project. This class will also manage the network operation queue. For a demo implementation, refer to this chapter's source code on the book's website.

2. Create a property of type ASINetworkQueue in this RESTEngine and initialize it inside the initialization method. For using ASINetworkQueue you should add the ASIHTTPRequest framework into your project. Refer to the "Further Reading" section at the end of this chapter for a link to information about how to integrate ASIHTTPRequest with your project.

The networkQueue Initialization in RESTEngine.h

```
@interface RESTEngine : NSObject {}
+ (RESTEngine*) sharedInstance;
@property (nonatomic, retain) ASINetworkQueue *networkQueue;
```

The networkQueue Initialization in RESTEngine.m

```
@synthesize delegate;
@synthesize networkQueue;
```

You will set the maximum number of concurrent operation count to 6. Setting this number correctly has a huge performance impact, which is explained in the "Tips to Improve Performance on iOS" section later in this chapter.

Adding Authentication to the RESTEngine

Now that the class is ready, you will add methods to handle web service calls; first and foremost, authentication. ASIHTTPRequest provides wrapper methods for a variety of authentication schemes including, but not limited to, HTTP Basic Authentication, HTTP Digest Authentication scheme, NTLM Authentication, and so on. I won't go through the details of the authentication mechanisms in this chapter, so simply assume that you exchange an access token with the server by sending the username and password to the /loginwaiter request or to the /logintable request. You need to define macros for these URL endpoints. Add the following code to the RESTEngine class header file:

The Constants in RESTEngine.h

```
#define BASE_URL @"http://api.example.com"
#define LOGIN_URL [NSString stringWithFormat:@"%@%@", BASE_URL, @"/
loginwaiter"]
```

Next, create a property in RESTEngine to hold the access token and then create a new method, initWithLoginName:password:, as in the following code:

The init Method (and Property Declaration) in RESTEngine.h

```
@property (nonatomic, retain) NSString *sessionKey;

-(id) initWithLoginName:(NSString*) loginName password:(NSString*)
password;
```

The init Method (and Property Declaration) in RESTEngine.m

```
@synthesize networkQueue;
@synthesize sessionKey;
...
...
-(id) initWithLoginName:(NSString*) loginName password:(NSString*)
password
{
  self.networkQueue = [ASINetworkQueue queue];
  [self.networkQueue setMaxConcurrentOperationCount:6];
  [self.networkQueue setDelegate:self];
  [self.networkQueue go];

  ASIFormDataRequest *request = [ASIFormDataRequest requestWithURL:[NSURL
URLWithString:LOGIN_URL]];

  [request setUsername:loginName];
  [request setPassword:password];

  [request setDelegate:self];

  [request setDidFinishSelector:@selector(loginDone:)];
  [request setDidFailSelector:@selector(loginFailed:)];

  [self.networkQueue addOperation:request];

  return self;
}
```

That completes your web service call. Now you should notify the caller, (which is usually the view controller) about the outcome of the web service call. You will use delegates for this.

Adding Delegates to the RESTEngine

For every web service call this RESTEngine class exposes two delegate methods, one for notifying a successful call and another for error notification. Usually this delegate is implemented by the view controller that calls the methods in the RESTEngine.

> Another, arguably cleaner way to notify the caller is by using blocks. Blocks have their own advantages and drawbacks, as discussed in Chapter 16, which also covers when to use blocks and when to use delegates. In that chapter, you modify this RESTEngine to return data and errors using blocks.

1. Use the following code to add a delegate definition to your RESTEngine class:

Code showing the delegate in RESTEngine.h

```
@protocol RESTEngineDelegate <NSObject>
@optional
-(void) loginSucceeded:(NSString*) accessToken;
-(void) loginFailedWithError:(NSError*) error;
@end

..
..

//DELEGATES
+(id)delegate;
+(void)setDelegate:(id)newDelegate;
```

Code showing the delegate in RESTEngine.m

```
+ (id)delegate {
  return _delegate;
}

+ (void)setDelegate:(id)newDelegate {
  _delegate = newDelegate;
}
```

2. Now change the loginDone and loginFailed methods to call this delegate. Because the delegate is marked optional in the delegate declaration, you should check if the delegate responds to it before sending the message.

Login Request Handling in RESTEngine.m

```
- (void)loginDone:(ASIHTTPRequest *)request  {
  NSDictionary *responseDict = [[request responseString]
mutableObjectFromJSONString];
    self.accessToken = [responseDict objectForKey:@"accessToken"];
```

```
if([_delegate respondsToSelector:@selector(loginSucceeded:)])

    [_delegate performSelector:@selector(loginSucceeded:) withObject:self.
accessToken];
}

- (void)loginFailed:(ASIHTTPRequest *)request  {
  self.accessToken = nil;
  if([_delegate respondsToSelector:@selector(loginFailedWithError:)])
    [_delegate performSelector:@selector(loginFailedWithError:)
withObject:[request error]];
}
```

3. Now that the RESTEgine class implementation is complete, you can call the initialize method from the view controller (which is usually the login page that shows the user name and password fields):

Login Button Event Handling in iHotelAppViewController.m

```
-(IBAction) loginButtonTapped:(id) sender  {
    [[RESTEngine sharedInstance] initWithLoginName:@"mugunth"
password:@"abracadabra"];
}

-(void) loginSucceeded:(NSString*) accessToken  {
    NSLog(@"Login is successful and this is the access token %@",
accessToken);
}

-(void) loginFailedWithError:(NSError*) error  {
    NSLog(@"Login failed. Check your password. Error is :%@", [error
localizedDescription]);
}
```

Thus, with just a few lines of code, you are able to implement the login functionality of the web service.

4. Remember the access token. If your access token is simply a string, you can store it in keychain or in NSUserDefaults. Storing it in keychain is more secure than NSUserDefaults. Choose one based on your security requirements. The easiest and probably the cleanest way to do this is to remove the synthesize method for accessToken and write it manually like this:

Access Token Custom Accessor in RESTEngine.m

```
-(NSString*) accessToken
{
    if(!_accessToken)
    {
        _accessToken = [[NSUserDefaults standardUserDefaults] stringForKey
:kAccessTokenDefaultsKey];
        [_accessToken retain];
    }

    return [[_accessToken retain] autorelease];
}
```

```objc
-(void) setAccessToken:(NSString *) aAccessToken
{
    [_accessToken release];
    _accessToken = [aAccessToken retain];

    [[NSUserDefaults standardUserDefaults] setObject:self.accessToken
forKey:kAccessTokenDefaultsKey];
    [[NSUserDefaults standardUserDefaults] synchronize];
}
```

> When you write a custom accessor, ensure that the method sends KVO notifications by sending `willChangeValueForKey` and `didChangeValueForKey` messages. This is omitted here for the sake of clarity. Get the full source code from the book's website.

If your web server sends user profile information at login, you might need a bit more sophisticated mechanism to cache the data. You look at caching in Chapter 17.

Whew! That completes your first endpoint, but you are not done yet! Next you create a second endpoint, `/menuitems`, which is used to download a list of menu items from the server.

Authenticating Your API Calls with Access Tokens

In most web services, every call after login is probably protected and can be accessed only by passing the access token. Instead of sending the access token in every method, a cleaner way is to write a factory method in your `RestEngine` that creates a request object. This request object can then be filled with parameters specific to the call.

In the following example, you create a new method called `prepareRequestWithURLString:`. It returns an `ASIFormDataRequest` for a given URL. Did I mention that the entire method is going to be under five lines long?

Preparing a URL Request Using a Factory Method in RESTEngine.m

```objc
- (ASIFormDataRequest*) prepareRequestForURLString:(NSString*) urlString
{
  ASIFormDataRequest *request = [ASIFormDataRequest requestWithURL:[NSURL
URLWithString:urlString]];

  if(self.accessToken)
    [request setPostValue:self.accessToken forKey:@"AccessToken"];

  return request;
}
```

If you need a request object from any other method, you can call this factory method. You will never again have a buggy API call where you accidentally forgot to set the access token. Note that this factory method can also have additional parameters set depending on your web service requirements. Should your web service require you to turn on gzip encoding for all calls, or need you to send the application version number and the device-related information, this factory method is the best place to add it.

Now add a method to your `RESTEngine` class for fetching menu items from the server:

Method to Fetch the List of Menu Items in RESTEngine.m

```
-(ASIFormDataRequest*) fetchMenuItems  {
   ASIFormDataRequest *request = [self prepareRequestForURLString:MENU_
ITEMS_URL];

   [request setDidFinishSelector:@selector(menuFetchDone:)];
   [request setDidFailSelector:@selector(menuFetchFailed:)];
   [self.networkQueue addOperation:request];

   return request;
}
```

If your method accepts post parameters, this is the method to add them. Your view controller code remains clean of any unnecessary strings/dictionaries.

Canceling Requests

View controllers that need to display the information from your web service call methods like `fetchMenuItems:` on the `RestEngine`. To ensure that it plays nicely with others, it is the responsibility of the view controller to cancel any request it creates when the user navigates out of the view. For example, tapping the Back button means that even if the request returns, the response is not used. Canceling the request at this point means that other requests queued in the `RESTEngine` get a chance to run, and your subsequent views' requests get executed faster. To enable this behavior, every method that is written on your `RestEngine` class should return the request object back to the view controller. Canceling a running request speeds up the execution waiting time for the request submitted by the next view. A good example of this scenario from the foursquare app is the user tapping on a profile view and then tapping on the Mayorships button. In this case, the profile view submits a request to fetch the user's profile, but the user has already navigated to the Mayorship view without viewing the profile. It's now the responsibility of the profile view to cancel its request. Canceling the profile fetch request naturally speeds up the Mayorship fetch request by freeing up the bandwidth. This is applicable not just to foursquare, but to every web service apps you develop.

Request Responses

When you call the `fetchMenuItems:` method, the response from server for this is a list of menu items. In the last web service call example, the response was an access token, a simple string, so you didn't need to design a model. In this case, you create a model class. Assume that the JSON returned by the server is of the following format:

```
{
"menuitems" : [{
  "id": "JAP122",
  "image": "http://d1.myhotel.com/food_image1.jpg",
  "name": "Teriyaki Bento",
```

```
    "spicyLevel": 2,
    "rating" : 4,
    "description" : "Teriyaki Bento is one of the best lorem ipsum dolor
sit",
    "waitingTime" : "930",
    "reviewCount" : 4
}]
```

One easy way to create a model from a JSON is to write verbose code to fill in your model class with the JSON. The other, much more elegant way is to piggyback on Objective-C's arguably most important feature: key-value coding. The JSONKit classes (or any other JSON parsing framework, including Apple's NSJSONSerialization) discussed earlier, converts a JSON-formatted string into a NSMutableDictionary (or a NSMutableArray). In this case, you get a dictionary with two entries, "status" and "menuitems". The call shown in the following code can extract the menu items dictionary from the response.

```
NSMutableDictionary *responseDict = [[request responseString]
mutableObjectFromJSONString];
NSMutableArray *menuItems = [responseDict objectForKey:@"menuitems"];
```

Now that you have an array of menu items, you can iterate through them, extract the JSON dictionary of every menuitem, and use KVO to convert them into model objects. This process is covered in the next section. I come back to the "status" entry in the "Error Handling" section later in this chapter.

Key Coding JSONs

Before you start writing your first model class, you need to learn a bit about the model class inheritance architecture. Any web service-based app includes more than one model. In fact, a count of ten models for a single app is not uncommon. Instead of writing the KVC code in ten different classes, you write a base class that does the bulk of KVC and delegates very little work to the subclasses. Call this base class JSONModel. Any model class in the app that models a JSON and needs JSON observing will inherit from this JSONModel.

> Because you will be making copies and/or mutable copies of your model classes, implement NSCopying and NSMutableCopying in this base class. Derived classes must override this base class implementation and provide their own deep copy methods.

To start, add a method called initWithDictionary: to the base class. Your JSONModel.h should look similar to the following.

JSONModel.h

```
@interface JSONModel : NSObject <NSCopying, NSMutableCopying> {

}

-(id) initWithDictionary:(NSMutableDictionary*) jsonDictionary;

@end
```

Then implement the `initWithDictionary:` method:

JSONModel.m

```
-(id) initWithDictionary:(NSMutableDictionary*) jsonObject
{
    if((self = [super init]))
    {
        [self init];
        [self setValuesForKeysWithDictionary:jsonObject];
    }
    return self;
}
```

The important part of this procedure is the method `setValuesForKeysWithDictionary:` This method is a part of Objective-C KVC that matches each property in the class that has the same name as a key in the dictionary, and sets its value to the value of that entry. Most importantly, if `self` is a derived class, it automatically matches the derived class properties and sets their values. There are some exception cases to be handled, which are covered shortly.

Voilá! With just one line of code, you have "mapped" the JSON into your model class. But will everything work automatically when you have a derived class? Isn't there a catch here? Before going into details, you should understand how the method `setValuesForKeysWithDictionary:` works. Your `MenuItem` dictionary looks like this:

```
"id": "JAP122",
"image": "http://d1.myhotel.com/food_image1.jpg",
"name": "Teriyaki Bento",
"spicyLevel": 2,
"rating" : 4,
"description" : "Teriyaki Bento is one of the best lorem ipsum dolor sit",
"waitingTime" : "930",
"reviewCount" : 4
```

When you pass this dictionary to the `setValuesForKeysWithDictionary:` method, it sends the following messages along with their corresponding values: `setId`, `setImage`, `setName`, `setSpicyLevel`, `setRating`, `setDescription`, `setWaitingTime`, and `setReviewCount`. So a class modeling this JSON should implement these methods. The easiest way to implement this is to use the Objective-C's built-in `@property` and `@synthesize`, so your `MenuItem.h` model class should look like the following:

MenuItem.h

```
@interface MenuItem : JSONModel
@property (nonatomic, strong) NSString *itemId;
@property (nonatomic, strong) NSString *image;
@property (nonatomic, strong) NSString *name;
@property (nonatomic, strong) NSString *spicyLevel;
@property (nonatomic, strong) NSString *rating;
@property (nonatomic, strong) NSString *itemDescription;
@property (nonatomic, strong) NSString *waitingTime;
```

```
@property (nonatomic, strong) NSString *reviewCount;

@end
```

MenuItem.m

```
@synthesize itemId;
@synthesize image;
@synthesize name;
@synthesize spicyLevel;
@synthesize rating;
@synthesize itemDescription;
@synthesize waitingTime;
@synthesize reviewCount;
```

Note that the property names for id and description have been changed to itemId and item Description. That's because id is a reserved keyword and description is a method in NSObject that prints out the address of the object. To avoid conflicts you have to rename them. However, you should handle these exception cases because the default implementation of the setValuesForKeysWithDictionary: method crashes with a familiar error message stating, "This class is not key value coding-compliant for the key: id." To handle this case, KVC provides a method called setValue:forUndefinedKey:.

In fact, it is the default implementation of this method that raises the NSUndefinedKeyException. Override this method in your derived class and set the values accordingly.

Your MenuItem.m should look like this now:

MenuItem.m

```
- (void)setValue:(id)value forUndefinedKey:(NSString *)key
{
    if([key isEqualToString:@"id"])
        self.itemId = value;
    if([key isEqualToString:@"description"])
        self.itemDescription = value;
    else
        [super setValue:value forKey:key];
}
```

To avoid crashes in the future because of spurious keys in JSON, and be a bit more defensive in your programming style, you could override this setValue:forUndefinedKey: method in the base class, JSONModel.m, like this:

```
- (void)setValue:(id)value forUndefinedKey:(NSString *)key {
    NSLog(@"Undefined Key: %@", key);
}
```

Now in your RESTEngine, add the handlers for the fetchMenuItems method to convert the JSON to model objects:

RESTEngine.m

```
- (void)menuFetchDone:(ASIHTTPRequest *)request
{
  NSMutableArray *responseArray = [[request responseString]
mutableObjectFromJSONString];
  NSMutableArray *menuItems = [NSMutableArray array];

  for(NSMutableDictionary *menuItemDict in responseArray)
     [menuItems addObject:[[[MenuItem alloc] initWithDictionary:menuItem
Dict] autorelease]];

  if([_delegate respondsToSelector:@selector(menuFetchSucceeded:)])
     [_delegate performSelector:@selector(menuFetchSucceeded:)
withObject:menuItems];
}

- (void)menuFetchFailed:(ASIHTTPRequest *)request
{
  if([_delegate respondsToSelector:@selector(loginFailedWithError:)])
     [_delegate performSelector:@selector(loginFailedWithError:)
withObject:[request error]];
}
```

As you see, you call the `MenuItem init` method with a JSON dictionary to initialize itself from the dictionary keys. In short, by overriding a method *only* for special cases, you have successfully mapped a JSON dictionary to your custom model and this model is clean of any JSON key strings! That's the power of KVC. The code is also inherently defensive, in the sense that whenever there is a change in JSON keys that the server sends (probably rising from a bug on server side), you see `NSLog` statements displaying the wrong undefined key on the console, and you can probably notify the server developers or make changes to your client to support the new keys.

It's also a good idea to add methods for performing deep copy to the derived class. Just override methods in `NSCopying` and `NSMutableCopying` and you are done. Tools like Accessorizer available from the Mac App Store can help you with that. (See the "Further Reading" section for a link to the app.)

List Versus Detail JSON Objects

A JSON object is a payload that gets transferred from the server to the client. To improve performance and reduce payload size, it's common for server developers to use two kinds of payload for the same object. One is a large payload format that contains all information about the object; the second is a small payload that contains information that is needed just to display the information on a list. For the example in this chapter, a minimal amount of information about the menu item will be displayed on the listing page, and most of the other content, including images, photos, and reviews, will be displayed on the detail page.

This technique goes a long way toward improving an iOS app's perceived performance. On the implementation side, the iOS app doesn't have to be changed for mapping two kinds of JSON. You get either a complete JSON, or a JSON that fills your object partially. The code written to map the detailed JSON should work without any modification in this scenario. For example, the server can send the small payload JSON for `/menuitems`, and a detailed payload for `/menuitems/<menuitemid>`. The detailed payload will contain exactly the same data plus the first page of reviews and links to the photos of the dishes and so on.

Nested JSON Objects

In the example, every menu item is going to have an array of reviews left by the user. If you depend on the default implementation of KVC, and declare an `NSMutableArray` property on your model, the KVC binding will set it to an array of `NSMutableDictionary`. But what you actually want is to map that dictionary as well in a recursive fashion. This case is handled by the overriding the `setValue:forKey:` method.

Assume that the following represents the format of JSON sent by the `/menuitems/<itemid>` method:

```
{
"menuitems" : [{
  "id": "JAP122",
  "image": "http://d1.myhotel.com/food_image1.jpg",
  "name": "Teriyaki Bento",
  "spicyLevel": 2,
  "rating" : 4,
  "description" : "Teriyaki Bento is one of the best lorem ipsum dolor
sit",
  "waitingTime" : "930",
  "reviewCount" : 4,
  "reviews": [{
    "id": "rev1",
    "reviewText": "This is an awesome place to eat",
      "reviewerName": "Awesome Man",
    "reviewedDate": "10229274633",
    "rating": "5"
  }]
}],
"status" : "OK"
}
```

This code is very similar to what you already saw, but has one additional payload: an array of reviews. In a real-life scenario, there might be multiple such additions, like a list of photos, a list of "likes," and so on. But for the sake of simplicity, just assume that the detailed listing of a menu item has only one additional piece of information, which is the array of reviews. Now before overriding the `setValue:forKey:` method, create a model object for a review entry. This class's header file will look similar to the one below. The implementation contains nothing but synthesizers and overridden `NSCopying` and `NSMutableCopying` (deep copy) methods.

Review.m

```
@property (nonatomic, strong) NSString *rating;
@property (nonatomic, strong) NSString *reviewDate;
@property (nonatomic, strong) NSString *reviewerName;
@property (nonatomic, strong) NSString *reviewId;
@property (nonatomic, strong) NSString *reviewText;
```

Again, you can generate these accessors using tools like Accessorizer. Your review JSON doesn't have any special keys that might be in conflict with Objective-C's reserved list, so you don't even have to write any explicit code for converting JSON to a review model. The initialization code is in the base class and the KVC compliant code is generated by the property/synthesizers. That's the power of KVC.

Next, override the `setValue:forKey:` method in the `MenuItem` model to convert review dictionaries to `Review` models:

Custom Handling of KVC's setValue:forKey: Method in MenuItem.m

```
-(void) setValue:(id)value forKey:(NSString *)key
{
   if([key isEqualToString:@"reviews"])
   {
     for(NSMutableDictionary *reviewArrayDict in value)
     {
        Review *thisReview = [[[Review alloc] initWithDictionary:reviewArray
Dict] autorelease];
        [self.reviews addObject:thisReview];
     }
   }
   else
     [super setValue:value forKey:key];
}
```

The idea behind this code is to handle the `reviews` key of the JSON in a specialized way and to let the other keys be handled by the default superclass implementation.

Less Is More

You might have heard about KVC and KVO, on the Internet from blogs of veteran Objective-C developers explaining how great they are. Now that you have understood them, you can put these concepts to use in your next app. You will realize how powerful they are and how easily they allow you to write less code in a more efficient way. Next, you move on to error handling.

Error Handling

Recall that you saw a key called `status` in the JSON payload. Every web service has some way to communicate error messages to the client. In some cases it's sent through a special key, like `status`. In other cases, the web server sends an `error` key with more information about the actual error and no such key is sent for a successful call. This section shows you how to model this on iOS, so that you write as little code as possible, yet write it in a way that is clear to read and understand.

The first thing to understand is that not all API errors can be mapped to a custom HTTP error code. In fact, a server might throw errors even when everything is perfectly fine, but the user input is wrong. A website registration web service might throw an error if the user tries to register with an email address that's already taken. This is just one example, and in most cases, you need specialized error handling for handling your own internal business logic errors. In this example, for instance, a missing menu item results in a 404 error. Most web services send a custom error message along with the 404 notice so that clients can understand what caused that 404. A client implementation should not just report the HTTP error as a error message to the user, but also understand the internal business logic error for elegant error reporting and do proper error reporting. Otherwise, the only error you can ever show is "Sorry, something bad happened, please try again later" and no one, including your customer, is interested in seeing that kind of vague message. This section shows you how to handle these cases in an elegant fashion.

In the following steps you subclass `ASIHTTPRequest` or `ASIFormDataRequest` to handle custom API errors. If your app needs to make only "form post" kinds of requests, subclass `ASIFormDataRequest`, otherwise subclass its parent, `ASIHTTPRequest`.

1. Create a subclass of `ASIFormDataRequest`. This subclass will have a property to store the business logic errors thrown from the server.

2. Create an `NSError*` property called `restError` in the subclass.

3. Override two methods to handle error conditions. The first method to override is the `failWithError`:

Code in RESTRequest.m that illustrate error handling

```objc
-(void) failWithError:(NSError *)theError
{
   NSMutableDictionary *errorDict = [[self responseDictionary]
objectForKey:@"error"];

   if(errorDict == nil)
   {
     self.restError = [[NSError alloc] initWithDomain:kRequestErrorDomain
code:[theError code]
userInfo:[theError userInfo]];
   }
   else
   {
     self.restError = [[NSError alloc] initWithDomain:kBusinessErrorDomain
code:[[errorDict objectForKey:@"code"] intValue]userInfo:errorDict];
   }
   [super failWithError:theError];
}
```

Using this class, you check for the presence of the `"error"` JSON key and process it appropriately. The `failWithError` method will be called when there is a HTTP error. You should handle non-HTTP, business logic errors in the same manner. As you saw earlier, not every business logic error can be mapped to an equivalent HTTP error code. Moreover, in some cases, there might be a benign error that is sent along with your response and the server might delegate the responsibility of treating that as an error or normal condition to the client. For handling both these cases you have to override another method, `requestFinished:`, as shown in the following code:

Code in RESTRequest.m that illustrate request handling
for successful conditions and report business logic error if any

```objc
- (void)requestFinished
{
```

```
   NSMutableDictionary *errorDict = [[self responseDictionary]
objectForKey:@"error"];

   if(errorDict)
   {
      self.restError = [[NSError alloc] initWithDomain:kBusinessErrorDomain
code:[[errorDict objectForKey:@"code"] intValue] userInfo:errorDict];
      [super failWithError:self.restError];
   }
   else
   {
      [super requestFinished];
   }
}
```

Both these methods remember the business logic errors in the `restError` property of your subclassed request object. This enables the client to know both the HTTP error (by accessing the `RestRequest`'s superclass's error object) and the business layer error, from the local property `restError`.

Because this handling is done on a subclass, the class `RestEngine` doesn't have to do any additional error handling. All it gets is a nicely wrapped `NSError` object for both kinds of error, HTTP or business logic. The view controller implementation will now be as simple as checking whether the error is `nil`; if it's not `nil`, show the message inside the `[[request restError] userInfo]`.

With that, I move on to a discussion of localization.

Localization

This section is about localizing web service-related error messages and not localizing your app. Adding internationalization and localization support to your app is explained in detail in Chapter 13.

Some implementations require you to localize error messages in multiple languages. For errors generated within the app, this is simple and can be handled using the foundation classes and macros. For server-related errors, the previous implementation just showed the server errors on the UI. The best way to show localized errors is for the server to return errors in agreed upon codes. The iOS client can then look into a localized string table and show the correct error for a given code.

RESTError.m

```
+ (void) initialize
{
   NSString *fileName = [NSString stringWithFormat:@"Errors_%@", [[NSLocale
currentLocale] localeIdentifier]];
   NSString *filePath = [[NSBundle mainBundle] pathForResource:fileName
ofType:@"plist"];

   if(filePath != nil)
   {
      errorCodes = [[NSMutableDictionary alloc] initWithContentsOfFile:file
Path];
```

```
    }
    else
    {
        // fall back to English for unsupported languages
        NSString *filePath = [[NSBundle mainBundle] pathForResource:@"Errors_
en_US" ofType:@"plist"];
        errorCodes = [[NSMutableDictionary alloc] initWithContentsOfFile:file
Path];
    }
}
```

This `RESTError` class can again by initialized with the error dictionary you get from the server using the KVC technique you learned earlier in this chapter. Override `NSError`'s `localizedDescription` and `localizedRecoverySuggestion` methods to provide proper user-readable error methods. In case your web service provides error codes to you along with error messages, this is the best way to handle and show error messages instead of showing the server error from the `userInfo` dictionary.

Handling Additional Formats Using Category Classes

Assume that you have written and delivered your app, and for some reason, your client wants to move the server implementation to a Windows-based system and the server now sends you XML data instead of JSON. With this current architecture in place, it's easy to add an additional format parsing to your model. The recommended way to do so is to write a category extension on your model that has a method to convert XML to dictionaries. In short, write a method in your category extension to convert an XML tree into a NSMutableDictionary and pass this dictionary to the `initWithDictionary:` method, which you previously wrote. Category classes like this provide a very powerful way to extend and add features to your existing implementation without creating any unwanted side effects.

Tips to Improve Performance on iOS

The best tip for improving performance for a web service-based app is to avoid sending data that's not immediately necessary. Unlike a web-based app, an iPhone app has very limited bandwidth, and in most cases it will be connected to a 3G network. Trying to implement techniques like prefetching contents for what could be the user's next page will only slow down your app.

Avoid multiple small AJAX-like API calls. In the "Creating the RESTEngine" section earlier in this chapter, you initialized the `networkQueue` to run six concurrent operations because most servers don't allow more than six parallel HTTP connections from a single IP address. Running more than six operations will only result in the seventh and subsequent operations timing out. On a 3G network, at least in 2011, most network operators throttle the bandwidth and limit the number of outbound connections from a mobile device to two. This is usually one on EDGE. As such you can even listen for reachability notifications using the Reachability classes provided by Apple (Apple 2011) and change the queue size dynamically as and when the connectivity changes. Again, this count of two on 3G and one on EDGE is not absolute and you should test the network of your customer base and use the results accordingly.

If you have control over the server development, the following tips might help to get the best out of the iOS app you develop.

- A server that caters to a web-based client should almost always have multiple small web service calls that are usually performed using AJAX. On iOS, it's best to avoid these APIs and possibly use or develop a custom API that gives more customized data per call.

- Unlike a browser, most carrier networks throttle the number of parallel data connections. Again, it's safe to assume that you shouldn't run more than one network operation on an EDGE connection, more than two parallel network operations on a 3G network, and six on a wi-fi connection.

Summary

In this chapter you learned how to architect a iOS application that uses a web service. The chapter also presented the different data exchange formats and ways to parse them in Objective-C, and you learned a very powerful method of processing responses from a RESTful service using Objective-C's powerful method, KVC. You then learned about using queues for handing concurrent requests and how to maximize performance by altering the maximum concurrent operations on the queue-based available network.

Further Reading

Apple Documentation

The following documents are available in the iOS Developer Library at `developer.apple.com` or through the Xcode Documentation and API Reference.

Reachability. Apple Developer Documentation.

Apple XMLPerformance Sample Code

Apple. NSXMLDocument Class Reference

Other Resources

Callahan, Kevin. *Mac App Store.* 2011
`http://itunes.apple.com/gb/app/accessorizer/id402866670?mt=12`

Cocoanetics. *JSON vs Plist, the ultimate showdown* 2011
`http://www.cocoanetics.com/2011/03/json-versus-plist-the-ultimate-showdown/`

Crockford, Douglas. *RFC 4627.* 07 01, 2006
`http://tools.ietf.org/html/rfc4627`

W3C. *Web Services Architecture.* 2 11, 2004
`http://www.w3.org/TR/ws-arch/#relwwwrest`

Copsey, Ben. *ASIHTTPRequest Documentation*. 2011
`http://allseeing-i.com/ASIHTTPRequest/`

ASIHTTPRequest - How To Use. 2011
`http://allseeing-i.com/ASIHTTPRequest/How-to-use#handling_http_`
`authentication`

Brautaset, Stig. *JSON Framework*. 1 1, 2011
`http://stig.github.com/json-framework/`

Wight, Jonathan. *TouchCode/TouchJSON*. 1 1, 2011
`https://github.com/TouchCode/TouchJSON`

Gabriel. *YAJL-ObjC*. 2011
`https://github.com/gabriel/yajl-objc`

Johnezang. *JSONKit*. 2011
`https://github.com/johnezang/JSONKit`

mbrugger json-benchmarks on Github
`https://github.com/mbrugger/json-benchmarks/`

## Chapter 11

Batten the Hatches with Security Services

iOS is likely the first platform that most developers encounter that employs a true least-privilege security model. Most modern operating systems employ some kind of privilege separation, allowing different processes to run with different permissions, but this is almost always used in a very coarse way. Most applications on Unix, OS X, and Windows run as either the current user or a superuser, which can do nearly anything. Attempts to segment this further, whether with Security Enhanced Linux (SELinux) or Windows User Account Control (UAC), have generally led to developer revolt. The most common questions about SELinux are not how to best develop for it, but how to turn it off.

Coming from these backgrounds, developers tend to be shocked when encountering the iOS security model. Rather than ensure maximal flexibility, Apple's approach has been to give developers the least privileges it can and see what software developers are *incapable* of making with those privileges. Then Apple provides the least additional privileges that allow the kinds of software it wants for the platform. This can be very restrictive on developers, but it's also kept iOS quite stable and free of malware. Apple is unlikely to change its stance on this, so understanding and dealing with the security model is critical to iOS development.

This chapter shows the way around the iOS security model, dives into the numerous security services that iOS offers, and provides the fundamentals you need to really understand Apple's security documentation. Along the way you'll gain a deeper understanding of how certificates and encryption work in practice, so that you can leverage these features to really improve the security of your products.

The code for this chapter is available in the online sample code. There is also a simple project called `FileExplorer` so you can investigate the public parts of the file system.

Understanding the iOS Sandbox

The heart of the iOS security model is the sandbox. When an application is installed, it is given its own home directory in the file system, readable only by that application. This makes it difficult to share information between applications, but also makes it difficult for malicious or poorly written software to read or modify your data.

Applications are not separated from each other using standard Unix file permissions. All applications run as the same user ID (501, `mobile`). Calling `stat` on another application's home directory fails, however, because of operating system restrictions. Similar restrictions prevent your application from reading `/var/log` while allowing access to `/System/Library/Frameworks`.

Within your sandbox, there are four important top-level directories: your `.app` bundle, `Documents`, `Library`, and `tmp`. While you can create new directories within your sandbox, it is not well defined how iTunes will deal with them. I recommend keeping everything in one of these top-level directories. You can always create subdirectories under `Library` if you need more organization.

Your `.app` bundle is the package built by Xcode and copied to the device. Everything within it is digitally signed, so you can't modify it. In particular, this includes your `Resources` directory. If you want to modify files that you install as part of your bundle, you'll need to copy them elsewhere first, usually somewhere in `Library`.

The `Documents` directory is where you store user-visible data, particularly files like word-processing documents or drawings that the user assigns a filename. These files can be made available to the desktop through file sharing if `UIFileSharingEnabled` is turned on in `Info.plist`.

The `Library` directory stores files that shouldn't be directly user visible. The `Library/Caches` directory is special because it isn't backed up, but is preserved between application upgrades. This is where you should put most things you don't want copied to the desktop.

The `tmp` directory is special because it is neither backed up nor preserved between application upgrades. This makes it ideal for temporary files, as the name implies.

When considering the security of the user's data, backups are an important consideration. Users may choose whether to encrypt the iTunes backup with a password. If there is data that shouldn't be stored unencrypted on the desktop machine, you should store it in the keychain (see the "Using Keychains" section later in this chapter). iTunes only backs up the keychain if backup encryption is enabled.

If you have information that you would rather the user not have access to, you can store it in the keychain or in `Library/Caches` because these are not backed up. This is weak protection, however, because the user can always jailbreak the phone to read any file or the keychain. There is no certain way to prevent the owner of a device from reading data on that device. iOS security is about protecting the user from attackers, not about protecting the application from the user.

Securing Network Communications

The greatest risk to most systems is their network communication. Attackers don't need access to the device, only to the device's network. The most dangerous areas are generally coffee shops, airports, and other public wi-fi networks. It's your responsibility to make sure that the user's information is safe, even on hostile networks.

The first and easiest solution is to use Hypertext Transfer Protocol Secure (HTTPS) for your network communication. Most iOS network APIs automatically handle HTTPS, and the protocol eliminates many of the easiest attacks. In the simplest deployment, you put a self-signed certificate on the web server, turn on HTTPS, and configure `NSURLConnection` to accept untrusted certificates, as discussed shortly. This is still vulnerable to several kinds of attacks, but it's easy to deploy and addresses the most basic attacks.

In iOS 5, the informal delegate protocol of `NSURLConnection` has been replaced with two formal protocols, `NSURLConnectionDelegate` and `NSURLConnectionDataDelegate`. Although there are now two protocols, there is still only a single delegate (of type `id`), so this mostly impacts how the documentation is organized.

The major `NSURLConnection` change in iOS 5 is to the authentication methods. Instead of three methods—
`connection:canAuthenticateAgainstProtectionSpace`, `connection:didReceive`
`AuthenticationChallenge`, and `connection:didCancelAuthenticationChallenge`—there is
now just one: `connection:willSendRequestForAuthenticationChallenge:`. In this method, you
are supposed to determine if you are willing to authenticate to this server, and if so, to provide the credentials.
The following code authenticates to any server that presents a noncorrupt certificate, whether or not the
certificate is valid or trusted:

```
- (void)connection:(NSURLConnection *)connection
  willSendRequestForAuthenticationChallenge:
  (NSURLAuthenticationChallenge *)challenge
{
  SecTrustRef trust = challenge.protectionSpace.serverTrust;
  NSURLCredential *cred;
  cred = [NSURLCredential credentialForTrust:trust];
  [challenge.sender useCredential:cred
        forAuthenticationChallenge:challenge];
}
```

This code extracts the trust object, discussed later, and creates a credential object for it. HTTPS connections
always require a credential object, even if you are not passing credentials to the server. The "Checking Certificate
Validity" section later in this chapter explains how to more carefully validate the certificate.

`ASIHTTPRequest`, **covered in Chapter 10, can support untrusted certificates without requiring you
to implement delegate methods. You can configure the request as follows:**

```
[request setValidatesSecureCertificate:NO];
```

How Certificates Work

Hopefully you have encountered public-private key infrastructure (PKI) systems before. This section gives a
quick overview of the technology, and then discusses how it affects the security of your application.

Asymmetric cryptography is based on the mathematical fact that you can find two very large numbers (call
them A and B) that are related in such a way that anything encrypted with one can be decrypted with the
other, and vice versa. Key A cannot decrypt things that key A encrypted, nor can key B decrypt things that key
B encrypted. Each can only decrypt the other's ciphertext. There is no real difference between key A and key
B, but for the purposes of public key cryptography, one is termed the *public key*, which generally everyone is
allowed to know, and the other is designated the *private key*, which is secret.

You can use a public key to encrypt data such that only a computer with the private key can decrypt it. This is an
important property that is used repeatedly in public key systems. If you want to prove that some entity (person
or machine) has the private key, you make up a random number, encrypt it with the entity's public key and send
it. That entity decrypts the message with the entity's private key, encrypts it with *your* public key and sends it
back to you. Because only the private key could have decrypted the message, the entity you're communicating
with must have the private key.

This property also allows you to *digitally sign* data. Given some data, you first hash it with some well-known hashing algorithm, and then encrypt it with your private key. The resulting ciphertext is the signature. To validate the signature, you hash the data again with the same algorithm, decrypt the signature using the public key, and compare the hashes. If they match, you know the signature was created by some entity that had access to the private key.

Just because an entity has access to the private key does not prove he is who he says he is. There are two questions you need to ask. First, how well is the private key protected? Anyone with access to the private key can forge a signature with it. Second, how do you know that the public key you have is related to the entity you care about? If I approach you on the street and hand you a business card that says I'm the President of the United States, it hardly proves anything. I'm the one who handed you the business card. Similarly, if a server presents you a public key that claims to be for `www.apple.com`, why should you believe it? This is where a *certificate chain* comes in, and it's relevant to both questions.

A certificate is made up of a public key, some metadata about the certificate (more on that later), and a collection of signatures from other certificates. In most cases, there is a short chain of certificates, each signing the one below it. In very rare cases, there may be multiple signatures on one certificate. An example of a certificate chain is shown in Figure 11-1.

In this example, the server `daw.apple.com` presents a certificate that includes its own public key, signed by an intermediate certificate from VeriSign, which is signed by a root certificate from VeriSign. Mathematically, you can determine that the controllers of each of these certificates did sign the next certificate in the chain, but why would you trust any of them? You trust them because Apple trusts the VeriSign root certificate, which has signed the intermediate certificate, which has signed the Apple certificate. Apple ships the VeriSign root certificate in the trusted root store of every iOS device, along with more than a hundred other trusted root certificates. The *trusted root store* is a list of certificates that is treated as explicitly trustworthy. Explicitly trusted certificates are called *anchors*. You can set your own anchors if don't want to trust Apple's list.

This brings you to the much-misused term *self-signed certificate*. For cryptographic reasons, every certificate includes a signature from itself. A certificate that only has this signature is called self-signed. Often, when people talk about a self-signed certificate, they mean a certificate that you shouldn't trust. But the VeriSign root certificate is a self-signed certificate, and it's one of the most trusted certificates in the world. Every root certificate, by definition, is a self-signed certificate. What's the difference? It isn't how many signatures a certificate has in its chain that matters, but how well all of the private keys in the chain are protected, and whether the identity of the owner has been authenticated.

If you generate your own self-signed certificate and protect the private key very well, then that's more secure than a certificate that VeriSign issues you. In both cases, you're dependent on protecting your private key, but in the latter case you also have to worry about VeriSign protecting *its* private key. VeriSign spends a lot of money and effort doing that, but protecting two keys is always more risky than protecting just one of them.

This isn't to say that commercial certificates from VeriSign, DigiTrust, and other providers are bad. But you don't get a commercial certificate to improve the security of your system. You get one for convenience because the commercial certs are already in the root key store. But remember, you control the root key store in your own application. This leads to a surprising fact: *There is no security reason to purchase a commercial certificate to secure your application's network protocol to your own server.*

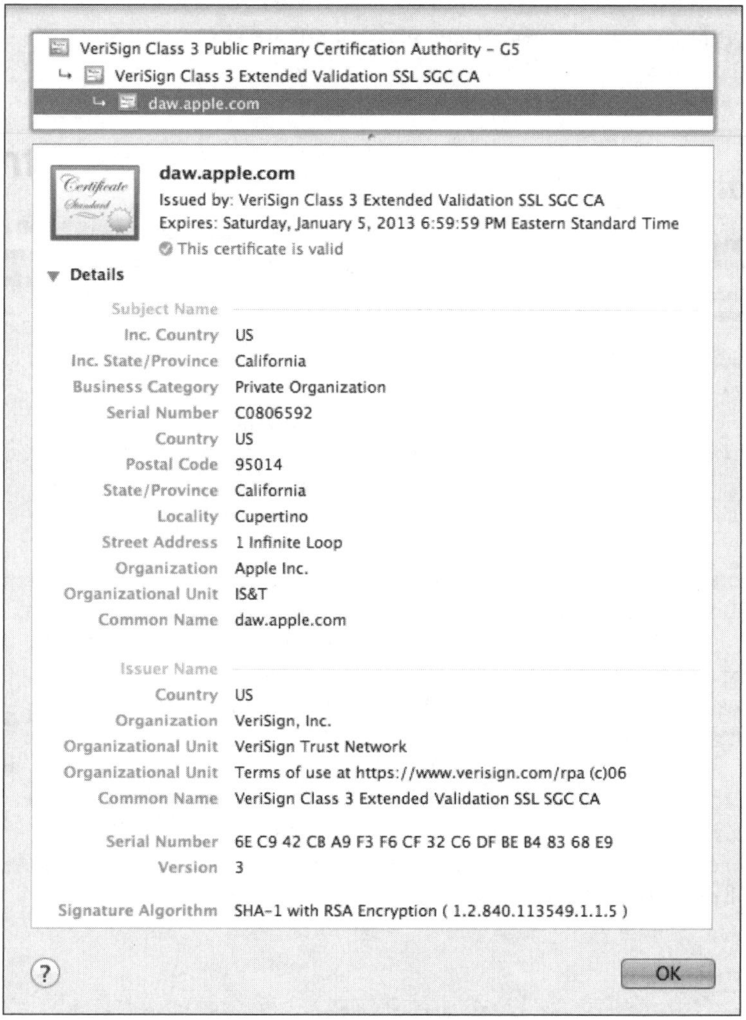

Figure 11-1 The certificate chain for daw.apple.com

Commercial certificates are valuable only for websites visited by browsers or other software you don't control. Generating your own certificate and shipping the public key in your application is marginally more secure than using a commercial certificate. If you already have a commercial certificate for your server, it is somewhat more convenient to use it for your application's network protocol, it's just not more secure. This is not to say that it's okay to trust random certificates (that is, turning off certificate validation). It's to say that it's okay to trust only *your* certificates rather than trusting commercial certificates.

Certificates can be corrupt or not, valid or not, and trusted or not. These are separate attributes that need to be understood individually. The first question is whether a certificate is corrupt. A certificate is corrupt if it does not conform to the X.509 data format, or if its signatures are incorrectly computed. A corrupt certificate should never be used for anything, and the iOS certificate function generally rejects them automatically.

> **X.509 refers to the data format specification and semantics originally defined by ITU-T** (`itu.int/ITU-T`). **The current version (v3) is defined by IETF RFC 5280** (`ietf.org/rfc/rfc5280.txt`).

Checking Certificate Validity

Given that a certificate is not corrupt, is it valid? Certificates contain a great deal of metadata about the public key they contain. The public key is just a very large number. It doesn't represent anything by itself. It's the metadata that gives that number meaning.

The most important piece of metadata is the subject. For servers, this is generally the fully qualified domain name (FQDN) such as `www.example.org`. The first test of validity is a name match. If you walk into a bank and identify yourself as "John Smith," you might be asked for your driver's license. If you hand over a license that says "Susan Jones," that would not help in identifying you no matter how authentic the driver's license. Similarly, if you are visiting a site named `www.example.org`, and the site presents a certificate with a common name `www.badguy.com`, you should generally reject it. Unfortunately it's not always that simple.

What if you visit `example.org`, and it presents a certificate that says `www.example.org`? Should you accept that certificate? Most humans would assume that `example.org` and `www.example.org` refer to the same server (which may or may not be true), but certificates use a simple string match. If the strings don't match, the certificate is invalid. Some servers present wild card certificates with subjects like `*.example.org` and iOS will accept that, but there are still some cases when it will reject a certificate because of a name mismatch you believe it should accept. Unfortunately, iOS does not make this easy to manage, but it can be done.

In this example, you're trying to connect to the IP address 72.14.204.113, which is `encrypted.google.com`. The certificate you receive is `*.google.com`, which is a mismatch. The string `72.14.204.113` does not include the string `.google.com`. You decide to accept any trusted certificate that includes `google.com` in its subject. To compile this example, you will need to link `Security.framework` into your project.

ConnectionViewController.m (Connection)

```
- (void)connection:(NSURLConnection *)connection
  willSendRequestForAuthenticationChallenge:
  (NSURLAuthenticationChallenge *)challenge
{
  NSURLProtectionSpace *protSpace = challenge.protectionSpace;
  SecTrustRef trust = protSpace.serverTrust;
  SecTrustResultType result = kSecTrustResultFatalTrustFailure;

  OSStatus status = SecTrustEvaluate(trust, &result);
  if (status == errSecSuccess &&
      result == kSecTrustResultRecoverableTrustFailure) {
    SecCertificateRef cert = SecTrustGetCertificateAtIndex(trust,
                                                           0);
    CFStringRef subject = SecCertificateCopySubjectSummary(cert);

    NSLog(@"Trying to access %@. Got %@.", protSpace.host,
          (__bridge id)subject);
```

```
      CFRange range = CFStringFind(subject, CFSTR(".google.com"),
                                  kCFCompareAnchored|
                                  kCFCompareBackwards);
      if (range.location != kCFNotFound) {
        status = RNSecTrustEvaluateAsX509(trust, &result);
      }
      CFRelease(subject);
    }

    if (status == errSecSuccess) {
      switch (result) {
        case kSecTrustResultInvalid:
        case kSecTrustResultDeny:
        case kSecTrustResultFatalTrustFailure:
        case kSecTrustResultOtherError:
// We've tried everything:
        case kSecTrustResultRecoverableTrustFailure:
          NSLog(@"Failing due to result: %lu", result);
          [challenge.sender cancelAuthenticationChallenge:challenge];
          break;

        case kSecTrustResultProceed:
        case kSecTrustResultConfirm:
        case kSecTrustResultUnspecified: {
          NSLog(@"Successing with result: %lu", result);
          NSURLCredential *cred;
          cred = [NSURLCredential credentialForTrust:trust];
          [challenge.sender useCredential:cred
                forAuthenticationChallenge:challenge];
        }
        break;

        default:
          NSAssert(NO, @"Unexpected result from trust evaluation:%d",
                   result);
          break;
      }
    }
    else {
      // Something was broken
      NSLog(@"Complete failure with code: %lu", status);
      [challenge.sender cancelAuthenticationChallenge:challenge];
    }
  }
```

In this routine, you are passed a challenge object and extract the trust object. You evaluate the trust object (`SecTrustEvaluate`) and receive a recoverable failure. You fetch the subject and determine if it's "close enough" (in this case, checking if it includes `.google.com`). If you're okay with the name you were passed, you reevaluate the certificate as a simple X.509 certificate rather than as part of an SSL handshake (that is, you evaluate it while ignoring the hostname). This is done with a custom function `RNSecTrustEvaluateAsX509`.

```
static OSStatus RNSecTrustEvaluateAsX509(SecTrustRef trust,
                                         SecTrustResultType *result
                                         )
 {
  OSStatus status = errSecSuccess;

  SecPolicyRef policy = SecPolicyCreateBasicX509();
  SecTrustRef newTrust;
  CFIndex numberOfCerts = SecTrustGetCertificateCount(trust);
  CFMutableArrayRef certs;
  certs = CFArrayCreateMutable(NULL,
                               numberOfCerts,
                               &kCFTypeArrayCallBacks);
  for (NSUInteger index = 0; index < numberOfCerts; ++index) {
    SecCertificateRef cert;
    cert = SecTrustGetCertificateAtIndex(trust, index);
    CFArrayAppendValue(certs, cert);
  }

  status = SecTrustCreateWithCertificates(certs,
                                          policy,
                                          &newTrust);
  if (status == errSecSuccess) {
    status = SecTrustEvaluate(newTrust, result);
  }

  CFRelease(policy);
  CFRelease(newTrust);
  CFRelease(certs);

  return status;
}
```

This function creates a new trust object by copying all the certificates from the original trust object created by the URL loading system. This trust object uses the simpler X.509 policy, which only checks the validity and trust of the certificate itself, without considering the hostname as the original SSL policy does.

A certificate may also be invalid because it has expired. Unfortunately, while you can reevaluate the certificate using any date you want using SecTrustSetVerifyDate, there is no easy, public way to determine the validity dates for the certificate. The following private methods allow you to work out the valid range:

```
CFAbsoluteTime SecCertificateNotValidBefore(SecCertificateRef);
CFAbsoluteTime SecCertificateNotValidAfter(SecCertificateRef);
```

As with all private methods, these may change at any time, and may be rejected by Apple. The only other practical way to parse the certificate is to export it with SecCertificateCopyData and parse it again using OpenSSL. Building and using OpenSSL on iOS is beyond the scope of this book. Search the Web for "OpenSSL iOS" for several explanations of how to build this library.

After evaluating the trust object, the final result will be a `SecTrustResultType`. There are several results that represent "good" or "possibly good" certificates:

- `kSecTrustResultProceed`—The certificate is valid, and the user has explicitly accepted it.

- `kSecTrustResultConfirm`—The certificate is valid, and you should ask the user whether to accept it.

- `kSecTrustResultUnspecified`—The certificate is valid, and the user has not explicitly accepted or rejected it. Generally you accept it in this case.

- `kSecTrustResultRecoverableTrustFailure`—The certificate is invalid, but in a way that may be acceptable, such as a name mismatch, expiration, or lack of trust (such as a self-signed certificate).

The following results indicate that the certificate should not be accepted:

- `kSecTrustResultDeny`—The certificate is valid, and the user has explicitly rejected it.

- `kSecTrustResultInvalid`—The validation was unable to complete, likely because of a bug in your code.

- `kSecTrustResultFatalTrustFailure`—The certificate itself was defective or corrupted.

- `kSecTrustResultOtherError`—The validation was unable to complete, likely because of a bug in Apple's code. You should never see this error.

Determining Certificate Trust

So far, you've learned to determine if a certificate is valid, but that doesn't mean it's trusted. Returning to the example of identifying yourself at the bank, if you present your Metallica fan club membership card, it probably would not be accepted as identification. The bank has no reason to believe that your fan club has done a good job making sure you are who you say you are. That's the same situation that an application faces when presented with a certificate signed by an unknown authority.

To be trusted, a certificate must ultimately be signed by one of the certificates in the trust object's list of *anchor certificates*. Anchor certificates are those certificates that are explicitly trusted by the system. iOS ships with more than a hundred of them from companies and government agencies. Some are global names like VeriSign and DigiTrust; others are more localized like QuoVadis and Vaestorekisterikeskus. Each of these organizations went through a complex audit process and paid significant amounts of money to be in the root store, but that doesn't mean your application needs to trust them.

If you generate your own certificate, you can embed the public key in your application and configure your trust object to accept only that certificate or certificates signed by it. This gives you greater control over your security and can save you some money.

For this example, you create a self-signed root certificate.

1. Open Keychain Access.

2. Select Keychain Access menu → Certificate Assistant → Create a Certificate.

3. Enter any name you like, set the Identity Type to Self Signed Root, set the Certificate Type to SSL Client, and create the certificate. You will receive a warning that this is a self-signed certificate. That is the intent of this

process, so you should click Continue. Your newly created certificate will display a warning that "This root certificate is not trusted." That is also as expected because it is not in the root keychain.

4. Back in the Keychain Access window, select the login keychain and select the category Certificates.

5. Find your certificate and drag it to the desktop to export it. This file includes only the public key. Keychain does not export the private key by default. Drag the public key file into your Xcode project.

You can test that the certificate presented is signed by your certificate as follows:

```
NSError *error;
NSString *path = [[NSBundle mainBundle] pathForResource:@"MyCert"
                                                 ofType:@"cer"];
NSData *certData = [NSData dataWithContentsOfFile:path
                                          options:0
                                            error:&error];

SecCertificateRef certificate;
certificate = SecCertificateCreateWithData(NULL,
                            (__bridge CFDataRef)certData);
CFArrayRef certs = CFArrayCreate(NULL,
                            (const void**)&certificate,
                            1,
                            &kCFTypeArrayCallBacks);

SecTrustSetAnchorCertificates(trust, certs);

CFRelease(certs);
CFRelease(certificate);
```

You load the certificate from your resource bundle into an `NSData`, convert it into a `SecCertificate`, and set it as the anchor for the trust object. The trust object will now only accept the certificates passed to `SecTrustSetAnchorCertificates` and will ignore the system's anchors. If you would like to accept both, you can use `SecTrustSetAnchorCertificatesOnly` to reconfigure the trust object.

Using these techniques, you can correctly respond to any certificate in your `connection:willSendRequest ForAuthenticationChallenge:` method, and control which certificates you accept or reject.

Employing File Protection

iOS provides hardware-level encryption of files. Files marked for protection are encrypted using a per-device key, which itself is encrypted using the user's password or PIN. Ten seconds after the device is locked, the unencrypted per-device key is removed from memory. When the user unlocks the device, the password or personal identification number (PIN) is used to decrypt the per-device key again, which is then used to decrypt the files.

The weakest link in this scheme is the user's password. On an iPhone, users almost exclusively use a 4-digit PIN, which offers only 10,000 combinations (far fewer are used in practice). In May 2011, ElcomSoft Co. Ltd demonstrated that it could brute-force a 4-digit PIN in about 20–40 minutes. This doesn't protect against forensics or device theft, but does protect against attackers who only have access to the device for a few minutes. On iPad, typing a real password is much more convenient, so the security is similar to file encryption on a laptop.

For a developer, the specifics of the iOS encryption scheme aren't critical. The scheme is effective enough for users to expect it from any application that holds sensitive information.

You can configure the protection of individual files that you create with NSFileManager or NSData. The options, shown in the following list, have slightly different names. NSFileManager applies string attributes to the file, while NSData uses numeric options during creation, but the meanings are the same. The FileManager constants begin with NSFileProtection..., and the NSData constants begin with NSDataWritingFileProtection....

- ...None—The file is not protected and can be read or written at any time. This is the default value.

- ...Complete—Any file with this setting is protected 10 seconds after the device is locked. This is the highest level of protection, and the setting you should generally use. Files with this setting may not be available when your program is running in the background. When the device is unlocked, these files are unprotected.

- ...CompleteUnlessOpen—Files with this setting are protected 10 seconds after the device is locked unless they are currently open. This allows your program to continue accessing the file while running in the background. When the file is closed, it will be protected if the device is locked.

- ...CompleteUntilFirstUserAuthentication—Files with this setting are only protected between the time the device boots and the first time the user unlocks the device. The files are unprotected from that point until the device is rebooted. This allows your application to open existing files while running in the background. You can create open new files using ...CompleteUnlessOpen. This is better than the None setting, but should be avoided if at all possible because it provides very limited protection.

To create a new file with file protection turned on, convert it to an NSData and then use writeToFile: options:error:. This is preferable to creating the file and then using NSFileManager to set its protection attribute.

```
[data writeToFile:dataPath
        options:NSDataWritingFileProtectionComplete
        error:&writeError];
```

To create a protected file in the background, you can apply the option ...CompleteUnlessOpen, which allows you to read as long as it is open when the device locks. You should generally avoid this unless you're actually in the background. The easiest way to achieve this is like this:

```
[data writeToFile: path
        options: NSDataWritingFileProtectionComplete
        error: &error] ||
[data writeToFile: path
        options: NSDataWritingFileProtectionCompleteUnlessOpen
        error: &error];
```

If you use this technique, upgrade your file protection at startup with a routine like this:

```
-(void)upgradeFilesInDirectory:(NSString *)dir
                        error:(NSError **)error {
  NSFileManager *fm = [NSFileManager defaultManager];
  NSDirectoryEnumerator *dirEnum = [fm enumeratorAtPath:dir];
  for (NSString *path in dirEnum) {
    NSDictionary *attrs = [dirEnum fileAttributes];
    if (![[attrs objectForKey: NSFileProtectionKey]
        isEqual:NSFileProtectionComplete]) {
      attrs = [NSDictionary dictionaryWithObject:
              NSFileProtectionComplete forKey:NSFileProtectionKey];
      [fm setAttributes:attrs ofItemAtPath:path error:error];
    }
  }
}
```

If your application needs to know whether protected data is available or not, you can use one of the following:

▨ Implement the methods `applicationProtectedDataWillBecomeUnavailable:` and `applicationProtectedDataDidBecomeAvailable:` in your application delegate,

▨ Observe the notifications `UIApplicationProtectedDataWillBecomeUnavailable` and `UIApplicationProtectedDataDidBecomeAvailable` (these constants lack the traditional `Notification` suffix),

▨ Check `[[UIApplication sharedApplication] protectedDataAvailable]`.

For foreground-only applications, file protection is very easy. Because it's so simple and it's hardware optimized, you should generally protect your files unless you have a good reason not to. If your application runs in the background, you need to give more careful thought to how to apply file protection, but you should still make sure to protect all sensitive information as well as possible.

Using Keychains

File protection is intended to protect *data*. Keychain is intended to protect *secrets*. In this context, a secret is a small piece of data used to access other data. The most common secrets are passwords and private keys.

The keychain is protected by the operating system and is encrypted when the device is locked. In practice, it works very similarly to file protection. Unfortunately, the Keychain API is anything but friendly. Many people have written wrappers around the Keychain API, but my recommendation is Apple's `KeyChainItemWrapper` from the `GenericKeychain` sample code (2010). This is what I'll discuss in this section, after a brief introduction to the low-level data structures.

An item in the keychain is called a `SecItem`, but is stored in a `CFDictionary`. There is no `SecItemRef` type. There are five classes of `SecItem`: generic password, Internet password, certificate, key, and identity. In most cases, you want to use a generic password. Many problems come from developers trying to use an Internet password, which is more complicated and provides little benefit. `KeyChainItemWrapper` only uses generic password items, which is one reason I like it. Storing private keys and identities is rare in iOS applications and it won't be discussed in this book. Certificates that contain only public keys should generally be stored in files rather than in keychain.

You eventually need to search the keychain for the item you want. There are many pieces of the key to search for, but the best way is to assign your own identifier and search for that. Generic password items include an attribute `kSecAttrGeneric`, which you can use to store your identifier. This is how `KeyChainItemWrapper` operates.

Keychain items have several searchable *attributes* and a single encrypted *value*. For a generic password item, some of the more important attributes are the account (`kSecAttrAccount`), service (`kSecAttrService`), and identifier (`kSecAttrGeneric`). The value is generally the password.

So with that background, let's see how to use `KeychainItemWrapper`. First, as shown in the following code, you create one with `initWithIdentifier:accessGroup:`. I discuss access groups in the section "Sharing Data with Access Groups," but for now leave it `nil`.

```
KeychainItemWrapper *
wrapper = [[KeychainItemWrapper alloc]
                        initWithIdentifier:@"MyKeychainItem"
                            accessGroup:nil];
```

You can now read from and write to `wrapper` like you would an `NSDictionary`. It automatically synchronizes with the keychain. The `__bridge` casts are to allow you to pass Core Foundation constants to a Cocoa method under ARC.

```
id kUsernameKey = (__bridge id)kSecAttrAccount;
id kPasswordKey = (__bridge id)kSecValueData;

NSString *username = [wrapper objectForKey:kUsernameKey];
[wrapper setObject:password forKey:kPasswordKey];
```

`KeychainItemWrapper` caches reads, but not writes. Writing to the keychain can be expensive, so you shouldn't do it too often. The keychain is not a place to store sensitive data that changes often. That should be written an encrypted file as described in the section "Employing File Protection."

Sharing Data with Access Groups

The iOS sandbox creates a significant headache for application suites. If you have multiple applications that work together, there is no easy way to share information among them. Of course you can save the data on a server, but the user still needs to enter credentials for each of your applications.

iOS offers a solution to this with access groups. Multiple applications can share keychain data as long as they share an access group. To create an access group, open the target in Xcode. At the bottom of the summary pane enable Entitlements. Then add a new keychain access group as shown in Figure 11-2.

Using `KeychainItemWrapper`, you can use this access group by passing the identifier to `initWith Identifier:accessGroup:`. For more information on this feature, see the documentation for `SecItemAdd` in the *Keychain Services Reference* (`developer.apple.com`).

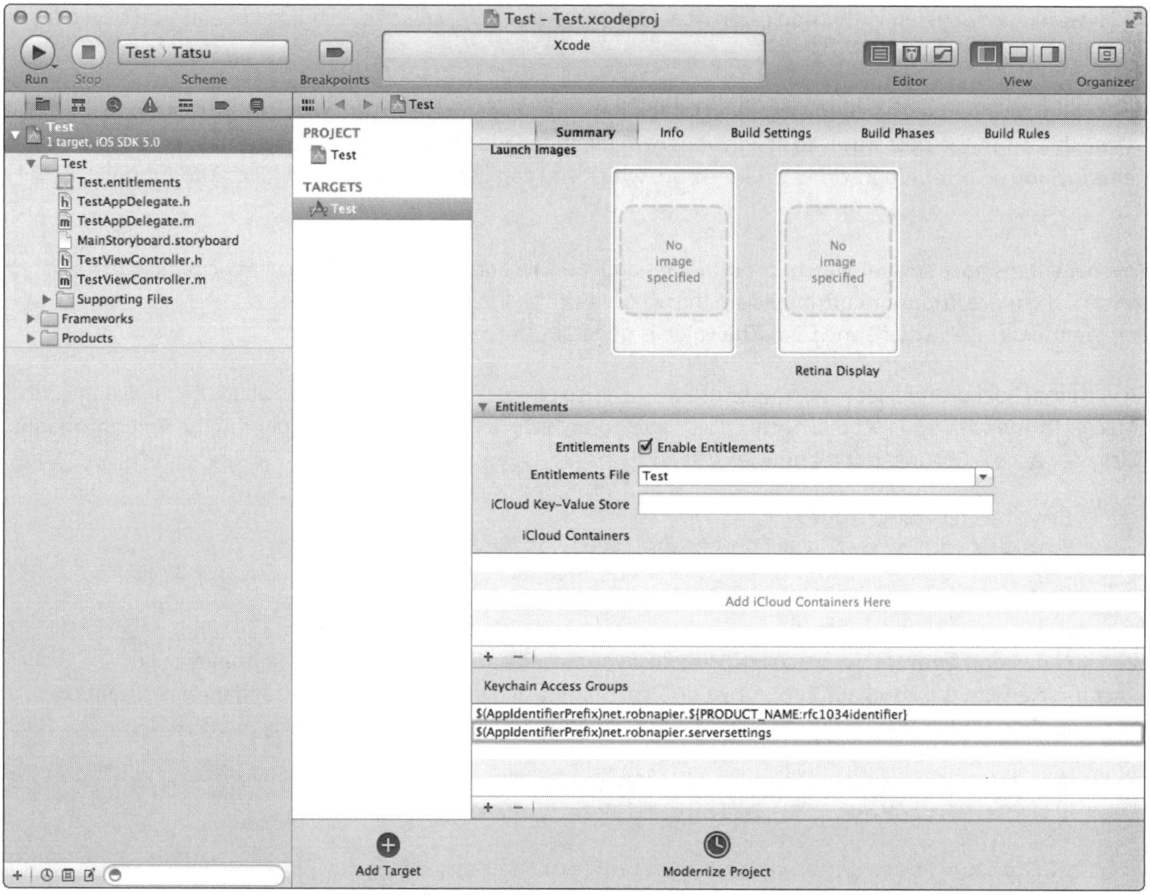

Figure 11-2 Creating the serversettings access group

Storing small pieces of sensitive information in the keychain is quite simple with `KeychainItemWrapper`. Unless you have a very good reason, I recommend using it instead of directly accessing the Keychain API, which is much more complicated.

Using Encryption

Most of the time, iOS handles all your encryption needs for you. It automatically encrypts and decrypts HTTPS for network traffic and manages encrypted files using file protections. If you have certificates, `SecKeyEncrypt` and `SecKeyDecrypt` handle asymmetric (public/private key) encryption for you.

But what about simple, symmetric encryption using a password? iOS has good support for this, but limited documentation. The available documentation is in `/usr/include/CommonCrypto`. Most of it assumes that you have some background in cryptography. This section covers what you need to use it successfully.

Overview of AES

The *Advanced Encryption Standard*, or AES, is a symmetric encryption algorithm. Given a key, it converts *plaintext* into *ciphertext*. The same key is used to convert ciphertext back into plaintext. Originally named Rijndael, in 2001 the algorithm was selected by the U.S. government as its standard for encryption.

It's a very good algorithm. Unless you need another algorithm for compatibility with an existing system, you should always use AES for symmetric encryption. The best cryptographers in the world have carefully scrutinized it, and it's hardware optimized on iOS devices, making it extremely fast.

Converting Passwords to Keys with PBKDF2

AES offers three key lengths: 128, 192, and 256 bits. There are slight differences in the algorithm for each length. Unless you have very specialized needs, I recommend AES-128. It offers an excellent trade-off of security and performance, including time performance and battery life performance.

A *key* is not the same thing as a *password*. A key is a very large number, used to encrypt and decrypt data. All possible keys for an encryption system are called its *key space*. A password is something a human can type. Long passwords that include spaces are sometimes called *passphrases*, but for simplicity I just use the word "password" no matter the construction. If you try to use a password as an AES key, you significantly shrink the number of available keys. If the user selects a random 16-character password using the 94 characters on a standard keyboard, that only creates about a 104-bit key space, approximately one ten-millionth the size of the full AES key space. Real users select passwords from a much smaller set of characters. Worse yet, if the user has a password longer than 16 bytes (16 single-byte characters or 8 double-byte characters), you will throw away part of it when using AES 128.

You need a way to convert a password into a useable key that makes it as hard as possible on the attacker to search every possible password. The answer is a *password-based key derivation function*. Specifically, you will use PBKDF2, which is defined by RSA Laboratories' Public-Key Cryptography Standards (PKCS) #5. You don't need to know the internals of PBKDF2 or PKCS #5, but it's important to know the names because they show up in the documentation. What is important is that PBKDF2 converts a password into a key.

To use PBKDF2, you need to generate a *salt*, which is just a large random number. The standard recommends at least 64 bits. The salt is combined with the password to prevent identical passwords from generating identical keys. You then iterate through the PBKDF2 function a specific number of times, and the resulting data is your key. To decrypt the data, you need to preserve the salt and the number of iterations. Typically the salt is saved with the encrypted data, and the number of iterations is a constant in your source code, but you can also save the number of iterations with the encrypted data.

The important fact here is that the salt, the number of iterations, and the final ciphertext are all public information. Only the key and the original password are secrets.

Generating the salt is easy. It's just a large random number. You can create it with a method like `randomDataOfLength:`, shown in the following code:

RNCryptManager.m (CryptPic)

```
const NSUInteger kPBKDFSaltSize = 8;

+ (NSData *)randomDataOfLength:(size_t)length {
  NSMutableData *data = [NSMutableData dataWithLength:length];

  int result = SecRandomCopyBytes(kSecRandomDefault,
                                  length,
                                  data.mutableBytes);
  NSAssert(result == 0, @"Unable to generate random bytes: %d",
           errno);

  return data;
}
...
NSData *salt = [self randomDataOfLength:kPBKDFSaltSize];
```

Originally, the standard called for 1,000 iterations of PBKDF2, but this has gone up as CPUs have improved. I recommend between 10,000 and 100,000 iterations on an iPhone 4 and 50,000 to 500,000 iterations on a modern MacBook Pro. The reason for the large number is to slow down brute-force attacks. An attacker generally tries passwords rather than raw AES keys because the number of practical passwords is much smaller. By requiring 10,000 iterations of the PBKDF2 function, the attacker must waste about 80ms per attempt on an iPhone 4. That adds up to 13 minutes of search time for a 4-digit PIN, and months or years to search for even a very simple password. The extra 80ms for a single key generation is generally negligible. Going up to 100,000 iterations adds nearly a second to key generation on an iPhone, but provides much better protection if the password guessing is done on a desktop, even if the password is very weak.

PBKDF2 requires a *pseudorandom function* (PRF), which is just a function that can generate a very long series of statistically random numbers. The only algorithm supported on iOS for this purpose is SHA1, so you always pass kCCPRFHmacAlgSHA1 for this parameter.

Luckily it's easier to use PBKDF2 than it is to explain it. The following method accepts a password string and salt data and returns an AES key.

RNCryptManager.m (CryptPic)

```
#import <CommonCrypto/CommonKeyDerivation.h>
const NSUInteger kAlgorithmKeySize = kCCKeySizeAES128;
const NSUInteger kPBKDFRounds = 10000;  // ~80ms on an iPhone 4

+ (NSData *)AESKeyForPassword:(NSString *)password
                         salt:(NSData *)salt {
  NSMutableData *
  derivedKey = [NSMutableData dataWithLength:kAlgorithmKeySize];

  int
  result = CCKeyDerivationPBKDF(kCCPBKDF2,          // algorithm
                                password.UTF8String, // password
                                password.length,     // passwordLength
                                salt.bytes,          // salt
```

```
                        salt.length,            // saltLen
                        kCCPRFHmacAlgSHA1,      // PRF
                        kPBKDFRounds,           // rounds
                        derivedKey.mutableBytes, // derivedKey
                        derivedKey.length);      // derivedKeyLen

    // Do not log password here
    NSAssert(result == kCCSuccess,
             @"Unable to create AES key for password: %d", result);

    return derivedKey;
}
```

Applying PKCS7 Padding

AES is a *block cipher*, which means that it operates on a fixed-sized block of data. AES works on exactly 128 bits (16 bytes) of input at a time. Because the data you want to encrypt may not be an exact multiple of 16 bytes, it may be necessary to pad the last block with extra data. PKCS #7 defines a standard way to do this, and you generally request it by passing the `kCCOptionPKCS7Padding` option.

Selecting the Mode and the Initialization Vector (IV)

AES can operate in two modes, *electronic codebook* (ECB) and *cipher-block chaining* (CBC). Unless you have special requirements, you should always use CBC, and it is the default in iOS. In this mode, each block influences the encryption of the next block, which greatly improves overall security.

> ECB is faster than CBC. The one case where ECB makes sense is if you are encrypting a large number of small (16 byte or less) random numbers. An example of this is using AES to encrypt other AES keys. In that one case, ECB is no less secure than CBC. It is extremely uncommon to encounter this situation in iOS, so you should always use CBC.

The first block is a special case because there is no previous block. CBC allows you to define an extra block called the *initialization vector* (IV) to begin the chain. This is often labeled optional, but you should always provide one. Otherwise, an all-zero block is used, and that leaves your data vulnerable to certain attacks. The IV is very similar to the salt discussed in the section "Converting Passwords to Keys with PBKDF2." It ensures that if the same plaintext is encrypted with the same key, the resulting ciphertext will still be different.

As with the salt, the IV is just a random series of bytes that you save with the ciphertext and use during decryption.

```
    iv = [self randomDataOfLength:kAlgorithmIVSize];
```

Performing One-Shot Encryption

That's really all the theory you need. iOS provides all the math functions, so you can ignore the implementation details. Key generation with PBKDF2 was added in iOS 5.

The first example is one-shot encryption and decryption routines. These take an `NSData` and return an `NSData`. They use the convenience function `CCCrypt` from `CommonCryptor`.

The encryption routine accepts plaintext data and a password, and returns ciphertext data, an IV, and a salt.

RNCryptManager.m (CryptPic)

```
#import <CommonCrypto/CommonCryptor.h>
const CCAlgorithm kAlgorithm = kCCAlgorithmAES128;
const NSUInteger kAlgorithmKeySize = kCCKeySizeAES128;
const NSUInteger kAlgorithmBlockSize = kCCBlockSizeAES128;
const NSUInteger kAlgorithmIVSize = kCCBlockSizeAES128;
const NSUInteger kPBKDFSaltSize = 8;
const NSUInteger kPBKDFRounds = 10000;  // ~80ms on an iPhone 4

+ (NSData *)encryptedDataForData:(NSData *)data
                        password:(NSString *)password
                              iv:(NSData **)iv
                            salt:(NSData **)salt
                           error:(NSError **)error {
  NSAssert(iv, @"IV must not be NULL");
  NSAssert(salt, @"salt must not be NULL");

  *iv = [self randomDataOfLength:kAlgorithmIVSize];
  *salt = [self randomDataOfLength:kPBKDFSaltSize];

  NSData *key = [self AESKeyForPassword:password salt:*salt];

  size_t outLength;
  NSMutableData *
  cipherData = [NSMutableData dataWithLength:data.length +
                kAlgorithmBlockSize];

  CCCryptorStatus
  result = CCCrypt(kCCEncrypt, // operation
                   kAlgorithm, // Algorithm
                   kCCOptionPKCS7Padding, // options
                   key.bytes, // key
                   key.length, // keylength
                   (*iv).bytes,// iv
                   data.bytes, // dataIn
                   data.length, // dataInLength,
                   cipherData.mutableBytes, // dataOut
                   cipherData.length, // dataOutAvailable
                   &outLength); // dataOutMoved

  if (result == kCCSuccess) {
    cipherData.length = outLength;
  }
  else {
   // ... Handle Error ...
    return nil;
  }
```

```
   return cipherData;
}
```

The decryption routine accepts ciphertext data, a password, IV, and salt. The IV and salt are the same values returned from the encryption method.

RNCryptManager.m (CryptPic)

```
+ (NSData *)decryptedDataForData:(NSData *)data
                       password:(NSString *)password
                             iv:(NSData *)iv
                           salt:(NSData *)salt
                          error:(NSError **)error {

   NSData *key = [self AESKeyForPassword:password salt:salt];

   size_t outLength;
   NSMutableData *
   decryptedData = [NSMutableData dataWithLength:data.length];
   CCCryptorStatus
   result = CCCrypt(kCCDecrypt, // operation
                    kAlgorithm, // Algorithm
                    kCCOptionPKCS7Padding, // options
                    key.bytes, // key
                    key.length, // keylength
                    iv.bytes,// iv
                    data.bytes, // dataIn
                    data.length, // dataInLength,
                    decryptedData.mutableBytes, // dataOut
                    decryptedData.length, // dataOutAvailable
                    &outLength); // dataOutMoved

   if (result == kCCSuccess) {
     [decryptedData setLength:outLength];
   }
   else {
     if (result != kCCSuccess) {
       // ... Handle Error ...
       return nil;
     }
   }

   return decryptedData;
}
```

Improving CommonCrypto Performance

The CCCrypt function is fairly straightforward. It has a lot of parameters and you need to generate a key, but once you have your data in place, it's just one function call. As presented in in the section "Performing One-Shot Encryption," however, CCCrypt requires enough memory to hold two copies of your plaintext. It also requires that all the plaintext be available when it gets started.

You can save half the memory by reusing the buffer in CCCrypt. The dataIn and dataOut parameters can point to the same buffer as long as it's as large as the ciphertext. For AES that's the size of the plaintext plus one 16-byte block.

This still requires that all the plaintext be available in memory at the same time. That can be expensive for large files, especially on a mobile device. It also prevents you from decrypting as the data is read from the network. This is particularly useful in cases when you want to store data on an untrusted server. HTTPS protects it on the network but that doesn't help if you don't trust the server. It's easiest to use file protection locally on the device and use AES to protect the file remotely.

CCCrypt is just a convenience function around the normal CommonCrypto routines: CCCryptorCreate, CCCryptorUpdate, and CCCryptorFinal. In this example, you use these to handle encryption and decryption with NSStream objects. The full source code is available in the CryptPic sample code for this chapter.

This routine handles either encrypting or decrypting, based on the operation parameter (kCCEncrypt or kCCDecrypt). First, it reads or writes the IV and salt at the beginning of the stream. The _CM...Data methods are helpers for dealing with NSStream. They're available in the sample code.

RNCryptManager.m (CryptPic)

```
switch (operation) {
  case kCCEncrypt:
    // Generate a random IV for this file.
    iv = [self randomDataOfLength:kAlgorithmIVSize];
    salt = [self randomDataOfLength:kPBKDFSaltSize];

    if (! [outStream _CMwriteData:iv error:error] ||
        ! [outStream _CMwriteData:salt error:error]) {
      return NO;
    }
    break;
  case kCCDecrypt:
    // Read the IV and salt from the encrypted file
    if (! [inStream _CMgetData:&iv
                    maxLength:kAlgorithmIVSize
                        error:error] ||
        ! [inStream _CMgetData:&salt
                    maxLength:kPBKDFSaltSize
                        error:error]) {
      return NO;
    }
    break;
  default:
    NSAssert(NO, @"Unknown operation: %d", operation);
    break;
}
```

Next, it generates the key from the password and creates the CCCryptor object. This is the object that performs the encryption or decryption.

```
NSData *key = [self AESKeyForPassword:password salt:salt];

// Create the cryptor
CCCryptorRef cryptor = NULL;
CCCryptorStatus result;
result = CCCryptorCreate(operation,              // operation
                        kAlgorithm,              // algorithim
                        kCCOptionPKCS7Padding,   // options
                        key.bytes,               // key
                        key.length,              // keylength
                        iv.bytes,                // IV
                        &cryptor);               // OUT cryptorRef
```

Next, it allocates some buffers to use. According to the documentation, you should be able to use a single buffer to manage the plaintext and ciphertext, but there is a bug in CCCryptorUpdate that prevents this (radar://9930555). If you use padding and call CCCryptorUpdate multiple times, you can't do "in place" encryption. That isn't a major problem in this case because the buffer size is small.

CCCryptorGetOutputLength returns the size of the buffer required to process the requested number of bytes, including any extra data that may be needed for the final block. You could also use kMaxReadSize + kAlgorithmBlockSize, which are always greater than or equal to the result of CCCryptorGetOutputLength. There's no problem with allocating a little too much memory here. Using NSMutableData rather than malloc lets ARC take care of the memory management for you, even if there's an error.

```
dstBufferSize = CCCryptorGetOutputLength(cryptor, // cryptor
                                        kMaxReadSize, // input length
                                            true); // final

NSMutableData *
dstData = [NSMutableData dataWithLength:dstBufferSize];

NSMutableData *
srcData = [NSMutableData dataWithLength:kMaxReadSize];

uint8_t *srcBytes = srcData.mutableBytes;
uint8_t *dstBytes = dstData.mutableBytes;
```

Now the routine reads a block of data, encrypts or decrypts it, and writes it to the output stream. process Result:bytes:length:toStream:error: just checks the result and handles the file writing in a way that simplifies error handling. The important call is CCCryptorUpdate. This reads data from srcBytes and writes them to dstBytes. It updates dstLength with the number of bytes written.

```
ssize_t srcLength;
size_t dstLength = 0;

while ((srcLength = [inStream read:srcBytes
                    maxLength:kMaxReadSize]) > 0 ) {
  result = CCCryptorUpdate(cryptor,           // cryptor
                        srcBytes,              // dataIn
                        srcLength,             // dataInLength
```

```
                                 dstBytes,        // dataOut
                                 dstBufferSize,   // dataOutAvailable
                                 &dstLength);     // dataOutMoved

    if (![self processResult:result
                       bytes:dstBytes
                      length:dstLength
                    toStream:outStream
                       error:error]) {
      CCCryptorRelease(cryptor);
      return NO;
    }
}
```

When you've read the entire file (`srcLength == 0`), there may still be some unprocessed data in the `CCCryptor`. `CCCryptorUpdate` only processes data in block-sized units (16 bytes for AES). If padding was enabled, you need to call `CCCryptorFinal` to deal with whatever's left over. If you did not enable padding, then you can skip this step, but it's generally not worth writing special code to avoid it.

```
    result = CCCryptorFinal(cryptor,         // cryptor
                            dstBytes,        // dataOut
                            dstBufferSize,   // dataOutAvailable
                            &dstLength);     // dataOutMoved
    if (![self processResult:result
                       bytes:dstBytes
                      length:dstLength
                    toStream:outStream
                       error:error]) {
      CCCryptorRelease(cryptor);
      return NO;
    }

    CCCryptorRelease(cryptor);
    return YES;
```

Note the calls to `CCCryptorRelease`. Unlike other `...Release` functions, this immediately frees the memory. There is no retain counting on `CCCryptor`. `CCCryptorRelease` also overwrites the memory with zeros, which is good security practice for sensitive data structures.

> The fact that `CCCryptorRelease` **overwrites the memory with zeros is not documented in** `CCCommonCryptor.h`, **but can be verified in the source code.** `CommonCrypto` **is open source, and the source is available from** `http://opensource.apple.com/`. **Look in the OS X tree, not the iOS tree.**

You can use this routine to encrypt and decrypt from any `NSStream`, which can handle file paths, URLs, or `NSData`. You would normally wrap it in a method like this one:

```
+ (BOOL)encryptFromStream:(NSInputStream *)fromStream
                 toStream:(NSOutputStream *)toStream
```

```
                    password:(NSString *)password
                        error:(NSError **)error {
    return [self applyOperation:kCCEncrypt
                   fromStream:fromStream
                     toStream:toStream
                     password:password
                        error:error];
}
```

You would then use it like this to encrypt an NSData directly to disk.

CPCryptController.m (CryptPic)

```
NSInputStream *pictureStream = [NSInputStream
                                 inputStreamWithData:data];
[pictureStream open];

NSOutputStream *
outputStream = [NSOutputStream
               outputStreamToFileAtPath:encryptedPath
               append:NO];
[outputStream open];

BOOL result = [RNCryptManager encryptFromStream:pictureStream
                                       toStream:outputStream
                                       password:password
                                          error:error];

[pictureStream close];
[outputStream close];
```

Combining Encryption and Compression

It's sometimes a good idea to compress data before encrypting it. There is a theoretical security benefit to doing this, but generally it's just to make the data smaller. The important thing to remember is that you must compress before you encrypt. You can't compress encrypted data. If you could, that would suggest patterns in the ciphertext, which would indicate a poor encryption algorithm. In most cases, encrypting and then compressing leads to a larger output than the original plaintext.

Summary

iOS provides a rich collection of security frameworks to make it as easy as possible to secure your users' data. This chapter showed you how to secure network communications, files, and passwords. You also learned how to properly validate certificates so that you can ensure your application only communicates with trusted sources. Securing your application requires a few extra lines of code, but taking care of the basics is generally not difficult using the code provided in this chapter.

Further Reading

Apple Documentation

The following documents are available in the iOS Developer Library at `developer.apple.com` or through the Xcode Documentation and API Reference.

Certificate, Key, and Trust Services Programming Guide

iOS Application Programming Guide, "The Application Runtime Environment"

Secure Coding Guide (`/usr/lib/CommonCrypto`)

WWDC Sessions

The following session videos are available at `developer.apple.com`.

WWDC 2010, "Session 204: Creating Secure Applications"

WWDC 2011, "Session 208: Securing iOS Applications"

Other Resources

Aleph One, *Phrack vol. 7, issue 49*, "Smashing The Stack For Fun And Profit," 1996. Fifteen years later, this is still one of the best introductions to buffer overflows available, with examples.
`www.phrack.org/issues.html?issue=49&id=14#article`

Schneier, Bruce, *Applied Cryptography*. 1996. Anyone interested in the guts of cryptography should read this book. The main problem is that after reading it, you may think you can create your own cryptography implementations. You shouldn't. Read this book as a fascinating, if dated, introduction to cryptography. Then put it down and use a well-established implementation.

Chapter 12

Running on Multiple iPlatforms and iDevices

The iOS SDK was announced to the public in February 2008. At that time there were only two devices using it: iPhone and iPod touch. Apple has since been innovating vigorously and in 2010, it introduced another bigger brother to the family, the iPad. In 2010, another new device running iOS was introduced: the Apple TV. Who knows what the future might hold—Apple might even announce an SDK for Apple TV development and may even enable running games from Apple TV controlled by your iPhone on iPod touch.

Every year, a new version of the SDK comes out along with at least two or three new device updates, and these new devices often come with additional sensors. The GPS sensor debuted with iPhone 3G, the magnetometer—a sensor used to show the direction of magnetic north (more commonly known as a compass)—debuted in iPhone 3GS, and the gyroscope (for lifelike game play) in iPhone 4. The iPad was introduced later with a whole new UI, a far bigger screen than the iPhone, but without a camera. iPad added a couple of cameras (including a front-facing camera) in the second iteration, iPad 2.

Similarly every version of the SDK comes with powerful new features: In App Purchases, Push Notification Service, Core Data, and MapKit support in iOS 3; multitasking, blocks, and Grand Central Dispatch in iOS 4; iCloud, Twitter integration, and Storyboards in iOS 5, to name a few. When you use one of these features, you might be interested in providing backward compatibility to users running an older version of the operating system. Keep in mind, however, that if you are using a feature available in a newer version of the SDK, you must either forget about old users (not a good idea) or write code that adapts to both users (either by supporting an equivalent feature for older users or by prompting them that additional features are available if they run a newer version).

As a developer you should know how to write code that easily adapts to any device (known or unknown) and platform. For that purpose, it's easier to depend on Cocoa framework APIs to detect capabilities than writing code assuming that a certain sensor would be present on a given hardware. In short, developers should avoid making assumptions about hardware capabilities based on device model strings.

This chapter looks at some strategies that can help you write code that adapts easily to multiple platforms and devices using the various APIs provided by Cocoa framework. In the course of this chapter, you write a category extension on the UIDevice class, and add methods that check for features that are not readily exposed by the framework.

Developing for Multiple Platforms

The iOS debuted with a public SDK in version 2.0, and version 5.0 is the fourth iteration that is available for developers. One important advantage of iOS over competing platforms is that users don't have to wait for carriers to "approve" their OS updates and, because the updates are free of charge, most users (more than 75%)

get the latest available OS within a month. As an iOS developer, it's usually fine to support just the two latest iterations of the SDK. That is, in late 2010 and early 2011, it was enough to support iOS 4 and iOS 3; now, in late 2011–early 2012, it should be enough to support iOS 5 and iOS 4. That makes life easier for developers.

Configurable Target Settings: Base SDK Versus Deployment Target

To customize all features your app can use and all devices and OS versions your app can run, Xcode provides two configurable settings for the target you build. The first is your base SDK setting and the second is the iOS Deployment Target.

Configuring the Base SDK Setting

The first configurable setting is called Base SDK. You can configure this setting by editing your target. To do so, follow these steps:

1. Open your project and select the project file on the project navigator.

2. On the editor pane, select the target and select the Build Settings tab. The Base SDK setting is usually the third option here, but the easiest way to look for a setting in this pane is to search for it in the search bar.

You can change the value to "Latest iOS SDK" or any version of SDK installed on your development machine. The Base SDK setting instructs the compiler to use that version of SDK to compile and build your app and this means it directly controls which APIs are available for your app. By default, new projects created with Xcode always use the latest-available SDK and Apple handles API deprecation. Unless you have very specific reasons not to, stick to this default value.

Configuring the Deployment Target Setting

The second setting is the Deployment Target, which governs the minimum required OS version necessary for using your app. If you set this to a particular version, say 5.0, the AppStore app automatically prevents users running previous operating systems from downloading or installing your app. To cater to a wider audience, I recommend providing backward compatibility for at least one previous version of the OS. For example, if iOS 5 is the latest version, you should also support at least iOS 4. You can set the Deployment Target on the same Build Settings tab as the Base SDK setting.

When you are using a feature available in iOS 5 SDK, but still want to support older versions, your Base SDK setting should be set to the latest SDK (or iOS 5) and your Deployment Target should be set to at least iOS 4. However, when your app is running on iOS 4 devices, some frameworks and features might not be available. It's your responsibility as a developer to adapt your app to work properly without crashing.

Considerations for Multiple SDK Support: Frameworks, Classes, and Methods

There are three cases that you need to handle when you support multiple SDKs: frameworks, classes, and methods. In the following sections, you learn about the ways to make this possible.

Framework Availability

Sometimes a new SDK might add a whole new framework, which means that a complete framework is not available on older operating systems. An example from iOS 4 is the `EventKit.framework`. This framework is available only to users running iOS 4 and above. You have two choices here. Either set the deployment target to iOS 4 and build your app only for customers running iOS 4 and above, or check if the given framework is present on the user's operating system and hide necessary UI elements that invoke a call to this framework. Clearly, the second choice is the optimal.

When you use a symbol that's defined in a framework that is not available on older versions, your app will not load. To avoid this and to selectively load a framework, you must weak-link it. To weak-link a framework, open the target settings page from the project settings editor. Then open the Build Phases tab and expand the fourth section (Link Binary With Libraries). You will see a list of frameworks that are currently linked to your target. If you haven't yet changed a setting here, all the frameworks are set to Required by default. Click the Required combo box and change it to Optional, which will weak-link a framework.

When you weak-link a framework, missing symbols automatically become null pointers and you can use this null check to enable or disable UI elements.

An example on iOS 5 is the `Twitter.Framework`. When you use the built-in Twitter framework for sending tweets, you should weak-link it and do a runtime check to see if it is available. If not, you have to show your own Tweet Composer UIs instead.

> When you link a framework that is present only on a newer version of the SDK, but still specify the iOS Deployment target to a SDK older than that, your application will fail to launch and crash almost immediately. This will cause your app to be rejected. When you receive a crash report from the Apple review team stating that the app crashes immediately on launch (mostly without any useful crash dumps), this is what you have to look for.

Class Availability

Sometimes a new SDK might add new classes to an existing framework. This means that even if the framework gets linked, not all symbols would be available to you on older operating systems. An example from iOS 4 is the `UILocalNotification` class defined in `UIKit.Framework`. This framework is linked with every iOS app, so when you are using this class, you should check for its presence by instantiating an object using the `NSClassFromString` method. If it returns `nil`, that class is not present on the target device. An example from iOS 5 is the `UIStepper` control. If you are using this class, check for its existence.

Another method to check for class availability is to use the `class` method instead of `NSClassFromString`, as shown in the following code.

Checking for Availability of the UIStepper Control

```
if ([UIStepper class]) {
    // Create an instance and add it to the subview
} else {
    // create instance of a equivalent control and add it to subview
}
```

> To use the `class` method, you should use the LLVM Clang compiler and the deployment target should be 3.1 or later.

Method Availability

In some cases, new methods are added to an existing class in the new SDK. A classic example from iOS 4 is multitasking support. The class `UIDevice` has a method called `isMultiTaskingAvailable`. The following code checks for this class.

Code for Checking Whether a Method Is Available in a Class

```
if ([[UIDevice currentDevice] respondsToSelector:@selector(isMultitasking
Supported)]) {
if([UIDevice currentDevice].isMultitaskingSupported) {
    // Code to support multitasking goes here
  }
}
```

To check if a method is available in a given class, use the `respondsToSelector:` method. If it returns YES, you can use the method you checked for.

If the method you are checking is a global C function, you should equate it to NULL instead, as shown in the following code.

Checking Availability of a C Function

```
if (CFunction != NULL) {
  CFunction(a);
}
```

> You have to equate the function name explicitly to NULL. Implicitly assuming pointers as nil or NULL will not work.

Checking the Availability of Frameworks, Classes, and Methods

Although it should quite easy to remember framework availability, it can be challenging to remember the availability of every single class and method. Equally difficult is reading through the complete iOS documentation to learn which method is available and which method is not. I recommend two different ways to check the availability of a framework, class, or method.

Developer Documentation

The straightforward way to check the availability of symbols or frameworks is to search in the Availability section of the developer documentation. Figure 12-1 is a screenshot from the developer documentation showing how to look for multitasking availability.

---

multitaskingSupported

A Boolean value indicating whether multitasking is supported on the current device. (read-only)

```
@property (nonatomic, readonly,
getter=isMultitaskingSupported) BOOL multitaskingSupported
```

Availability
Available in iOS 4.0 and later.
Declared In
UIDevice.h

Figure 12-1 Multitasking availability in developer documentation

Macros in iOS Header Files

The other method for checking the availability of a method or class is to read through the header files. I find this easier than fiddling through the documentation. Just command-click the symbol from your source code and Xcode opens the header file where it's defined. Most newly added methods have either one of the macro decorations shown in Figure 12-2:

Availability Macros

```
UIKIT_CLASS_AVAILABLE
__OSX_AVAILABLE_STARTING
__OSX_AVAILABLE_BUT_DEPRECATED
```

```
@property(nonatomic,readonly,getter=isMultitaskingSupported) BOOL multitaskingSupported __OSX_AVAILABLE_STARTING
    (__MAC_NA,__IPHONE_4_0);
```

Figure 12-2 Multitasking availability in header file

It's usually easier and faster to check availability of a class or method for a given SDK version from the header file. But not all methods will have this macro decoration. If it doesn't, you have to look at the developer documentation.

If a method doesn't have a macro decoration, it probably means that the method was added ages ago to the SDK and you normally don't have to worry if you are targeting the two most recent SDKs.

Now that you know how to support multiple SDK versions, let's focus on the meat of the chapter: supporting multiple devices. In the next section, you learn about the subtle differences between the devices and learn the right way to check for availability of a particular feature. In parallel, you also write a category extension class on `UIDevice` that adds methods and properties for checking features not exposed by the framework.

Detecting Device Capabilities

The first and most common mistake that developers made in the past, when there were only two devices (iPod touch and iPhone), was to detect the model name and check if it was an "iPhone," thereby assuming capabilities. This worked well for a year or so. But soon, when new devices with new hardware sensors became available, the method became highly error prone. For example, the initial version of the iPod touch didn't have a microphone; however, after the iPhone OS 2.2 software update, users can add one by connecting an external microphone/ headset. If your code assumes device capabilities based on model name, it will still work, but it's not correct and not the right thing to do.

Detecting Devices and Assuming Capabilities

Consider the following code fragment, which assumes the capabilities of the iPhone.

Detecting a Microphone the Wrong Way

```
if(![[UIDevice currentDevice].model isEqualToString:@"iPhone"])  {
        UIAlertView *alertView = [[UIAlertView alloc]
initWithTitle:@"Error"
message:@"Microphone not present"
delegate:self
        cancelButtonTitle:@"Dismiss"
otherButtonTitles: nil];
        [alertView show];
    }
```

The problem with the preceding code is that the developer has made a broad assumption that only iPhones will ever have microphones. This code worked well initially. But with the iOS software 2.2 update, when Apple added external microphone capability to iPod touch, the above code prevents users from using the app. Another problem is that this code shows an error for any new device introduced later, say iPad.

You should instead use some other method for detecting hardware or sensor availability than assuming devices' capabilities. Fortunately or unfortunately, these methods are scattered around on various frameworks. Let's now start looking at various methods for checking device capabilities the right way and grouping them under a `UIDevice` category class.

Detecting Hardware and Sensors

The first thing to understand is that instead of assuming capabilities, you should check for the presence of the exact hardware or sensor you need. For example, instead of assuming that only iPhones have a microphone, use APIs to check for the presence of a microphone. The first advantage of the following code is that it automatically works for new devices to be introduced in the future and for externally connected microphones.

What's the second advantage? The code is a one-liner.

Correct Way to Check for Microphone Availability

```
- (BOOL) microphoneAvailable  {
 AVAudioSession *session = [AVAudioSession sharedInstance];
 return session.inputIsAvailable;
}
```

In the case of a microphone, you should also consider detecting input device change notifications. That is, enable your Record button on the UI when the user plugs in a microphone, in addition to `viewDidAppear`. Sounds cool, right? Here's how to do that.

Detecting Whether a Microphone Is Being Plugged In

```
void audioInputPropertyListener(void* inClientData,
AudioSessionPropertyID inID, UInt32 inDataSize, const void *inData)  {

    UInt32 isAvailable = *(UInt32*)inData;
    BOOL micAvailable = (isAvailable > 0);
    // update your UI here
}

- (void)viewDidLoad  {
    [super viewDidLoad];
AudioSessionAddPropertyListener(
kAudioSessionProperty_AudioInputAvailable,
audioInputPropertyListener, nil);
}
```

All you need to do here is to add a property listener for `kAudioSessionProperty_AudioInput Available` and on the call back check for the value.

With just few extra lines of code, you are able to write the correct version of device detection code. Next you extend this for other hardware and sensors.

> `AudioSessionPropertyListeners` **behave much like observing** `NSNotification` **events. When you add a property listener to a class, it's your responsibility to remove it at the right time. In the example above, because you added the property listener in** `viewDidLoad`, **you should remove it in** `viewDidUnload`.

Detecting Camera Types

The iPhone shipped with a single camera originally and added a front-facing camera later in iPhone 4. The iPod touch had no camera until the fourth generation. While the iPhone 4 has a front-facing camera, the iPad 1 (its bigger brother) doesn't have one, while the newer iPad 2 has both a front-facing and a back-facing camera. All this means that you should not write code with device-based assumptions. It is actually far easier to use the API.

The `UIImagePickerController` class has class methods to detect source type availability.

Checking for Camera Presence

```
- (BOOL) cameraAvailable  {
  return [UIImagePickerController isSourceTypeAvailable:
UIImagePickerControllerSourceTypeCamera];
}
```

Checking for a Front-Facing Camera

```
- (BOOL) frontCameraAvailable
{
#ifdef __IPHONE_4_0
  return [UIImagePickerController isCameraDeviceAvailable:
UIImagePickerControllerCameraDeviceFront];
#else
  return NO;
#endif
}
```

For detecting a front-facing camera, you should be running on iOS 4 and above. The enumeration `UIImage PickerControllerCameraDeviceFront` is available only on iOS 4 and above because any device that has a front-facing camera (iPhone 4 and iPad 2) always runs iOS 4 and above. So you use a macro and return `NO` if the device runs iOS 3 or below.

Similarly, you can check if the camera attached has video-recording capabilities. Cameras on iPhone 3GS and above can record videos. You can check that using the following code.

Checking for a Video-Recording Capable Camera

```
- (BOOL) videoCameraAvailable  {
  UIImagePickerController *picker =
[[UIImagePickerController alloc] init];
// First call our previous method to check for camera presence.
if(![self cameraAvailable])   return NO;
NSArray *sourceTypes = [UIImagePickerControlleravailableMediaTypesFor
SourceType:
UIImagePickerControllerSourceTypeCamera];

  if (![sourceTypes containsObject:(NSString *)kUTTypeMovie]){

    return NO;
  }

  return YES;
}
```

This enumerates the available media types for a given camera and determines if it contains `kUTTypeMovie`.

Detecting Whether a Photo Library Is Empty

If you are using a camera, you will almost always use the user's photo library. Before calling `UIImagePicker` to show the user's photo album, you should ensure that there are photos in it. You can check this the same way as you check for camera presence. Just pass `UIImagePickerControllerSourceTypePhotoLibrary` or `UIImagePickerControllerSourceTypeSavedPhotosAlbum` for the source type.

Detecting the Presence of a Camera Flash

So far, the only device to have a camera flash is the iPhone 4. In coming years, more and more devices will have this. It's easy to check for camera flash presence using `UIImagePickerController`'s class method:

Checking for a Camera Flash

```
- (BOOL) cameraFlashAvailable  {
#ifdef __IPHONE_4_0
  return [UIImagePickerController isFlashAvailableForCameraDevice:
UIImagePickerControllerCameraDeviceRear];
#else
  return NO;
#endif
}
```

Detecting a Gyroscope

The gyroscope is an interesting addition to the iPhone 4. It allows developers to measure relative changes to the physical position of the device. By comparison, an accelerometer, can measure only force. Twisting movements cannot be measured by accelerometer. Using a gyroscope, it's possible for game developers to implement 6-axis control like that found in Sony's PlayStation 3 controller or Nintendo's Wii controller. You can detect the presence of a gyroscope using an API provided in the `CoreMotion.framework`.

Code to Detect the Presence of a Gyroscope

```
- (BOOL) gyroscopeAvailable  {
#ifdef __IPHONE_4_0
  CMMotionManager *motionManager = [[CMMotionManager alloc] init];
  BOOL gyroAvailable = motionManager.gyroAvailable;
  return gyroAvailable;
#else
  return NO;
#endif
}
```

If a gyroscope is a core feature of your app but your target device doesn't have a gyroscope, you have to design your app with alternative input methods, or you can specify them in the `UIRequiredDeviceCapablities` key in your app's `info.plist`, preventing devices without a gyroscope from installing the app. You learn more about this key later in the chapter.

Detecting a Compass or Magnetometer

Compass availability can be checked using the `CoreLocation.framework` class `CLLocationManager`. Call the method `headingAvailable` in `CLLocationManager` and if it returns true, you can use compass in your app. A compass is more useful in a location-based application and augmented reality-based applications.

Detecting a Retina Display

As an iOS developer, you already know that catering to a retina display is as easy as adding an @2x image file for every resource you use in the app. But in cases where you download the image from a remote server, you should download images at twice the resolution on devices with retina display.

A good example of this is a photo browser app like, say, a Flickr viewer or Instagram. When your user launches the app in iPhone 4 (the only device with a retina display as of this writing) you should be downloading images of double the resolution you do for non-retina display devices. Some developers choose to ignore this and download higher resolution images for all devices, but that is a waste of bandwidth and might even be slower to download over EDGE. Instead, download higher-resolution files after determining that the device has a retina display. Checking for this is easy.

Retina Display Capable

```
- (BOOL) retinaDisplayCapable  {
 int scale = 1.0;
 UIScreen *screen = [UIScreen mainScreen];
 if([screen respondsToSelector:@selector(scale)])
  scale = screen.scale;
 if(scale == 2.0f) return YES;
 else return NO;
}
```

With this code you look for the `mainScreen` of the device and check if the device is capable of showing high-resolution retina display-capable graphics. This way, if Apple introduces an external retina display (maybe the newer Apple Cinema Displays) and allows the current generation iPads to project to it in retina mode, your app will still work without changes.

Detecting Alert Vibration Capability

As of this writing, only iPhones are capable of vibrating to alert the user. Unfortunately, there is no public API for checking if the device is vibration capable. However, the `AudioToolbox.framework` has methods (shown below) to selectively vibrate only iPhones.

```
AudioServicesPlayAlertSound(kSystemSoundID_Vibrate);

AudioServicesPlaySystemSound(kSystemSoundID_Vibrate);
```

The first method vibrates the iPhone and plays a beep sound on iPod touch. The second method just vibrates the iPhone. On devices not capable of vibrating, they don't do anything. If you are developing a game that vibrates the device to signify danger or a Labyrinth game where you want to vibrate whenever the player hits the wall, you should use the second method. The first method is for alerting the user, which includes vibration plus beeps while the second is just for vibrations.

Detecting Remote Control Capability

iOS apps can handle remote control events generated by buttons pressed on the external headset. To handle this, use the following method to start receiving notifications:

```
[[UIApplication sharedApplication] beginReceivingRemoteControlEvents];
```

Implement the following method in your `firstResponder`:

```
remoteControlReceivedWithEvent:
```

Be sure to turn this off when you no longer need the events by calling

```
[[UIApplication sharedApplication]

endReceivingRemoteControlEvents];
```

Detecting Phone Call Capability

You can check if a device can make phone calls by checking if it can open URLs of type `tel:`. The `UIApplication` class's `canOpenURL:` method is handy for checking if a device has an app that can handle URLs of a specific type. `tel:` URLs are handled by the phone app on iPhone. The same method can also be used to check if a specific app that can handle a given URL is installed on a device.

Phone Call Capabilities

```
- (BOOL) canMakePhoneCalls  {
  return [[UIApplication sharedApplication]
canOpenURL:[NSURL URLWithString:@"tel://"]];
}
```

> **A word about usability:** Developers should completely hide features specific to phones on iPod touch devices. For example, if you are developing a Yellow Pages app that lists phone numbers from the Internet, show the button to place a call only on devices that are capable of making phone calls. Do not simply disable it (because nothing can be done by the user to enable it) or show an error alert. There have been cases where showing a "Not an iPhone" error on an iPod touch leads to rejection of the app by the app review team.

In App Email and SMS

While In App email and In App SMS are technically not sensors or hardware, not every device can send emails or SMSs. This includes iPhones as well—even those that run iOS 4 and above. Although `MFMessageViewController` and `MFMailComposeViewController` are available from iOS 4, and even if your app's minimum deployment target is set to iOS 4, you still need to know and understand the common pitfalls when using these classes.

For example, an iOS device with no configured email accounts cannot send email, even when it's technically capable of sending one. The same applies to SMS/MMS. An iPhone that doesn't have a SIM card cannot send text messages. You should be aware of this and always check for capabilities before attempting to use this feature.

Checking for this capability is easy. Both `MFMessageComposeViewController` (for In App SMS) and `MFMailComposeViewController` (for In App email) have class methods `canSendText` and `canSendMail`, respectively, that can be used.

Checking Multitasking Awareness

Checking if a device can multitask is straightforward. As you saw earlier in this chapter, you have to check if the method `isMultitaskingSupported` is available, as shown in the following code. If it returns `YES`, you can write multitasking-related code. Otherwise, you should remember your app's state and continue when the app is launched again.

Is Multitasking Available?

```
if ([[UIDevice currentDevice] respondsToSelector:
@selector(isMultitaskingSupported)])  {
   if([UIDevice currentDevice].isMultitaskingSupported)  {
      // Code to support multitasking goes here
   }
}
```

But there is something more. On devices that don't support multitasking, your application delegate will not receive the following callbacks.

– `applicationDidEnterBackground:`

– `applicationWillEnterForeground:`

This means that any part of your startup code and initialization sequence you write in `application WillEnterForeground:` should be written in `applicationDidFinishLaunchingWithOptions:` as well for nonmultitasking capable devices.

Similarly, the teardown code (including your Core Data-managed context save methods) that you write in `applicationDidEnterBackground:` should be written in `applicationWillTerminate:` as well.

Obtaining the UIDevice+Additions Category

The code fragments you've seen so far in this chapter are available as a UIDevice category addition. You can download that from the book's website.

It has just two files: `UIDevice+Additions.h` and `UIDevice+Additions.m`. You have to link necessary frameworks to avoid those pesky linker errors because this class links to various Apple library frameworks. But don't worry; they are dynamically loaded so they don't bloat your app.

UIRequiredDeviceCapabilities

So far, you've learned how to conditionally check a device for specific capabilities and use them if they are present. In some cases, your app depends solely on the presence of particular hardware and without that hardware your app will be unusable. Examples include a camera app like Instagram or Camera+. The core functionality of the app doesn't work without a camera. In this case, you need something more than just checking for device capabilities and hiding specific parts of your app. You normally won't need devices without a camera to use or download your app.

Apple provides a way to ensure this using the `UIRequiredDeviceCapablities` key in the Info plist file. The following values are supported for this key: `telephony`, `wifi`, `sms`, `still-camera`, `auto-focus-camera`, `front-facing-camera`, `camera-flash`, `video-camera`, `accelerometer`, `gyroscope`, `location-services`, `gps`, `magnetometer`, `gamekit`, `opengles-1`, `opengles-2`, `armv6`, `armv7`, `peer-peer`.

You can explicitly require particular device capabilities or prohibit installation of your app on devices without a specific capability. For example, you can prevent your apps from running on devices with `video-camera` by setting the `video-camera` key to `NO`. Alternatively, you can mandate the presence of `video-camera` by setting the `video-camera` key to `YES`.

> **Apple doesn't allow you to submit an update to an existing app and prevent it from running on a specific device that was supported before the update. For example, if your app supported both iPhone and iPod touch in version 1.0, you cannot submit an update that prevents it from running on either device. Put another way, you cannot introduce a mandate for the presence of particular hardware later in your app's product life cycle. The submission process on iTunes connect will fail and show you an error. The converse is allowed, however. That is, if you have been excluding a device previously, you can allow installations on it in a subsequent version. In other words, if version 1 of your app supported only iPhones, you can submit a version 2 to support all devices.**

Adding values to the `UIRequiredDeviceCapablities` key will prohibit your app from being installed on devices without the capabilities you requested. If you specify that telephony is needed, users cannot even download the app on their iPod touch or iPad. You must be certain that this is your expected behavior before using this key.

Summary

This chapter discussed various techniques and tricks to help run your app on multiple platforms. It also looked at the various hardware and sensors available for iOS developers and how to detect their presence the right way. You incrementally wrote a category extension on `UIDevice` that could be used for detecting most device capabilities. Finally, you learned about the `UIRequiredDeviceCapablities` key and how to completely exclude devices without a required capability. My recommendation is to depend on the methods explained in this chapter and use the `UIRequiredDeviceCapablities` key sparingly.

Further Reading

Apple Documentation

The following documents are available in the iOS Developer Library at `developer.apple.com` or through the Xcode Documentation and API Reference.

Understanding the UIRequiredDeviceCapablities key

iOS Build Time Configuration Details

Other Resources

MKBlog, "iPhone Tutorial: Better way to check capabilities of iOS devices"
`http://blog.mugunthkumar.com/coding/iphone-tutorial-better-way-to-check-capabilities-of-ios-devices/`

Github. "MugunthKumar/DeviceHelper"
`https://github.com/MugunthKumar/DeviceHelper`

Chapter 13

Internationalization and Localization

Localization is a key concern for any application with a global market. Users want to interact in their own languages, with their familiar formatting. Supporting this in your application is called *internationalization* (sometimes abbreviated "i18n" for the 18 characters between the "i" and the "n") and *localization* ("L10n"). The differences between i18n and L10n aren't really important or consistently agreed upon. Apple says, "Internationalization is the process of designing and building an application to facilitate localization. Localization, in turn, is the cultural and linguistic adaptation of an internationalized application to two or more culturally-distinct markets." (See *"Internationalization Programming Topics"* at `developer.apple.com`.) This chapter uses the terms interchangeably.

After reading this chapter, you will have a solid understanding of what localization is and how to approach it. Even if you're not ready to localize your application yet, this chapter provides easy steps to dramatically simplify localization later. You learn how to localize strings, numbers, dates and nib files, and how to regularly audit your project to make sure it stays localizable.

What is Localization?

Localization is more than just translating strings. Localization means making your application culturally appropriate to your target audience. iOS requires that nib files be localized for each language individually rather than providing an auto-layout framework like Adobe's Adam and Eve. This is generally on purpose. Auto-layout tends to create layouts that look mediocre in all languages. Apple wants your layouts to look ideal in all languages, which means laying them out manually and individually rather than by algorithm. Russian and German are bigger languages than English. Chinese is smaller but denser. Arabic and Hebrew run right to left. Different languages need different layouts to look their best.

That said, there are many things you can do to make iOS localization easier.

- Keep nib files simple. This isn't difficult on iOS because there aren't as many complicated things you can do in a nib as you can on Mac. But just remember that every `IBOutlet` and `IBAction` connection you make has to be made in every localized nib file.

- Separate nib files that require localization from ones that don't. Many iOS nib files have no strings or localized images in them at all. You don't need to localize these. If you just need a localized title, then make it an `IBOutlet` and set the localized value at runtime rather than localizing the nib file. String localization is much easier to maintain than nib file localization.

- Remember right-to-left languages. This is one of the hardest things to fix later, especially if you have custom text views.

- Don't assume that comma is the thousands separator or dot is the decimal point. These are different in different languages, so build your regular expressions using `NSLocale`.

- Glyphs (drawn symbols) and characters do not always map one-to-one. If you're doing custom text layout, this can be particularly surprising. Apple's frameworks generally handle this well automatically, but don't try to circumvent systems like Core Text when they force you to calculate the number of glyphs in a string rather than using `length`. This issue is particularly common in Thai, but exists in many languages (even occasionally in English, as I'll discuss in Chapter 18).

In my experience, it is best to do all of your development up to the point of release and then translate rather than try to translate as you go. The cost of localization is best absorbed at fixed points during development, generally at the end. It's expensive to retranslate things every time you tweak the UI.

While translation is best done near the time of release, you should line up your localization provider fairly early in the development cycle and prepare for localization throughout the process. A good localization provider does more than just translate a bunch of strings you send it. Ideally your localization provider will provide testing services to make sure your application "makes sense" in the target culture. Getting the provider involved early in the process can save expensive rework later if your interface is hard to localize.

An example of a "hard-to-localize" application is one that includes large blocks of text. Translating large blocks of text can play havoc with layout, particularly on iPhone. Remembering that you will often pay by the word for translation may help you focus on reducing the number of words you use. Redesign your UI so it doesn't need so much text to let the user know what to do. Rely on Apple's UI elements and icons as much as possible. Apple's done the hard and expensive work for you to make them internationally appropriate. Don't waste that. For example, when using a `UIToolBarItem`, you should use a system item whenever appropriate rather than drawing your own icons. If the icon's meaning matches your intent, you should always try to use the system icon, even you believe you could create a better one. In my opinion, the "action" icon (an arrow coming out of a box) is incomprehensible, but users are used to it. Apple has trained them in what it means, so you should use it. Never use a system icon for something other than its intended meaning, however. For example, do not use `UIBarButtonSystemItemReply` to mean "go left" or "go back."

Another frequent localization problem is icons that assume a cultural background, such as a decorated tree to indicate "winter." Checkmarks can also cause problems, because they are not used in all cultures (French for instance), and in some cultures a checkmark means "incorrect" (Finnish for instance). Involving a good localization provider before producing your final artwork can save you a lot of money re-creating your assets.

Localizing Strings

The most common tool for localizing strings is `NSLocalizedString`. This function looks up the given key in `Localizeable.strings` and returns the value found there, or the key itself if no value is found. `Localizeable.strings` is a localized file, so there is a different version for each language, and `NSLocalizedString` automatically selects the correct one based on the current locale. A command-line tool called `genstrings` automatically searches your files for calls to `NSLocalizedString` and writes your initial `Localizeable.strings` file for you.

The easiest approach is to use the string as its own key (the second parameter is a comment to the localizer):

```
NSString *string =
    NSLocalizedString(@"Welcome to the show.",
                      @"Welcome message");
```

To run `genstrings`, you should open a terminal, change to your source code directory, and run it as shown here (assuming an English localization):

```
genstrings -o en.lproj *.m
```

This will create a file called `en.lproj/Localizeable.string` that contains the following:

```
/* Welcome message */
"Welcome to the show." = "Welcome to the show.";
```

Even if you don't run `genstrings`, this works in the developer's language because it automatically returns the key as the localized string.

In most cases I recommend using the string as its own key and automatically generating the `Localizeable.strings` file when you're ready to hand the project off to localizers. This approach simplifies development and helps keep the `Localizeable.strings` file from accumulating keys that are no longer used.

Auditing for Nonlocalized Strings

During development, you should periodically audit your program to make sure that you're using `NSLocalizedString` as you should. I recommend a script like this:

find_nonlocalized

```perl
#!/usr/bin/perl -w
# Usage:
#     find_nonlocalized [<directory> ...]
#
# Scans .m and .mm files for potentially nonlocalized
#   strings that should be.
# Lines marked with DNL (Do Not Localize) are ignored.
# String constant assignments of this form are ignored if
#   they have no spaces in the value:
#   NSString * const <...> = @"...";
# Strings on the same line as NSLocalizedString are
#   ignored.
# Certain common methods that take nonlocalized strings are
#   ignored
# URLs are ignored
#
# Exits with 1 if there were strings found

use File::Basename;
use File::Find;
```

```perl
use strict;

# Include the basenames of any files to ignore
my @EXCLUDE_FILENAMES = qw();

# Regular expressions to ignore
my @EXCLUDE_REGEXES = (
    qr/\bDNL\b/,
    qr/NSLocalizedString/,
    qr/NSString\s*\*\s*const\s[^@]*@"[^ ]*";/,
    qr/NSLog\(/,
    qr/@"http/, qr/@"mailto/, qr/@"ldap/,
    qr/predicateWithFormat:@"/,
    qr/Key(?:[pP]ath)?:@"/,
    qr/setDateFormat:@"/,
    qr/NSAssert/,
    qr/imageNamed:@"/,
    qr/NibNamed?:@"/,
    qr/pathForResource:@"/,
    qr/fileURLWithPath:@"/,
    qr/fontWithName:@"/,
    qr/stringByAppendingPathComponent:@"/,
);

my $FoundNonLocalized = 0;

sub find_nonlocalized {
    return unless $File::Find::name =~ /\.mm?$/;
    return if grep($_, @EXCLUDE_FILENAMES);

    open(FILE, $_);

    LINE:
    while (<FILE>) {
        if (/@"[^"]*[a-z]{3,}/) {
            foreach my $regex (@EXCLUDE_REGEXES) {
                next LINE if $_ =~ $regex;
            }
            print „$File::Find::name:$.:$_";
            $FoundNonLocalized = 1;
        }
    }
    close(FILE);
}

my @dirs = scalar @ARGV ? @ARGV : („.");
find(\&find_nonlocalized, @dirs);
exit $FoundNonLocalized ? 1 : 0;
```

Periodically run this script over your source to make sure that there are no nonlocalized strings. If you use Jenkins (jenkins-ci.org) or another continuous-integration tool, you can make this script part of the build process, or you can add it as a script step in your Xcode build. Whenever it returns a new string, you can decide whether to fix it, update the regular expressions to ignore it, or mark the specific line with DNL (Do Not Localize).

Formatting Numbers and Dates

Numbers and dates are displayed differently in different locales. This is generally straightforward using `NSDateFormatter` and `NSNumberFormatter`, which you are likely already familiar with.

> **For an introduction to** `NSDateFormatter` **and** `NSNumberFormatter`, **see the** *"Data Formatting Guide"* **in Apple's documentation at** `developer.apple.com`.

There are a few things to keep in mind, however. First, formatters are needed for input as well as output. Most developers remember to use a formatter for date input, but may forget to use one for numeric input. The decimal point is not universally used to separate whole from fractional digits on input. Some countries use a comma or an apostrophe. It's best to validate number input using an `NSDateFormatter` rather than custom logic.

Digit groupings have a bewildering variety. Some countries split thousands groups with space, comma, or apostrophe. China sometimes groups ten thousands (four digits). Don't guess. Use a formatter. Remember that this can impact the length of your string. If you only leave room for seven characters for one hundred thousand ("100,000") you may overflow in India, which uses eight ("1,00,000" or one lakh).

Percentages are another place that you should be careful because different cultures place the percent sign at the beginning or end of the number, and some use a slightly different symbol. Using `NSNumberFormatterPercentStyle` will behave correctly.

Be especially careful with currency. Don't store currency as a float because that can lead to rounding errors as you convert between binary and decimal. Always store currency as an `NSDecimalNumber`, which does its math in decimal. Keep track of the currency you're working in. If your user switches locale from the U.S. to France, you shouldn't switch his $1 purchase to €1. Generally you need to persist what currency a given value is expressed in. The `RNMoney` class is an example of how to do this. First, the following code demonstrates how to use the class to store Rubles and Euros.

main.m (Money)

```
NSLocale *russiaLocale = [[NSLocale alloc]
                      initWithLocaleIdentifier:@"ru_RU"];

RNMoney *money = [[RNMoney alloc]
                  initWithIntegerAmount:100];
NSLog(@"Local display of local currency: %@", money);
NSLog(@"Russian display of local currency: %@",
      [money localizedStringForLocale:russiaLocale]);


RNMoney *euro =[[RNMoney alloc] initWithIntegerAmount:200
                              currencyCode:@"EUR"];
NSLog(@"Local display of Euro: %@", euro);
NSLog(@"Russian display of Euro: %@",
      [euro localizedStringForLocale:russiaLocale]);
```

RNMoney is an immutable object that stores an amount and a currency code. If you do not provide a currency code, it defaults to the current locale's currency. It is a very simple data class designed to be simple to initialize, serialize, and format. Here is the code.

RNMoney.h (Money)

```
#import <Foundation/Foundation.h>

@interface RNMoney : NSObject <NSCoding>
@property (nonatomic, readonly, strong)
                                NSDecimalNumber *amount;
@property (nonatomic, readonly, strong)
                                NSString *currencyCode;

- (RNMoney *)initWithAmount:(NSDecimalNumber *)anAmount
        currencyCode:(NSString *)aCode;
- (RNMoney *)initWithAmount:(NSDecimalNumber *)anAmount;

- (RNMoney *)initWithIntegerAmount:(NSInteger)anAmount
                    currencyCode:(NSString *)aCode;
- (RNMoney *)initWithIntegerAmount:(NSInteger)anAmount;

- (NSString *)localizedStringForLocale:(NSLocale *)aLocale;
- (NSString *)localizedString;

@end
```

RNMoney.m (Money)

```
#import "RNMoney.h"

@implementation RNMoney

@synthesize amount=amount_;
@synthesize currencyCode=currencyCode_;

static NSString * const kRNMoneyAmountKey = @"amount";
static NSString * const kRNMoneyCurrencyCodeKey =
                                        @"currencyCode";

- (RNMoney *)initWithAmount:(NSDecimalNumber *)anAmount
                currencyCode:(NSString *)aCode {
  if ((self = [super init])) {
    amount_ = anAmount;
    if (aCode == nil) {
      NSNumberFormatter *formatter = [[NSNumberFormatter alloc] init];
      currencyCode_ = [formatter currencyCode];
    }
    else {
      currencyCode_ = aCode;
    }
  }
  return self;
```

```
}

- (RNMoney *)initWithAmount:(NSDecimalNumber *)anAmount {
  return [self initWithAmount:anAmount
               currencyCode:nil];
}

- (RNMoney *)initWithIntegerAmount:(NSInteger)anAmount
                     currencyCode:(NSString *)aCode {
   return [self initWithAmount:
            [NSDecimalNumber decimalNumberWithDecimal:
             [[NSNumber numberWithInteger:anAmount]
             decimalValue]]
                 currencyCode:aCode];
}

- (RNMoney *)initWithIntegerAmount:(NSInteger)anAmount {
  return [self initWithIntegerAmount:anAmount
                      currencyCode:nil];
}

- (id)init {
  return [self initWithAmount:[NSDecimalNumber zero]];
}

- (id)initWithCoder:(NSCoder *)coder {

  NSDecimalNumber *amount = [coder decodeObjectForKey:
                               kRNMoneyAmountKey];
  NSString *currencyCode = [coder decodeObjectForKey:
                               kRNMoneyCurrencyCodeKey];
  return [self initWithAmount:amount
               currencyCode:currencyCode];
}

- (void)encodeWithCoder:(NSCoder *)aCoder {
  [aCoder encodeObject:amount_ forKey:kRNMoneyAmountKey];
  [aCoder encodeObject:currencyCode_
             forKey:kRNMoneyCurrencyCodeKey];
}

- (NSString *)localizedStringForLocale:(NSLocale *)aLocale
{
  NSNumberFormatter *formatter = [[NSNumberFormatter alloc]
                                   init];
  [formatter setLocale:aLocale];
  [formatter setCurrencyCode:self.currencyCode];
  [formatter setNumberStyle:NSNumberFormatterCurrencyStyle];
  return [formatter stringFromNumber:self.amount];
}

- (NSString *)localizedString {
  return [self localizedStringForLocale:
           [NSLocale currentLocale]];
```

```
}

- (NSString *)description {
  return [self localizedString];
}

@end
```

Localizing Nib Files

Localizing nib files is one of the most tedious and risky parts of localization. Consider the following common case:

- Your project has a nib file with a button connected to the method `doThis:`.

- You send your nib file off to be translated and receive back a dozen versions of it.

- Now you want to change the button's action to `doThat:`.

You open your master nib file (usually English) and make the change, but now you have 11 other versions of the nib file that are incorrect, and you don't discover this until someone clicks on the button in another language and the application crashes.

About that time you start to think that nib files are a terrible idea and swear you'll never use them again, but that's the wrong conclusion. Nib files are incredibly powerful and an important part of iOS development. They're worth the trouble once you learn some best practices for managing them.

First, don't localize a nib file if you don't have to. If there's nothing to localize, then you only need one copy. iOS will automatically load your master nib file if there is no localized version available.

If the localizable parts of a nib file don't require layout changes, then you may want to use an `IBOutlet` and plug in the localized value in `viewDidLoad`. It's easier to localize programmatic strings than nib files. This is particularly good for handling titles and items such as `UINavigationItem` and `UITabBarItem` that are automatically sized. You can usually get away with this technique for `UIButton` if it stretches across the entire view.

`UILabel` generally requires individual localization because the label will almost certainly need to be resized.

Sentence structure is radically different between languages. This means that you can almost never safely compose a string from parts like this:

```
NSString *intro = @"There was an error deleting";
NSString *num = [NSString stringWithFormat:@"%d", 5];
NSString *tail = @"objects.";
NSString *str = [NSString stringWithFormat:@"%@ %@ %@",
                 intro, num, tail]; // Wrong
```

The problem with this code is that when you translate "There was an error deleting" and "objects" into other languages, you may not be able to glue them together in the same order. Instead, you need to localize the entire string together like this:

```
NSString *format = NSLocalizedString(
            @"There was an error deleting %d objects",
            @"Error when deleting objects.");
NSString *str = [NSString stringWithFormat:format, 5];
```

Some languages have more complex plurals than English. For instance, there may be special word forms for describing two of something versus more than two. Don't assume you can check for greater-than-one and easily determine linguistic plurals. Solving this well can be very difficult, so try to avoid it instead. Don't have special code that tries to add an *s* to the end of plurals because this is almost impossible to translate. A good translator will help you word your messages in ways that translate better in your target languages.

Talk with your localization provider early on to understand its process and how to adjust your development practice to facilitate working with it. Figure 13-1 demonstrates a good approach.

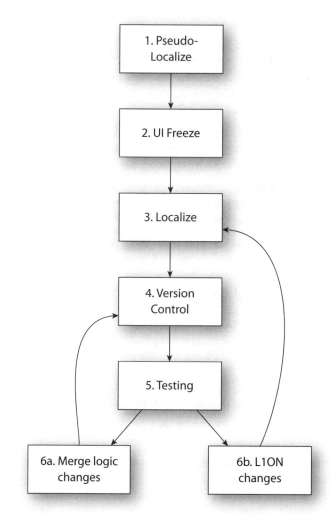

Figure 13-1 Localization workflow

1. **Pseudo-Localize**—During development, it's a good idea to start doing experimental localization to work out any localization bugs early in the process. Pseudo-localization is the process of localizing into a nonsense language. A common nonsense language is one that substitutes all vowels with the letter *x*. For example, "Press here to continue" would become "Prxss hxrx tx cxntxnxx." This kind of "translation" can be done by developers, generally with a simple Perl script, and will make it more obvious where you have used nonlocalized strings. This won't find every problem. In particular, it is not good at discovering strings that are pieced together from other strings, but it can find many simple problems before you pay for real translation services. You will need a language code for this localization. Pick a language that you do not plan to localize your application for. If you're an American English speaker and don't plan to localize for British English, it is particularly useful to use the British English slot for this purpose because you'll still be able to easily read the rest of the iPhone's interface.

2. **UI Freeze**—There should be a clear point in the development cycle that you freeze the UI. After that point, you should strongly avoid any changes that affect localizable resources. Many teams ship a monolingual version of their product at this point and then ship a localization update. That's the easiest approach if your market is tolerant of the delay.

3. **Localize**—You will send your resource files to your localizers and they will send you back localized files. Nib files can be locked in Xcode to prevent changing localizable, nonlocalizable, or all properties. Before sending nib files to a localizer, lock nonlocalizable properties to protect your nib files against changes to connections, class names, and other nonvisible attributes of the nib file. Figure 13-2 shows the lock option in Interface Builder.

4. **Version Control**—As you make changes to your nib files, you will need to keep track of the original files your localizer sent to you. Lock the localizable properties in the nib files (unlocking the nonlocalizable properties). Then put these into a version control system or save them in a separate directory.

5. **Testing**—You'll need to do extensive testing to make sure that everything is correct. Ideally you will have native speakers of each of your localized languages test all your UI elements to ensure they make sense and that there aren't any leftover nonlocalized strings. A good localizer can assist in this.

6a. **Merge Logic Changes**—Certain nib file changes do not affect localization. Changes to connections or class names don't change the layout or the resources. These are logic changes rather than localization (L10N) changes. You can merge the localized nib files like this:

```
ibtool --previous-file ${OLD}/en.lproj/MyNib.nib
       --incremental-file ${OLD}/fr.lproj/MyNib.nib
       --strings-file ${NEW}/fr.lproj/Localizeable.strings
       --localize-incremental
       --write ${NEW}/fr.lproj/MyNib.nib
       ${NEW}/en.lproj/MyNib.nib
```

This computes the nonlocalization changes between the old and new English `MyNib.nib`. It then applies these changes to the old French `MyNib.nib` and writes it as the new French nib file. As long as you keep track of the original files you were sent by the localizer, this works quite well for nonlayout changes, and can be scripted fairly easily.

6b. **L10N Changes**—If you make localization changes such as changing the layout of a localized nib file or changing a string, you'll need to start the process over and send the changes to the localizer. You can reuse the previous string translations, which makes things much cheaper, but it is still a lot of work so avoid making these changes late in the development cycle.

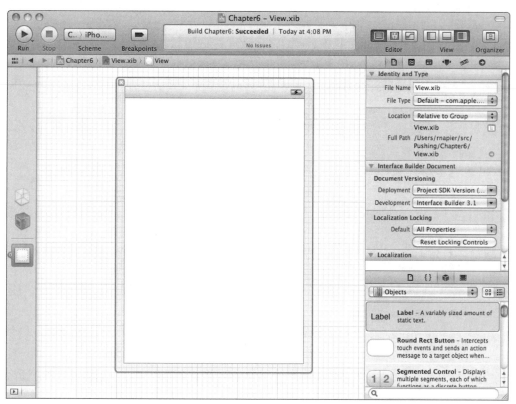

Figure 13-2 Interface Builder localization locking option

Summary

Localization is never an easy subject, but if you work with a good localization partner early and follow the best practices detailed here, you can greatly expand the market for your applications.

Further Reading

Apple Documentation

The following documents are available in the iOS Developer Library at `developer.apple.com` or through the Xcode Documentation and API Reference.

Data Formatting Guide

Internationalization Programming Topics

Locales Programming Guide

## Chapter 14

Selling Past the Sale with In App Purchases

The iOS SDK makes it possible for many developers to make a living independently, and there are a variety of business models from which to choose. The first model is easily understandable (and arguably the most profitable): Make an app and sell it on the App Store. Another model is to release two versions—a free lite version and a pro (paid) version of the same app. Yet another model, probably pioneered by Web 2.0, is advertisement based. Developers use a third-party advertiser's SDK (or iAds) to show advertisements and developers get paid for impressions or click-throughs. While all these augment the earnings of a developer, the first model, selling apps on the App Store, has been by far the most successful model. In App Purchases offer yet another unique way to sell premium content or features on your iOS app. Some apps take advantage of this and make money only through In App Purchases. They fall into a category called freemium apps and they have been quite successful, at least when you look at the top-grossing apps list on the U.S. App Store.

This chapter introduces you to Apple's In App Purchase framework, `StoreKit.framework`, and moves on to a wrapper framework, the MKStoreKit. You learn how to use it to integrate a mini In App Store within your app. This chapter also provides solutions to the problems that developers most commonly face while integrating StoreKit within their apps.

Before You Start

The chapter is broadly divided into two major sections. The first half focuses on creating and customizing products on iTunes Connect, and the second half tackles the programming aspects. You will use MKStoreKit and will go through the features it offers, including how to customize it for every allowed business model. At the end of the chapter you look at the most common issues and problems faced by developers and at solutions to get around them. Throughout the chapter, pay special attention to the shaded boxes, which offer helpful tips and important warnings. The information in those boxes explains what could go awry during implementation when you do something wrong. Let's start the journey.

In App Purchase Products

Products that can be sold using In App Purchases broadly fall under the following four categories: content, functionality, service, and subscription. The latest SDK provides support for all of these. Apple allows four different product types, namely: consumable, non-consumable, auto-renewable subscriptions, and non-renewable subscriptions. In a generic sense, a consumable is a product that depletes when it is used. A nonconsumable, on the other hand, is a product that is available for use any number of times after purchase. Your printer is an example of a non-consumable while the ink it uses is a common example of a consumable. Subscriptions, both auto-renewable and non-renewable, are analogous to real world subscriptions. You should match the following category of product to one of these four based on your business model.

- **Content**—Products that are categorized as content include digital books, magazines, additional level packs, music, ringtones, and a variety of other data. Content can be sold as either consumable or non-consumable depending on your business model. Thinking from the user's perspective, content is generally considered non-consumable. For example, when a user gets a book, it's your responsibility as a developer to remember his purchase and make it available to him for free. The SDK, in most cases, provides this feature for free.

- **Functionality**—Products that are categorized as functionality mainly include locked features. For example, a task manager app can allow users to create a maximum of n tasks; to create tasks after that limit, the user has to unlock by paying a fee. Functionality is almost always considered non-consumable.

- **Service**—Products that are categorized as service are mostly functionality that incurs a recurring expense to the developer. Service is very similar to the functionality category, except that it involves serious computation power and is done on a remote server. A classic example of this is push notifications. A Twitter client, for instance, may provide push notifications as a consumable selling, say a 1,000 notifications for a dollar.

  Service can also be subscription based if your business model requires it to be so.

- **Subscription**—Products that are categorized as subscription are mostly content or service. Subscriptions usually provide the said content or service over a period of time as opposed to at the time of purchase. For example, a Twitter client may provide unlimited push notifications as a subscription costing 99 cents every three months.

Treating a product as a consumable or a subscription or a non-consumable is up to the business owner.

> Subscriptions were originally available in iOS 3.0, but they were complicated to use and the burden of renewing and/or restoring them to other devices relied on the developer. As such, adoption was low and very few developers used this. With iOS 4.3, Apple introduced a new kind of product called *auto-renewable subscription*, for which restoring and renewing subscriptions happens automatically and is taken care of by Apple. From now on, you should almost always use auto-renewable subscriptions. Use the older subscription style only if your business already has proper server-side subscription handling in place and customers are already using it.

Prohibited Items

The previous section explained about the products that you can sell via In App Purchase. While Apple is okay with most kinds of business models, there are a couple kinds of items that you cannot sell via the App Store as of this writing.

The first kind of item (and this is arguably the most important point to remember) you cannot sell through In App Purchases is physical goods or services. For example, if you develop a wallpaper app, you can sell digital wallpapers, but you cannot sell printed posters of the same wallpapers through In App Purchase. Similarly, if you are a hotel owner and make an app for booking reservations, you cannot collect reservation fees or booking fees through In App Purchase.

The second kind of item that is not allowed is *intermediate currency*. If you make a music subscription app, you have to sell music directly. You cannot sell "points" and allow the user to download music for those points. Subscription passes, prepurchasable coupons, and anything that is not offering the product at the time of purchase is not allowed.

> **Warning:** There might be some app that already does this on the App Store. That doesn't automatically entitle you. You run the risk of being rejected by Apple. If you see an app that sells an item that is prohibited by rule, chances are that it slipped past the App Store review. Such apps risk the chance of getting approved during every subsequent product update.

Lotteries or sweepstakes are allowed in some cases, if the developer is permitted by law to run a lottery business. Again, you can only sell those apps in countries where you have the legal right to do so. Having a lottery app on the U.S. App Store doesn't automatically entitle you to sell the same app on the U.K. App Store or the Australian App Store. You might need to submit additional documents to the Apple review process along with your app.

> Apple's developer documentation doesn't contain any information on what is allowed and what is not allowed. Read the *App Store Review Guidelines* on `developer.apple.com` and your iOS developer license agreement to understand what is and is not permitted.

Rethinking Your Business Model

All items that you are planning to sell through In App Purchase (especially content) have to go through Apple's formal review process, which usually take a week and sometimes longer. Remember this when coming up with your business plan.

If you are making an app that provides premium wallpapers for download, you probably won't be able to sell a "wallpaper of the day" through In App Purchases—at least not easily. You can, however, think of different business plans, like offering a free download for any wallpaper of the day if the user is subscribed to a premium membership. Another suggestion is to submit your app's "wallpaper of the day" for at least the next 30 days so that you have full control of releasing it on the correct dates. Ensure that your buffer is bigger than the worst-case approval times.

Finally, every product you submit to the App Store needs to be configured on iTunes Connect. This configuration might take anywhere from a couple of minutes to an hour (if complex screenshots are needed). If you are selling digital books or any other digital content like wallpapers, it might not be feasible (timewise) to configure every product on iTunes Connect. Moreover, there is a limit of 5,000 Stock Keeping Units (SKUs) that you can add to your product via In App Purchases. A recommended alternative in such a case is to make them consumable.

At this point you should have decided whether to sell your In App product as a consumable, non-consumable, or subscription.

Setting Up Products on iTunes Connect

Implementing In App Purchases in your app is 20% configuration, 10% getting the right business model for your app, and 70% implementation. With MKStoreKit that 70% coding reduces to somewhere near zero. However, the addition of new types of products has made configuration confusing and changes to rules and lack of proper documentation on what is acceptable and what is not acceptable has made choosing the right business model difficult, so configuration remains the most challenging aspect of the integration.

This section walks you through the steps involved in setting up products on iTunes Connect. I assume that you are already signed up with the iOS developer program and have the necessary credentials to log in to various portals like iOS developer program portal and iTunes Connect.

I refer to the iOS developer program portal and iTunes Connect throughout the next few pages. The following links will be of help. The URLs are pretty easy to remember:

iOS developer program portal—`http://developer.apple.com/devcenter/ios/index.action`

iTunes Connect—`http://itunesconnect.apple.com`

Step 1: Create a New App ID for Your App

Every app that requires In App Purchases should have an App ID that is unique to the application. The ID cannot include a wild card character (*). The recommended convention for this is reverse DNS notation. Here are a couple of examples:

```
com.mycompany.myapp.levelpack1
org.mycompany.myapp.levelpack2
```

To create a new App ID, log in to iOS Developer Program portal and navigate to the iOS Provisioning Portal, as shown in Figure 14-1.

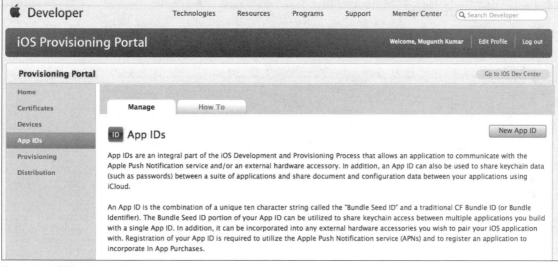

Figure 14-1 iOS Provisioning Portal

Click the New App ID button and follow the wizard to create an App ID. Ensure that you use a fully qualified App ID without any wild card characters.

> **Warning:** A wild card character in your App ID will prevent you from adding products for In App Purchase later. If you already have a product on App Store and want to integrate In App Purchases in the next release, but the live app isn't using a unique App ID, it will still work, but your users will not be notified about this update automatically through the App Store; they have to download it again. To push update notifications, the App Store relies on the fact that subsequent updates to a product use the same App ID and incrementing version numbers. While there are workarounds to associate a new App ID to an existing Bundle ID (Apple Technical Note QA1680), I would still recommend using a unique product ID for each app you develop. As of this writing, with iOS 5, there are several features that rely on a unique App ID including but not limited to push notifications, Game Center integration, and iCloud integration. If your app might use any one of these features (even in a future release), you should use a unique App ID from the beginning.

Step 2: Generate Provisioning Profiles

In App Purchases cannot be run on a simulator; you need a device to run and test them. This means you should create a provisioning profile for running your app on a device. That's the second step. Go to the fifth link on the left navigation pane in the iOS Provisioning Portal. This step is done in exactly same way as for any other app. Remember to choose the same App ID that you created in step 1.

Step 3: Create the App's Product Entry

Before you create In App Purchase products, you need to have an app that sells your In App Purchase products. Let's start by creating an application on iTunes Connect. Open iTunes Connect and click Manage Your Applications. That's the first link in the right column, as shown in Figure 14-2.

Sales and Trends
Preview or download your daily and weekly sales information here.

Contracts, Tax, and Banking
Manage your contracts, tax, and banking information.

Payments and Financial Reports
View and download your monthly financial reports and payments.

Manage Users
Create and manage both iTunes Connect and In App Purchase Test User accounts.

Manage Your Applications
Add, view, and manage your applications in the iTunes Store.

Contact Us
Having a problem uploading your application? Can't find a Finance Report? Use our Contact Us system to find an answer to your question or to generate a question to an iTunes Rep

Download the Developer Guide.

(?) FAQs Review our answers to common inquiries.

Figure 14-2 iTunes Connect home page

Create a new application from the Manage Your Applications link. It's most important for you to choose your Bundle ID correctly. Choose the App ID you created in step 1 as your Bundle ID here, as shown in Figure 14-3.

The Bundle ID and App ID are the same. Apple just uses a different name here.

Later in your app you query the App Store for information about your product. This information includes the price in the currency of the user's App Store account, the localized product name, and the product description. Making a mistake in this step means that you will not be able to get detailed information about an In App Product programmatically later. The product identifiers will be returned as Invalid Product Ids, described later in this chapter. This is because your In App Purchase products are tied to an app using the Bundle ID (App ID).

An app with a specific Bundle ID cannot sell In App Purchase products that are meant for a different app that uses a different Bundle ID.

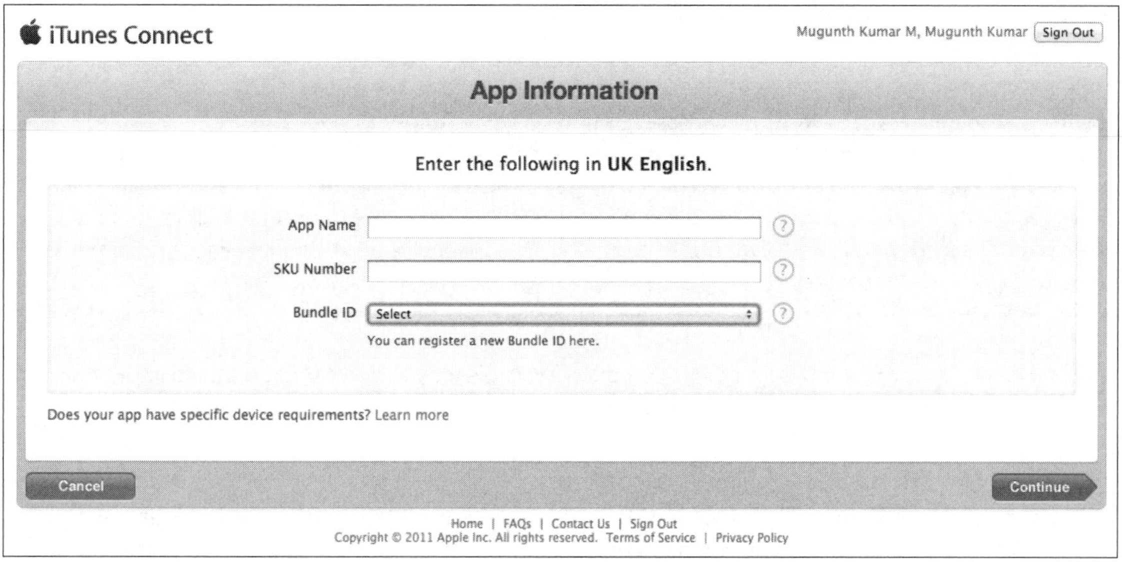

iTunes Connect

Mugunth Kumar M, Mugunth Kumar [Sign Out]

App Information

Enter the following in **UK English**.

App Name

SKU Number

Bundle ID [Select ⬧] (?)
You can register a new Bundle ID here.

Does your app have specific device requirements? Learn more

[Cancel]   [Continue]

Home | FAQs | Contact Us | Sign Out
Copyright © 2011 Apple Inc. All rights reserved. Terms of Service | Privacy Policy

Figure 14-3 New application form

Step 4: Create the In App Purchase Product Entries

Click on the app and you will see a screen like that shown in Figure 14-4.

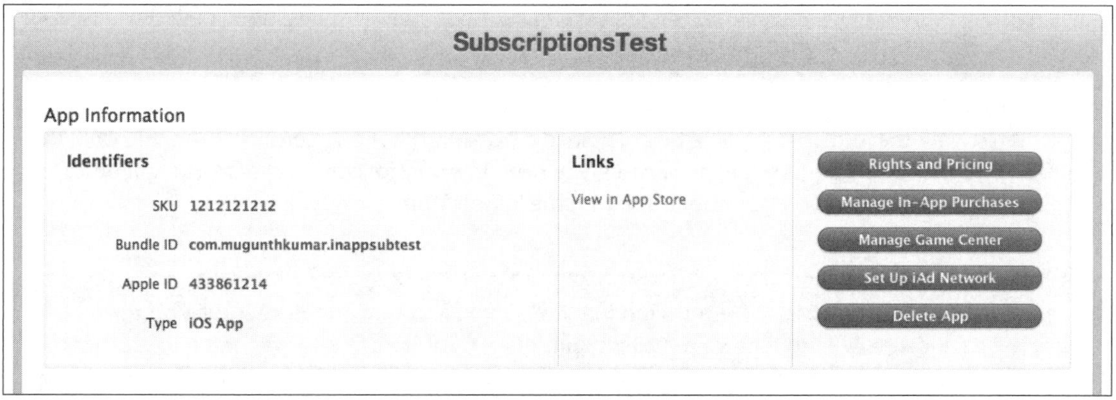

SubscriptionsTest

App Information

Identifiers

SKU 1212121212

Bundle ID com.mugunthkumar.inappsubtest

Apple ID 433861214

Type iOS App

Links

View in App Store

[Rights and Pricing]

[Manage In-App Purchases]

[Manage Game Center]

[Set Up iAd Network]

[Delete App]

Figure 14-4 App information

Click the Manage In-App Purchases link to create your first In App Purchase product.

> If you don't see the Manage In-App Purchases option on your iTunes Connect, be sure your iTunes Connect account has Admin privileges. Then, check that your Contract Tax and Banking information is correct. If this is your first app and you haven't yet submitted your tax documents and/or haven't accepted the Paid Applications Contract, you will not see this link on the page. In that case, correct the situation appropriately and wait; Apple normally takes a week or two to approve your documents, depending on your location.

On the first page, you see four different types of products available for you to create. You should know what kind of product you are creating (discussed earlier in the chapter). Choose that product type and proceed.

> To create the Product ID for your In App products, I recommend suffixing the product identifier with your Bundle ID. For example, if your Bundle ID is `com.mycompany.myapp`, your In App product ID would be `com.mycompany.myapp.inapp`. This will ensure that product IDs across your other apps don't clash with each other.

Consumables, Non-consumables, Non-renewing Subscriptions

For all product types except auto-renewable subscriptions, you have to enter a product identifier and choose its price tier. Add a description that shows up when the user buys your product. If your product is multilingual, add descriptions in all supported languages in this page.

You now have to add a screenshot of the product (yes, that's for the product you have not yet created) before you can submit the form. For the time being, upload a 320×480 iPhone screenshot. This screenshot is only for iOS App Store review purposes. In most cases, you need this only for content. For features or other consumables, it's okay to upload a screenshot displaying the In App Store.

> Nonrenewing subscriptions are not recommended after Apple announced the new auto-renewing subscriptions. Functionally, auto-renewing subscriptions offer everything that nonrenewing subscriptions offer and add features like automatic renewal without user intervention, and restoring subscriptions on customers' other devices.

Auto-renewable Subscriptions

Auto-renewable subscriptions are slightly different. You create a subscription family and add duration of the subscription to that family. This allows you to create the same magazine subscription with different durations. For instance, you can create a weekly subscription at $5 or a monthly subscription at $20 or a yearly subscription at $300. Other options within a subscription family are similar to consumables.

Step 5: Generating the Shared Secret

For auto-renewable subscriptions, you need to do one more very important step: Generate a shared secret.

In the App Information page (shown in Figure 14-4), click the Manage In App Purchases link. On this page, you will see a link titled, "View or generate a shared secret." Copy the shared secret safely. You will need it when you write the real code.

Step 6: Creating Test User Accounts

The final step is to create user accounts that you will use for testing In App Purchases after implemention. You can do this later, after implementation, but doing it now completes all steps needed for configuring In App Purchases.

To create test user accounts, open the iTunes Connect home page (see Figure 14-2) and click Manage Users. You will see two links, one for creating an iTunes Connect user and another for creating a Test User. Click the second link and create a Test User. This should be fairly simple.

That completes the configuration part of In App Purchasing. If you have done all the steps correctly, you have completed 30% of the In App Purchase integration. The remaining 70% is the real code, which you dive into next.

In App Purchase Implementation

The configuration of In App Purchases was hard, and so is the programming involved in the implementation. In App Purchase implementation requires you to complete some tedious coding. The following is a comprehensive list of the important tasks that you have to do for implementing In App Purchases in your app.

- First and foremost, your app could be closed (probably by a phone call) while a transaction is in progress. Given that transactions can continue outside of your app, you should have a Store Observer class that initializes at application launch and receives any purchases made while the app is in the background.

- Remember the actual number of consumable items purchased.

- Remember the non-consumable purchase and allow the user to restore it on his other devices.

- Remembering these purchases should be done securely using iOS keychain.

- Post nonrenewing subscriptions to your server and "remember" them there. You should also have the capability to restore them on any other device when the user logs into your app from another device.

- Consumable contents can be occasionally delivered digitally from your server. In that case, your server should be able to verify the authenticity of the receipt and provide content. This also means that your iOS app should post App Store purchase receipts to your server before it starts downloading content.

- Verify whether auto-renewing subscription receipts are still valid. Even though auto-renewing subscriptions are renewed automatically without manual user intervention, you are still required to check this because a user might have cancelled the subscription. A cancelled subscription remains valid only until the end of the current subscription period. This means that you as a developer should remember purchases, purchase receipts, and verify the receipts' validity, probably during app launch. If they are no longer valid, stop providing the content.

- To validate auto-renewing subscriptions, post your receipt and the shared secret you generated in step 5 of the previous section to the App Store, parse the returned JSON (JavaScript Object Notation), and get the subscription's latest purchase date.

- The `StoreKit.framework` doesn't tell you when an auto-renewable subscription ends. Instead, the API returns the actual date of the latest receipt. From this date, you should calculate the actual date of expiry.

- Display localized product prices and descriptions on your Store View Controller.

While this might sound complicated, MKStoreKit wraps most of these functionalities. Next you see how to add MKStoreKit into your app and build it.

Introduction to MKStoreKit

MKStoreKit is an open source framework (In App Purchases Tutorial | MKBlog, 2011) that makes integrating In App Purchases simpler. As of this writing, the latest version is 4.0 and that's the version used in this chapter. You can download the source code for this from the book's website or from Github (see the "Further Reading" section at the end of this chapter).

Why MKStoreKit?

MKStoreKit automatically takes care of the following items you saw in the list in the preceding section.

- When your app is closed while a transaction is in progress, MKStoreKit automatically tracks this, continues to observe StoreKit delegates, and remembers any purchases made outside of your app. This takes care of the first item.

- For consumables and nonconsumables, MKStoreKit automatically remembers your purchases in iOS keychain. Purchases are remembered using your product identifiers as the key so in most cases you don't have to customize anything here. Items 2, 3, and 4 are thus taken care of automatically.

- The MKSKProduct class posts nonrenewing subscriptions to your server. So the fifth item is taken care of, if you do the server customization with the PHP code that comes with MKStoreKit. You learn about this later in the "Customizing MKStoreKit" section.

- For consumables or any content you deliver digitally from your server, you have to post the App Store receipt to your server. The server should verify the receipt and validate it. If it's valid, it should deliver the content to your app. The `MKSKProduct` class takes care of this in tandem with some server configuration, which you learn about later in this chapter. This handles item 6.

- For auto-renewing subscriptions, you need to verify the latest receipt when your app is launched and disable access to content when the user has cancelled the subscription. The `MKSKSubscriptionProduct` class does this automatically, including parsing the response JSON from the App Store and verifying that the subscriptions are still valid; it notifies you via NSNotificationCenter. You should tell MKStoreKit how many days a subscription is valid. You learn how to do this later in this chapter. This takes care of items 7, 8, and 9.

- MKStoreKit has helper methods that return your product descriptions and price formatted in the local currency of the user. That takes care of the last item.

Customizing MKStoreKit to work with your app takes less than 25 lines of code. In some cases it should be less than ten lines of code.

Now, before you actually integrate the framework, it's always good to know how it works internally. The next section explains this.

Design of MKStoreKit

MKStoreKit uses blocks instead of delegates to notify you of product purchases. (You learn more about blocks in Chapter 16.) Other notifications like subscription expiry are posted to `NSNotificationCenter`. The framework comprises a main singleton class, the `MKStoreManager`, and several other support classes listed here:

- **MKStoreManager.h and MKStoreManager.m**—This is the main singleton class that handles most of the implementation. You have to initialize this singleton in your AppDelegate's `applicationDidFinish LaunchingWithOptions:` method.

- **MKStoreObserver.h and MKStoreObserver.m**—This is the class that implements of the `StoreKit`. framework's `SKPaymentTransactionObserver`. It notifies product purchases, or restores notifications to `MKStoreManager` singleton.

- **MKSKProduct.h and MKSKProduct.m**—This is an internal class used by MKStoreKit to validate purchases. `MKStoreManager` uses this class to communicate with your server to check whether the receipt is valid and the actual product can be downloaded. This is used only for Server Product Model, where you verify receipts on server and deliver content digitally.

- **MKSKSubscriptionProduct.h and MKSKSubscriptionProduct.m**—This is another internal class used by MKStoreKit to validate your auto-renewable subscription purchases. `MKStoreManager` uses this class to communicate with your server to check if the latest subscription receipts are still valid. If the user has cancelled his subscription, this class notifies `MKStoreManager` that the subscription is no longer valid and `MKStoreManager` posts a notification. You have to observe these notifications (shown below) on your view controller and enable or disable your Subscribe buttons accordingly. If your app doesn't use auto-renewable subscriptions, you don't have to do this.

  ```
  kSubscriptionsPurchasedNotification
  kSubscriptionsInvalidNotification
  ```

- **MKStoreKitConfigs.h and MKStoreKitConfigs.plist**—These two files in the framework require customization based on your app. You will learn about customizing them later in this chapter.

- **Remembering purchases**—MKStoreKit uses iOS keychain to remember a purchase automatically when it's purchased.

Customizing MKStoreKit

Two important files in MKStoreKit that you should change are

- `MKStoreKitConfigs.h`
- `MKStoreKitConfigs.plist`

The plist file contains the list of products that you configured on iTunes Connect. You add your products under the corresponding keys in the plist depending on the product type. You should add your consumables under the consumable key, nonconsumables under the nonconsumable key, and subscriptions under the subscriptions key. Every type of key has its own suboptions. You learn how to configure them later in this chapter.

Initializing MKStoreKit

Before you configure MKStoreKit, initialize it in your AppDelegate's `applicationDidFinishLaunching WithOptions:` method. This ensures that the StoreObservers are initialized properly to receive transactions completed outside of the app. Just initialize the singleton by calling the following in your AppDelegate:

```
[MKStoreManager sharedManager];
```

Configuring for Use with Server Product Model

When you sell content in your app and allow users to stream or download the content from your server, you should use the Server Product Model. In the Server Product Model, the iOS app makes a purchase and sends the transaction receipt over to the server for verification. The server then verifies the receipt with Apple's receipt verification server and if the receipt is valid, redirects the request to the requested content.

Server Setup

MKStoreKit comes with server code in PHP ready to verify receipts from the server. Copy the Server Code directory and open it up for access. Copy the public URL for this directory. Let's assume that it can be accessed at this location:

```
http://api.example.com/servercode
```

Now go back to your iOS source, open the file `MKStoreKitConfigs.h`, and locate these lines:

```
#define SERVER_PRODUCT_MODEL 0
#define OWN_SERVER nil
#define REVIEW_ALLOWED 1
```

Set the `OWN_SERVER` value to `@"http://api.example.com/servercode"`.

You are all set. MKStoreKit will ping the `featureCheck.php` endpoint in this directory to verify receipts and remember the purchase only when the server says receipts are valid. Receipt validation is done by posting the receipt to Apple's receipt validation URL:

```
https://buy.itunes.apple.com/verifyReceipt
```

For sandbox testing, you should use

```
https://sandbox.itunes.apple.com/verifyReceipt
```

The server code automatically switches this based on the configuration you defined. The default implementation of `featureCheck.php` returns plain strings—YES or NO—based on whether the receipts are valid or not. You might need to modify it to return in JSONs along with the URL of the content location.

Configuring for Use with Consumables

In a generic sense, a consumable is a product that depletes when it is used. Printer ink is a common example. In App Purchases consumables behave the same way. When a user purchases a consumable product, it's stored on the device and stays there until he uses it. You are not obliged to restore consumables on other devices. When implementing consumables, you often encounter a business case where bulk purchases are subsidized to the user, just like real world consumables.

For example, you might have two products in your game, a small box of ammo containing one hundred bullets at 99 cents, and a larger box containing a thousand at $5.99. Within your game, both the products are synonymous. However, SKU wise, they are treated differently and they cost differently. To implement this model, MKStoreKit allows you to specify names for your products. That way you can tell MKStoreKit to treat them separately during purchase, but treat them the same when consumed. Essentially, this means that buying either of the products increases the count of the same item. To configure MKStoreKit this way, use the suboptions inside the consumable key in `MKStoreKitConfigs.plist` illustrated in Figure 14-5.

▼ Consumables	Diction...	(1 item)
▼ com.mugunthkumar.inappsubtest.consumable1	Diction...	(2 items)
Count	Number	500
Name	String	EggBasket

Figure 14-5 Configuring consumables in MKStoreKit

You add the product identifier of every consumable within the Consumables dictionary. Every product has a Name and Count. From the previous example (the ammo box case), imagine you have two products: `com.myapp.mygame.ammopackSmall` and `com.myapp.mygame.ammopackLarge`. The Count key will let you set the count of the virtual consumable for this product purchase. The Name key will let you set the real name of the consumable. MKStoreKit normally remembers purchases with product identifier. But for consumables, it uses the Name key because multiple SKUs can actually mean the same within your app.

Now, in the course of your game/app, if the user consumes your product, you should first check if it's available by calling these methods:

```
- (BOOL) canConsumeProduct:(NSString*) productName quantity:(int)
quantity;
- (BOOL) consumeProduct:(NSString*) productName quantity:(int) quantity;
```

`consumeProduct` will properly deduct the quantity of the product consumed from the purchased quantity and stores the remaining available quantity in the keychain, all automatically.

Configuring for Use with Auto-renewable Subscriptions

Auto-renewable subscription configuration is very similar to consumables configuration. The first step is to specify your shared secret. Copy the shared secret you generated earlier in the chapter and paste it here in the file `MKStoreKitConfigs.h`:

```
#warning Shared Secret Missing Ignore this warning if you don't use auto-
renewable subscriptions
#define kSharedSecret @"<FILL IN YOUR SHARED SECRET HERE>"
```

You can now remove the `#warning` line. Also, if you don't use auto-renewable subscriptions (and thus don't have a shared secret), you can ignore this warning. Just remove the `#warning` line.

Now open the plist file and as you would for consumables, instead of specifying the count, specify the duration of the subscription. Now, on your view controllers that display the store, you should observe the `kSubscriptionsPurchasedNotification` and/or `kSubscriptionsInvalidNotification` and enable or disable your subscribe buttons accordingly.

Making the Purchase

Now that you have configured MKStoreKit, making the real purchase is very simple. It's just a single method call like this:

```
    [[MKStoreManager sharedManager] buyFeature:@"com.myapp.myfeature"
           onComplete:^(NSString*) purchasedProduct
{
  // provide the content for the product "purchasedProduct".
}
        onCancelled:^
{
  // optionally display an error
}];
```

Once you configure MKStoreKit properly, it takes just a single method call to initiate a purchase. Remembering the purchase is automatically done for you. To check if a product has been purchased previously, you can call this method:

```
[MKStoreManager isProductPurchased:@"com.myapp.feature1"];
```

This returns a `Boolean` that states if the product is purchased or not. Restoring purchases is done with another one-liner. Read the `MKStoreManger.h` file to see the functionalities exposed by MKStoreKit.

Now that's fewer than 10 lines to get it all running, and maybe another 15 lines of configuration, as I promised at the beginning of the chapter.

Testing Your In App Purchase

Now that you have implemented In App Purchasing, let's go ahead and test if they work. You will need the credentials of the test user account you created earlier in this chapter for testing. Before you start, open the settings app on the device you will be using for testing and tap on the Store menu. Log out of the App Store and ensure that no user is logged into the store.

Run the app on a device and initiate a purchase. You are prompted to enter or create a new iTunes account or use an existing account. Choose to use an existing account and enter the Test User name and password you created previously. The App Store will now ask you to confirm the purchase of your In App Purchase product. Tap on Buy (or Subscribe), and your product is now purchased. You have successfully completed the In App Purchase integration in your app.

All this sounds good, but what happens when there is a problem? Let's see about some quick troubleshooting techniques in the next section.

Troubleshooting

Even after all the explanation on this chapter, In App Purchases remains one of the most difficult frameworks to troubleshoot.

Invalid Product IDs

The most common problem occurs when the App Store returns your product as invalid. If you have been following the chapter closely, reading every tip and warning, you shouldn't encounter this. However, the problem could happen if you have any of the following issues.

- The product Bundle ID in `Info.plist` file doesn't match the App ID you created.

- Your contract and tax statements are not yet submitted and or you have not yet accepted the iOS developer paid applications contract. To correct these issues, go to iTunes Connect and click the Contracts, Tax, and Banking link. It's very important to check this when you submit your first app.

- Jailbroken devices sometimes don't work well with the App Store. An app called AppSync from Cydia seems to be the cause of most problems associated with In App Purchasing. In App Purchases are best tested with a device running an unmodified operating system.

Sometimes, even after you ensure that none of these issues is a problem, the App Store still indicates that your products are invalid. This happens more often to non-U.S. based developers. Wait several hours before retrying (see *"Retrieving Store Information"* in the Apple Developer Documentation, 2011). Apple uses distributed servers and it might take several hours to migrate the products you created from the U.S. servers to other mirror servers near your country.

Cannot Connect to iTunes Store

The other common problem is when you get the message "Cannot connect to iTunes store: Code: -1003." This happens when your firewall blocks iTunes. Test the In App Purchases by connecting to a different network or ensure if you have proper Internet connectivity.

You Have Already Purchased This Product, but It's Still Not Downloaded

This error is common when you work with consumables. It happens mostly when you tap on the Buy button too often. The workaround is to disable the Buy button once the purchase is initiated and reenable it after the transaction completes. Follow the interaction pattern similar to the built-in App Store.

If your problem is still not solved, the old school method of deleting the app and redoing all the steps often works.

Summary

In App Purchases, although tricky to implement, offer an innovative and unique way to monetize your apps. Carefully deciding on your business model and implementing In App Purchases can vastly increase the money you make from the App Store. A quick look at the top-grossing apps on the U.S. App Store shows that at least 25% follow the freemium model whereby the app is free but content and features are provided through In App Purchases. This clearly proves that freemium is successful on the App Store. With frameworks like MKStoreKit minimizing your coding efforts, why not give it a try?

Further Reading

Apple Documentation

The following documents are available in the iOS Developer Library at `developer.apple.com` or through the Xcode Documentation and API Reference.

App Store Review Guidelines

In App Purchase Programming Guide

Retrieving Store Information

Blogs

iPhone Tutorial: In App Purchases | MKBlog
`http://blog.mugunthkumar.com/coding/iphone-tutorial---in-app-purchases/`

MKStoreKit 4.0 – Supporting Auto Renewable Subscriptions | MKBlog
`http://blog.mugunthkumar.com/coding/mkstorekit-4-0-supporting-auto-renewable-subscriptions/`

Other Resources

MKStoreKit on Github
`https://github.com/MugunthKumar/MKStoreKit`

Can't use in-app purchase: This is not a test user account / Boxcar support
`http://help.boxcar.io/kb/general/cant-use-in-app-purchase-this-is-not-a-test-user-account`

Part IV

Pushing the Limits

Chapter 15

Cocoa's Biggest Trick: Key-Value Coding and Observing

There is no magic in Cocoa. It's just C. But there's one particular trick that borders on magic, and that's key-value observing (KVO). This chapter explores how and when to use KVO, as well as its nonmagical cousin, key-value coding (KVC).

Key-value coding is a mechanism that allows you to access an object's properties by name rather than by calling explicit accessors. This allows you to determine property bindings at run time rather than at compile time. For instance, you can request the value of the property named by the string variable `someProperty` using `[object valueForKey:someProperty]`. You can set the value of `someProperty` using `[object setValue:someValue forKey:someProperty]`. This indirection allows you to determine the specific properties to access at run time rather than at compile time, allowing more flexible and reusable objects. To get this flexibility, your objects need to name their methods in specific ways. This naming convention is called key-value coding, and in this chapter you learn these rules to create indirect getters and setters, access items in collections, and manage KVC with nonobjects. You also learn to implement advanced KVC techniques such as Higher Order Messaging and collection operators.

If your objects follow the KVC naming rules, then you can also make use of *key-value observing*. KVO is a mechanism for notifying objects of changes in the properties of other objects. Cocoa has several observer mechanisms including delegation and `NSNotification`, but KVO is the fastest. The observed object does not have to include any special code to notify observers, and if there are no observers, KVO has no run time cost. The KVO system adds the notification code only when the class is actually observed. This makes it very attractive for situations where performance is at a premium. In this chapter you learn how to use KVO with properties and collections, and the trick Cocoa uses to make KVO so transparent.

All code samples in this chapter can be found in the online files for Chapter 15 in the projects `KVC`, `KVC-Collection`, and `KVO`.

Key-Value Coding

Key-value coding is a standard part of Cocoa that allows your properties to be accessed by name ("key") rather than by calling an explicit accessor. It allows other parts of the system to ask for "the property named `foo`" rather than calling `foo` directly. This permits dynamic access by parts of the system that do not know your keys at compile time. This particularly supports nib file loading and Core Data in iOS. On Mac, KVC is a fundamental part of the AppleScript interface.

The following code listings demonstrate how KVC works with an example of a cell that can display any object using `valueForKeyPath:`.

KVCTableViewCell.h (KVC)

```
@interface KVCTableViewCell : UITableViewCell
- (id)initWithReuseIdentifier:(NSString*)identifier;

// Object to display.
@property (nonatomic, readwrite, strong) id target;

// Name of property of object to display
@property (nonatomic, readwrite, copy) NSString *property;
@end
```

KVCTableViewCell.m (KVC)

```
@implementation KVCTableViewCell
@synthesize target=target_;
@synthesize property=property_;

- (BOOL)isReady {
  // Only display something if configured
  return (self.target && [self.property length] > 0);
}

- (void)update {
  NSString *text;
  if (self.isReady) {
    // Ask the target for the value of its property that has the
    // name given in self.property. Then convert that into a human
    // readable string
    id value = [self.target valueForKeyPath:self.property];
    text = [value description];
  }
  else {
    text = @"";
  }
  self.textLabel.text = text;
}

- (id)initWithReuseIdentifier:(NSString *)identifier {
  return [self initWithStyle:UITableViewCellStyleDefault
          reuseIdentifier:identifier];
}

- (void)setTarget:(id)aTarget {
  target_ = aTarget;
  [self update];
```

```
}

- (void)setProperty:(NSString *)aProperty {
  property_ = aProperty;
  [self update];
}
@end
```

KVCTableViewController.m (KVC)

```
@implementation KVCTableViewController

- (NSInteger)tableView:(UITableView *)tableView
 numberOfRowsInSection:(NSInteger)section {
  return 100;
}

- (UITableViewCell *)tableView:(UITableView *)tableView
        cellForRowAtIndexPath:(NSIndexPath *)indexPath {

  static NSString *CellIdentifier = @"KVCTableViewCell";

  KVCTableViewCell *cell = [tableView
        dequeueReusableCellWithIdentifier:CellIdentifier];

  if (cell == nil) {
    cell = [[KVCTableViewCell alloc]
            initWithReuseIdentifier:CellIdentifier];
    // You want the "intValue" of the row's NSNumber.
    // The property will be the same for every row, so you set it
    // here in the cell construction section.
    cell.property = @"intValue";
  }

  // Each row's target is an NSNumber representing that integer
  // Since each row has a different object (NSNumber), you set
  // the target here, in the cell configuration section.
  cell.target = [NSNumber numberWithInt:indexPath.row];

  return cell;
}

@end
```

This example is quite simple, displaying 100 rows of integers, but imagine if KVCTableViewCell had animation effects or special selection behaviors. You could apply those to arbitrary objects without the object or the cell needing to know anything about the other. That's the ultimate goal of a good model-view-controller (MVC) design, which is the heart of Cocoa's architecture. (See Chapter 4 for more information on the MVC pattern.)

The `update` method of `KVCTableViewCell` demonstrates `valueForKeyPath:`, which is the main KVC method you use in this example. Here is the important section:

```
id value = [self.target valueForKeyPath:self.property];
text = [value description];
```

In this example, `self.property` is the string `"intValue"` and `self.target` is an `NSNumber` object representing the row index. So the first line is effectively the same as this code:

```
id value = [NSNumber numberWithInt:[self.target intValue]];
```

The call to `numberWithInt:` is automatically inserted by `valueForKeyPath:`, which automatically converts number types (`int`, `float`, etc.) into `NSNumber` objects, and all other nonobject types (structs, pointers) into `NSValue` objects.

While this example utilizes an `NSNumber`, the key take-away is that `target` could be any object, and `property` could be the name of any property of `target`.

Setting Values with KVC

KVC can also modify writable properties using `setValue:forKey:`. For example, the following two lines are roughly identical:

```
cell.property = @"intValue";
[cell setValue:@"intValue" forKey:@"property"];
```

Both of these will call `setProperty:`, as long as `property` is an object. See the section "KVC and Nonobjects" for a discussion of how to handle `nil` and nonobject properties.

Methods that modify properties are generally called *mutators* in the Apple documentation.

Traversing Properties

You may have noticed that KVC methods have `key` and `keyPath` versions. For instance, there is `valueForKey:` and `valueForKeyPath:`. The difference between a key and a key path is that a key path can have nested relationships, separated by a period. The `valueForKeyPath:` method traverses the relationships. For instance, the following two lines are roughly identical:

```
[[self department] name];
[self valueForKeyPath:@"department.name"];
```

On the other hand, `valueForKey:@"department.name"` would try to retrieve the property `department.name`, which in many cases would throw an exception.

The `keyPath` version is more flexible, while the `key` version is slightly faster. If the key is passed to me, I generally use `valueForKeyPath:` to provide the most flexibility to my caller. If the key is hard-coded, I generally use `valueForKey:`.

KVC and Collections

Object properties can be one-to-one or one-to-many. One-to-many properties are either ordered (arrays) or unordered (sets).

Immutable ordered (NSArray) and unordered (NSSet) collection properties can be fetched normally using valueForKey:. If you have an NSArray property called items, then valueForKey:@"items" returns it as you'd expect. But there are more flexible ways of managing this.

For this example, you create a table of multiples of two. The data model object only keeps track of the number of rows, not the actual results, but it provides the results as though it were an NSArray. This project is available as KVC-Collection in the sample code. Here is how to create it:

▨ Create a new iPhone project in Xcode using the Model-Detail Application template with storyboard and automatic reference counting.

▨ Select MainStoryboard.storyboard and remove the "Master View Controller" and "Detail View Controller."

▨ Drag a view controller from the library and set its class to RootViewController. Click-drag from the navigation controller to your new view controller and set the relationship to rootViewController.

▨ Add labels and buttons as shown in Figure 15-1. The hash marks (###) are separate labels from the titles.

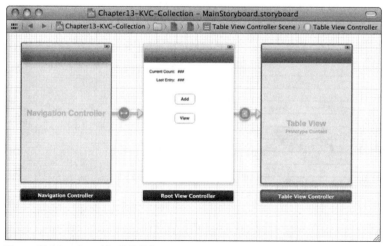

Figure 15-1 Storyboard for KVC-Collection project

▨ Delete the MasterViewController and DetailViewController source files.

▨ Add a new source file using the UIViewController template and name it RootViewController. Do not use a XIB for its user interface.

In the storyboard, select the root view controller and show the assistant editor. Click-drag from the labels and buttons to `RootViewController.h` to create the outlets shown in Figure 15-2. For the "View" button, click-drag to the table view controller and select the push segue.

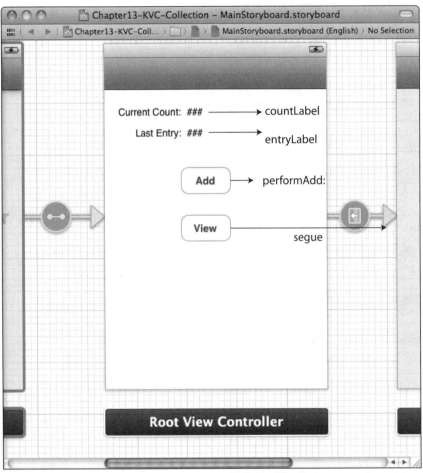

Figure 15-2 KVC-Collection Root View Controller layout

The following code implements the example project and demonstrates KVC access to a collection. When you press the Add button, the number of items stored in `DataModel` will be incremented. When you press the View button, a table view will be constructed to display the information in the `DataModel` using KVC proxy collections in `RootViewController`, and KVC collection accessors in `KVCTableViewController`. After the code I explain how both of these access mechanism work.

RootViewController.h

```
@interface RootViewController : UIViewController
@property (nonatomic, strong) IBOutlet UILabel *countLabel;
@property (nonatomic, strong) IBOutlet UILabel *entryLabel;
- (IBAction)performAdd;
@end
```

RootViewController.m

```
@implementation RootViewController
@synthesize countLabel=countLabel_;
@synthesize entryLabel=entryLabel_;

- (void)refresh {
  DataModel *model = [DataModel sharedModel];

  // There is no property called "items" in DataModel. KVC will
  // automatically create a proxy for you.
  NSArray *items = [model valueForKey:@"items"];
  NSUInteger count = [items count];
  self.countLabel.text = [NSString stringWithFormat:@"%d",
                          count];

  if (count > 0) {
    self.entryLabel.text = [[items objectAtIndex:(count-1)]
                            description];
  } else {
    self.entryLabel.text = @"";
  }
}

- (void)viewWillAppear:(BOOL)animated {
  [self refresh];
  [super viewWillAppear:animated];
}

- (IBAction)performAdd {
  [[DataModel sharedModel] addItem];
  [self refresh];
}

@end
```

KVCTableViewController.m

```
@implementation KVCTableViewController

- (NSInteger)tableView:(UITableView *)tableView
 numberOfRowsInSection:(NSInteger)section {

  // countOfItems is a KVC method, but you can call it directly
```

```
    // rather than creating an "items" proxy.
    return [[DataModel sharedModel] countOfItems];
}

- (UITableViewCell *)tableView:(UITableView *)tableView
        cellForRowAtIndexPath:(NSIndexPath *)indexPath {
    static NSString *CellIdentifier = @"Cell";

    UITableViewCell *cell = [tableView
        dequeueReusableCellWithIdentifier:CellIdentifier];

    if (cell == nil) {
      cell = [[UITableViewCell alloc]
            initWithStyle:UITableViewCellStyleDefault
            reuseIdentifier:CellIdentifier];
    }

    DataModel *model = [DataModel sharedModel];
    id object = [model objectInItemsAtIndex:indexPath.row];
    cell.textLabel.text = [object description];

    return cell;
}
 @end
```

DataModel.h

```
@interface DataModel : NSObject

+ (DataModel*)sharedModel;

- (void)addItem;
- (NSUInteger)countOfItems;
- (id)objectInItemsAtIndex:(NSUInteger)index;
@end
```

DataModel.m

```
@interface DataModel ()
@property (nonatomic, readwrite, assign) NSUInteger count;
@end

@implementation DataModel
@synthesize count=count_;

+ (DataModel*)sharedModel {
    static DataModel *sharedModel;
    static dispatch_once_t onceToken;
    dispatch_once(&onceToken, ^{ sharedModel = [DataModel new]; });
    return sharedModel;
```

```
}

- (NSUInteger)countOfItems {
  return self.count;
}

- (id)objectInItemsAtIndex:(NSUInteger)index {
  return [NSNumber numberWithInt:index * 2];
}

- (void)addItem {
  self.count++;
}

@end
```

Note how `RootViewController` accesses the array of items from `DataModel`:

```
NSArray *items = [model valueForKey:@"items"];
```

Normally you would expect this to call `[DataModel items]`, but there is no such method. `DataModel` doesn't ever create an array. So where does this `NSArray` come from?

`DataModel` implements `countOfItems` and `objectInItemsAtIndex:`. These are very specially named methods. When `valueForKey:` looks for `items`, it searches for the following methods:

- `getItems` or `items` or `isItems`—If any of these are found, it is used to return the value.

- `countOfItems` and either `objectInItemsAtIndex:` or `itemsAtIndexes`—This is the combination you use in this example. KVC generates a proxy array that is discussed shortly.

- `countOfItems` and `enumeratorOfItems` and `memberOfItems`—This combination causes KVC to return a proxy set.

- An instance variable named `_items`, `_isItems`, `items` or `isItems`—KVC will directly access the ivar. You generally should avoid this behavior, and it's a good reason to name your ivars with something other than a leading underscore. Direct instance variable access breaks encapsulation and makes the code more fragile.

In this example, `valueForKey:` automatically generates and returns a proxy `NSKeyValueArray`. This is a subclass of `NSArray`, and you can use it like any other array, but calls to `count`, `objectAtIndex:` and related methods are forwarded to the appropriate KVC methods. The proxy caches its requests, making it very efficient. See the *Key-Value Coding Programming Guide* in the iOS Developer Library for the full set of methods you can implement for this form.

In this example, the property is `items`, so KVC looks for `countOfItems` for instance. Had the property been `boxes`, then KVC would look for `countOfBoxes`. KVC requires that you name your methods in a standard way so that it can construct these method names. This is why getters must begin with a lowercase letter.

For mutable collection properties, there are two options. You can use the mutator (property-changing) methods such as the following (again, see the *Key-Value Coding Programming Guide* for the full list):

```
- (void)insertObject:(id)object
    inChildrenAtIndex:(NSUInteger)index;
- (void)removeObject:(id)object
    inChildrenAtIndex:(NSUInteger)index;
```

Or you can return a special proxy object by calling `mutableArrayValueForKey:` or `mutableSetValueForKey:`. Modifying this object automatically calls the appropriate KVC methods on your object.

KVC and Dictionaries

Dictionaries are just a special kind of nested relationship. For most keys, calling `valueForKey:` is the same as calling `objectForKey:` (the exception is if the key begins with @, which is used to refer to the `NSDictionary` itself if needed).

KVC and Nonobjects

Not every method returns an object, but `valueForKey:` always returns an `id`. Nonobject return values are wrapped in an `NSValue` or `NSNumber`. These two classes can handle just about anything from numbers and Booleans to pointers and structures. While `valueForKey:` will automatically wrap scalar values into objects, you cannot pass nonobjects to `setValue:forKey:`. You must wrap scalars in `NSValue` or `NSNumber` yourself.

Setting a nonobject property to `nil` presents a special case. Whether that is legal or not depends on the situation, so KVC does not guess. If you call `setValue:forKey:` with a value of `nil`, the key will be passed to `setNilValueForKey:`. You need to override this method to do the right thing if you want to handle setting `nil` for a nonobject property.

Higher-Order Messaging with KVC

`setValue:forKey:` is filled with useful special cases, such as the fact that it is overridden for collections like `NSArray` and `NSSet`. Rather than operating on the collection itself, `setValue:forKey:` is passed to each member of the collection. The results are added to the returned collection. This allows you to easily construct collections from other collections such as

```
NSArray *array = [NSArray arrayWithObjects:@"foo",
                    @"bar", @"baz", nil];
NSArray *capitals =
            [array valueForKey:@"capitalizedString"];
```

This passes the method `capitalizedString` to each item in the `NSArray` and returns a new `NSArray` with the results. Passing messages (`capitalizedString`) as parameters is called Higher Order Messaging. Multiple messages can be passed using key paths:

```
NSArray *array = [NSArray arrayWithObjects:@"foo",
                @"bar", @"baz", nil];
NSArray *capitalLengths =
      [array valueForKeyPath:@"capitalizedString.length"];
```

The above code calls `capitalizedString` on each element of `array`, then calls `length`, and wraps the return into an `NSNumber` object. The results are collected into a new array called `capitalLengths`.

You looked at more flexible approaches using trampolines in Chapter 4, but KVC provides a very easy solution for many problems, as long as you don't need to pass parameters.

Collection Operators

KVC provides a few complex functions as well. It can, for instance, sum or average a list of numbers automatically. Consider this:

```
NSArray *array = [NSArray arrayWithObjects:@"foo",
                @"bar", @"baz", nil];
NSUInteger totalLength =
      [[array valueForKeyPath:@"@sum.length"] intValue];
```

`@sum` is an operator that sums the indicated property (`length`). Note that this can be hundreds of times slower than the equivalent loop:

```
NSArray *array = [NSArray arrayWithObjects:@"foo",
                @"bar", @"baz", nil];
NSUInteger totalLength = 0;
for (NSString *string in array) {
  totalLength += [string length];
}
```

The performance issues are generally significant when dealing with arrays of thousands or tens of thousands of elements. Beyond `@sum`, there are many other operators that you can find in the *Key-Value Coding Programming Guide* in the iOS Developer Library. The operations are particularly valuable when working with Core Data, and can be faster than the equivalent loop, because they can be optimized into database queries. You cannot create your own operations, however.

Key-Value Observing

Key-value observing is a mechanism for transparently notifying observers of changes in object properties. At the beginning of the "Key-Value Coding" section, you built a table view cell that could display any object. In that example, the data was static. If you changed the data, the cell wouldn't update. Let's improve that now.

You can make the cell automatically update whenever its object changes. You need a changeable object, so use the current date and time. You use key-value observing to get a callback every time a property you care about changes.

KVO has a lot of similarities to NSNotificationCenter. You start observing using addObserver:forKey Path:options:context:. To stop observing, you use removeObserver:forKeyPath:. The callback is always observeValueForKeyPath:ofObject:change:context:. Here are the modifications required to create 1,000 rows of date cells that automatically update every second.

KVCTableViewCell.m (KVO)

```objc
@implementation KVCTableViewCell

...

- (void)removeObservation {
  if (self.isReady) {
    [self.target removeObserver:self
                     forKeyPath:self.property];
  }
}

- (void)addObservation {
  if (self.isReady) {
    [self.target addObserver:self forKeyPath:self.property
                     options:0
                     context:(__bridge void*)self];
  }
}

- (void)observeValueForKeyPath:(NSString *)keyPath
                      ofObject:(id)object
                        change:(NSDictionary *)change
                       context:(void *)context {

  if ((__bridge id)context == self) {
    // Our notification, not our superclass's
      [self update];
  }
  else {
    [super observeValueForKeyPath:keyPath ofObject:object
                           change:change context:context];
  }
}

- (void)dealloc {
  if (target_ && [property_ length] > 0) {
    [target_ removeObserver:self forKeyPath:property_];
  }
}

- (void)setTarget:(id)aTarget {
```

```objc
  [self removeObservation];
  target_ = aTarget;
  [self addObservation];
  [self update];
}

- (void)setProperty:(NSString *)aProperty {
  [self removeObservation];
  property_ = aProperty;
  [self addObservation];
  [self update];
}

@end
```

KVCTableViewController.m (KVO)

```objc
@interface KVCTableViewController ()
@property (readwrite, retain) NSTimer *timer;
@property (readwrite, retain) NSDate *now;
@end

@implementation KVCTableViewController
@synthesize timer = timer_;
@synthesize now = now_;

- (void)updateNow {
  self.now = [NSDate date];
}

- (void)viewDidLoad {
  [self updateNow];
  self.timer = [NSTimer
    scheduledTimerWithTimeInterval:1
                            target:self
                          selector:@selector(updateNow)
                          userInfo:nil
                           repeats:YES];
}

- (void)viewDidUnload {
  [self.timer invalidate];
  self.timer = nil;
  self.now = nil;
}

...

- (UITableViewCell *)tableView:(UITableView *)tableView
        cellForRowAtIndexPath:(NSIndexPath *)indexPath {

  static NSString *CellIdentifier = @"KVCTableViewCell";
```

```
   id cell = [tableView
     dequeueReusableCellWithIdentifier:CellIdentifier];

   if (cell == nil) {
     cell = [[[KVCTableViewCell alloc]
       initWithReuseIdentifier:CellIdentifier] autorelease];
     [cell setProperty:@"now"];
     [cell setTarget:self];
   }

   return cell;
}

- (void)dealloc {
  [timer_ invalidate];
}

@end
```

In `KVCTableViewCell`, you observe the requested property on your target in `addObservation`. When you register for KVO, you pass `self` as the `context` pointer (after casting to `void*` for ARC) so that in the callback you can determine if this was your observation. Because there is only one KVO callback for a class, you may be receiving a callback for a property your superclass registered for. If so, you need to pass it along to `super`. Unfortunately, you can't always pass to `super` because `NSObject` will throw an exception. So you use a unique `context` to identify your observations. There's more about this in "KVO Tradeoffs."

In `RootViewController`, you create a property `now` and ask the cell to observe it. Once a second, you update it. Observers are notified and the cells update. This is all quite efficient because at any given time there is only about one screen's worth of cells because of cell reuse.

The real power of KVO is seen in `[KVCTableViewController updateNow]`:

```
- (void)updateNow {
  self.now = [NSDate date];
}
```

The only thing you have to do is update your data. You don't have to worry that someone might be observing you, and if no one is observing you, then you don't pay any overhead like you would for `NSNotificationCenter`. This is discussed further in "KVO Tradeoffs," but the incredible simplicity on the part of the model class is the real benefit of KVO. As long as you use accessors to modify your ivars, all the observation mechanism is handled automatically, with no cost when you don't need it. All the complexity is moved into the observer rather than the observed. It's no wonder that KVO is becoming very popular in low-level Apple frameworks.

KVO and Collections

Observing collections often causes confusion. The thing to remember is that observing a collection is not the same as observing the objects in it. If a collection contains Adam, Bob, and Carol, then adding Denise changes the collection. Changes to Adam do not change the collection. If you want to observe changes to the objects in a collection, you must observe those objects, not the collection. Generally that's done by observing the collection, and then observing objects as they are added, and stopping when they're removed.

How Is KVO Implemented?

Key-value observing notifications rely on two NSObject methods: willChangeValueForKey: and didChangeValueForKey:. Before an observed property change is made, something must call willChangeValueForKey:. This will record the old value. After the change is made, something must call didChangeValueForKey:, which calls observeValueForKeyPath:ofObject:change:context:. You can do this by hand, but that's fairly uncommon. Generally you only do this if you're trying to control when the callbacks are made. Most of the time, it's handled automatically.

There is very little magic in Objective-C. Even message dispatching, which can seem mysterious at first, is actually pretty straightforward. (Message dispatching is covered in Chapter 20.) However, KVO borders on magic. Somehow when you call setNow:, there is an extra call to willChangeValueForKey:, didChangeValueForKey:, and observeValueForKeyPath:ofObject:change:context: in the middle. You might think that this is because you synthesized setNow:, and occasionally you'll see people write code like this:

```
- (void)setNow:(NSDate *)aDate {
    [self willChangeValueForKey:@"now"]; // Unnecessary
    now_ = aDate;
    [self didChangeValueForKey:@"now"]; // Unnecessary
}
```

This is redundant and you shouldn't do it because then the KVO methods will be called twice. KVO always calls willChangeValueForKey: before an accessor and didChangeValueForKey: afterward. How? The answer is class swizzling. Swizzling is discussed further in Chapter 20, but when you first call addObserver: forKeyPath:options:context: on an object, the framework creates a new KVO subclass of the class and converts the observed object to that new subclass. In that special KVO subclass, it creates setters for the observed properties that work effectively like this:

```
- (void)setNow:(NSDate *)aDate {
    [self willChangeValueForKey:@"now"];
    [super setValue:aDate forKey:@"now"];
    [self didChangeValueForKey:@"now"];
}
```

This is done at run time, not compile time. That's why it's so important that you name things correctly. KVO can figure this out only if you use the KVC naming convention.

It's difficult to detect the KVO class swizzling. It overrides class to return the original class. But occasionally you'll see references to NSKVONotifying_MYClass instead of MYClass.

KVO Tradeoffs

KVC is powerful technology, but other than possibly being slower than direct method calls, it generally is a good thing. The one major downside is that you lose compile-time checks of your property names. You should always code following KVC naming conventions, whether you use KVC directly or not. That will save you a lot of grief when you want to instantiate objects from a nib file, which requires KVC. It also makes your code readable by other Objective-C developers, who expect certain names to mean certain things. For the most part, this means naming your getters and setters `property` and `setProperty:` respectively.

KVO, on the other hand, is a mixed bag. It can be useful and it can cause trouble. It's implemented in a highly magical way and some of its usage is quite awkward. Calls to `addObserver:forKeyPath:options:context:` do not exactly balance with calls to `removeObserver:forKeyPath:`. Consider the following code:

```
[target addObserver:self forKeyPath:@"foo" options:0
        context:@"first"];
[target addObserver:self forKeyPath:@"foo" options:0
        context:@"second"];
[target removeObserver:self forKeyPath:@"foo"];
[target removeObserver:self forKeyPath:@"foo"];
```

The first call to `removeObsever:forKeyPath:` removes both previous observers. The second call will crash. This may sound contrived, but consider the case where both you and your superclass are observing the same object's property. There is no easy way to implement that without special knowledge about your superclass's implementation. If your superclass is a UIKit class, you don't have the source code to even find out what it's observing. You just have to hope it doesn't collide with you now or in the future.

This problem alone makes it difficult to use KVO as easily as `NSNotification`. Similarly, because `removeObsever:forKeyPath:` will crash if you are not an observer for that key path, you must keep track of exactly which properties you are observing. KVO has no equivalent to `NSNotificationCenter` `removeObserver:`, which conveniently cleans up all observations you might have.

KVO creates subtle code-path surprises. When you call `postNotification:`, you know that some other code may run. You can search your code for the notification name and generally find all of the things that might happen. It can be quite surprising that just setting one of your own properties can cause arbitrary code in an unknown part of the program to execute, and it can be even harder to search the code to discover this. That can make it very difficult to solve bugs. KVO bugs in general are difficult to solve because so much of the activity "just happens" without there being any visible code causing it.

So KVO's greatest strength is also its greatest danger. It can sometimes dramatically reduce the amount of common code you write. In particular, it can get rid of the common problem of hand-building all your setters just so you can call some `updateSelf` method. In this way it can reduce bugs because of incorrectly cut-and-pasted code. But it can also inject really confusing bugs, and with the introduction of Automatic Reference Counting, handwritten setters are even easier to write correctly.

My recommendation is to use KVO sparingly, simply, and only in places where it's a real benefit. Its performance scales much better than `NSNotification` if you need a very large number of observations (a few hundred or more). It lets you get the advantages of `NSNotification` without modifying the observed class. And it sometimes requires less code, although you need to include all the special-case code you may need to work around subtle KVO problems. In the `KVCTableViewCell` example, hand-coding `setProperty:` and `setTarget:` saves about 15 lines versus the equivalent KVO solution that observes `property` and `target`.

Avoid KVO in situations where you have complex interdependencies or a complicated class hierarchy. Simple solutions with delegates and `NSNotification` are often better than excessively clever solutions using KVO.

On the other hand, Apple is clearly moving toward KVO in performance-critical frameworks. It is the primary way to deal with `CALayer` and `NSOperation`. You should expect to see it more often in new low-level classes. It has the advantage of zero-overhead observation. If there are no observers of a given instance, then KVO is free. Delegate methods and `NSNotification` still have to do work even if there are no observers. For low-level, performance-critical objects, KVO is a clear win. Use it wisely.

Summary

In this chapter you have learned two of the most powerful techniques in Objective-C, KVC and KVO. These techniques provide a level of run-time flexibility that is difficult to achieve in other languages. Writing your code to conform to KVC is a critical part of a Cocoa program, whether you call `valueForKey:` directly or not. KVO can be challenging to use well, but is a powerful tool when you need high-performance observations. As a Cocoa developer, you need to keep KVC and KVO in mind when designing your classes. Following a few simple naming rules will make all the difference.

Further Reading

Apple Documentation

The following documents are available in the iOS Developer Library at `developer.apple.com` or through the Xcode Documentation and API Reference.

Key-Value Coding Programming Guide

Key-Value Observing Programming Guide

NSKeyValueCoding Protocol Reference

NSKeyValueObserving Protocol Reference

## Chapter 16

Think Different: Blocks and Functional Programming

Programming paradigms fall into three major categories: procedural programming, object-oriented programming, and functional programming. Most modern programming languages—such as Java, C#, or Objective-C—don't fall purely into a specific paradigm. They are usually inclined to one while including some methodologies from the others. Objective-C is primarily object-oriented, yet it borrows some functional aspects using *blocks*. This chapter is about the functional programming aspects in Objective-C.

The functional programming (FP) paradigm is easy to explain theoretically, but its highly abstract nature makes it hard to understand and realize its power. The easiest way to really comprehend and appreciate FP is to implement a practical system. Later in this chapter, you dirty your hands with a dash of FP by writing an FP equivalent of a commonly used Cocoa method, and then go deeper by refactoring the RESTEngine you wrote in Chapter 10 to use blocks. Finally, you learn about some of the block-based methods added to the Cocoa framework from iOS 4 onward. Now let's get started.

What Is a Block?

Simply defined, a *block* is an ad hoc piece of code. Just as you would with a primitive data type like an integer or double, you declare a block and start using it. You can pass blocks as parameters, "copy" them for use later, and do pretty much anything that you would normally do to a primitive data type. Veteran C programmers have been using function pointers to do pretty much what I just explained. What sets a block apart from a function pointer (which is different enough to be called a programming paradigm by itself) is that it can be declared within the lexical scope of another method, and that it can "capture the state" of the variables in that scope. This means that a block has contextual information without the programmer needing to do anything, unlike a function pointer.

> A block differs from a function pointer by the way it is written and by its inherent nature to capture the state of local variables and optionally modify them.

Now, that paragraph doesn't really help you to understand the concept. It is analogous to a chapter about object-oriented programming that says: An object is an "entity" that encapsulates code with data. You will be hesitant to use blocks and the functional programming paradigm if you don't comprehend it conceptually. So, before I talk about another abstract point, let's get this one straight by thinking outside the box. To do that, I'll show you a practical, nonprogramming–related example.

Why Use Functional Programming?

To understand why you should use functional programming paradigm, it might help to relate it to something outside of the programming world. I'm going to digress a bit here, but I promise it will take fewer than a couple of minutes of your reading time.

The Human Brain Versus the Microprocessor

A microprocessor stores data in an addressable fashion and executes instructions to process them. The human brain, on the other hand, thinks and stores "data" associatively. Here's an example: On a microprocessor, you "store" a number, the value 10, and access it by its address, 0x8BADF00D. When you ask the microprocessor about the location of the number, it returns the address. The human brain works differently. The answer to the question, "Where is my iPhone?" would probably be similar to, "It's in the living room on top of the DVD player." The human answer won't even remotely be like "It's 5.04 meters northeast at an angle 27.23 degrees from the main entrance to the living room." Humans associate the location of the iPhone to the location of the DVD player and the location of the DVD player to the location of the living room. That's a huge difference in the thought processes between how a microprocessor works and how a human brain works. This difference in thought process is akin to the difference between the procedural and functional programming paradigm.

Procedural Versus Functional Paradigm

Procedural programming is all about feeding your microprocessor with instructions. While that has worked very well for decades, some real-world programming tasks are easier to think about and express as abstract concepts than as a bunch of instructions. Let me give you an example. (No, not that clichéd factorial example; read on, this is going to be Objective-C).

A 'Functional' UIAlertView

For this example, you want to show a `UIAlertView` and take an action when the user taps on the Affirmative button. The procedural way of doing this is to create a `UIAlertView` object, own its delegate and implement the callbacks, show the `UIAlertView`, and release it.

UIAlertView Example (The Procedural Way)

```
-(IBAction) buttonTapped:(id) sender  {
  UIAlertView *alert = [[UIAlertView alloc] initWithTitle:@"Send email"
  message:@"Are you sure you want to send it now?"
  delegate:self
  cancelButtonTitle:@"Cancel"
  otherButtonTitles:@"Send", nil];

  [alert show];
  [alert release];
}

-(void)alertView:(UIAlertView*) alertView didDismissWithButtonIndex:(NSInt
eger) buttonIndex  {
```

```
    if(buttonIndex != [alertView cancelButtonIndex])   {
      [self sendTheMail];
    }
}

-(void) sendTheMail  {
    // write actual code for sending the mail
}
```

Implementation (and syntax) aside, let's now look at how you would call a `UIAlertView` that adheres to the functional paradigm.

UIAlertView Example (The Functional Way)

```
[UIAlertView showAlertViewWithTitle:@"Send email"
message:@"Are you sure you want to send it now?"
cancelButtonTitle:@"Cancel"
otherButtonTitles:[NSArray arrayWithObjects:@"Send", nil] onCompletion:^{
    // write actual code for sending the mail
}
onCancel:^{
    // write code for handling other cases
}];
```

That's much cleaner.

■ You don't have to implement a delegate.

■ You don't have to allocate or release objects.

■ You don't have to explicitly show the alert.

Instead, you specify your intent and things happen behind the scenes automatically for you.

In the functional paradigm example, your code reads like English. You declaratively say what your title is, and what the message you need to show is. When the user closes the alert, you declaratively say what code to execute for both cases, closing by accepting the alert and closing by cancelling the alert instead of implementing a delegate.

The point is that instead of instructing, you specify your intent and the code becomes much cleaner to read and follow.

You will appreciate this code when you show multiple alerts in a single view controller and use tags to differentiate the alert views on the callback delegate. If you understand this, you have grasped the essence of the functional programming paradigm.

Later in this chapter you learn about implementing this method as a category addition to `UIAlertView` along with syntax and other associated stuff.

> You might wonder why, because microprocessors still execute instructions one by one, you should bother about functional programming. That's a valid question. The functional paradigm is almost always for writing software that's easy for co-developers to read and understand. In nearly every case, an equivalent imperative logic is less expensive to execute, but with Moore's law, and the rate at which microprocessor speed increases, code clarity is often more important than writing efficient code. Again, that doesn't always mean you should adhere to a functional paradigm. Not every real-world problem can be represented in a functional way.

I hope I've persuaded you to learn and use the functional paradigm, so let's dive into the technical bits of it.

Declaring a Block

You declare a block using the ^ (caret) character.

```
int (^MyBlock) (int parameter1, double parameter2);
```

This syntax is for a block called `MyBlock` that takes an `int` and `double` as parameters and returns an integer. In most applications, you would `typedef` a block like this:

```
typedef int (^MyBlock) (int parameter1, double parameter2);
```

You can now declare instances of your block as you would declare any other data type.

```
MyBlock firstBlock, secondBlock;
```

You assign a block like this:

```
firstBlock = ^(int parameter1, double parameter2)  {
// your block code here
NSLog(@"%d, %f", parameter1, parameter2);
}
```

Because the block takes in an `integer` and a `double` as parameters, you can invoke them like this:

```
firstBlock(5, 2.3);
```

Invoking this block in this case will `NSLog` the numbers to the console. That's pretty much all for the syntax.

Scope of Variables

You learned earlier in this chapter that, compared to a function pointer, a block has access to the variables in its lexical scope. Optionally, a block can modify a variable in the lexical scope even if the variable goes out of scope. To allow a block to access variables within a lexical scope, the Objective-C runtime allocates blocks on the stack.

When you are passing a block as a parameter to other methods, you should copy the block to the heap. This is because, blocks, when used as parameters, will be invoked after the stack in which it was originally created is deallocated. You can use the normal Objective-C copy message to copy a block. This also copies/retains variables in its lexical scope. This is a very important concept you should understand when you use blocks in your code. In the next section, you learn the scenarios for when a variable would be copied and when it would be retained.

> **Warning:** A block cannot be retained. Sending a retain message is a no-op and doesn't increase the retain count. Normally you wouldn't send a retain message explicitly. But you should keep an eye on the storage semantics you use, when you declare a block as a property. Even the omniscient LLVM compiler doesn't warn you when you use retain as a storage type for a block property.

Stack Versus Heap

A block is a different kind of Objective-C object. Unlike traditional objects, blocks are not created on the heap. This is primarily for two reasons. The first is performance: A stack allocation is almost always faster than heap. The second reason is the necessity to access other local variables.

Now, a stack gets destroyed when the scope of the function ends. If your block is passed to a method that needs it even after its scope is destroyed, you should copy your block. This is where Objective-C runtime performs some magic behind the scenes. When a block is copied, it's moved from stack to heap. Along with the block, the local variables defined in its scope are copied when you reference it within your block. All NSObject subclasses that are referenced are retained instead of copied (because they are already on heap and retain is less time-consuming than a copy). The Objective-C runtime gives a const reference to every local variable to a block. This also means that a block cannot modify the contextual data by default, and code like the following will result in a compilation error.

```
int statusCode  = -1;

Myblock b = ^{
  statusCode = 4;
};
```

But I previously said that blocks could "optionally" modify the local variables. To allow modification, you declare variables with a __block modifier. So the declaration of statusCode is now

```
__block int statusCode = -1;
```

The reason for this additional modifier is to instruct the compiler to copy the __block variables when the block is copied. Copying is a more time-consuming operation than either retain or passing by a const reference and the implementers decided to leave this in the hands of the developer.

__block **variables are copied instead of being retained.**

Now, coming back to the previous example of a blocks-based UIAlertView, your block has all contextual information available without declaring any additional data structures. Your UIAlertView onDismiss or onCancel block methods can access the local variables without the developer managing them (through context parameters).

However, it comes with a minor catch that you should be wary of: the retain cycle.

The Retain Cycle Problem

```
__block TWTweetComposeViewController *controller =
[[TWTweetComposeViewController alloc] init];
        [controller setInitialText:@"Test Tweet"];

    controller.completionHandler =
     ^(TWTweetComposeViewControllerResult result)  {

        controller = nil; // retain cycle issue
        [self dismissModalViewControllerAnimated:YES];
    };
```

If you attempt to capture a variable within a block like the preceding code, you end up with a retain cycle that never gets deallocated. With the new LLVM compiler, you normally don't have to worry much about this because it's clever enough to point the issue.

Implementing a Block

Now that you know the workings of a block, let's implement the UIAlertView block-based example I showed you in the previous section. After this, you refactor your RESTEngine to use blocks.

Blocks-based UIAlertView

You want the syntax for this example to be like the following:

```
[UIAlertView showAlertViewWithTitle:(NSString*)title
message:(NSString*) message
cancelButtonTitle: (NSString*) cancelTitle
otherButtonTitles: (NSArrat*) otherButtons
onCompletion:^{
```

```
  // write actual code for sending the mail
}
onCancel:^{
  // write code for handling other cases

}];
```

Follow these steps to implement the `UIAlertView` block-based example.

1. Add a Category class on `UIAlertView`. You can use the Category template provided in Xcode 4.2. Call the Category class `UIAlertView` (Blocks).

2. Typedef your Dismiss and Cancel blocks.

```
typedef void (^DismissBlock) (int buttonIndex);
typedef void (^CancelBlock) ();
```

3. Add the method definition to the header file:

```
+ (UIAlertView*) showAlertViewWithTitle:(NSString*) title
                    message:(NSString*) message
           cancelButtonTitle:(NSString*) cancelButtonTitle
            otherButtonTitles:(NSArray*) otherButtons
                   onDismiss:(DismissBlock) dismissed
                    onCancel:(CancelBlock) cancelled;
```

4. Declare static storage for the blocks on the implementation.

```
static DismissBlock _dismissBlock;
static CancelBlock _cancelBlock;
```

5. Implement your block-based method.

```
+ (UIAlertView*) showAlertViewWithTitle:(NSString*) title
                    message:(NSString*) message
           cancelButtonTitle:(NSString*) cancelButtonTitle
            otherButtonTitles:(NSArray*) otherButtons
                   onDismiss:(DismissBlock) dismissed
                    onCancel:(CancelBlock) cancelled {

  [_cancelBlock release];
  _cancelBlock  = [cancelled copy];

  [_dismissBlock release];
  _dismissBlock  = [dismissed copy];

  UIAlertView *alert = [[UIAlertView alloc] initWithTitle:title
                                   message:message
                                  delegate:[self self]
                         cancelButtonTitle:cancelButtonTitle
                         otherButtonTitles:nil];

  for(NSString *buttonTitle in otherButtons)
```

```
        [alert addButtonWithTitle:buttonTitle];

    [alert show];
    return [alert autorelease];
}
```

Note that you have copied the block parameters passed to the method to the static storage. That's because you have to invoke those block methods later in the `UIAlertViewDelegate`.

6. Handle the `UIAlertViewDelegate`:

```
+ (void)alertView:(UIAlertView*) alertView didDismissWithButtonIndex:(NSInteger) buttonIndex {

    if(buttonIndex == [alertView cancelButtonIndex])   {
      _cancelBlock();
    }
    else   {
      _dismissBlock(buttonIndex - 1);// cancel button is button 0
    }

    [_cancelBlock autorelease];
    [_dismissBlock autorelease];
}
```

The delegate method is nothing fancy. Just handle it and call the appropriate block method.

With about 50 lines of code, you implemented a block-based `UIAlertView`. This should help write clean, readable code on your view controllers. You can implement similar methods for `UIActionSheet` as well.

You can download the complete source code from the book's website. In the next section, you refactor your RESTEngine by following the same methodology.

Blocks-based RESTEngine

In Chapter 10 you implemented a class to talk to a REST-based web service. As shown in the following code, the login method took a username and password as parameters and returned success or failure on delegates.

Login Method in RESTEngine

```
-(IBAction) loginButtonTapped:(id) sender   {
    [[RESTEngine sharedInstance] initWithLoginName:@"mugunth"
password:@"abracadabra"];
}

-(void) loginSucceeded:(NSString*) accessToken   {
    NSLog(@"Login is successful and this is the access token %@",
    accessToken);
}

-(void) loginFailedWithError:(NSError*) error   {
    NSLog(@"Login failed. Check your password. Error is :%@",
    [error localizedDescription]);
}
```

Wouldn't it be cleaner and more elegant if you refactor the code like you did for the UIAlertView? That is, instead of implementing delegates, wouldn't be great if you could just pass a block of code that should be executed when login succeeds and another block of code that should be executed when login fails? That's the calling code, which should look like the following.

RESTEngine Login Method (Functional Paradigm)

```
-(IBAction) loginButtonTapped:(id) sender
{
  AppDelegate.engine =
  [[[RESTEngine alloc] initWithLoginName:@"mugunth"
                         password:@"abracadabra"
                 onLoginSucceeded:^(NSString* accessToken)   {
                    NSLog(@"Login is successful and this is the
                       access token %@", accessToken);
                 }

                          onError:^(NSError* error)   {

                             NSLog(@"Login failed. Check your
                             password. Error is :%@", [error
                             localizedDescription]);

                          }] autorelease];
    AppDelegate.engine.delegate = self;
}
```

That code reads like English and looks as if the complete network operation is synchronous. To refactor your RESTEngine code so that your view controller code looks like this, you are going to remove some code. Yes, remove code to make it adhere to the functional pardigm.

Removing is the best form of refactoring. Remove as much code as possible until you can't remove any more.

The following code shows the login method's implementation in RESTEngine class.

RESTEngine Login Method Implementation

```
-(id) initWithLoginName:(NSString*) loginName password:(NSString*)
password
  onLoginSucceeded:(StringBlock) loginSucceeded onError:(ErrorBlock) error
  {

  self.networkQueue = [ASINetworkQueue queue];
  [self.networkQueue setMaxConcurrentOperationCount:6];
  [self.networkQueue setDelegate:self];
```

```
[self.networkQueue go];

ASIFormDataRequest *request = [ASIFormDataRequest
    requestWithURL:[NSURL URLWithString:LOGIN_URL]];

[request setUsername:loginName];
[request setPassword:password];

[request setCompletionBlock:^ {

    NSDictionary *responseDict = [[request responseString] JSONValue];
    self.accessToken = [responseDict objectForKey:@"accessToken"];
    loginSucceeded(self.accessToken);
  }];

[request setFailedBlock:^ {
    self.accessToken = nil;
    error([request error]);
  }];
[self.networkQueue addOperation:request];

    return self;
}
```

As you see, the code that has to be executed is passed along as a block parameter, making your view controller much cleaner. In any normal case, your delegate almost always has to differentiate the request using tags (or request objects) and then switch code accordingly. With blocks, this is no longer necessary. Instead of setting the completion and error selectors and calling delegates from there, you are invoking the blocks from the operation's `completionBlock` and `failedBlock`.

The complete code for this example is available for download on the book's website.

By refactoring the RESTEngine, you removed at least four methods from your project: the `requestSucceeded:` and `requestFailed:` callback methods of your request in RESTEngine class and the `loginDone:` and `loginFailed:` methods in your view controller class, and this is for just one web service call. Now multiply this by the number of web service calls you have and imagine the obvious code cleanup you can do using blocks!

This should give you a complete understanding of how to use blocks in a much more sophisticated example. That completes the example; in the next section, you learn about Cocoa functions that take blocks as parameters.

Blocks and Concurrency

By now, you have learned enough to know how to use blocks and should be comfortable with the syntax. Let's now talk about one other important benefit you get from blocks: concurrency.

Managing concurrency has always been the hardest part of programming. Blocks are an excellent use case here because they can be used for creating units of programming or tasks that can be executed independently. Blocks can be used with dispatch queues in Grand Central Dispatch (GCD) or NSOperationQueue without needing to create threads explicitly. Using an NSOperationQueue is something you have already done before in the RESTEngine implementation.

In the next section, you briefly go through a feature of iOS and OS X called GCD and learn how blocks and dispatch queues in GCD work together to make concurrency implementation easier. Later on, I'll compare GCD with NSOperationQueue and provide suggestions on when to use what.

Dispatch Queues in GCD

Grand Central Dispatch is a very powerful feature that allows you to write concurrent code easily. It shifts the burden of managing multiple threads and thread synchronization to the operating system (iOS or OS X). When you use GCD, you create units that can be executed independently of each other and let the operating system handle the queuing and synchronization for you. The GCD implementation on iOS (and OS X) consists of a set of C language extensions, APIs, and a runtime engine. GCD automatically ensures that your independent units are executed on multiple processors if available (like iPad 2). As a developer, the only thing you have to focus on is designing your heavy worker processes so that they work independently of each other (as opposed to threads with shared synchronized data). GCD also provides context pointers to share data across your blocks, but discussing them is outside the scope of this chapter.

GCD provides three types of dispatch queues—serial, concurrent, and main—to which you can enqueue your task. The serial queue executes one task at a time in first-in-first-out (FIFO) order and the concurrent queue executes them in parallel, also in FIFO order. The main dispatch queue executes operations on the main thread, which is usually used to synchronize execution across threads executing in different serial/concurrent queues. Let's now see how to create a dispatch queue and submit tasks to it.

Creating a dispatch queue is as easy as one C function call:

```
myQueue = dispatch_queue_create("com.mycompany.myapp.myfirstqueue", NULL);
```

To dispatch tasks asynchronously to this queue, use the dispatch_async method. That method takes your block as the second parameter. It essentially queues your block to the queue specified in the first parameter. This is yet another few lines of code.

```
dispatch_async(myQueue, ^(void) {
  [self doHeavyWork];
});
```

That's it. Without explicitly using a thread and in less than ten lines of code, you have implemented GCD in your app! Designing your blocks in an independent way already solved most of the complexities involved around synchronization. For example in the preceding code, the doHeavyWork method is designed to work independently with its own data.

Imagine that the `doHeavyWork` method is an image manipulation method. To design it so that it runs independently, slice the image (vertically or horizontally), pass each slice to a block, and send this to a dispatch queue instead of using the complete image data on a shared synchronized variable. That's if you have a 3200×2000-pixels image and you want to apply a filter on it, slice it to 10 different images of 320×2000 pixels each and process them independently. After processing is done, stitch them back together on the main dispatch queue and notify the relevant observers.

NSOperationQueue Versus GCD Dispatch Queue

You already know that iOS provides another queuing mechanism called `NSOperationQueue`. This also takes blocks as parameters and queues them just like a dispatch queue. Now, you might have a question: When should I use GCD and when should I use `NSOperationQueue`?

There are some similarities and differences between `NSOperationQueue` and GCD.

- `NSOperationQueue` is built using GCD and is a higher-level abstraction of it.

- GCD supports only FIFO queues whereas operations queued to an `NSOperationQueue` can be reordered (reprioritized).

- Setting dependencies between operations is possible with `NSOperationQueue` but not with GCD. If one of your operations needs data that is generated by the other, you can set the operation to be dependent on the other operation and `NSOperationQueue` automatically executes them in the correct order. With GCD, there is no built-in support to set dependencies.

- `NSOperationQueue` is KVO compliant. This means you can observe the state of the tasks. Does that mean you should always use `NSOperationQueue` instead of GCD? The answer is no. `NSOperationQueue` is slower than GCD in terms of execution speeds. If you profile your code using Instruments and you think you need more performance, use GCD. Usually in lower-level code, you might not have task dependencies or a necessity to observe state using KVO. As always, follow Donald Knuth's quote: "We should forget about small efficiencies, say about 97% of the time: premature optimization is the root of all evil," and use the lower-level GCD only if it improves performance gains when profiled with Instruments.

Block-based Cocoa Methods

With iOS 4 and the introduction of blocks, many of the built-in Cocoa framework methods have block-based equivalents. Covering every single block-based method is impossible in a single chapter and demands a complete book of its own. But Apple follows a pattern. In this section, I briefly explain some of the methods that take block parameters and give some hints and tips on when to look out for a block-based equivalent method in the framework.

UIView Animations using Blocks

Prior to iOS 4, view-based animations were usually done using UIView's class methods, beginAnimations and commitAnimations. You write the code you want to be animated within these two statements and the animation is performed after the call to commitAnimations.

Code to animate the alpha value of a view will look something like the following.

Animation in iOS 3 (without Blocks)

```
  [UIView beginAnimations:@"com.mycompany.myapp.animation1"
context:&myContext];
[UIView setAnimationCurve:UIViewAnimationCurveEaseInOut];
[UIView setAnimationDuration:1.0f];
[UIView setAnimationDelay:1.0f]; // start after 1 second
[UIView setAnimationDidStopSelector:@selector(animationDidStop:finish
ed:)];
   self.imageView.alpha = 0.0;
[UIView commitAnimations];
```

Starting with iOS 4, UIView has several equivalent block-based animation methods. One method that you will quite commonly use is animateWithDuration:delay:options:animations:completion: The previous code snippet can be expressed using this method as follows.

Animation in iOS 4 and above (with Blocks)

```
[UIView animateWithDuration:1.0 delay:1.0 options:UIViewAnimationCurveEase
InOut
                    animations:^ {
                        self.imageView.alpha = 0.0;
                    }
                    completion:^(BOOL finished) {
                        [self. imageView removeFromSuperView];
                    }];
```

Note that the blocks version also removes the imageView after animation is complete, something that is done on the callback method animationDidStop:animated: in the iOS 3 version (not illustrated). Other block-based animation methods are permutations of this method, omitting parameters like delay, options, and completion block. A huge advantage of this method is that you don't have to maintain context you normally set with the methods setAnimationWillStartSelector: and setAnimationDidStopSelector:. Because a block is aware of the local context, you don't even need a context parameter.

Presenting and Dismissing View Controllers

iOS 5 introduces a new method for presenting and dismissing view controllers that takes a block parameter that must be called when the presenting (or dismissing) animation is completed. This block parameter is called after `viewDidDisappear` is called. Prior to iOS 5, you might have done some cleanup code in `viewDidDisappear`. With this method in iOS 5, you can easily do that in the completion block. The methods can be invoked like this.

Presenting

```
[self presentViewController:myViewController animated:YES completion:^  {
   //Add code that should be executed after view is presented
       }];
```

Dismissing

```
[self dismissViewControllerAnimated:YES completion:^  {
   //Add code that should be executed after view is presented
}];
```

TweetComposer Versus In App Email/SMS

In iOS 5, Apple added native support for Twitter, and apps that need to send out a tweet could just instantiate a `TWTweetComposerViewController`, prepopulated with the text to be tweeted, and present it to the user. The implementation is very similar to how you normally send an in app email or SMS. However, the `TWTweetComposeViewController` reports completion by a block parameter instead of a delegate. Your completion handler will look something like the following code.

TwTweetComposeViewController completion handler

```
controller.completionHandler = ^(TWTweetComposeViewControllerResult
result)
  {
            [self dismissModalViewControllerAnimated:YES];
            switch (result) {
                case TWTweetComposeViewControllerResultCancelled:
                    break;
                case TWTweetComposeViewControllerResultDone:
                    break;
            }
        };
```

Dictionary Enumeration Using NSDictionary enumerateWithBlock

Dictionary enumeration using block-based methods is sure to make your code cleaner. You no longer have to deal with `keyEnumerator` or `objectForKey` methods. With block-based equivalents, it's much easier, as shown here:

```
[dictionary enumerateKeysAndObjectsUsingBlock:^(id key, id val, BOOL
   *stop)  {

     //NSLog(@"%@, %@", key, val);
}];
```

Looking for Block-based Methods

The Cocoa framework follows a pattern when using blocks. I've listed a few of these that would help you in searching for equivalent block-based methods in the Cocoa framework.

- Check whether the current method has a context parameter for a Cocoa method. If it does, then the chances are that there will be a block-based equivalent.

- Look for delegates with one or two optional methods. You might find a `completionHandler` for classes that were previously notifying results via delegates.

- Enumeration, sorting, and filtering methods mostly have block equivalents. Examples include, `NSArray`, `NSDictionary`, `NSString`, `NSAttributedString`, `NSFileManager`, and several others.

Once you get used to the Cocoa framework design pattern and functional programming paradigm, you should be able to intuitively guess whether a method might have an equivalent block-based method.

Supported Platforms

Blocks are fairly new and are supported from iOS 4 and Snow Leopard onward. This means that when you use blocks, you should raise your minimum deployment target to iOS 4.0 for iOS projects and Mac OS X 10.6 for Mac projects. Statistics from various blogs show that more than 95% of devices run iOS 4 and above. (See, for example, Cocoanetics August 2011 discussion of Marco Arment's published statistics about users of Instapaper [see the "Further Reading" section].)This is going to approach 100% soon. On iOS projects, there should be nothing that stops you from using blocks. On Mac, Leopard and prior operating systems don't support blocks natively. But there is a third-party, open-source block-based runtime called PLBlocks (see "Further Reading" section) that allows support for blocks on those operating systems. For Mac projects, my recommendation is to start using Apple's equivalent block-based Cocoa methods using conditional compilation and then remove it altogether when Snow Leopard/Lion usage is high enough. My prediction is that that isn't more than a year away.

Summary

This chapter discussed the functional paradigm, a very powerful paradigm that can make your code more readable (as in case of the `UIAlertView` example) and help you write less code (as in case on the RESTEngine example). Functional programming will be the next big programming paradigm change after object-oriented programming, and you will be seeing more and more Cocoa methods using and accepting blocks.

Apple usually makes older technologies obsolete faster than its competitors. As much as it is true for products it makes, it holds good for its API too. The `TWTweetComposeViewController` class is a perfect example of this. While it is similar to the `MFMailComposeViewController` class, handling responses from `TWTweetComposeViewController` is via a `completionHandler` block, unlike `MFMailComposeViewController` that uses a `MFMailComposeViewControllerDelegate`. Note that `TWTweetComposeViewController` doesn't even support delegates.

On similar lines, for maybe another couple of years, there will be block-based additions to existing methods, but newer classes will have only block-based parameters and you will be eventually forced to use them. A paradigm change like this is tough. But the sooner you get accustomed, the better.

Further Reading

Apple Documentation

The following documents are available in the iOS Developer Library at `developer.apple.com` or through the Xcode Documentation and API Reference.

> Blocks Programming topics - iOS Programming Guide
>
> Concurrency Programming Guide - Migrating away from threads – Apple Developer

Blogs

> mikeash.com: Friday Q&A 2009-08-14: Practical Blocks
> `http://www.mikeash.com/pyblog/friday-qa-2009-08-14-practical-blocks.html`
>
> How blocks are implemented (and the consequences) | Cocoawithlove
> `http://cocoawithlove.com/2009/10/how-blocks-are-implemented-and.html`
>
> Cocoanetics – iOS versions in the wild (2011-08)
> `http://www.cocoanetics.com/2011/08/ios-versions-in-the-wild/`
>
> iOS device and OS version stats from Instapaper 3.0
> `http://www.marco.org/2011/03/24/ios-device-and-os-version-stats-from-instapaper-3-0`
>
> Is it worth supporting iOS 3 devices? – JCMultimedia
> `http://blog.jcmultimedia.com.au/2011/03/is-it-worth-supporting-ios-3-in-2011.html`
>
> Plblocks Block-capable Toolchain/Runtime for Mac OS X 10.5 and iPhone OS 2.2+
> `http://code.google.com/p/plblocks/`
>
> When to use NSOperation vs. GCD – Eschatology
> `http://eschatologist.net/blog/?p=232`

Source Code References

> UIKitCategoryAdditions - Github
> `https://github.com/MugunthKumar/UIKitCategoryAdditions`

Chapter 17

Going Offline

The iPhone can connect to the Internet from nearly anywhere. Most iOS apps use this capability, which makes it one of the best Internet-powered devices ever made. However, because it's constantly on the move, connectivity, reception, or both can be poor. This poses a problem for iOS developers, who should ensure that their apps' perceived response time remains more or less constant, as though the complete content were available locally. You do this by caching your data locally. Caching data means saving it temporarily so that it can be accessed faster than making a round trip to the server.

This chapter shows you the caching techniques you could use for solving the problem of slow performance caused when connectivity is poor or unavailable. As you saw in Chapter 10, Internet-connected apps fall into two major categories. In the first category are apps that behave like a front end to an online web service, and in this chapter you begin by designing a caching subsystem for the web service-based app you developed in Chapter 10 (the iHotel app). The second category of apps synchronizes user-generated content with a remote server. In iOS 5, Apple introduced a new cloud platform for syncing data across all Apple devices the user owns, and later in this chapter you look at different ways of syncing users' data across their devices through the new iCloud service.

Reasons for Going Offline

The main reason why your app might need to work offline is to improve the perceived speed of the app. You go offline by caching your app's content. There are two kinds of caching that can be used to make your app work offline. The first is on-demand caching, where the app caches request responses as and when they are made, much like your web browser does. The second is precaching, where you cache your contents completely for offline access.

Web service apps like the one we developed in Chapter 10 use on demand caching techniques to improve the perceived speed of the app rather than to provide offline access. Offline access just happens to be an added advantage. Twitter, Facebook, and foursquare are great examples of this. The data that these apps bring in often quickly becomes stale. How often are you interested in a tweet that was posted a couple of days ago, or in knowing where a friend was last week? Generally, the relevance of a tweet or a check-in is important only for a couple of hours, but loses some or all of its importance after 24 hours. Nevertheless, most Twitter clients cache tweets, and the official foursquare client shows you the last state of the app when you open it without an active Internet connection. You can even try this on your favorite twitter client, Twitter for iPhone, Tweetbot, or whatever you prefer; open one of your friends' profiles, and view his timeline. The app fetches the timeline and populates the page. While it loads the timeline, you see a loading spinner. Now go to a different page and come back again and open the timeline. You will see that it is loaded instantly. The app still refreshes the content in the background (based on when you previously opened it), but instead of showing a rather uninteresting spinner, it shows previously cached content, thereby making it appear fast. Without this caching, users will see the spinner for every single page, which slowly frustrates them. Whether the Internet connection is fast or slow, it's your responsibility as an iOS developer to mitigate this effect and provide the perception that the app is loading fast. This goes a long way toward improving your customers' satisfaction and thereby boosting your app's ratings on the App Store.

The other kind of caching gives more importance to the data being cached. Examples include apps like Google Reader clients, read-later apps like Instapaper, and so on. Now you have the background; in the next section you learn how to add a caching layer to the iHotel app you designed and developed in Chapter 10.

Strategies for Caching

The two caching techniques discussed in the previous section—on-demand caching and precaching—are quite different when it comes to design and implementation. With on-demand caching, you store the content fetched from the web service locally on the file system (in some format) and then, for every request, you check for the presence of this data in the cache and perform a fetch from the server only if the data is not available (or is stale). Hence your cache layer should behave more or less like cache memory on your processor. The speed of fetching the data is more important than the data itself. On the other hand, when you precache, you save content locally for future access. With precaching, a loss of data is not acceptable. For example, consider a scenario where the user has downloaded articles for reading in the subway, only to find that they are no longer present on his device.

Apps like Twitter, Facebook, and foursquare fall into the on-demand category, whereas apps like Instapaper and Google Reader clients fall into the precache type.

To implement precaching, you will probably use a background thread that accesses data and stores it locally in a meaningful representation. By "meaningful," I mean you should save your contents in a way that allows you to make modifications locally. Core Data is one way to do this. On-demand caching doesn't mandate this requirement. Implementation is very specific to the app you are building.

On-demand caching works like caching on your browser, allowing you to view content that you have viewed before. Caching happens as and when you open a view controller (on-demand), rather than on a background thread.

The next section discusses and compares both these caching techniques.

Methods for Storing Your Cache

When an app saves information, it normally saves it to the application's sandbox. Because cached data is not user created, it should not be saved to the `NSDocumentsDirectory`, but rather to the `NSCachesDirectory`. A good practice is to create a self-contained directory for all your cached data. In this example, you will create in the caches folder a directory named `MyAppCache`. You can create this directory using the following code:

```
NSArray *paths = NSSearchPathForDirectoriesInDomains(NSCachesDirectory,
NSUserDomainMask, YES);
NSString *cachesDirectory = [paths objectAtIndex:0];
cachesDirectory = [cachesDirectory stringByAppendingPathComponent:@"MyApp
Cache"];
```

The reason for creating this directory in the caches folder is that iCloud (and iTunes) backups don't include this directory. If you create large cache files in the Documents directory, they get uploaded to iCloud during backup and use up the limited space (~5GB at the time of writing) fairly quickly. You don't want to do that—you want to be a good citizen on your user's iPhone, right? NSCachesDirectory is meant for that.

Caching or saving data can be done either by storing it as archives of your data models (using NSKeyed Archiver) or using a higher-level database like raw SQLite or using object serialization framework like Core Data. You should carefully choose the technology based on your requirements. I offer suggestions on when to use NSKeyedArchiver and when to use Core Data in the "NSKeyedArchiver versus Core Data" section later in this chapter. Before that, you work through the implementation-level details of NSKeyedArchiver and Core Data.

Implementing NSKeyedArchiver

NSKeyedArchiver is implemented by implementing the NSCoding protocol. Conform your model classes to the NSCoding protocol, as shown in the following code:

NSCoding Protocol Methods

```
-  (void)encodeWithCoder:(NSCoder *)aCoder;
-  (id)initWithCoder:(NSCoder *)aDecoder;
```

When your models conform to NSCoding, archiving them is as easy as calling one of the following methods:

```
[NSKeyedArchiver archiveRootObject:objectForArchiving
toFile:archiveFilePath];

[NSKeyedArchiver archivedDataWithRootObject:objectForArchiving];
```

The first method creates an archive file specified at the path archiveFilePath. The second method returns an NSData object. NSData is usually faster because there is no file access overhead, but it is stored in your application's memory and would soon use up memory if it is not periodically checked. Periodic caching to flash memory on the iPhone is also not advisable because cache memory, unlike hard drives, comes with limited read/write cycles. You should balance both in an optimized way. You get a detailed look at this later in the "AppCache Architecture" section of this chapter.

Creating your model object from the archive is another one-liner. You can use either one of the following class methods, depending from where you have to unarchive.

```
[NSKeyedUnarchiver unarchiveObjectWithData:data];

[NSKeyedUnarchiver unarchiveObjectWithFile:archiveFilePath];
```

These two methods come in handy when converting to and from serialized data.

Using any of the NSArchiving methods requires your models to implement the NSCoding protocol, as shown above.

However, this is very easy, and simple enough that you can even automate it using tools like Accessorizer. (See the "Further Reading" section for a link to Accessorizer on the Mac App Store.)

The next sections describe using a more structured data format, Core Data and SQLite.

Core Data

Core Data, as Marcus Zarra says, is more of an object serialization framework than just a database API:

> *It's a common misconception that Core Data is a database API for Cocoa. […] It's an object framework that can be persisted to disk (Zarra, 2009).*

> **For a good, in-depth explanation of Core Data, read *Core Data: Apple's API for Persisting Data on Mac OS X* by Marcus Zarra (Pragmatic Bookshelf, 2009. ISBN 9781934356326).**

To store data in Core Data, first create a Core Data model file and design your Entities and Relationships; then write methods to save and retrieve data. Core Data isn't simple stuff to be explained in a couple of pages.

While technically Core Data can be used to cache data, I advise that you use it only if you are going to do pre-caching, not on-demand caching. The benefit Core Data offers over `NSKeyedArchiver` is individual access to the models' properties without unarchiving the complete data. But the complexity of implementing Core Data in your app defeats the benefits, especially when you want to implement on-demand caching. Moreover, as you learned previously, precaching requires you to store data in a meaningful representation that allows you to make local changes easily. Core Data is meant for that.

Raw SQLite

SQLite can be embedded into your app by linking against the libsqlite3 libraries, but it has significant drawbacks. Any sqlite3 library or an Object Relational Mapping (ORM) is almost always going to be slower than Core Data. In addition, while sqlite3 is thread-safe, the binary bundled with iOS is not. So unless you ship a custom-built sqlite3 library (compiled with the thread-safe flag), it becomes your responsibility to ensure that data access to and from the sqlite3 database is thread-safe. Because Core Data has so much more to offer and is thread-safe, I suggest avoiding native SQLite as far as possible on iOS.

> **The only exception to using Raw SQLite over Core Data in your iOS app is when you have application-specific data in the resource bundle that is shared by all other third-party platforms your app supports—for example, a location database for an app that runs on iPhone, Android, BlackBerry, and, say, Windows Phone. But again, that's not caching either.**

NSKeyedArchiver versus Core Data

Of the different techniques available to save data locally, two of them stand out: `NSKeyedArchiver` and Core Data. In this section, you'll see when to use each of them.

If you are developing an app that needs to cache data only to improve its perceived performance, it's advisable to use NSKeyedArchiver. The only drawback to this is that an archive created by NSKeyedArchiver needs to be completely unarchived and brought into memory before accessing even one variable inside. Core Data makes it easy to access individual models or even search for a list of items matching a given predicate, but if your application needs to cache just for performance improvements, you will not be required to access individual properties from the cached models. You will mostly use the complete cached contents at one go.

On the other hand, if you need your data to be available offline and in a more meaningful way than in just a raw serialized form, use a higher-level serialization like Core Data. In short, if your app requires precaching rather than on-demand caching, consider using Core Data. Note, however, that Core Data-based caching is extremely complicated and requires heavy changes to your iOS app. Use this only if you want true offline access for your app like the Apple's built-in Mail or Calendar app.

When you use Core Data, you must periodically delete data that's no longer needed, otherwise your cache will start growing and slow down the app's speed.

A programmer's quick-and-dirty way of deciding whether to go for Core Data or stay with NSKeyedArchiver is to determine whether you would ever download data in a background thread or perform any post-processing of data after downloading (precaching). If you download data in a background thread, that probably means you need the data in a more meaningful format than an archive and should use Core Data. If you are post-processing the downloaded data, (for example caching an HTML web page for offline access and rewriting image links to point to locally cached images) you might need to save the HTML text in Core Data and cache images later on, and then edit the HTML text to point to your locally cached images.

Because Core Data-based caching is highly specific to the app you develop, this chapter focuses more on the NSKeyedArchiver technique.

Cache Versioning

When you cache data, you need to decide whether to support version migration. If you are using an on-demand caching technique, no version migration is necessary: You can delete your cache when the user downloads the new version because old data is not important. On the other hand, if your app needs a precaching technique, chances are that you have cached multiple megabytes of data, which only makes sense if you migrate them to the new version. With Core Data, data migration across versions is easy (at least compared to raw sqlite).

AppCache Architecture

In this section you add caching support to the iHotelApp from Chapter 10. The iHotelApp doesn't need true offline access; what it needs is on-demand caching. On-demand caching is done as and when the view disappears from the hierarchy (technically in your viewWillDisappear: method). The basic construct of the view controller that supports caching is shown in Figure 17-1. The complete code that has AppCache Architecture can be obtained from the downloaded source code for this chapter. This chapter, from here on, assumes you have this code ready.

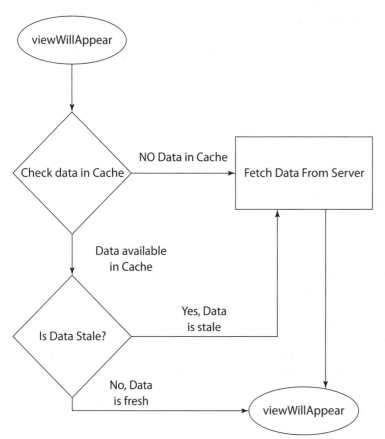

Figure 17-1 Control flow in your view controller that implements on-demand caching

In your `viewWillAppear` method, check your cache for the data necessary to display this view. If it is available, fetch it and update your user interface with cached data. Now check whether your data from the cache is old. Your business rule should dictate what's new and what's old. If you decide that the content is old, show the data on the UI and, in the background, fetch data from the server and update the UI again. If the data is not available in cache, fetch the data from the server while showing a loading spinner. After fetching data, update your UI.

The flowchart shown above assumes that what you show on the UI are models that can be archived. Implement the `NSCoding` protocol in the `MenuItem` model in the iHotelApp. The `NSKeyedArchiver` mandates that this protocol be implemented. The code snippets shown below illustrate this.

NSCoding encodeWithCoder Method for the MenuItem Class (MenuItem.m)

```
-  (void)encodeWithCoder:(NSCoder *)encoder
{
    [encoder encodeObject:self.itemId forKey:@"ItemId"];
    [encoder encodeObject:self.image forKey:@"Image"];
    [encoder encodeObject:self.name forKey:@"Name"];
    [encoder encodeObject:self.spicyLevel forKey:@"SpicyLevel"];
    [encoder encodeObject:self.rating forKey:@"Rating"];
    [encoder encodeObject:self.itemDescription forKey:@"ItemDescription"];
```

```
    [encoder encodeObject:self.waitingTime forKey:@"WaitingTime"];
    [encoder encodeObject:self.reviewCount forKey:@"ReviewCount"];
}
```

initWithCoder Method for the MenuItem Class (MenuItem.m)

```
- (id)initWithCoder:(NSCoder *)decoder
{
    if ((self = [super init])) {
        self.itemId = [decoder decodeObjectForKey:@"ItemId"];
        self.image = [decoder decodeObjectForKey:@"Image"];
        self.name = [decoder decodeObjectForKey:@"Name"];
        self.spicyLevel = [decoder decodeObjectForKey:@"SpicyLevel"];
        self.rating = [decoder decodeObjectForKey:@"Rating"];
        self.itemDescription = [decoder decodeObjectForKey:@"ItemDescripti
on"];
        self.waitingTime = [decoder decodeObjectForKey:@"WaitingTime"];
        self.reviewCount = [decoder decodeObjectForKey:@"ReviewCount"];
    }
    return self;
}
```

As I mentioned previously, you can generate the NSCoding protocol implementation using Accessorizer.

Based on the cache flow flowchart you saw in Figure 17-1, you have to implement the actual caching logic in the `viewWillAppear:` method. The following code added to `viewWillAppear:` implements that.

Code Snippet in the viewWillAppear: of Your View Controller that Restores Your Model Objects from Cache

```
NSArray *paths = NSSearchPathForDirectoriesInDomains(NSCachesDirectory,
NSUserDomainMask, YES);
NSString *cachesDirectory = [paths objectAtIndex:0];
NSString *archivePath = [cachesDirectory stringByAppendingPathComponent:@"
AppCache/MenuItems.archive"];

NSMutableArray *cachedItems = [NSKeyedUnarchiver unarchiveObjectWithFile:a
rchivePath];

if(cachedItems == nil)
  self.menuItems = [AppDelegate.engine localMenuItems];
else
  self.menuItems = cachedItems;

NSTimeInterval stalenessLevel = [[[[NSFileManager defaultManager] attribut
esOfItemAtPath:archivePath error:nil]
fileModificationDate] timeIntervalSinceNow];

if(stalenessLevel > THRESHOLD)
  self.menuItems = [AppDelegate.engine localMenuItems];

[self updateUI];
```

The logical flow of the caching mechanism is

1. The view controller checks for previously cached items in the archive file `MenuItems.archive` and unarchives it.

2. If the `MenuItems.archive` is not present it makes a call to fetch data from server.

3. If `MenuItems.archive` is present, it checks the archive file modification date to determine how stale this cached data is. If it's old (as determined by your business requirements), fetch the data again from the server. Otherwise display the cached data.

Next, the following code added to the `viewDidDisappear` method saves (as `NSKeyedArchiver` archives) your models to the caches directory.

Code Snippet in the viewWillDisappear: of Your View Controller that Caches Your Models

```
NSArray *paths = NSSearchPathForDirectoriesInDomains(NSCachesDirectory,
NSUserDomainMask, YES);
NSString *cachesDirectory = [paths objectAtIndex:0];
NSString *archivePath = [cachesDirectory stringByAppendingPathComponent:@"
AppCache/MenuItems.archive"];

[NSKeyedArchiver archiveRootObject:self.menuItems toFile:archivePath];
```

As the view disappears, you save the contents of the `menuItems` array to an archive file. Take care not to cache this if you didn't fetch from the server in `viewWillAppear`.

So just by adding fewer than ten lines in the view controller (and a bunch of Accessorizer generated lines in the model), you add caching support to your app.

Refactoring

You will be using this caching logic in several view controllers in your app. This means that you will have lots of duplicated code in `viewWillAppear` and `viewWillDisappear`. To make this easier, you will learn how to refactor this code and extract the filenames into a different class. Let's call that class `AppCache`. Refactor this code so that your view controller's `viewWillAppear/viewWillDisappear` block looks like the following code. The lines in bold show the changes made while refactoring, and are explained following the code.

Refactored Code Snippet in the viewWillAppear: of Your View Controller that Caches Your Models Using the AppCache Class. (MenuItemsViewController.m)

```
- (void)viewWillAppear:(BOOL)animated
{
  NSMutableArray *cachedItems = [AppCache getCachedMenuItems];

  if(cachedItems == nil)
    self.menuItems = [AppDelegate.engine localMenuItems];
  else
```

```
        self.menuItems = cachedItems;

    if([AppCache isMenuItemsStale])
        self.menuItems = [AppDelegate.engine localMenuItems];

    [self updateUI];

    [super viewWillAppear:animated];
}

- (void)viewWillDisappear:(BOOL)animated
{
    [AppCache cacheMenuItems:self.menuItems];
    [super viewWillDisappear:animated];
}
```

There are a couple of major changes in your view controller that include adding the AppCache class. The AppCache class abstracts the knowledge of staleness from the view controller. It also abstracts exactly where the cache is stored. Later in this chapter you modify this AppCache to introduce another layer of cache where the content is stored in memory.

Because the AppCache class abstracts out where the cache is exactly stored, you don't have to worry about copying and pasting code that gets the application's cache directory. In case your app is like the iHotelApp example, you also easily add security to the cached data by creating subdirectories for every user. The helper method in AppCache then currently returns the cache directory that can be modified to return the correct subdirectory for the currently logged-in user. This way, data cached by user 1 will not be visible to user 2, who logs in later.

The complete code listing is available from the source code download for Chapter 17 on the book's website.

Cache Versioning

The AppCache class implemented on-demand caching. When the view appears and disappears, caching happens behind the scenes. However, when you update the app, you might change your model classes. That means that any previously archived data will no longer be restored on your new models. As you learned earlier, in on-demand caching your data is not that important and you can delete it when you update the app. In the sample code, you do that by just deleting the cache folder and rebuilding it again on-demand. You don't really have to migrate data because the data might already be stale across version updates.

Invalidating the Cache

In this section you add the necessary methods to delete the cache directory contents when the app is updated. To detect version updates, you have to save your application version inside NSUserDefaults every time the app launches, and check whether the previously saved version is older than the app's current version. If yes, delete the cache folder and resave the new version to NSUserDefaults.

The following is the code for doing this. Add it to your AppCache init method.

Code Snippet in the AppCache Initialize Method that Handles Cache Versioning (AppCache.m)

```
+(void) initialize
{
  NSString *cacheDirectory = [AppCache cacheDirectory];
  if(![[NSFileManager defaultManager] fileExistsAtPath:cacheDirectory])
  {
    [[NSFileManager defaultManager]  createDirectoryAtPath:cacheDirectory
    withIntermediateDirectories:YES
    attributes:nil
    error:nil];
  }

  double lastSavedCacheVersion = [[NSUserDefaults standardUserDefaults]
doubleForKey:@"CACHE_VERSION"];
  double currentAppVersion = [[AppCache appVersion] doubleValue];

  if( lastSavedCacheVersion == 0.0f || lastSavedCacheVersion <
currentAppVersion)
  {
    [AppCache clearCache];
    // assigning current version to preference
    [[NSUserDefaults standardUserDefaults] setDouble:currentAppVersion
forKey:@"CACHE_VERSION"];
    [[NSUserDefaults standardUserDefaults] synchronize];
  }
}
```

Note that this code depends on a helper method that gets the application's current version. You can read the version from your app's `Info.plist` file using this block of code:

Code to Get the Current App Version from the Info.plist file (AppCache.m)

```
+(NSString*) appVersion
{
  CFStringRef versStr = (CFStringRef)CFBundleGetValueForInfoDictionaryKey(
CFBundleGetMainBundle(), kCFBundleVersionKey);
  NSString *version = [NSString stringWithUTF8String:CFStringGetCStringPtr
(versStr,kCFStringEncodingMacRoman)];

  return version;
}
```

The preceding code calls a method to clear the cache directory. The following snippet illustrates that.

Code Snippet that Clears All Cached Files from the Cache Directory (AppCache.m)

```
+(void) clearCache
{
  NSArray *cachedItems = [[NSFileManager defaultManager] contentsOfDirectory
AtPath:[AppCache cacheDirectory] error:nil];
```

```
    for(NSString *path in cachedItems)
        [[NSFileManager defaultManager] removeItemAtPath:path error:nil];
}
```

Creating an In-Memory Cache

Every iOS device shipped so far has included flash memory, and this flash memory has one little problem: It has limited read-write cycles before it wears out. While this limit is generally very high compared to the device's life span, it's still important to avoid writing to and reading from flash memory too often. In the previous example, you were caching directly to disk when the view hides and reading directly from disk whenever the view is shown. This could be taxing to the flash memory on users' devices. To avoid this, you can introduce another cache layer, which stores your archives in memory (NSMutableDictionary). In the "Implementing NSKeyedArchiver" section, you learned two methods for creating archives: one for saving them to a file and one for saving them as NSData objects. You will use the second method, which gives you a NSData pointer that you can store in a NSMutableDictionary rather than as flat files in file system. The other advantage you get by introducing an in-memory cache layer is slightly higher performance when you archive and unarchive contents. While this sounds complicated, it isn't really. In this section you look at how to add a transparent in-memory cache to the AppCache class. (In-memory cache is transparent in the sense that the calling code—the ViewController—doesn't even know about its presence and doesn't need any code changes.) You also design a least-recently-used algorithm to save the cached data back to disk if it hasn't been used recently.

The following list outlines the steps you follow to create the in-memory cache. These steps are explained in more detail in the following sections.

1. Add some variables to hold your cached data in memory.

2. Limit the size of the in-memory cache and write the least-recently-used items to a file and remove it from in-memory. RAM is limited, and when you hit the limit, you will get a memory warning. Failing to release memory when you receive this warning will crash your app. You obviously don't want that to happen, right? So you set a maximum threshold for the memory cache. When anything is added to the cache after it's full, the last used object should be saved to file (flash memory).

3. Handle memory warnings and write the in-memory cache to flash memory (as files).

4. Write all in-memory cache to flash memory (files) when the app is closed or quit.

Designing the AppCache

Let's start designing the AppCache class by adding the variables to hold the cache data. Add an NSMutableDictionary for storing your cache data, an NSMutableArray to keep track of recently used items, in chronological order, and an integer that limits the maximum size of this cache, as shown in the following code.

Variables in AppCache

```
static NSMutableDictionary *memoryCache;
static NSMutableArray *recentlyAccessedKeys;
static int kCacheMemoryLimit;
```

Now you have to make changes to the `cacheMenuItems:` and `getCachedMenuItems` methods in `AppCache` to save the model objects transparently to this in-memory cache.

```
+(void) cacheMenuItems:(NSMutableArray*) menuItems
{
   [self cacheData:[NSKeyedArchiver archivedDataWithRootObject:menuItems]
           toFile:@"MenuItems.archive"];
}

+(NSMutableArray*) getCachedMenuItems
{
   return [NSKeyedUnarchiver unarchiveObjectWithData:[self
dataForFile:@"MenuItems.archive"]];
}
```

Instead of writing directly to file, the preceding code calls a helper method, `cacheData:toFile:`. This method will save the `NSData` from the `NSKeyedArchiver` to the in-memory cache. It also checks and removes the least-recently-accessed data and save it to file when the prefixed memory limit for the number of in-memory items is reached. The implementation for this is shown in the following code.

Helper Method that Transparently Caches Data to In-Memory Cache (AppCache.m)

```
+(void) cacheData:(NSData*) data toFile:(NSString*) fileName
{
   [memoryCache setObject:data forKey:fileName];
   if([recentlyAccessedKeys containsObject:fileName])
   {
      [recentlyAccessedKeys removeObject:fileName];
   }

   [recentlyAccessedKeys insertObject:fileName atIndex:0];

   if([recentlyAccessedKeys count] > kCacheMemoryLimit)
   {
      NSString *leastRecentlyUsedDataFilename = [recentlyAccessedKeys
lastObject];
      NSData *leastRecentlyUsedCacheData = [memoryCache objectForKey:leastRe
centlyUsedDataFilename];
      NSString *archivePath = [[AppCache cacheDirectory] stringByAppendingPa
thComponent:fileName];
      [leastRecentlyUsedCacheData writeToFile:archivePath atomically:YES];

      [recentlyAccessedKeys removeLastObject];
      [memoryCache removeObjectForKey:leastRecentlyUsedDataFilename];
   }
}
```

Similar to the preceding code, which caches data (`cacheData:toFile:`), you should write a method that checks the in-memory cache and returns this data, instead of directly reading from a file. The method should access the file only if it isn't.

Helper Method that Transparently Retrieves the Cached Data from In-Memory Cache (AppCache.m)

```objc
+(NSData*) dataForFile:(NSString*) fileName
{
  NSData *data = [memoryCache objectForKey:fileName];
  if(data) return data; // data is present in memory cache

   NSString *archivePath = [[AppCache cacheDirectory] stringByAppendingPath
Component:fileName];
  data = [NSData dataWithContentsOfFile:archivePath];

  if(data)
    [self cacheData:data toFile:fileName]; // put the recently accessed
data to memory cache

  return data;
}
```

This method also saves the data read from flash memory back to in-memory cache, which is just like how a least-recently-used caching algorithm works.

Handling Memory Warnings

For the most part, the AppCache is now complete and you have added a transparent in-memory cache without modifying the calling code. However, there is one more important thing that you should do. Because you are retaining data used by views in AppCache, the memory consumption of your app continues to grow, and the chances of receiving a memory warning become very high. To avoid this, you handle the memory warning notifications in AppCache. In the static initialize method, add a notification observer to UIApplication DidReceiveMemoryWarningNotification:

```objc
[[NSNotificationCenter defaultCenter] addObserver:self selector:@selector(
saveMemoryCacheToDisk:)
name:UIApplicationDidReceiveMemoryWarningNotification object:nil];
```

Now write a method to save the in-memory cache items to files:

```objc
+(void) saveMemoryCacheToDisk:(NSNotification *)notification
{
  for(NSString *filename in [memoryCache allKeys])
  {
    NSString *archivePath = [[AppCache cacheDirectory] stringByAppending
PathComponent:filename];
    NSData *cacheData = [memoryCache objectForKey:filename];
    [cacheData writeToFile:archivePath atomically:YES];
  }

  [memoryCache removeAllObjects];
}
```

This method ensures that your AppCache doesn't eat up the available system memory, yet be faster than writing directly to files from your view controller.

Handling Termination and Enter Background Notifications

You should also ensure that your in-memory cache is saved when the app quits or enters background. This gives an added advantage to your on-demand caching: offline access. Let's add the third and final step, which is to observe for app's resigning active or closing notifications and do the same thing as above. No extra methods are needed; just add observers in the initialize method for `UIApplicationDidEnterBackgroundNotification` and `UIApplicationWillTerminateNotification`: This is to ensure that your in-memory cache is saved to file system.

Observing Notifications and Saving In-Memory Cache to Disk (AppCache.m)

```
[[NSNotificationCenter defaultCenter] addObserver:self selector:@selector(
saveMemoryCacheToDisk:)
name: UIApplicationDidEnterBackgroundNotification object:nil];

[[NSNotificationCenter defaultCenter] addObserver:self selector:@selector(
saveMemoryCacheToDisk:)
name: UIApplicationWillTerminateNotification object:nil];
```

Remember to call `removeObserver` in `dealloc` as well. For the complete AppCache code, download the code sample from the book's website.

The next section presents a popular use for caching (caching thumbnails/avatars) as well as guidance on how to design an ImageCache utility based on what you've learned in this chapter.

Caching Images

In most of the web service-related apps, the data you display often contains images and thumbnails attached to it. iOS by default doesn't provide a built-in mechanism to cache these images and thumbnails. To make these thumbnails load faster, you have to cache them. Invalidating these caches can be done when the cached image is "stale." "Stale" here is again business-rule specific. In an app that sells wallpapers, thumbnails older than 30 minutes might be considered "old," whereas in a social networking app that caches your friends' avatar thumbnails, 2- or 3-day-old avatars are still acceptable. This section offers suggestions for designing an ImageCache utility that is configurable and works in a way that's very similar to the AppCache you wrote earlier.

Components of ImageCache

The image cache you are going to write is very similar to `AppCache` in architecture. It's composed of two major components. The first component is a singleton class that encapsulates the complete caching logic like the `AppCache`. The second component (that is different from `AppCache`) is an `NSOperation` that performs the actual download. In many ways this singleton behaves like the `AppCache` you wrote in the previous section. The same way that `AppCache` has public methods to read and write data to it, the `ImageCache` singleton will expose methods to request a new image. In the "Implementing NSKeyedArchiver" section you learned two methods for creating archives: one for saving them to a file and one for saving them as `NSData` objects.

Any such cache component should check whether the requested file is already present before attempting a download. Similar to the design of `AppCache`, the `ImageCache` should have two levels of cache. One is the file system (the flash storage) and the other is the in-memory cache.

Creating the ImageCache Singleton

In this section you create the singleton class and add a public method to accept URLs for fetching images. In addition, the method also encapsulates certain state variables like the list of images cached in-memory. This in-memory cache should be shared across every instance (as though it weren't a singleton) of `ImageCache` that's created in the app. This was not a requirement for `AppCache`, which is why it wasn't a singleton.

One difference between `AppCache` and `ImageCache` is that `AppCache` returns data immediately when you request it. The data you fetch is either in memory or in a file. If the data is not present, `AppCache` just returns `nil`, which is perfectly acceptable in that scenario. That's not the case for `ImageCache`. If the image you requested is not present locally, you have to fetch it from the URL. This also means that `ImageCache` cannot return data on the same method that called it. In Chapter 16, you learned about blocks and how to pass function blocks as parameters. You will use the techniques learned there to design your `ImageCache`. `ImageCache` will return data by invoking a block after the image is fetched from the remote source. The caller will be notified of the image fetch asynchronously after the image is fetched.

Here's the first and only public method of the ImageCache singleton:

```
-(void) imageAtURL:(NSURL*) url onCompletion:(void(^)(UIImage* image,
NSURL* url)) imageFetchedBlock;
```

Now you have a method that accepts two parameters: a URL and a block. The following list outlines the flow of the method.

1. The ImageCache singleton checks whether the image at this URL is already present in the memory cache. If it's present, return the image by invoking the block method.

2. Check whether the image is present in the file system (cached previously). Then, depending on the result of this check, do one of the following:

   - If it's present, the image should be brought back and stored in the memory cache and then returned to the caller by invoking the block method.

   - If the image is not present in any of the local caches, fetch it from the remote source. For this, you write an `NSOperation` subclass (`ImageFetchOperation`), and queue image requests coming in. When the operation completes, the `ImageFetchOperation` notifies the caller by invoking the block method. `ImageCache` should pass the block to the `ImageFetchOperation` class so that `ImageFetchOperation` can directly pass the fetched image to the caller.

One important step that you must do to improve the performance is to check whether the image request has been queued previously. If the requested URL is currently in the queue, but not yet downloaded, just add the new block to that `ImageFetchOperation`. This ensures that both callers are notified when the image is fetched, yet performs the actual fetch operation exactly once. This is essentially a performance enhancement to the `ImageCache`.

The properties in the `ImageCache` singleton are

Properties in the ImageCache Singleton (ImageCache.m)

```
@property (nonatomic, strong) NSOperationQueue *imageFetchQueue;
@property (nonatomic, strong)
NSMutableDictionary *runningOperations;
@property (nonatomic, strong) NSMutableDictionary *memoryCache;
@property (nonatomic, strong) NSMutableArray *memoryCacheKeys;
```

ImageFetchOperation – NSOperation Subclass

The `NSOperation` subclass is fairly simple and straightforward in implementation. All it does is accept a URL and a couple of blocks to be invoked. One is a block that is invoked when the operation ends so that the ImageCache singleton can mark this URL as complete, and the other is a block that passes the fetched image to the caller. This is the same block received by `ImageCache` from its caller, copied to this operation.

The basic methods in the ImageFetchOperation header looks like this:

Properties and Methods in ImageFetchOperation (ImageFetchOperation.m)

```
@property (nonatomic, strong) NSURL *photoURL;
@property (nonatomic, strong) NSMutableArray *observerBlocks;

-(id) initWithURL:(NSURL*) url onCompletion:(void(^)()) completionBlock;
-(void) addImageFetchObserverBlock:(void(^)(UIImage* image, NSURL* url))
observerBlock;
```

The implementation is fairly simple. Fetch the URL and check whether the returned mime-type is an image. If it's an image, construct a `UIImage` object and invoke all the blocks. If it is not an image, log a message.

Based on what you learned in the last few sections and in the previous section on `AppCache`, try implementing `ImageCache` on your own. If you need help, there is always the complete source code for this chapter waiting for you on the book's website.

Using iCloud

In iOS 5 (and Mac OS X Lion), Apple introduced a new and arguably most important feature, or service, called iCloud. iCloud stores your content and continuously pushes it to all devices associated with a specific Apple account. To the end user, the integration is seamless and happens "automatically." However, to give your customers that kind of user experience, some hard development work must be done.

Prior to iCloud, developers supported Dropbox Sync to synchronize data across user devices. While this handles the problem of syncing data in the iOS 4 era, it's still limited to flat files, and most importantly, your users should have a Dropbox account and they should sign in with their Dropbox credentials on your app. With iCloud, no such signing in is necessary. You get access to the iCloud data store you declare for your app if the user is running iOS 5. No extra steps or actions are necessary from your user. Moreover, iCloud has support for key-value data storage and excellent support for your Core Data-managed app. If your app is data-centric, iCloud alone should be a reason to migrate your app to iOS 5.

Managing Document and Key-Value Data Storage on iCloud

You can store two kinds of data on iCloud: traditional files (document file storage) and key-value data. If your app currently uses `NSUserDefaults` to store app-specific settings, you might consider using iCloud key-value data storage to sync those settings across the user's devices. The preferred way to store documents on iCloud is to design your persistent models as subclasses of `UIDocument` or `UIManagedDocument`. The next sections discuss the differences between them.

UIDocument

Using `UIDocument` is not a prerequisite for iCloud; however, if you manage individual files yourself, you should also manage file presenters and coordinators to support the iCloud's locking mechanism. `UIDocument` has built-in support for this. Additionally, it helps resolve version conflicts made by updates on other devices.

Another important feature provided by `UIDocument` is its excellent support for managing *file packages*. (A file package is a directory of files that appear to the user as a single file. On your Mac, applications in your /Applications folder are file packages.) File packages can store individual components in your app as separate files, so a change to one of those components means that only the changed file needs to be sent to iCloud. For example, in a drawing app you might consider saving the actual drawing in a file, and sets of custom brushes and fonts in separate files within the same file package. You can still manage the entire file package using just one `UIDocument` subclass. Now when a user opens a large drawing and edits a custom brush, only the file representing the custom brush needs to be sent, and that is usually far smaller than the drawing.

UIManagedDocument

`UIManagedDocument` is a concrete subclass of `UIDocument` that integrates with Core Data. You initialize it with the URL of your persistent store and the document object does the rest. It then creates a Core Data stack based on your core data model file (.xcdatamodeld file). If you are currently using Core Data to store your user content, you should adopt `UIManagedDocument` in your app to support iCloud data syncing. This is arguably the easiest way to migrate apps that currently use Core Data.

Key-Value Data Storage

The second type of data you can store is key-value data. If your app currently stores app-specific settings in `NSUserDefaults`, consider using the iCloud's key-value data storage to sync these settings across users' devices. The total size of data you store here cannot exceed 64KB and no key can be more than 4KB. In most cases, you will be saving a Boolean or an integer or a string, which usually is less than 4KB. If you are storing serialized models, however, ensure that they're less than 4KB, or use `UIDocument` as discussed in the previous section.

Understanding the iCloud Data Store

To start using iCloud in your app, you first need to configure your App ID for iCloud usage. After doing so, generate your provisioning profile and request entitlements in your app. Depending on the data storage requirements in your app, you need to request either one or both of the following entitlements.

iCloud Entitlements key

```
com.apple.developer.ubiquity-container-identifiers
com.apple.developer.ubiquity-kvstore-identifier
```

The first one is used for document storage and the second is used for key-value storage. Once this is done, you can start moving documents from your application's sandbox to iCloud storage. The entitlements ensure that data generated by your app is sandboxed and will not be accessible to other apps.

Sharing Data within Apps (or App Suites)

On iCloud, you identify and request a data store container by its unique id. This is normally your application's App ID, but not necessarily. You can use the same iCloud data store container for two of your apps and share data within them. This is a very powerful feature, especially if you are developing a "lite" and "pro" versions of an app. You can now use the same ubiquitous container identifier, which means that data created by a user using the lite version becomes automatically available if he purchases your pro version, making the migration process easier. You can also use this technique to share data among a suite of apps you build.

The iCloud data store resides initially on the user's iPhone until it's moved to iCloud by the iCloud daemon running on the iOS device. Once you move the document to iCloud storage, you can safely delete the original copy because all subsequent edits will happen directly to the file stored on iCloud. As a developer, you don't have to worry about uploading to a remote source or be bothered about network disconnection. The iCloud daemon automatically takes care of this syncing. You should, however, handle conflict resolutions. The default conflict resolution strategy iCloud follows is to choose the "last modified" document. While this might be okay in some cases, you should evaluate this strategy on a case-by-case basis for your app.

Storing Data within Your iCloud Container

With iOS 5, the Settings app on every device has an iCloud section that allows users to see how much data they have used on iCloud for backup and how much data apps syncing with iCloud use. When you store your files inside the iCloud container, it appears as a big blob of data to the user. When you store them inside the Documents directory, users can see the individual files and their sizes. Files inside this Documents directory can be deleted one by one, whereas data stored outside of this directory appears as a big blob and can be deleted only all at once. To avoid confusion and to play nice, always store any user-generated files inside this Documents directory, and store miscellaneous metadata that you don't want the users to see outside of this directory.

A Word about iCloud Backup

With versions of iOS prior to iOS 5, when the device syncs with iTunes, the contents of your app's documents folder is automatically backed up. With iOS 5 devices, the same contents are backed up to the iCloud, but documents you store on iCloud manually are not included in the backup because they are already on iCloud. Do note that, this automatic backup is different from iCloud syncing. Backed-up documents are treated as opaque data that can be used only to completely restore an iOS device. Individual file access is not possible programmatically or by the user.

Summary

In this chapter you designed a very powerful yet simple way to implement caching in your app. You also designed a similar utility class to cache image thumbnails. Finally, you learned about the new iCloud service and explained a fairly important technique for sharing data across your own apps and among a user's devices. The techniques discussed here will help you take your app to the next level by improving its overall usability.

Further Reading

Apple Documentation

The following documents are available in the iOS Developer Library at `developer.apple.com` or through the Xcode Documentation and API Reference.

Archives and Serializations Programming Guide

iCloud – Apple Developer

Books

The Pragmatic Bookshelf | Core Data
`http://pragprog.com/titles/mzcd/core-data`

Other Resources

Callahan, Kevin. *Mac App Store.* 2011
`http://itunes.apple.com/gb/app/accessorizer/id402866670?mt=12`

## Chapter 18

Fancy Text Layout

There are several options for displaying text in iOS. There are simple controls like UILabel and full rendering engines like UIWebView. For complete control, including laying out columns or drawing text along a path, you can implement your own layout engine with Core Text. Unfortunately, there is no easy-to-use rich text control available. Each option has significant restrictions. In this chapter you explore the choices available and learn how to make the most of them within their limitations, while we all wait for the day that Apple finally provides UIRichTextView. You also take a brief look at some of the third-party options available.

The Normal Stuff: Fields, Views, and Labels

You're probably already familiar with UILabel, UITextField, and UITextView, so I discuss them only briefly here. They are the basic controls you use for day-to-day text layout.

UILabel is a lightweight, static text control. It is very common for developers to have problems with dynamic labels (labels with contents set programmatically) they create in Interface Builder. Here are a few tips for using UILabel:

- UILabel can display multiline text. Just set its numberOfLines property in code or the Lines property in Interface Builder. This is the maximum number of lines. If you want it to be unbounded, set it to zero.

- By default, Interface Builder turns on adjustsFontSizeToFitWidth. This can be surprising if you assign text that is wider than the label. Rather than truncating or overflowing the label, the text shrinks. Generally it's a good idea to make your dynamic labels very wide to avoid truncating or resizing.

- Unlike other views, user interaction is disabled by default for UILabel. If you attach a UIGestureRecognizer to a UILabel, it won't work unless you remember to set userInteractionEnabled to YES. Don't confuse this with the enabled property, which only controls the appearance of the label.

- UILabel is not a UIControl and does not have a contentVerticalAlignment property. Text is always vertically centered. If you want to adjust the vertical location of the text, you need to resize the label with sizeToFit and then adjust the label's frame.origin.

UITextField provides simple, single-line text entry. It includes an optional "clear" button and optional overlay views on the left and right (leftView and rightView). The overlay views can be used to provide hints about the field's purpose. For instance, a search icon on the left is a very space-efficient way of indicating a search field. Remember that the overlay views are UIView objects. You can use a UIButton here or any other kind of interactive view. Just make sure they're large enough for the user to touch easily. You generally should not move these views with setFrame:. Override the methods leftViewRectForBounds: or rightViewRectForBounds:. UITextField then lays them out appropriately. The text rectangle (textRectForBounds:) is clipped automatically so it does not overlap these rectangles.

A common problem with `UITextField` is detecting when the user presses the Return key. In many cases you would like to use this to automatically process the data and dismiss the keyboard. To do so, you need to implement a `UITextFieldDelegate` method, as shown here:

ViewController.m (AutoReturn)

```
- (BOOL)textField:(UITextField *)textField
        shouldChangeCharactersInRange:(NSRange)range
        replacementString:(NSString *)string {
  if ([string isEqualToString:@"\n"]) {
    self.outputLabel.text = [textField text];
    [textField resignFirstResponder];
    return NO;
  }
  return YES;
}
```

Whenever the user presses the Return key, a newline character (\n) is sent to this method. When that happens, you apply whatever processing you would like (in this case, setting the text of another label), and then call `resignFirstResponder` to dismiss the keyboard. A similar technique can be used with `UITextView`.

`UITextView` is easily confused with `UITextField`, but serves a somewhat different function. It is intended for multiline, scrolling text, editing, or viewing. It is a type of `UIScrollView`, not a `UIControl`. You can apply a font to the text, but the same font is used for the entire view. `UITextView` cannot display rich text from an `NSAttributedString`. There is no Apple-provided view that can do that. Generally the choice between `UITextField` and `UITextView` is obvious based on how much text the user is going to type.

Web Views for Rich Text

Apple's recommendation for viewing rich text is to use `UIWebView`. This is unfortunate because while `UIWebView` is well adapted to displaying web pages, it's not ideal for displaying rich text. First, `UIWebView` requires HTML. The native rich-text data structure in Cocoa is `NSAttributedString`, but iOS provides no mechanism for converting between `NSAttributedString` and HTML. Furthermore, `UIWebView` is slow, its loading API is asynchronous, and it provides no easy access to its current contents. In short, `UIWebView` is almost the opposite of what you'd want in a good rich-text viewer. Regrettably, it is often the best option available. This section shows you how to use it most effectively.

Displaying and Accessing HTML in a Web View

The code to load HTML into a `UIWebView` is fairly straightforward:

```
NSString *html = @"This is <i>some</i> <b>rich</b> text";
[self.webView loadHTMLString:html baseURL:nil];
```

`webView` does not yet contain the HTML string. This is only a request to load the string at some point in the future. You need to wait for the delegate callback `webViewDidFinishLoad:`. At that point, you can read the data in the web view using JavaScript:

```
- (void)webViewDidFinishLoad:(UIWebView *)webView {
  NSString *
  body = [self.webView
          stringByEvaluatingJavaScriptFromString:
          @"document.body.innerHTML"];
  // Use body
}
```

The only way to access the data inside the web view is through JavaScript and `stringByEvaluatingJava ScriptFromString:`. I recommend isolating this JavaScript to a single object to provide a simpler interface. For instance, you could create a `MyWebViewController` object that owns the `UIWebView` and provides a `body` property to set and retrieve the contents.

Responding to User Interaction

It is fairly common in a rich-text viewer to support some kind of user interaction. When the user taps on a button or link, you may want to run some Objective-C code. You can achieve this by creating a special URL scheme. Rather than `http`, pick a custom scheme identifier. For example, you might have the following HTML:

```
<p>Click <a href='do-something:First'>here</a> to do something.</p>
```

In this example the URL scheme is `do-something` and the resource specifier is `First`. When this link is tapped, the entire URL is sent to the delegate and you can act on it like this:

```
- (BOOL)webView:(UIWebView *)webView
shouldStartLoadWithRequest:(NSURLRequest *)request
 navigationType:(UIWebViewNavigationType)navigationType {
  NSURL *URL = request.URL;
  if ([URL.scheme isEqualToString:@"do-something"]) {
    NSString *message = URL.resourceSpecifier;
    // Do something with message
    return NO;
  }
  return YES;
}
```

Returning `YES` from this delegate method allows `UIWebView` to load the request. You should return `NO` for your custom scheme. Otherwise, `UIWebView` will try to load it and pass an error to `webView:didFailLoadWithError:`.

URL schemes are case-insensitive. The result of `request.URL.scheme` will always be lowercase, even if you use mixed-case in the HTML. I recommend using a hyphen (–) to separate words in the scheme. You can also use a period (.) or plus (+). The rest of the URL is case-sensitive.

Drawing Web Views in Scroll and Table Views

`UIWebView` cannot be embedded in a `UIScrollView` or `UITableView` because the web view's event handling will interfere with the scroll view. This makes it effectively unusable for table view cells. Because web views have significant performance issues, they're not appropriate for table view cells in any case. You should generally draw table view cells using UIKit drawing (`drawInRect:withFont:`) or Core Text.

Instead of directly embedding the web view, you can capture the web view as a `UIImage` and then draw that image in the scroll view or table view. To capture a web view as a `UIImage`, you need to call `renderInContext:` on its layer as shown here:

```
UIGraphicsBeginImageContext(self.webView.bounds.size);
[webView.layer renderInContext:UIGraphicsGetCurrentContext()];
UIImage *image = UIGraphicsGetImageFromCurrentImageContext();
UIGraphicsEndImageContext();
```

For web views larger than 1024×1024, you need to break them up into smaller pieces and render them individually.

Rich Editing with Web Views

There are several options for rich-text editing with `UIWebView`. Recent versions of WebKit have added significant new features to facilitate rich-text editing. Most important is the `contentEditable` DOM attribute. Applying this to the `body` or any `div` automatically makes the element editable. If you are interested in the approach, you should generally go with an established web-based editor like TinyMCE or CKEditor. Both of these include good WebKit optimizations. See "Further Reading" at the end of the chapter for links to more information on these.

Web views are useful for their intended purpose of displaying web pages and work fairly well for rich-text editing. They are somewhat slow and complicated to use, though, particularly if there is significant interaction between Objective-C and JavaScript. If you choose to develop parts of your application in JavaScript, I recommend that you separate the parts that are in Objective-C from the parts in JavaScript, and try to move data between them as infrequently as possible. If you make portions of your application pure JavaScript, you can develop those using normal web-development tools and techniques, including the features in Safari's Develop menu. This is much easier to develop and debug than code that includes both Objective-C and JavaScript.

The ultimate extension of this is to use a framework like PhoneGap (see "Further Reading") to develop a web application with a thin Objective-C wrapper. It is difficult to get the full power of iOS this way, but it could simplify development for applications that rely heavily on JavaScript.

Core Text

Core Text is the low-level text layout and font-handling engine in iOS. It is extremely fast and powerful. With it you can handle complex layouts like multicolumn text and even curved text.

Core Text is a C-based API that uses Core Foundation naming and memory management. If you're not familiar with Core Foundation patterns, see Chapter 19.

Understanding Bold, Italic, and Underline

Before diving into text layout, be sure you understand the three most common rich-text attributes: bold, italic, and underline. These are generally presented to the user as simple attributes, but they are quite different from each other.

In typography, you do not "bold" a font by drawing it with thicker lines. Instead, the font designer provides a heavier weight version of the font, called a *variation*. In iOS the Helvetica font has a variation called Helvetica-Bold. While these fonts are related, they are completely different CTFont objects. To find font variations, you use CTFontCreateCopyWithSymbolicTraits.

Italic is similar, but there are two related typefaces that are commonly treated as "italic." True italic type is based on calligraphy and uses different shapes (*glyphs*) than the regular (or *roman*) font. Some fonts do not have a true italic variation and merely slant the roman type to the right. This is called *oblique*. When users request italic, they generally mean either italic or oblique. If you pass kCTFontItalicTrait to CTFontCreateCopyWith SymbolicTraits, it returns the best font that matches this looser definition. Text with both bold and italic requires yet another font variation such as Helvetica-BoldOblique.

Unlike bold and italic, underline is a decoration like color or shadow. You do not change font when you add decorations. See Figure 18-1 for examples of bold, italic, and underline. Note carefully the significant difference between the glyphs of the roman font and the italic variation, while the underlined glyphs are identical to the roman font. Also note that underline is not as simple as drawing a line under the text. Proper underline includes breaks for descenders like *p*. All of these small details greatly improve the appearance and legibility of text in iOS.

> Example Baskerville
> Example Underline
> **Example Bold**
> *Example Italic*

Figure 18-1 Variations and decorations of Baskerville

You generally do not need to be aware of these subtleties when developing for iOS, but when using Core Text these issues can be important.

Attributed Strings

The fundamental data type in Core Text is CFAttributedString. An *attributed string* is a string that applies attributes to ranges of characters. The attributes can be any key-value pair, but for the purposes of Core Text, they usually contain style information such as font, color, and indentation.

It is usually best to use CFMutableAttributedString so you can modify the attributes of various parts of the string. CFAttributedString requires that all of the string have the same attributes.

In the following example, you create a basic, rectangular layout to display some rich text. First, you create an `NSAttributedString` and apply attributes to it. In later examples, you will use this `NSAttributedString`. You must link with `CoreText.framework` and `CoreGraphics.framework` for the examples in this section.

ViewController.m (SimpleLayout)

```
CFMutableAttributedStringRef attrString;
CTFontRef baseFont, boldFont, italicFont;

// Create the base string.
// Note how you can define a string over multiple lines.
CFStringRef string = CFSTR
(
  "Here is some simple text that includes bold and italics.\n"
  "\n"
  "We can even include some color."
  );

// Create the mutable attributed string
attrString = CFAttributedStringCreateMutable(NULL, 0);
CFAttributedStringReplaceString(attrString,
                                CFRangeMake(0, 0),
                                string);

// Set the base font
baseFont = CTFontCreateUIFontForLanguage(kCTFontUserFontType,
                                         16.0,
                                         NULL);
CFIndex length = CFStringGetLength(string);
CFAttributedStringSetAttribute(attrString,
                               CFRangeMake(0, length),
                               kCTFontAttributeName,
                               baseFont);

// Apply bold by finding the bold version of the current font.
boldFont = CTFontCreateCopyWithSymbolicTraits(baseFont,
                                              0,
                                              NULL,
                                              kCTFontBoldTrait,
                                              kCTFontBoldTrait);
CFAttributedStringSetAttribute(attrString,
                               CFStringFind(string,
                                            CFSTR("bold"),
                                            0),
                               kCTFontAttributeName,
                               boldFont);

// ... Apply italics the same way ...

// Apply color
CGColorRef color = [[UIColor redColor] CGColor];
```

```
CFAttributedStringSetAttribute(attrString,
                               CFStringFind(string,
                                            CFSTR("color"),
                                            0),
                               kCTForegroundColorAttributeName,
                               color);
```

// ... Use the attributed string ...

```
CFRelease(attrString);
CFRelease(baseFont);
CFRelease(boldFont);
CFRelease(italicFont);
```

CFAttributedString is toll-free bridged with NSAttributedString if you'd rather do more of this in Objective-C. Because Core Text constants are Core Foundation types, this can require a lot of type casting, but either approach is fine.

Paragraph Styles

Some styles apply to paragraphs rather than characters. These include alignment, line break, and spacing. Paragraph attributes are bundled into a CTParagraphStyle object. To create a CTParagraphStyle, you first need a collection of CTParagraphStyleSetting structures. Each of these includes the setting key (such as kCTParagraphStyleSpecifierAlignment), the size of the value, and a pointer to the value. This is somewhat complicated to declare, but allows Core Text to process it very quickly. Here's an example of how to center a paragraph of text:

ViewController.m (SimpleLayer)

```
CTTextAlignment alignment = kCTCenterTextAlignment;
CTParagraphStyleSetting setting = {
  kCTParagraphStyleSpecifierAlignment,
  sizeof(alignment), &alignment };

CTParagraphStyleRef style = CTParagraphStyleCreate(&setting, 1);
CFRange lastLineRange = // ... Range of text to center ...
CFAttributedStringSetAttribute(attrString, lastLineRange,
                               kCTParagraphStyleAttributeName,
                               style);
```

The call to CTParagraphStyleCreate takes a pointer to a C array of CTParagraphStyleSetting structs, and the number of structs in that C array. This is not a problem for static formatting, but it can be a little more challenging for dynamic formatting because CTParagraphStyle is immutable. One way to address this problem is by allocating an array of styles, and resizing it as needed with realloc, as shown here:

```
NSUInteger countOfSettings = 0;
CTParagraphStyleSetting *settings = NULL;
...
// Center if needed
if (isCentered(...)) {
```

```
      CTTextAlignment alignment = kCTCenterTextAlignment;
      ++countOfSettings;
    settings = realloc(settings,
                        countOfSettings * sizeof(*settings));
      CTParagraphStyleSetting setting = {
        kCTParagraphStyleSpecifierAlignment,
        sizeof(alignment), &alignment };

      settings[countOfSettings - 1] = setting;
    }
    ...
    // Apply the accumulated settings, and release memory
    if (countOfSettings > 0) {
      CTParagraphStyleRef style = CTParagraphStyleCreate(settings,
                                                countOfSettings);
      free(settings), settings = NULL;
      CFAttributedStringSetAttribute(attrString, range,
                            kCTParagraphStyleAttributeName, style);
    }
```

Paragraph settings are a little more complicated to manage, but provide very powerful layout options including centering, justification, indentation, and spacing. Making the most of them is worth the few extra lines of code.

Simple Layout with CTFramesetter

Once you have an attributed string, you generally lay out the text using CTFramesetter. A *framesetter* is responsible for creating frames of text. A CTFrame (*frame*) is an area enclosed by a CGPath containing one or more lines of text. Once you generate a frame, you draw it into a graphics context using CTFrameDraw. In the next example, you draw an attributed string into the current view using drawRect:.

First, you need to flip the view context. Core Text was originally designed on the Mac, and it performs all calculations in Mac coordinates. The origin is in the lower-left corner—lower-left origin (LLO)—and the y-coordinates run from bottom to top like in a mathematical graph. CTFramesetter does not work properly unless you invert the coordinate space, as shown in the following code.

CoreTextLabel.m (SimpleLayout)

```
- (id)initWithFrame:(CGRect)frame {
  if ((self = [super initWithFrame:frame])) {
    CGAffineTransform
    transform = CGAffineTransformMakeScale(1, -1);
    CGAffineTransformTranslate(transform,
                               0, -self.bounds.size.height);
    self.transform = transform;
    self.backgroundColor = [UIColor whiteColor];
  }
  return self;
}
```

Before drawing the text, you need to set the text transform, or *matrix*. The text matrix is not part of the graphics state and is not always initialized the way you would expect. It is not included in the state saved by CGContextSaveGState. If you are going to draw text, you should always call CGContextSetTextMatrix in drawRect:.

```
- (void)drawRect:(CGRect)rect {
  CGContextRef context = UIGraphicsGetCurrentContext();
  CGContextSetTextMatrix(context, CGAffineTransformIdentity);

  // Create a path to fill. In this case, use the whole view
  CGPathRef path = CGPathCreateWithRect(self.bounds, NULL);

  CFAttributedStringRef
  attrString = (__bridge CFTypeRef)self.attributedString;

  // Create the framesetter using the attributed string
  CTFramesetterRef framesetter = CTFramesetterCreateWithAttributedString(a
ttrString);

  // Create a single frame using the entire string (CFRange(0,0))
  // that fits inside of path.
  CTFrameRef
  frame = CTFramesetterCreateFrame(framesetter,
                                   CFRangeMake(0, 0),
                                   path,
                                   NULL);

  // Draw the frame into the current context
  CTFrameDraw(frame, context);

  CFRelease(frame);
  CFRelease(framesetter);
  CGPathRelease(path);
}
```

There is no guarantee that all of the text will fit within the frame. CTFramesetterCreateFrame simply lays out text within the path until it runs out of space or runs out of text.

Creating Frames for Noncontiguous Paths

Since at least iOS 4.2, CTFramesetterCreateFrame has accepted nonrectangular and noncontiguous frames. The *Core Text Programming Guide* has not been updated since before the release of iPhoneOS 3.2 and is occasionally ambiguous on this point. Because CTFramePathFillRule was added in iOS 4.2, Core Text has explicitly supported complex paths that cross themselves, including paths with embedded holes.

CTFramesetter always typesets the text from top to bottom (or right to left for vertical layouts such as Japanese). This works well for contiguous paths, but can be a problem for noncontiguous paths such as for multicolumn text. For example, you could define a series of columns this way:

ColumnView.m (Columns)

```
- (CGRect *)copyColumnRects {
  CGRect bounds = CGRectInset([self bounds], 20.0, 20.0);

  int column;
  CGRect* columnRects = (CGRect*)calloc(kColumnCount,
                                        sizeof(*columnRects));

  // Start by setting the first column to cover the entire view.
  columnRects[0] = bounds;
  // Divide the columns equally across the frame's width.
  CGFloat columnWidth = CGRectGetWidth(bounds) / kColumnCount;
  for (column = 0; column < kColumnCount - 1; column++) {
    CGRectDivide(columnRects[column], &columnRects[column],
            &columnRects[column + 1], columnWidth, CGRectMinXEdge);
  }

  // Inset all columns by a few pixels of margin.
  for (column = 0; column < kColumnCount; column++) {
    columnRects[column] = CGRectInset(columnRects[column],
                                      10.0, 10.0);
  }
  return columnRects;
}
```

You have two choices of how to combine these rectangles. First, you could create a single path that contains all of them, like this:

```
    CGRect *columnRects = [self copyColumnRects];

    // Create a single path that contains all columns
    CGMutablePathRef path = CGPathCreateMutable();
    for (int column = 0; column < kColumnCount; column++) {
      CGPathAddRect(path, NULL, columnRects[column]);
    }
    free(columnRects);
```

This would typeset the text as shown in Figure 18-2.

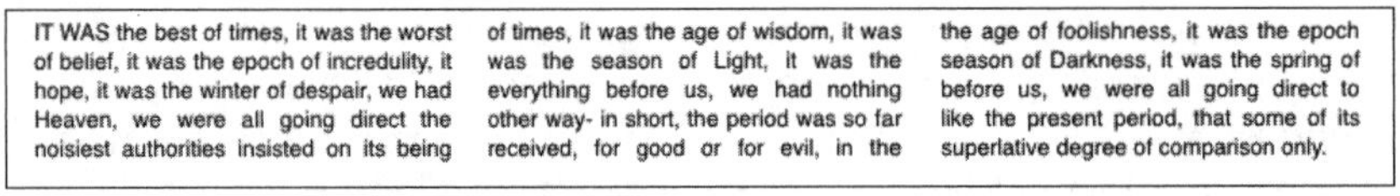

IT WAS the best of times, it was the worst of belief, it was the epoch of incredulity, it hope, it was the winter of despair, we had Heaven, we were all going direct the noisiest authorities insisted on its being of times, it was the age of wisdom, it was was the season of Light, it was the everything before us, we had nothing other way- in short, the period was so far received, for good or for evil, in the the age of foolishness, it was the epoch season of Darkness, it was the spring of before us, we were all going direct to like the present period, that some of its superlative degree of comparison only.

Figure 18-2 Column layout using a single path

Most of the time that isn't what you want. Instead, you need to typeset the first column, then the second column, and finally the third. To do so, you need to create three paths and add them to a CFMutableArray called paths:

```
CGRect *columnRects = [self copyColumnRects];
// Create an array of layout paths, one for each column.
for (int column = 0; column < kColumnCount; column++) {
  CGPathRef
  path = CGPathCreateWithRect(columnRects[column], NULL);
  CFArrayAppendValue(paths, path);
  CGPathRelease(path);
}
free(columnRects);
```

You then iterate over this array, typesetting the text that hasn't been drawn yet:

```
CFIndex pathCount = CFArrayGetCount(paths);
CFIndex charIndex = 0;
for (CFIndex pathIndex = 0; pathIndex < pathCount; ++pathIndex) {
  CGPathRef path = CFArrayGetValueAtIndex(paths, pathIndex);

  CTFrameRef
  frame = CTFramesetterCreateFrame(framesetter,
                                   CFRangeMake(charIndex, 0),
                                   path,
                                   NULL);
  CTFrameDraw(frame, context);
  CFRange frameRange = CTFrameGetVisibleStringRange(frame);
  charIndex += frameRange.length;
  CFRelease(frame);
}
```

The call to CTFrameGetVisibleStringRange returns the range of characters within the attributed string that are included in this frame. That lets you know where to start the next frame. The zero-length range passed to CTFramesetterCreateFrame indicates that the framesetter should typeset as much of the attributed string as will fit.

Using these techniques, you can typeset text into any shape you can draw with CGPath, as long as the text fits into lines. You learn how to handle more complicated cases in "Drawing Text Along a Curve" later in this chapter.

Typesetters, Lines, Runs, and Glyphs

The framesetter is responsible for combining typeset lines into frames that can be drawn. The typesetter is responsible for choosing and positioning the glyphs in those lines. CTFramesetter automates this process so you generally don't need to deal with the underlying typesetter (CTTypesetter). In recent versions of iOS (since around 4.2), improvements in CTFramesetter have made it even less common to use CTTypesetter directly. You will generally use the framesetter, or move further down the stack to lines, runs, and glyphs.

Starting at the bottom of the stack, a *glyph* (CGGlyph) is a shape that represents some piece of language information. This includes letters, numbers, and punctuation. It also includes whitespace, ligatures, and other marks. A *ligature* is when letters or other fundamental language units (*graphemes*) are combined to form a single glyph. The most common in English is the *fi* ligature formed when the letter *f* is followed by the letter *i*. In many fonts, these are combined into a single glyph to improve readability. The important thing is that a string may have a different number of glyphs than characters; the number of glyphs depends on the font and the layout of the characters.

A font can be thought of as a collection of glyphs, along with some metadata such as the size and name. The CGGlyph type is implemented as an index into a CGFont. This should not be confused with CTFont or UIFont. Each drawing system has its own font type. Core Text also has a CTGlyphInfo type for controlling how Unicode characters are mapped to glyphs. This is rarely used.

The typesetter is responsible for choosing the glyphs for a given attributed string, and for collecting them into runs. A *run* (CTRun) is a series of glyphs that has the same attributes and direction (such as left-to-right or right-to-left). Attributes include font, color, shadow, and paragraph style. You cannot directly create CTRun objects, but you can draw them into a context with CTRunDraw. Each glyph is positioned in the run, taking into account individual glyph size and kerning. *Kerning* is small adjustments to the spacing between glyphs to make text more readable. For example, the letters *V* and *A* are often kerned very close together.

The typesetter combines runs into lines. A *line* (CTLine) is a series of runs oriented either horizontally or vertically (for languages such as Japanese). CTLine is the lowest-level typesetting object that you can directly create from an attributed string. This is convenient for drawing small blocks of rich text. You can directly draw a line into a context using CTLineDraw.

Generally in Core Text you work with either a CTFramesetter for large blocks or a CTLine for small labels. From any level in the hierarchy, you can fetch the lower-level objects. For example, given a CTFramesetter, you create a CTFrame, and from that you can fetch its array of CTLine objects. Each line includes an array of CTRun objects, and within each run is a series of glyphs, along with positioning information and attributes. Behind the scenes is the CTTypesetter doing most of the work, but you seldom interact with it directly.

In the next section, "Drawing Text Along a Curve," you put all of these pieces together to perform complex text layout.

Drawing Text Along a Curve

In this example you use all the major parts of Core Text. Apple provides a somewhat simple example called CoreTextArcCocoa that demonstrates how to draw text along a semicircular arc. The Apple sample code is not very flexible, however, and is difficult to use for shapes other than a perfect circle centered in the view. It also forces the text to be evenly spaced along the curve. In this example, you learn how to draw text on any Bézier curve, and the techniques are applicable to drawing on any path. You also preserve Core Text's kerning and ligatures. The end result is shown in Figure 18-3. This example is available from the downloads for this chapter, in CurvyTextView.m in the CurvyText project.

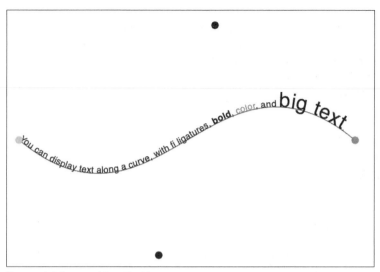

Figure 18-3 Output of CurvyTextView

While `CGPath` can represent a Bézier curve and Core Graphics can draw it, there are no functions in iOS that allow you to calculate the points along the curve. You need these points, provided by `Bezier()`, and the slope along the curve, provided by `BezierPrime()`:

```
static double Bezier(double t, double P0, double P1, double P2,
                     double P3) {
  return pow(1-t,3)*P0 + 3*pow(1-t,2)*t*P1 + 3*(1-t)*pow(t,2)*P2
         + pow(t,3)*P3;
}

static double BezierPrime(double t, double P0, double P1,
                          double P2, double P3) {
  return - 3*pow(1-t,2)*P0 + 3*pow(1-t,2)*P1 - 6*t*(1-t)*P1
         - 3*pow(t,2)*P2 + 6*t*(1-t)*P2 + 3*pow(t,2)*P3;
}
```

`P0` is the starting point, drawn in green by `CurvyTextView`. `P1` and `P2` are the control points, drawn in black. `P3` is the end point, drawn in red. You call these functions twice, once for the *x* coordinate, and once for *y* coordinate. To get a point and angle along the curve, you pass a number between 0 and 1 to `pointForOffset:` and `angleForOffset:`

```
- (CGPoint)pointForOffset:(double)t {
  double x = Bezier(t, P0_.x, P1_.x, P2_.x, P3_.x);
  double y = Bezier(t, P0_.y, P1_.y, P2_.y, P3_.y);
  return CGPointMake(x, y);
}
- (double)angleForOffset:(double)t {
  double dx = BezierPrime(t, P0_.x, P1_.x, P2_.x, P3_.x);
  double dy = BezierPrime(t, P0_.y, P1_.y, P2_.y, P3_.y);
  return atan2(dy, dx);
}
```

These methods are called so many times that I've made an exception to the rule always to use accessors. This is the major hotspot of this program, and optimizations to speed it up or call it less frequently are worthwhile. The Accelerate framework may be useful here by combining the *x* and *y* calculations into a single vector calculation. See *Taking Advantage of the Accelerate Framework* in the Apple documentation for more information.

With these two functions to define your path, you can now lay out the text. The following is a method to draw an attributed string into the current context along this path.

```
- (void)drawText {
  if ([self.attributedString length] == 0) { return; }

  // Initialize the text matrix (transform). This isn't reset
  // automatically, so it might be in any state.
  CGContextRef context = UIGraphicsGetCurrentContext();
  CGContextSetTextMatrix(context, CGAffineTransformIdentity);

  // Create a typeset line object
  CTLineRef line = CTLineCreateWithAttributedString(
                        (__bridge CFTypeRef)self.attributedString);

  // The offset is where you are in the curve, from [0, 1]
  double offset = 0.;

  // Fetch the runs and process one at a time
  CFArrayRef runs = CTLineGetGlyphRuns(line);
  CFIndex runCount = CFArrayGetCount(runs);
  for (CFIndex runIndex = 0; runIndex < runCount; ++runIndex) {
    CTRunRef run = CFArrayGetValueAtIndex(runs, runIndex);

    // Apply the attributes from the run to the current context
    [self prepareContext:context forRun:run];

    // Fetch the glyphs as a CGGlyph* array
    NSMutableData *glyphsData = [self glyphDataForRun:run];
    CGGlyph *glyphs = [glyphsData mutableBytes];

    // Fetch the advances as a CGSize* array. An advance is the
    // distance from one glyph to another.
    NSMutableData *advancesData = [self advanceDataForRun:run];
    CGSize *advances = [advancesData mutableBytes];

    // Loop through the glyphs and display them
    CFIndex glyphCount = CTRunGetGlyphCount(run);
    for (CFIndex glyphIndex = 0;
         glyphIndex < glyphCount && offset < 1.0;
         ++glyphIndex) {

      // You're going to modify the transform, so save the state
```

```
CGContextSaveGState(context);

// Calculate the location and angle. This could be any
// function, but here you use a Bezier curve
CGPoint glyphPoint = [self pointForOffset:offset];
double angle = [self angleForOffset:offset];

// Rotate the context
CGContextRotateCTM(context, angle);

// Translate the context after accounting for rotation
CGPoint
translatedPoint = CGPointApplyAffineTransform(glyphPoint,
                    CGAffineTransformMakeRotation(-angle));
CGContextTranslateCTM(context,
                    translatedPoint.x, translatedPoint.y);

// Draw the glyph
CGContextShowGlyphsAtPoint(context, 0, 0,
                    &glyphs[glyphIndex], 1);

// Move along the curve in proportion to the advance.
offset = [self offsetAtDistance:advances[glyphIndex].width
                    fromPoint:glyphPoint offset:offset];
CGContextRestoreGState(context);
        }
    }
}
```

The translation at the end of `drawText` is particularly important. All the glyphs are drawn at the origin. You use a transform to move the glyph into the correct position. The transform includes a rotation and a translation, and the order matters. If you rotate the context halfway around, and then translate the context up one point, the net effect would be to translate *down* one point. To account for this, you need to apply the inverse transform to the translation using `CGPointApplyAffineTransform`. The inverse of rotating by `angle` radians is to rotate by `-angle` radians. You could also use `CGAffineTransformInvert` to get the same effect.

There are a few more methods that you need. First, you need to apply the attributes to the context. In this example, you just set the font and color, but you could support any of the attributes listed in `CTStringAttributes.h`, or add your own.

```
- (void)prepareContext:(CGContextRef)context forRun:(CTRunRef)run {
    CFDictionaryRef attributes = CTRunGetAttributes(run);

// Set font
CTFontRef runFont = CFDictionaryGetValue(attributes,
                                    kCTFontAttributeName);
CGFontRef cgFont = CTFontCopyGraphicsFont(runFont, NULL);
CGContextSetFont(context, cgFont);
CGContextSetFontSize(context, CTFontGetSize(runFont));
CFRelease(cgFont);

// Set color
```

```
    CGColorRef color = (CGColorRef)CFDictionaryGetValue(attributes,
                                   kCTForegroundColorAttributeName);
    CGContextSetFillColorWithColor(context, color);
}
```

Fetching the glyph and advance information is easy. You just allocate a buffer and pass it to CTRunGetGlyphs or CTRunGetAdvances. The problem with these routines is that they copy all the data, which can be slow. There are faster versions (CTRunGetGlyphsPtr and CTRunGetAdvancesPtr) that return a pointer without making a copy. These versions can fail, however, if the data hasn't been calculated yet. glyphDataForRun:, shown in the following code, handles both cases and returns an NSMutableData that automatically handles memory management. advanceDataForRun: is nearly identical. You can find the source for it in CurvyTextView.m.

```
- (NSMutableData *)glyphDataForRun:(CTRunRef)run {
  NSMutableData *data;
  CFIndex glyphsCount = CTRunGetGlyphCount(run);
  const CGGlyph *glyphs = CTRunGetGlyphsPtr(run);
  size_t dataLength = glyphsCount * sizeof(*glyphs);
  if (glyphs) {
    data = [NSMutableData dataWithBytesNoCopy:(void*)glyphs
                             length:dataLength freeWhenDone:NO];
  }
  else {
    data = [NSMutableData dataWithLength:dataLength];
    CTRunGetGlyphs(run, CFRangeMake(0, 0), data.mutableBytes);
  }
  return data;
}
```

Finally, to maintain proper spacing, you need to find the point along the curve that is the same distance as the advance. This is not trivial for a Bézier curve. Offsets are not linear, and it is almost certain that the offset 0.25 will not be a quarter of the way along the curve. A simple solution is to repeatedly increment the offset and calculate a new point on the curve until the distance to that point is at least equal to your advance. The larger the increment you choose, the more characters tend to spread out. The smaller the increment you choose, the longer it takes to calculate. My experience is that values between 1/1000 (0.001) and 1/10,000 (0.0001) work well. While 1/1000 has visible errors when compared to 1/10,000, the speed improvement is generally worth it. You could try to optimize this with a binary search, but that can fail if the loop wraps back on itself or crosses itself. Here is a simple implementation of the search algorithm:

```
- (double)offsetAtDistance:(double)aDistance
                fromPoint:(CGPoint)aPoint
                   offset:(double)anOffset {
  const double kStep = 0.001; // 0.0001 - 0.001 work well
  double newDistance = 0;
  double newOffset = anOffset + kStep;
  while (newDistance <= aDistance && newOffset < 1.0) {
    newOffset += kStep;
    newDistance = Distance(aPoint,
                      [self pointForOffset:newOffset]);
  }
  return newOffset;
```

> For more information on finding lengths on a curve, search the Web for "arc length parameterization."

With these tools, you can typeset rich text along any path you can calculate.

Comparison of Rich Text Options

With all of these options available, which one is right for your project? In the vast majority of cases, UIKit views like `UILabel` are perfectly adequate. If you need a just few stylized words, you can break the sentence into multiple `UILabel` views.

For complex styles, UIKit views are insufficient. The next tool you should consider is custom view drawing with `NSString` methods such as `drawInRect:withFont:`. This approach is very good for static text.

If you need to draw highly stylized, dynamic text, then you basically have two options: web views and Core Text. For selectable and editable text, the best option is typically a web view. If you go this way, I recommend starting with a well-established JavaScript editor like TinyMCE or CKEditor. You should also try to make your editing code as standalone as possible so that you can develop and debug it in a web browser rather than in Xcode.

If you don't need to edit your rich text, then Core Text is a good choice. If you need to perform very complex layout, such as drawing along curves, Core Text may be your only option. Core Text does not include any capability for text selection, or copy and paste. If the user needs to select text, you need to implement that by hand.

Whichever option you choose, try to keep your text rendering isolated to a small number of classes so that you can swap out the engine later. Apple often tries out complicated APIs in its own code before making them public. The release of Pages, perhaps the most advanced rich-text application for iOS, suggests that an editable rich-text view may be on its way. When it comes, you'll want to be able to drop it in as easily as possible.

Third-Party Options

So far in this chapter, you've learned to use all the major text layout options that come with iOS. Each has trade-offs, however. The ideal solution would handle `NSAttributedString` or HTML simply, while preserving the capability to select text for copy and paste operations. There are several third-party attempts to achieve this ideal. None is perfect, but each can be useful in some situations.

NSAttributedString-Additions-for-HTML

As you've likely noticed, creating an `NSAttributedString` can be very tedious, and the code is difficult to read and understand. On Mac, you can create an `NSAttributedString` directly from HTML using `[NSAttributedString initWithHTML:documentAttributes:]`, but there is no equivalent on iOS.

Cocoanetics (Drobnik KG) has developed a category for `NSAttributedString` called `NSAttributedString-Additions-for-HTML` on iOS to provide similar functionality as on Mac. For simple conversions, the Cocoanetics version is better than the Mac solution (which is notorious for strange WebKit-related side effects). You should not consider this a general-purpose converter, but for many problems it is very useful.

CoreTextWrapper

Adrian Kosmaczewski maintains a nice Cocoa interface for Core Text called `CoreTextWrapper`, focused on multicolumn layout. This wrapper is fairly limited in what it provides, but it is very good at the problem it is intended to solve. It also provides a wrapper for loading custom fonts from your bundle.

OmniUI

Omni Group, the creators of OmniGraffle, OmniOutliner, and other popular products, makes much of its core code available under an open-source license. One of the many things in its library is `OUIEditableFrame`, a rich-text editor based on Core Text that includes cut and paste. In some ways, it is the mythical `UIRichTextView` that everyone would like Apple to provide. It is part of the larger `OmniUI` framework.

`OUIEditableFrame` is very powerful, but it has problems. First, at least in mid-2011, it isn't complete. There are a few pieces that are unimplemented and cause it to crash. Just as importantly, using Omni Group code is a commitment. It's difficult to use just a little of it. `OUIEditableFrame` relies on numerous other frameworks. Omni Group writes code for its products, and then generously makes it available to others. It doesn't spend a great deal of time making it is easy to use in your product. Just getting Omni Group code to compile successfully can be a challenge. Even so, if rich-text editing is important to your project, you should certainly consider `OUIEditableFrame`. If you just need text selection, look at `OUILoupeOverlay`, which provides the magnifying view. Build its `TextEditor` sample project to see it in action.

Summary

Apple provides a variety of powerful text-layout tools, from `UILabel` to `UIWebView` to Core Text. In this chapter you looked at the major options and how to choose among them. Most of all, you should have a good understanding of how to use Core Text to create beautiful text layout in even the most complex applications.

Further Reading

Apple Documentation

The following documents are available in the iOS Developer Library at `developer.apple.com` or through the Xcode Documentation and API Reference.

Core Text Programming Guide

Quartz 2D Programming Guide. "Text"

String Programming Guide. "Drawing Strings"

Text, Web, and Editing Programming Guide

WWDC Sessions

The following session videos are available at `developer.apple.com`.

WWDC 2011. "Session 511 – Rich Text Editing in Safari on iOS"

Other Resources

Clegg, Jay. *Jay's Projects*. "Warping Text to a Bézier curves." Useful background on techniques for laying out text along a curve. The article is in C# and GDI+, but the math is useful on any platform.
`planetclegg.com/projects/WarpingTextToSplines.html`

Drobnik, Oliver. *NSAttributedString-Additions-for-HTML*. Category to convert between formatted `NSAttributedString` objects and HTML.
`github.com/Cocoanetics/NSAttributedString-Additions-for-HTML`

Kosmaczewski, Adrian. *CoreTextWrapper* – Wrapper to simplify multicolumn layout using Core Text.
`github.com/akosma/CoreTextWrapper`

Knabben, Frederico. *CKEditor* – A major JavaScript-rich text editor. CKEditor is a major rewrite of FCKEditor.
`ckeditor.com`

Moxiecode Systems AB. *TinyMCE* – One of the most popular JavaScript rich-text editors available.
`tinymce.com`

Nitobi. *PhoneGap* – API that allows web applications to access native portions of the iOS device. This essentially allows web applications to behave as native applications.
`phonegap.com`

Omni Group. *OmniUI* – Rich text editor framework based using Core Text.
`github.com/omnigroup/OmniGroup/tree/master/Frameworks/OmniUI`

## Chapter 19

Building a (Core) Foundation

As an iOS developer, you will spend most of your time using the UIKit and Foundation frameworks. UIKit provides user interface elements like `UIView` and `UIButton`. Foundation provides basic data structures like `NSArray` and `NSDictionary`. These can handle the vast majority of problems the average iOS application will encounter. But there are some things that require lower-level frameworks. The names of these lower-level frameworks often start with the word "Core": Core Text, Core Graphics, and Core Video, for example. What they all have in common are C-based APIs based on Core Foundation.

Core Foundation provides a C API that is similar to the Objective-C Foundation framework. It provides a consistent object model with reference counting and containers, just like Foundation, and simplifies passing common data types to low-level frameworks. As you see later in this chapter, Core Foundation is tightly coupled with Foundation, making it easy to pass data between C and Objective-C.

In this chapter, you learn the Core Foundation data types and naming conventions. You learn about Core Foundation allocators and how they provide greater flexibility than `+alloc` provides in Objective-C. This chapter extensively covers Core Foundation string and binary data types. You discover Core Foundation collection types, which are more flexible than their Foundation counterparts and include some not found Objective-C like tree structures. Finally, you learn how to move data easily between Core Foundation and Objective-C using toll-free bridging. When you are finished, you will have the tools you need to use the powerful Core frameworks, as well as more flexible data structures to improve your own projects.

All code samples in this chapter can be found in `main.m` and `MYStringConversion.c` in the online files for Chapter 19.

Core Foundation Types

Core Foundation is made up primarily of *opaque types*, which are simply C structs. Opaque types are similar to classes in that they provide encapsulation, and some inheritance and polymorphism. The similarity should not be overstated, however. Core Foundation is implemented in pure C, where there is no language support for inheritance or polymorphism, so sometimes the class metaphor can become strained. But for general usage, Core Foundation can be thought of as an object model with `CFType` as its root "class."

Like Objective-C, Core Foundation deals with pointers to instances. In Core Foundation, these pointers are given the suffix `Ref`. For example, a pointer to a `CFType` is a `CFTypeRef` and a pointer to a string is a `CFStringRef`. Mutable versions of opaque types include the word `Mutable`, so a `CFMutableStringRef` is the mutable form of a `CFStringRef`. Generally mutable types can be treated as if they were a subclass of the nonmutable type, just as in Foundation. For simplicity, and to match the Apple documentation, this chapter uses the term `CFString` to refer to the thing a `CFStringRef` points to, even though Core Foundation does not define the symbol `CFString`.

Because Core Foundation is implemented in C, and C has no language support for inheritance or polymorphism, how does Core Foundation give the illusion of an object hierarchy? First, `CFTypeRef` is just a `void*`. This provides a crude kind of polymorphism because it allows arbitrary types to be passed to certain functions, particularly `CFCopyDescription`, `CFEqual`, `CFHash`, `CFRelease`, and `CFRetain`.

Except for `CFTypeRef`, opaque types are structs. A mutable and immutable pair is usually of the form

```
typedef const struct __CFString * CFStringRef;
typedef struct __CFString * CFMutableStringRef;
```

This way, the compiler can enforce `const` correctness to provide a kind of inheritance. It should be clear that this isn't real inheritance. There is no good way to provide arbitrary subclasses of `CFString` that the compiler will type check. For example, consider the following code:

```
CFStringRef errName = CFSTR("error");
CFErrorRef error = CFErrorCreate(NULL, errName, 0, NULL);
CFPropertyListRef propertyList = error;
```

A `CFError` is not a `CFPropertyList`, so line 3 should generate a warning. It doesn't because `CFPropertyListRef` is defined as `CFTypeRef`, which is required because it has several "subclasses" including `CFString`, `CFDate`, and `CFNumber`. Once something has several subclasses, it generally has to be treated as a `void*` (`CFTypeRef`) in Core Foundation. This isn't obvious from looking at the code, but luckily it doesn't come up that often. Most types are defined as a specific `struct` or `const struct`.

Naming and Memory Management

As in Cocoa, naming conventions are critical in Core Foundation. The most important rule is the Create Rule: If a function has the word `Create` or `Copy` in its name, you are an owner of the resulting object and must eventually release your ownership using `CFRelease`. Like Cocoa, objects are reference counted and can have multiple "owners." When the last owner calls `CFRelease`, the object is destroyed.

There is no equivalent of `NSAutoreleasePool` in Core Foundation, so functions with `Copy` in the name are much more common than in Cocoa. Some functions, however, return a reference to an internal data structure or to a constant object. These functions generally include the word `Get` in their name (the Get Rule). The caller is not an owner and does not need to release them.

> `Get` in Core Foundation is not the same as `get` in Cocoa. Core Foundation functions including `Get` return an opaque type or a C type. Cocoa methods that begin with `get` update a pointer passed by reference.

There is no automatic reference counting in Core Foundation. Memory management in Core Foundation is very similar to manual memory management in Cocoa:

- If you `Create` or `Copy` an object, you are an owner.

- If you do not `Create` or `Copy` an object, you are not an owner. If you want to prevent the object from being destroyed, you must become an owner by calling `CFRetain`.

- If you are an owner of an object, you must call `CFRelease` when you are done with it.

> `CFRelease` **is very similar to** `release` **in Objective-C, but there are important differences. The most critical is that you cannot call** `CFRelease(NULL)`**. This is somewhat unfortunate, and many specialized versions of** `CFRelease` **exist that do allow you to pass** `NULL` (`CGGradientRelease` **for instance).** `CFRelease` **also behaves differently than** `retain` **in garbage-collected environments. This doesn't apply to iOS, so it isn't covered here, but you can read Apple's** *Memory Management Programming Guide for Core Foundation* **for more information.**

Some functions have both `Create` and `Copy` in their name. For example, `CFStringCreateCopy` creates a copy of another `CFString`. Why not just `CFStringCopy`? That's because `Create` tells you other things about the function than just the ownership rule. It indicates that the first parameter is a `CFAllocatorRef`, which lets you customize how the newly created object is allocated. In almost all cases you pass `NULL` for this parameter, which specifies the default allocator: `kCFAllocatorDefault`. (I'll cover allocators in more depth in a moment.) Knowing that the function is a creator, the name also tells you that it makes a copy of the passed string.

Conversely, a function with `NoCopy` in its name does not make a copy. For example, `CFStringCreateWithBytesNoCopy` takes a pointer to a buffer and creates a string without copying the bytes. So who is now responsible for releasing the buffer? That brings us back to allocators.

Allocators

A `CFAllocatorRef` is a strategy for allocating and freeing memory. In almost all cases you want the default allocator, `kCFAllocatorDefault`, which is the same as passing `NULL`. This allocates and frees memory in "the normal way" according to Core Foundation. This way is subject to change, and you shouldn't rely on any particular behavior. It is rare to need a specialized allocator, but in a few cases it can be useful. Here are the standard allocators to give an idea of what they can do:

- `kCFAllocatorDefault`—The default allocator. Equivalent to passing `NULL`.

- `kCFAllocatorSystemDefault`—The original default system allocator. This is available in case you have changed the default allocator using `CFAllocatorSetDefault`. This is very rarely necessary.

- `kCFAllocatorMalloc`—Calls `malloc`, `realloc`, and `free`. This is particularly useful as a deallocator for `CFData` and `CFString` if you created the memory with `malloc`.

- `kCFAllocatorMallocZone`—Creates and frees memory in the default `malloc` zone. This can be useful with garbage collection on Mac, but is almost never useful in iOS.

▪ kCFAllocatorNull—Does nothing. Like kCFAllocatorMalloc, this can be useful with CFData or CFString as a deallocator if you do not want to free the memory.

▪ kCFAllocatorUseContext—Only used by the CFAllocatorCreate function. When you create a CFAllocator, the system needs to allocate memory. Like all other Create methods, this requires an allocator. This special allocator tells CFAllocatorCreate to use the functions passed to it to allocate the CFAllocator.

See the section "Backing Storage for Strings" for examples of how these would be used in a practical problem.

Introspection

Core Foundation allows a variety of type introspection, primarily for debugging purposes. The most fundamental is the CFTypeID, which uniquely identifies the opaque type of the object, similar to Class in Objective-C. You can determine the type of a Core Foundation instance by calling CFGetTypeID. The returned value is opaque and subject to change between versions of iOS. You can compare the CFTypeID of two instances, but most often you compare the result of CFGetTypeID to the value from a function like CFArrayGetTypeID. All opaque types have a related GetTypeID function.

As in Cocoa, Core Foundation instances have a description for debugging purposes, returned by CFCopyDescription. This returns a CFString that you are responsible for releasing. CFCopyTypeIDDescription provides a similar string that describes a CFTypeID. You should not rely on the format or content of these because they're subject to change.

To write debugging output to the console, use CFShow. It will display the value of a CFString, or the description of other types. To display the description of a CFString, use CFShowStr. For example, given the following definitions

```
CFStringRef string = CFSTR("Hello");
CFArrayRef array = CFArrayCreate(NULL, (const void**)&string, 1,
                                 &kCFTypeArrayCallBacks);
```

Here are the results for each kind of CFShow call:

```
CFShow(array);
<CFArray 0x6d47850 [0x1445b38]>{type = immutable, count = 1,
   values = (
      0 : <CFString 0x410c [0x1445b38]>{contents = "Hello"}
   )}

CFShow(string);
Hello

CFShowStr(string);
Length 5
IsEightBit 1
HasLengthByte 0
HasNullByte 1
InlineContents 0
```

```
Allocator SystemDefault
Mutable 0
Contents 0x3ba7
```

Strings and Data

`CFString` is a Unicode-based storage container that provides rich and efficient functionality for manipulating, searching, and converting international strings. Closely related are the `CFCharacterSet` and `CFAttributedString` classes. `CFCharacterSet` represents a set of characters for efficiently searching, including or excluding certain characters from a string. `CFAttributedString` combines a string with ranges of attributes. This is most commonly used to handle rich text, but can be used for a variety of metadata storage.

`CFString` is closely related to `NSString` and they are generally interchangeable, as you'll see in "Toll-free Bridging" later in this chapter. This section focuses on the differences between `CFString` and `NSString`.

Constant Strings

In Cocoa, a literal `NSString` is indicated by an ampersand, as in `@"string"`. In Core Foundation, a literal `CFString` is indicated by the macro `CFSTR`, as in `CFSTR("string")`. If you're using the Apple-provided `gcc` and the option `-fconstant-cfstrings`, this macro uses a special built-in compiler hook that creates constant `CFString` cobjects at compile time. `clang` also has this built-in compiler hook. If you're using standard `gcc`, then an explicit `CFStringMakeConstantString` function is used to create these objects at runtime.

Because `CFSTR` has neither `Create` nor `Copy` in its name, you do not need to call `CFRelease` on the result. You may, however, call `CFRetain` normally if you like. If you do, you should balance it with `CFRelease` as usual. This allows you to treat constant strings in the same way as programmatically created strings.

Creating Strings

A common way to generate a `CFString` is from a C string. For example

```
const char *cstring = "Hello World!";
CFStringRef string = CFStringCreateWithCString(NULL, cstring,
  kCFStringEncodingUTF8);
CFShow(string);
CFRelease(string);
```

While many developers are most familiar with `NULL`-terminated C strings, there are other ways to store strings, and understanding them can be useful in improving code efficiency. In network protocols, it can be very efficient to encode strings as a length value followed by a sequence of characters. If parsers are likely to need only a part of the packet, it is faster to use length bytes to skip over the parts you don't need than to read everything looking for `NULL`. If this length encoding is 1 byte long, then the buffer is a Pascal string and Core Foundation can use it directly as shown in the following code.

```
// A common type of network buffer
struct NetworkBuffer {
  UInt8 length;
```

```
    UInt8 data[];
};

// Some data we pulled off of the network into the buffer
static struct NetworkBuffer buffer = {
   4, {'T', 'e', 'x', 't'}};

CFStringRef string =
   CFStringCreateWithPascalString(NULL,
                           (ConstStr255Param)&buffer,
                           kCFStringEncodingUTF8);
CFShow(string);
CFRelease(string);
```

If you have length some other way, or if the length is not 1 byte long, you can use
`CFStringCreateWithBytes` similarly:

```
CFStringRef string = CFStringCreateWithBytes(NULL,
                                   buffer.data,
                                   buffer.length,
                                   kCFStringEncodingUTF8,
                                   false);
```

The final `false` indicates this string does not have a *byte order mark* (BOM) at the beginning. The BOM indicates whether the string was generated on a big endian or little endian system. A BOM is not needed or recommended for UTF-8 encodings. This is one of many reasons to prefer UTF-8 when possible.

Core Foundation constants begin with a k, unlike their Cocoa counterparts. For example, the Core Foundation counterpart to `NSUTF8StringEncoding` is `kCFStringEncodingUTF8`.

Converting to C Strings

While converting from C strings is very simple, converting back into C strings can be deceptively difficult. There are two ways to get a C string out of a `CFString`: Request the pointer to the internal C string representation, or copy the bytes out into your own buffer.

Obviously the easiest and fastest way to get the C string is to request the internal C string pointer:

```
const char *
cstring = CFStringGetCStringPtr(string, kCFStringEncodingUTF8);
```

This appears to be the best of all worlds. It's extremely fast and you don't have to allocate or free memory. Unfortunately, it may not work, depending on how the string is currently encoded inside of the `CFString`. If there isn't an internal C string representation available, then this routine returns `NULL` and you have to use `CFStringGetCString` and pass your own buffer although it is not obvious how large a buffer you need. Here's an example of how to solve this problem.

```
char * MYCFStringCopyUTF8String(CFStringRef aString) {
  if (aString == NULL) {
    return NULL;
  }

  CFIndex length = CFStringGetLength(aString);
  CFIndex maxSize =
    CFStringGetMaximumSizeForEncoding(length,
                                      kCFStringEncodingUTF8);
  char *buffer = (char *)malloc(maxSize);
  if (CFStringGetCString(aString, buffer, maxSize,
                         kCFStringEncodingUTF8)) {
    return buffer;
  }
  return NULL;
}

...

CFStringRef string = CFSTR("Hello");
char * cstring = MYCFStringCopyUTF8String(string);
printf("%s\n", cstring);
free(cstring);
```

MYCFStringCopyUTF8String is not the fastest way to convert a CFString to a C string because it allocates a new buffer for every conversion, but it is easy to use and quick enough for many problems. If you're converting a lot of strings and want to improve speed and minimize memory churn, you might use a function like this one that supports reusing a common buffer:

```
#import <malloc/malloc.h> // For malloc_size()

const char * MYCFStringGetUTF8String(CFStringRef aString,
                                     char **buffer) {
  if (aString == NULL) {
    return NULL;
  }

  const char *cstr = CFStringGetCStringPtr(aString,
                                           kCFStringEncodingUTF8);
  if (cstr == NULL) {
    CFIndex length = CFStringGetLength(aString);
    CFIndex maxSize =
      CFStringGetMaximumSizeForEncoding(length,
              kCFStringEncodingUTF8) + 1; // +1 for NULL
    if (maxSize > malloc_size(buffer)) {
      *buffer = realloc(*buffer, maxSize);
    }
    if (CFStringGetCString(aString, *buffer, maxSize,
                           kCFStringEncodingUTF8)) {
      cstr = *buffer;
    }
  }
  return cstr;
}
```

The caller of `MYCFStringGetUTF8String` is responsible for passing a reusable buffer. The buffer may point to `NULL` or to preallocated memory. Keep in mind that the returned C string points into either the `CFString` or into `buffer`, so invalidating either of those can cause the returned C string to become invalid. In particular, passing the same buffer repeatedly to this function may invalidate old results. That's the trade-off for its speed. Here's how it would be used.

```
CFStringRef strings[3] = { CFSTR("One"), CFSTR("Two"),
                           CFSTR("Three") };
char * buffer = NULL;
const char * cstring = NULL;
for (unsigned i = 0; i < 3; ++i) {
  cstring = MYCFStringGetUTF8String(strings[i], &buffer);
        printf("%s\n", cstring);
}
free(buffer);
```

If you need conversion to be as fast as possible, and you know the maximum string length, then the following is even faster.

```
CFStringRef string = ...;
const CFIndex kBufferSize = 1024;
char buffer[kBufferSize];
CFStringEncoding encoding = kCFStringEncodingUTF8;
const char *cstring;
cstring = CFStringGetCStringPtr(string, encoding);
if (cstring == NULL) {
  if (CFStringGetCString(string, buffer, kBufferSize,
                         encoding)) {
    cstring = buffer;
  }
}
printf("%s\n", cstring);
```

Because this approach relies on a stack variable (`buffer`), it is difficult to wrap this into a simple function call, but it avoids any extra memory allocations.

Other String Operations

To developers familiar with `NSString`, most of `CFString` should be fairly obvious. You can find ranges of characters, append, trim and replace characters, compare, search, and sort as in Cocoa. `CFStringCreateWithFormat` provides identical functionality to `stringWithFormat:`. I won't explore all the functions here. You can find them all in the documentation for `CFString` and `CFMutableString`.

Backing Storage for Strings

Generally a `CFString` will allocate the required memory to store its characters. This memory is called the *backing storage*. If you have an existing buffer, it is sometimes more efficient or convenient to continue using it rather than copying all the bytes into a new `CFString`. You might do this because you have a buffer of bytes you want to convert into a string, or because you want to continue to have access to the raw bytes while also using convenient string functions.

In the first case, where you already have a buffer, you generally use a function like

```
CFStringCreateWithBytesNoCopy.
const char *cstr = "Hello";
char *bytes = CFAllocatorAllocate(kCFAllocatorDefault,
                                  strlen(cstr) + 1, 0);
strcpy(bytes, cstr);
CFStringRef str =
    CFStringCreateWithCStringNoCopy(kCFAllocatorDefault,
                                    bytes,
                                    kCFStringEncodingUTF8,
                                    kCFAllocatorDefault);
CFShow(str);
CFRelease(str);
```

Because you passed the default allocator (`kCFAllocatorDefault`) as the destructor, the `CFString` owns the buffer and will free it when it's done using the default allocator. This matches the earlier call to `CFAllocatorAllocate`. If you had allocated the buffer with `malloc`, the code would look like this:

```
const char *cstr = "Hello";
char *bytes = malloc(strlen(cstr) + 1);
strcpy(bytes, cstr);
CFStringRef str =
    CFStringCreateWithCStringNoCopy(NULL, bytes,
                                    kCFStringEncodingUTF8,
                                    kCFAllocatorMalloc);
CFShow(str);
CFRelease(str);
```

In both cases, the allocated buffer would be freed when the string is destroyed. But what if you wanted to keep the buffer for other uses? Consider the following code:

```
const char *cstr = "Hello";
char *bytes = malloc(strlen(cstr) + 1);
strcpy(bytes, cstr);
CFStringRef str =
    CFStringCreateWithCStringNoCopy(NULL, bytes,
                                    kCFStringEncodingUTF8,
                                    kCFAllocatorNull);
CFShow(str);
CFRelease(str);
printf("%s\n", bytes);
free(bytes);
```

You pass `kCFAllocatorNull` as the destructor. You still release the string because you created it with a `Create` function. But now, the buffer pointed to by `bytes` is still valid after the call to `CFRelease`. You are responsible for calling `free` on bytes when you are done with it.

There is no guarantee that the buffer you pass will be the actual buffer used. Core Foundation may call the deallocator at any time and create its own internal buffer. Most critically, you must not modify the buffer after creating the string. If you have a buffer that you want to access as a `CFString` while allowing changes to it, then you need to use `CFStringCreateMutableWithExternalCharactersNoCopy`. This creates a mutable string that always uses the provided buffer as its backing store. If you change the buffer, you need to let the string know by calling `CFStringSetExternalCharactersNoCopy`. Using these functions bypasses many string optimizations, so they should be used with care.

CFData

`CFData` is the Core Foundation equivalent to `NSData`. It is much like `CFString` with similar creation functions, backing store management, and access functions. The primary difference is that `CFData` does not manage encodings like `CFString`. You can find the full list of functions in the `CFData` and `CFMutableData` references.

Collections

Core Foundation provides a rich set of object collection types. Most have Cocoa counterparts like `CFArray` and `NSArray`. There are a few specialized Core Foundation collections such as `CFTree` that have no Cocoa counterpart. Core Foundation collections provide greater flexibility in how they manage their contents. In this section you learn about the Core Foundation collections that have Objective-C equivalents: `CFArray`, `CFDictionary`, `CFSet`, and `CFBag`. The other Core Foundation collections are seldom used, but I will introduce them so that you're aware of what's available if you need it.

Cocoa collections can only hold Objective-C objects and must retain them. Core Foundation collections can hold anything that can fit in the size of a pointer (32 bits for the ARM processor), and can perform any action when adding or removing items. The default behavior is very similar to the Cocoa equivalents, and Core Foundation collections generally retain and release instances when adding and removing.

Core Foundation uses a structure of function pointers that define how to treat items in the collection. Configuring these callbacks allows you to highly customize your collection. You can store nonobjects like integers, create weak collections that do not retain their objects, or modify how objects are compared for equality. The "Callbacks" section covers this. Each collection type has a default set of callbacks defined in the header. For example, the default callbacks for `CFArray` are `kCFTypeArrayCallBacks`. While introducing the major collections, I will focus on these default behaviors.

CFArray

`CFArray` corresponds to `NSArray`, and holds an ordered list of items. Creating a `CFArray` takes an allocator, a series of values, and a set of callbacks, as shown in the following code.

```
CFStringRef strings[3] =
  { CFSTR("One"), CFSTR("Two"), CFSTR("Three") };
CFArrayRef array = CFArrayCreate(NULL, (void *)strings, 3,
                                 &kCFTypeArrayCallBacks);
CFShow(array);
CFRelease(array);
```

Creating a `CFMutableArray` takes an allocator, a size, and a set of callbacks. Unlike `NSMutableArray` capacity, which is only an initial size, the size passed to `CFMutableArray` is a fixed maximum. To allocate an array that can grow, pass a size of zero.

```
CFMutableArrayRef array = CFArrayCreateMutable(NULL, 0,
                             &kCFTypeArrayCallBacks);
```

CFDictionary

`CFDictionary` corresponds to `NSDictionary`, and hold key-value pairs. Creating a `CFDictionary` takes an allocator, a series of keys, a series of values, a set of callbacks for the keys, and a set of callbacks for the values.

```
#define kCount 3
CFStringRef keys[kCount] =
  { CFSTR("One"), CFSTR("Two"), CFSTR("Three") };
CFStringRef values[kCount] =
  { CFSTR("Foo"), CFSTR("Bar"), CFSTR("Baz") };
CFDictionaryRef dict =
  CFDictionaryCreate(NULL,
                     (void *)keys,
                     (void *)values,
                     kCount,
                     &kCFTypeDictionaryKeyCallBacks,
                     &kCFTypeDictionaryValueCallBacks);
```

Creating a `CFMutableDictionary` is like creating a `CFMutableArray`, except there are separate callbacks for the keys and values. As with `CFMutableArray`, the size is fixed if given. For a dictionary that can grow, pass a size of 0.

CFSet, CFBag

`CFSet` corresponds to `NSSet` and is an unordered collection of unique objects. `CFBag` corresponds to `NSCountedSet` and allows duplicate objects. As with their Cocoa counterparts, uniqueness is defined by equality. The function that determines equality is one of the callbacks.

Like `CFDictionary`, `CFSet` and `CFBag` can hold `NULL` values by passing `NULL` as their callback structure pointer.

Other Collections

Core Foundation includes several collections that do not have a Cocoa counterpart:

- `CFTree` provides a convenient way to manage tree structures that might otherwise be stored less efficiently in a `CFDictionary`. There is a short example of `CFTree` in the section "Toll-free Bridging."

- `CFBinaryHeap` provides a binary-searchable container, similar to a sorted queue.

- `CFBitVector` provides a convenient way to store bit values.

Full information on `CFTree` is available in Apple's *Collections Programming Topics for Core Foundation.* See the Apple documentation on `CFBinaryHeap` and `CFBitVector` for more information on their usage. These are not often used and are not heavily documented.

Callbacks

Core Foundation uses a structure of function pointers that define how to treat items in the collection. The structure includes the following members:

- `retain`—Called when an item is added to the collection. The default behavior is similar to `CFRetain` (you'll learn what "similar" means below). If it is `NULL`, no action is performed.

- `release`—Called when an item is removed from the collection, and when the collection is destroyed. The default behavior is similar to `CFRelease`. If it is `NULL`, no action is performed.

- `copyDescription`—Called for each object in response to functions that want a human-readable description for the entire collection, such as `CFShow` or `CFCopyDescription`. The default value is `CFCopyDescription`. If this is `NULL`, the collection has some built-in logic to construct a simple description.

- `equal`—Called to compare a collection object with another object to determine if they're equal. The default value is `CFEqual`. If this is `NULL`, the collection will use strict equality (`==`) of the values. If the items are pointers to objects (as is the usual case), then this means that objects are only equal to themselves.

- `hash`—This only applies to hashing collections like dictionaries and sets. This function is used to determine the hash value of an object. A hash is a fast way to compare objects. Given an object, a hash function returns an integer such that if two objects are equal, then their hashes are equal. This allows the collection to quickly determine unequal objects with a simple integer comparison, saving the expensive call to CFEqual for objects that are possibly equal. The default value is CFHash. If this is NULL, the value (usually a pointer) is used as its own hash.

The default values for `retain` and `release` act like `CFRetain` and `CFRelease`, but are actually pointers to the private functions `__CFTypeCollectionRetain` and `__CFTypeCollectionRelease`. The `retain` and `release` function pointers include the collection's allocator in case you would like to create a new object rather than retain an existing one. This is incompatible with `CFRetain` and `CFRelease`, which do not take an allocator. Usually this doesn't matter because in most cases you will either leave `retain` and `release` as default, or set them to `NULL`.

Each collection type has a default set of callbacks defined in the header. For example, the default callbacks for `CFArray` are `kCFTypeArrayCallBacks`. These can be used to easily modify default behavior. The following creates a nonretaining array, which could also hold nonobjects such as integers.

```
CFArrayCallBacks nrCallbacks = kCFTypeArrayCallBacks;
nrCallbacks.retain = NULL;
nrCallbacks.release = NULL;
CFMutableArrayRef nrArray = CFArrayCreateMutable(NULL, 0,
                            &nrCallbacks);
CFStringRef string =
  CFStringCreateWithCString(NULL, "Stuff",
                            kCFStringEncodingUTF8);
```

```
CFArrayAppendValue(nrArray, string);
CFRelease(nrArray);
CFRelease(string);
```

Another example of callback configuration is to allow NULL values or keys. Dictionaries, sets, and bags can hold NULL values or keys if the retain and release callbacks are NULL. These types have CFTypeGetValueIfPresent functions to handle this case. For example, the function CFDictionaryGetValueIfPresent() allows you to determine whether the value was NULL versus missing, as shown in the following code:

```
CFDictionaryKeyCallBacks cb = kCFTypeDictionaryKeyCallBacks;
cb.retain = NULL;
cb.release = NULL;
CFMutableDictionaryRef dict =
  CFDictionaryCreateMutable(NULL, 0, &cb,
                           &kCFTypeDictionaryValueCallBacks);
CFDictionarySetValue(dict, NULL, CFSTR("Foo"));

const void *value;
Boolean fooPresent =
  CFDictionaryGetValueIfPresent(dict, NULL, &value);
CFRelease(dict);
```

Other collections, such as CFArray, cannot hold NULL values. As in Foundation, you must use a special placeholder NULL constant called kCFNull. It is an opaque type (CFNull), so it can be retained and released.

Core Foundation collections are much more flexible than their Cocoa equivalents. As you see in the next section, however, you can bring this flexibility almost transparently Cocoa through the power of toll-free bridging.

Toll-free Bridging

One of the cleverest aspects of Core Foundation is its capability to transparently exchange data with Foundation. For example, any function or method that accepts an NSArray also accepts a CFArray with only a bridge cast. A *bridge cast* in an instruction to the compiler of how to apply automatic reference counting.

In many cases, you only need to use the __bridge modifier, as shown in the following code.

```
NSArray *nsArray = [NSArray arrayWithObject:@"Foo"];
printf("%ld\n", CFArrayGetCount((__bridge CFArrayRef)nsArray));
```

This essentially tells the compiler to do nothing special. It should simply cast nsArray as a CFArrayRef and pass it to CFArrayGetCount. There is no change to the reference count of nsArray.

This works in reverse as well:

```
CFMutableArrayRef cfArray =
  CFArrayCreateMutable(NULL, 0, &kCFTypeArrayCallBacks);
CFArrayAppendValue(cfArray, CFSTR("Foo"));
NSLog(@"%ld", [(__bridge id)cfArray count]);
CFRelease(cfArray);
```

The `__bridge` cast works as long as there is no Core Foundation memory management involved. In the preceding examples, you are not assigning the results to variables or returning them. Consider this case, however:

```
- (NSString *)firstName {
  CFStringRef cfString = CFStringCreate...;
  return (???)cfString;
}
```

How can you cast `cfString` correctly? Before ARC, you would have cast this to an `NSString` and called `autorelease`. With ARC, you can't call `autorelease`, and ARC doesn't know that `cfString` has an extra retain on it from `CFStringCreate....` You again use a bridge cast, this time in the form of a function as in this example:

```
return CFBridgingRelease(cfString);
```

This function transfers ownership from Core Foundation to ARC. In the process, it reduces the retain count by one to balance the `CFStringCreate....` You must use a bridge cast to achieve this. Calling `CFRelease` before returning the object would destroy the object.

When transferring an object from ARC to Core Foundation, you use `CFBridgingRetain`, which increases the retain count by one, as shown in the following code:

```
CFStringRef cfStr = CFBridgingRetain([nsString copy]);
...
CFRelease(cfStr);
```

The bridging functions can also be written in a typecast style as follows:

```
NSString *nsString = CFBridgingRelease(cfString);
NSString *nsString = (__bridge_transfer id)cfString;

CFStringRef cfString = CFBridgingRetain(nsString);
CFStringRef cfString = (__bridge_retained CFTypeRef)nsString;
```

> `CFTypeRef` **is a generic pointer to a Core Foundation object and** `id` **is a generic pointer to an Objective-C object. You could also use explicit types here like** `CFStringRef` **and** `NSString*`.

The function form is shorter, and in my opinion easier to understand. `CFBridgingRelease` and `CFBridgingRetain` should only be used when an object is being transferred between ARC and Core Foundation. They are not replacements for `CFRetain` or `CFRelease`, or a way to "trick" the compiler into adding an extra `retain` or `release` on Objective-C objects.

Not only is toll-free bridging very convenient for moving information between C and Objective-C, it enables Cocoa developers to make use of certain Core Foundation functions that have no Objective-C equivalent. For example, `CFURLCreateStringByAddingPercentEscapes` allows much more powerful transformations than the equivalent `NSURL stringByAddingPercentEscapesUsingEncoding:`.

Even types that are not explicitly toll-free bridged are still bridged to NSObject. This means that you can store Core Foundation objects (even ones with no Cocoa equivalent) in Cocoa collections, as shown in this example:

```
CFTreeContext ctx = {0, (void*)CFSTR("Info"), CFRetain,
                          CFRelease, CFCopyDescription};
CFTreeRef tree = CFTreeCreate(NULL, &ctx);
NSArray *array = [NSArray arrayWithObject:(__bridge id)tree];
CFRelease(tree);
NSLog(@"%@", array);
```

Toll-free bridging is implemented in a fairly straightforward way. Every Objective-C object structure begins with an ISA pointer to a Class:

```
typedef struct objc_class *Class;
typedef struct objc_object {
  Class isa;
} *id;
```

Core Foundation opaque types begin with a CFRuntimeBase, and the first element of that is also an ISA pointer:

```
typedef struct __CFRuntimeBase {
  uintptr_t _cfisa;
  uint8_t _cfinfo[4];
#if __LP64__
  uint32_t _rc;
#endif
} CFRuntimeBase;
```

_cfisa points to the toll-free bridged Cocoa class. These are subclasses of the equivalent Cocoa class; they forward Objective-C method calls to the equivalent Core Foundation function call. For instance, CFString is bridged to the private toll-free bridging class NSCFString.

If there is no explicit bridging class, then _cfisa points to __NSCFType, which is a subclass of NSObject, and forwards calls like retain and release.

To handle Objective-C classes passed to Core Foundation functions, all public toll-free functions look something like this:

```
CFIndex CFStringGetLength(CFStringRef str) {
  CF_OBJC_FUNCDISPATCH0(__kCFStringTypeID, CFIndex, str, "length");
  __CFAssertIsString(str);
  return __CFStrLength(str);
}
```

CF_OBJC_FUNCDISPATCH0 checks the _cfisa pointer. If it matches the Core Foundation bridging class for the given CFTypeID, then it passes the call along to the real Core Foundation function. Otherwise it translates the call into an Objective-C message (length in this case, given as a C string).

Summary

Core Foundation bridges the gap between C and Objective-C code, providing powerful data structures for C, and near-transparent data passing to and from low-level code. As Apple releases more low-level Core frameworks that require these types, Core Foundation is an increasingly important part of an iOS developer's toolkit.

Core Foundation data structures are generally more flexible than their Cocoa equivalents. They provide better control over how memory is managed through allocators, and often include functions for more specialized problems like handling Pascal strings or very configurable URL percent substitutions. Core Foundation collections can be configured to be nonretaining, and can even store nonobjects such as integers.

While Objective-C is extremely powerful, you can still generally write code that is faster and more efficient in pure C, which is why the lowest-level APIs are all C APIs. For those parts of your programs that require the kind of performance you can only get from C, Core Foundation provides an excellent collection of abstract data types that you can easily exchange with the higher-level parts of your program. The vast majority of problems in iOS are best solved in Cocoa and Objective-C, but for those places that C is appropriate, Core Foundation is a powerful tool.

Further Reading

Apple Documentation

The following documents are available in the iOS Developer Library at `developer.apple.com` or through the Xcode Documentation and API Reference.

> Collections Programming Topics for Core Foundation
>
> Core Foundation Design Concepts
>
> Data Formatting Guide for Core Foundation
>
> Dates and Times Programming Guide for Core Foundation
>
> "Managing Toll-Free Bridging," Programming With ARC Release Notes
>
> Memory Management Programming Guide for Core Foundation
>
> Property List Programming Topics for Core Foundation
>
> Strings Programming Guide for Core Foundation

Other Resources

> "Automatic Reference Counting," *Clang documentation*
> `clang.llvm.org/docs/AutomaticReferenceCounting.html`
>
> ridiculous_fish, "Bridge." An entertaining introduction to toll-free bridging internals by one of the AppKit and Foundation team at Apple.
> `ridiculousfish.com/blog/archives/2006/09/09/bridge`

Chapter 20
Deep Objective-C

Much of Objective-C is very straightforward in practice. There is no multiple inheritance or operator overloading like in C++. All objects have the same memory-management rules, which rely on a simple set of naming conventions. With the addition of ARC, you don't even need to worry about memory management in most cases. The Cocoa framework is designed with readability in mind, so most things do exactly what they say they do.

Still, there are many parts of Objective-C that can appear mysterious until you dig into them, such as creating new methods and classes at runtime, introspection, and message passing. Most of the time you don't need to understand how this works, but for some problems it is very useful to harness the full power of Objective-C. The flexibility of Core Data relies heavily on the dynamic nature of Objective-C.

The heart of this power is the *Objective-C runtime*, provided by `libobjc`. The Objective-C runtime is a collection of functions that provides the dynamic features of Objective-C. It includes such core functions as `objc_msgSend`, which is called every time you use the `[object message]` syntax. It also includes functions to allow you to inspect and modify the class hierarchy at runtime, including creating new classes and methods.

This chapter shows you how to use these features to achieve the same kind of flexibility, power, and speed as Core Data and other Apple frameworks. All code samples in this chapter can be found in the online files for Chapter 20.

Understanding Classes and Objects

The first thing to understand about Objective-C objects is that they are really C structs. Every Objective-C object has the same layout, as shown in Figure 20-1.

First there is a pointer to your class definition. Then each of your superclasses' *ivars* (instance variables) are laid out as struct properties, and then your class's ivars are laid out as struct properties. This structure is called `objc_object`, and a pointer to it is called `id`:

```
typedef struct objc_object {
    Class isa;
} *id;
```

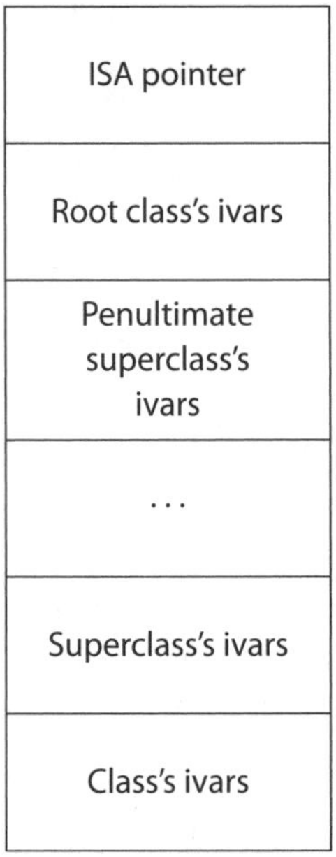

Figure 20-1 Layout of an Objective-C object

The `Class` structure contains a metaclass pointer (more on that in a moment), a superclass pointer, and data about the class. The data of particular interest are the name, ivars, methods, properties, and protocols. Don't worry too much about the internal structure of `Class`. There are public functions to access all the information you need.

> The Objective-C runtime is open source, so you can see exactly how it's implemented. Go to the Apple Open Source site (`opensource.apple.com`), and look for the package `objc` in the Mac code. It doesn't include it in the iOS packages, but the Mac code is identical or very similar. These particular structures are defined in `objc.h` and `objc-runtime-new.h`. There are two definitions of many things in these files because of the switch from Objective-C 1.0 to Objective-C 2.0. Look for things marked "new" when there is a conflict.

`Class` is itself much like an object. You can send messages to a `Class` instance—for example, when you call `[Foo alloc]`—so there has to be a place to store the list of class methods. These are stored in the metaclass, which is the `isa` pointer for a `Class`. It is extremely rare to need to access metaclasses, so let's not dwell on them here; see the "Further Reading" section at the end of this chapter for links to more information. See the section "How Message Passing Really Works" for more information on message passing.

The superclass pointer creates the hierarchy of classes, and the list of ivars, methods, properties, and protocols defines what the class can do. An important point here is that the methods, properties, and protocols are all stored in the writable section of the class definition. These can be changed at runtime, and that's exactly how categories are implemented (see Chapter 3 for more information about categories). Ivars are stored in the read-only section and cannot be modified (because that could impact existing instances). That's why categories cannot add ivars.

Notice in the definition of `objc_object` shown at the beginning of this section that the `isa` pointer is not `const`. That is not an oversight. The class of an object can be changed at runtime. The superclass pointer of `Class` is also not `const`. The hierarchy can be modified. This is covered in more detail in the "ISA Swizzling" section later in this chapter.

Now that you've seen the data structures underlying Objective-C objects, you next look at the kinds of functions you can use to inspect and manipulate them. These functions are written in C, and they use naming conventions somewhat similar to Core Foundation. All the functions shown here are public and are documented in the *Objective-C Runtime Reference*. The following is the simplest example:

```
#import <objc/objc-runtime.h>
...
const char *name = class_getName([NSObject class]);
printf("%s\n", name);
```

Runtime methods begin with the name of the thing they act upon, which is almost always also their first parameter. Because this example includes `get` rather than `copy`, you don't own the memory that is returned to you and should not call `free`.

The next example prints a list of the selectors that `NSObject` responds to. The call to `class_copyMethodList` returns a copied buffer that you must dispose of with `free`.

PrintObjectMethods.m (Runtime)

```
void PrintObjectMethods() {
  unsigned int count = 0;
  Method *methods = class_copyMethodList([NSObject class],
                                         &count);
  for (unsigned int i = 0; i < count; ++i) {
    SEL sel = method_getName(methods[i]);
    const char *name = sel_getName(sel);
    printf("%s\n", name);
  }
  free(methods);
}
```

There is no reference counting (automatic or otherwise) in the runtime, so there is no equivalent to `retain` or `release`. If you fetch a value with a function that includes the word `copy`, you should call `free` on it. If you don't use a function that includes the word `copy`, you must not call `free` on it.

Working with Methods and Properties

The Objective-C runtime defines several important types:

- `Class`—Defines an Objective-C class, as described in the section "Understanding Classes and Objects."

- `Ivar`—Defines an instance variable of an object, including its type and name.

- `Protocol`—Defines a formal protocol.

▨ `objc_property_t`—Defines a property. Its unusual name is probably to avoid colliding with user types defined in Objective-C 1.0 before properties existed.

▨ `Method`—Defines an object method or a class method. This provides the name of the method (its *selector*), the number and types of parameters it takes and its return type (collectively its *signature*), and a function pointer to its code (its *implementation*).

▨ `SEL`—Defines a selector. A selector is a unique identifier for the name of a method.

▨ `IMP`—Defines a method implementation. It's just a pointer to a function that takes an object, a selector, and a variable list of other parameters (varargs), and returns an object:

```
typedef id (*IMP)(id, SEL, ...);
```

Now you use this knowledge to build your own simplistic *message dispatcher*. A message dispatcher maps selectors to function pointers and calls the referenced function. The heart of the Objective-C runtime is the message dispatcher `objc_msgSend`, which you learn much more about in the section "How Message Passing Really Works." The example `myMsgSend` is how `objc_msgSend` might be implemented if it only needed to handle the simplest cases.

The following code is written in C just to prove that Objective-C runtime is really just C. I've added comments to demonstrate the equivalent Objective-C.

MyMsgSend.c (Runtime)

```
static const void *myMsgSend(id receiver, const char *name) {
  SEL selector = sel_registerName(name);
  IMP methodIMP =
  class_getMethodImplementation(object_getClass(receiver),
                                selector);
  return methodIMP(receiver, selector);
}

void RunMyMsgSend() {
  // NSObject *object = [[NSObject alloc] init];
  Class class = (Class)objc_getClass("NSObject");
  id object = class_createInstance(class, 0);
  myMsgSend(object, "init");

  // id description = [object description];
  id description = (__bridge id)myMsgSend(object, "description");

  // const char *cstr = [description UTF8String];
  const char *cstr = myMsgSend(description, "UTF8String");

  printf("%s\n", cstr);
}
```

With the addition of Automatic Reference Counting (ARC) in IOS 5, converting a `void*` to an `id` requires an appropriate bridging cast so that ARC knows where to add `retain` and `release` calls. You need to tell the compiler that the `NSString` returned by `description` is an auto-released object by using the cast `__bridge id`. `UTF8String` returns a nonobject, so you can use it as-is.

You can use this same technique in Objective-C using `methodForSelector:` to avoid the complex message dispatch of `objc_msgSend`. This only makes sense if you're going to call the same method thousands of times on an iPhone. On a Mac, you won't see much improvement unless you're calling the same method millions of times. Apple has highly optimized `objc_msgSend`. But for very simple methods called many times, you may be able to improve performance 5–10% this way if you are not using Automatic Reference Counting. With ARC, bypassing `objc_msgSend` can be slower because ARC adds an extra retain/release to the return value in some cases where it isn't required (such as a `void` method). This may be improved in later versions of LLVM (radar://10002493), but the point is that bypassing the normal message dispatch system is not an easy way to improve performance.

The following example demonstrates how to do this and shows the performance impact. Try it with and without ARC.

FastCall.m (Runtime)

```
const NSUInteger kTotalCount = 10000000;

void FastCall() {
  NSMutableString *string = [NSMutableString string];
  NSTimeInterval totalTime = 0;
  NSDate *start = nil;
  NSUInteger count = 0;

  // With objc_msgSend
  start = [NSDate date];
  for (count = 0; count < kTotalCount; ++count) {
    [string setString:@"stuff"];
  }

  totalTime = -[start timeIntervalSinceNow];
  printf("w/ objc_msgSend = %f\n", totalTime);

  // Skip objc_msgSend.
  start = [NSDate date];
  SEL selector = @selector(setString:);
  IMP setStringMethod =[string methodForSelector:selector];

  for (count = 0; count < kTotalCount; ++count) {
    setStringMethod(string, selector, @"stuff");
  }

  totalTime = -[start timeIntervalSinceNow];
  printf("w/o objc_msgSend  = %f\n", totalTime);
}
```

How Message Passing Really Works

As demonstrated in the "Working with Methods and Properties" section earlier in this chapter, calling a method in Objective-C eventually translates into calling a method implementation function pointer and passing it an object pointer, a selector, and a set of function parameters. Like the example `myMsgSend`, every Objective-C message expression is converted into a call to `objc_msgSend` (or a closely related function; I'll get to that in "The Flavors of `objc_msgSend`" later in this chapter). However, `objc_msgSend` is much more powerful than `myMsgSend`. Here is how it works:

1. Check if the receiver is `nil`. If so, then call the `nil`-handler. This is really obscure, undocumented, unsupported, and difficult to make useful. The default is to do nothing and I won't go into it more here. See the "Further Reading" section for more information.

2. In a garbage-collected environment (which iOS doesn't support, but I include for completeness), check for one of the short-circuited selectors (`retain`, `release`, `autorelease`, `retainCount`) and if it matches, return `self`. Yes, that means `retainCount` returns `self` in a garbage-collected environment. You shouldn't have been calling it anyway.

3. Check the class's cache to see if it's already worked out this method implementation. If so, call it.

4. Compare the requested selector to the selectors defined in the class. If the selector is found, call its method implementation.

5. Compare the requested selector to the selectors defined in the superclass, and then its superclass, and so on. If the selector is found, call its method implementation.

6. Call `resolveInstanceMethod:` (or `resolveClassMethod:`). If it returns `YES`, start over. The object is promising that the selector will resolve this time, generally because it has called `class_addMethod`.

7. Call `forwardingTargetForSelector:`. If it returns non-`nil`, send the message to the returned object. Don't return `self` here. That would be an infinite loop.

8. Call `methodSignatureForSelector:`, and if it returns non-`nil`, create an `NSInvocation` and pass it to `forwardInvocation:`.

9. Call `doesNotRecognizeSelector:`. The default implementation of this just throws an exception.

Dynamic Implementations

The first interesting thing you can do with message dispatch is provide an implementation at runtime using `resolveInstanceMethod:` and `resolveClassMethod:`. This is usually how `@dynamic` synthesis is handled. When you declare a property to be `@dynamic`, you are promising the compiler that there will be an implementation available at runtime even though the compiler can't find one now. This suppresses the compiler error indicating that you have failed to implement the required methods for a property.

Here's an example of how to use this to dynamically create getters and setters for properties stored in an `NSMutableDictionary`.

Person.h (Person)

```objc
@interface Person : NSObject
@property (copy) NSString *givenName;
@property (copy) NSString *surname;
@end
```

Person.m (Person)

```objc
@interface Person ()
@property (strong) NSMutableDictionary *properties;
@end

@implementation Person
@dynamic givenName, surname;
@synthesize properties = properties_;

- (id)init {
  if ((self = [super init])) {
    properties_ = [[NSMutableDictionary alloc] init];
  }
  return self;
}

static id propertyIMP(id self, SEL _cmd) {
  return [[self properties] valueForKey:
        NSStringFromSelector(_cmd)];
}

static void setPropertyIMP(id self, SEL _cmd, id aValue) {
  id value = [aValue copy];

  NSMutableString *key =
  [NSStringFromSelector(_cmd) mutableCopy];

  // Delete "set" and ":" and lowercase first letter
  [key deleteCharactersInRange:NSMakeRange(0, 3)];
  [key deleteCharactersInRange:
                     NSMakeRange([key length] - 1, 1)];
  NSString *firstChar = [key substringToIndex:1];
  [key replaceCharactersInRange:NSMakeRange(0, 1)
              withString:[firstChar lowercaseString]];

  [[self properties] setValue:value forKey:key];
}

+ (BOOL)resolveInstanceMethod:(SEL)aSEL {
  if ([NSStringFromSelector(aSEL) hasPrefix:@"set"]) {
    class_addMethod([self class], aSEL,
                  (IMP)setPropertyIMP, "v@:@");
```

```
    }
    else {
      class_addMethod([self class], aSEL,
                      (IMP)propertyIMP, "@@:");
    }
    return YES;
  }

@end
```

main.m (Person)

```
int main(int argc, char *argv[]) {
  @autoreleasepool {
    Person *person = [[Person alloc] init];
    [person setGivenName:@"Bob"];
    [person setSurname:@"Jones"];

    NSLog(@"%@ %@", [person givenName], [person surname]);
  }
}
```

In this example, you use `propertyIMP` as the generic getter and `setPropertyIMP` as the generic setter. Note how these functions make use of the selector to determine the name of the property. Also note that `resolveInstanceMethod:` assumes that any unrecognized selector is a property setter or getter. In many cases, this is okay. You still get compiler warnings if you pass unknown methods like this:

```
[person addObject:@"Bob"];
```

But if you do it this way, you get a slightly surprising result:

```
NSArray *persons = [NSArray arrayWithObject:person];
id object = [persons objectAtIndex:0];
[object addObject:@"Bob"];
```

You get no compiler warning because you can send any message to `id`. And you won't get a runtime error either. You just retrieve the key `addObject:` (including the colon) from the `properties` dictionary and do nothing with it. This kind of bug can be difficult to track down, and you may want to add additional checking in `resolveInstanceMethod:` to guard against it. But the approach is extremely powerful. Although dynamic getters and setters are the most common use of `resolveInstanceMethod:`, it can also be used to dynamically load code in environments that allow dynamic loading. iOS doesn't allow this approach, but on Mac you can use `resolveInstanceMethod:` to avoid loading entire libraries until the first time one of the library's classes is accessed. This can be useful for large but rarely used classes.

Fast Forwarding

The runtime gives you one more fast option before falling back to the standard forwarding system. You can implement `forwardingTargetForSelector:` and return another object to pass the message to. This is particularly useful for proxy objects or objects that add functionality to another object. The CacheProxy example demonstrates an object that caches the getters and setters for another object.

CacheProxy.h (Person)

```
@interface CacheProxy : NSProxy
- (id)initWithObject:(id)anObject
         properties:(NSArray *)properties;
@end

@interface CacheProxy ()
@property (readonly, strong) id object;
@property (readonly, strong)
                    NSMutableDictionary *valueForProperty;
@end
```

CacheProxy is a subclass of NSProxy rather than NSObject. NSProxy is a very thin root class designed for classes that forward most of their methods, particularly classes that forward their methods to objects hosted on another machine or on another thread. It is not a subclass of NSObject, but it does conform to the <NSObject> protocol. The NSObject class implements dozens of methods that might be very hard to proxy. For example, methods that require the local run loop like performSelector:withObject:afterDelay:, might not make sense for a proxied object. NSProxy avoids most of these methods.

To implement a subclass of NSProxy, you must override methodSignatureForSelector: and forwardInvocation:. These throw exceptions if they're called otherwise.

First, you should create the getter and setter implementations, as in the Person example. In this case, if the value is not found in the local cache dictionary, you will forward the request to the proxied object.

CacheProxy.m (Person)

```
@implementation CacheProxy
@synthesize object = object_;
@synthesize valueForProperty = valueForProperty_;

// setFoo: => foo
static NSString *propertyNameForSetter(SEL selector) {
  NSMutableString *name =
  [NSStringFromSelector(selector) mutableCopy];
  [name deleteCharactersInRange:NSMakeRange(0, 3)];
  [name deleteCharactersInRange:
                    NSMakeRange([name length] - 1, 1)];
  NSString *firstChar = [name substringToIndex:1];
  [name replaceCharactersInRange:NSMakeRange(0, 1)
                withString:[firstChar lowercaseString]];
  return name;
}

// foo => setFoo:
static SEL setterForPropertyName(NSString *property) {
  NSMutableString *name = [property mutableCopy];
  NSString *firstChar = [name substringToIndex:1];
  [name replaceCharactersInRange:NSMakeRange(0, 1)
                withString:[firstChar uppercaseString]];
  [name insertString:@"set" atIndex:0];
```

```
    [name appendString:@":"];
    return NSSelectorFromString(name);
}

// Getter implementation
static id propertyIMP(id self, SEL _cmd) {
    NSString *propertyName = NSStringFromSelector(_cmd);
    id value = [[self valueForProperty] valueForKey:propertyName];
    if (value == [NSNull null]) {
        return nil;
    }

    if (value) {
        return value;
    }

    value = [[self object] valueForKey:propertyName];
    [[self valueForProperty] setValue:value
                               forKey:propertyName];
    return value;
}

// Setter implementation
static void setPropertyIMP(id self, SEL _cmd, id aValue) {
    id value = [aValue copy];
    NSString *propertyName = propertyNameForSetter(_cmd);
    [[self valueForProperty] setValue:(value != nil ? value :
                                       [NSNull null])
                               forKey:propertyName];
    [[self object] setValue:value forKey:propertyName];
}
```

Note the usage of `[NSNull null]` to manage `nil` values. You cannot store `nil` in an `NSDictionary`. In the next block of code, you will synthesize accessors for the properties requested. All other methods will be forwarded to the proxied object.

```
- (id)initWithObject:(id)anObject
          properties:(NSArray *)properties {
    object_ = anObject;
    valueForProperty_ = [[NSMutableDictionary alloc] init];
    for (NSString *property in properties) {
        // Synthesize a getter
        class_addMethod([self class],
                        NSSelectorFromString(property),
                        (IMP)propertyIMP,
                        "@@:");
        // Synthesize a setter
        class_addMethod([self class],
                        setterForPropertyName(property),
                        (IMP)setPropertyIMP,
                        "v@:@");
    }
    return self;
}
```

The next block of code overrides methods that are implemented by `NSProxy`. Because `NSProxy` has default implementations for these methods, they won't be automatically forwarded by `forwardingTargetForSelector:`.

```objc
- (NSString *)description {
  return [NSString stringWithFormat:@"%@ (%@)",
          [super description], self.object];
}

- (BOOL)isEqual:(id)anObject {
  return [self.object isEqual:anObject];
}

- (NSUInteger)hash {
  return [self.object hash];
}

- (BOOL)respondsToSelector:(SEL)aSelector {
  return [self.object respondsToSelector:aSelector];
}

- (BOOL)isKindOfClass:(Class)aClass {
  return [self.object isKindOfClass:aClass];
}
```

Finally, you will implement the forwarding methods. Each of them simply passes unknown messages to the proxied object. See Chapter 4 for more details on message signatures and invocations.

Whenever an unknown selector is sent to `CacheProxy`, `objc_msgSend` will call `forwardingTarget ForSelector:`. If it returns an object, then `objc_msgSend` will try to send the selector to that object. This is called "fast forwarding." In this example, `CacheProxy` sends all unknown selectors to the proxied object. If the proxied object doesn't appear to respond to that selector, then `objc_msgSend` will fall back to normal forwarding by calling `methodSignatureForSelector:` and `forwardInvocation:`. This will be covered in the next section, "Normal Forwarding." `CacheProxy` forwards these requests to the proxied object as well.

```objc
- (id)forwardingTargetForSelector:(SEL)selector {
  return self.object;
}

- (NSMethodSignature *)methodSignatureForSelector:(SEL)sel
{
  return [self.object methodSignatureForSelector:sel];
}

- (void)forwardInvocation:(NSInvocation *)anInvocation {
  [anInvocation setTarget:self.object];
  [anInvocation invoke];
}
@end
```

Normal Forwarding

After trying everything described in the previous sections, the runtime tries the slowest of the forwarding options: `forwardInvocation:`. This can be tens to hundreds of times slower than the mechanisms covered in the previous sections, but it is also the most flexible. You are passed an `NSInvocation`, which bundles the target, the selector, the method signature, and the arguments. You may then do whatever you want with it. The most common thing to do is to change the target and `invoke` it, as demonstrated in the `CacheProxy` example. `NSInvocation` and `NSMethodSignature` are explained in Chapter 4.

If you implement `forwardInvocation:`, you also must implement `methodSignatureForSelector:`. That's how the runtime determines the method signature for the `NSInvocation` it passes to you. Often this is implemented by asking the object you're forwarding to.

There is a special limitation of `forwardInvocation:`. It doesn't support *vararg methods*. These are methods such as `arrayWithObjects:` that take a variable number of arguments. There's no way for the runtime to automatically construct an `NSInvocation` for this kind of method because it has no way to know how many parameters will be passed. While many vararg methods terminate their parameter list with a `nil`, that is not required or universal (`stringWithFormat:` does not), so determining the length of the parameter list is implementation dependent. The other forwarding methods, such as Fast Forwarding, do support vararg methods.

Even though `forwardInvocation:` returns nothing itself, the runtime system will return the result of the `NSInvocation` to the original caller. It does so by calling `getReturnValue:` on the `NSInvocation` after `forwardInvocation:` returns. Generally you call `invoke` and the `NSInvocation` stores the return value of the called method, but that isn't required. You could call `setReturnValue:` yourself and return. This can be handy for caching expensive calls.

Forwarding Failure

Okay, so you've made it through the entire message resolution chain, and haven't found a suitable method. What happens now? Technically, `forwardInvocation:` is the last link in the chain. If it does nothing, then nothing happens. You can use it to swallow certain methods if you want to. But the default implementation of `forwardInvocation:` does do something. It calls `doesNotRecognizeSelector:`. The default implementation of that method just raises an `NSInvalidArgumentException`, but you could override this behavior. That's not of particularly great utility because this method is required to raise `NSInvalidArgumentException` (either directly or by calling `super`), but it's legal.

You can also call `doesNotRecongizeSelector:` yourself in some situations. For example, if you do not want anyone to call your `init`, you could override it like this:

```
- (id)init {

[self doesNotRecognizeSelector:_cmd];
}
```

This makes calling `init` a runtime error. Personally, I often do it this way instead:

```
- (id)init {
  NSAssert(NO, @"Use -initWithOptions:");
  return nil;
}
```

That way it crashes when I'm developing, but not in the field. Which form you prefer is somewhat a matter of taste.

You should, of course, call `doesNotRecognizeSelector:` in methods like `forwardInvocation:` when the method is unknown. Don't just return unless you specifically mean to swallow the error. That can lead to very challenging bugs.

The Flavors of objc_msgSend

In this chapter, I've referred generally to `objc_msgSend`, but there are several related functions: `objc_msgSend_fpret`, `objc_msgSend_stret`, `objc_msgSendSuper`, and `objc_msgSendSuper_stret`. The `SendSuper` form is obvious. It sends the message to the superclass. The `stret` forms handle most cases when you return a struct. This is for processor-specific reasons related to how arguments are passed and returned in registers versus on the stack. I won't go into all the details here, but if you're interested in this kind of low-level detail, then you should read *Hamster Emporium* (see "Further Reading"). Similarly, the `fpret` form handles the case when you return a floating-point value on an Intel processor. It isn't used on the ARM-based processors that iOS runs on, but it is used when you compile for the simulator. There is no `objc_msgSendSuper_fpret` because the floating-point return only matters when the object you're messaging is `nil` (on an Intel processor), and that's not possible when you message `super`.

The point of all this is not, obviously, to address the processor-specific intricacies of message passing. If you're interested in that, read *Hamster Emporium*. The point is that not all message passing is handled by `objc_msgSend`, and you cannot use `objc_msgSend` to handle any arbitrary method call. In particular, you cannot return a "large" struct with `objc_msgSend` on any processor, and you cannot safely return a floating point with `objc_msgSend` on Intel processors (such as when compiling for the simulator). This generally translates into: Be careful when you try to bypass the compiler by calling `objc_msgSend` by hand.

Method Swizzling

In Objective-C, *swizzling* refers to transparently swapping one thing for another. Generally, it means replacing methods at runtime. Using method swizzling, you can modify the behavior of objects that you do not have the code for, including system objects. In practice, swizzling is fairly straightforward, but it can be a little confusing to read. For this example, you add logging every time you add an observer to `NSNotificationCenter`.

> **Since iOS 4.0, Apple has rejected some applications from the AppStore for using this technique.**

First you add a category on `NSObject` to simplify swizzling:

RNSwizzle.h (MethodSwizzle)

```
@interface NSObject (RNSwizzle)
+ (IMP)swizzleSelector:(SEL)origSelector
            withIMP:(IMP)newIMP;
@end
```

RNSwizzle.m (MethodSwizzle)

```
@implementation NSObject (RNSwizzle)
+ (IMP)swizzleSelector:(SEL)origSelector
                withIMP:(IMP)newIMP {
  Class class = [self class];
  Method origMethod = class_getInstanceMethod(class,
                                              origSelector);
  IMP origIMP = method_getImplementation(origMethod);

  if(!class_addMethod(self, origSelector, newIMP,
                    method_getTypeEncoding(origMethod))) {
    method_setImplementation(origMethod, newIMP);
  }

  return origIMP;
}
@end
```

Let's look at this in more detail. You pass a selector and a function pointer (IMP) to this method. What you want to do is to swap the current implementation of that method with the new implementation and return a pointer to the old implementation so you can call it later. You have to consider three cases: The class may implement this method directly, the method may be implemented by one of the superclass hierarchy, or the method may not be implemented at all. The call to class_getInstanceMethod returns an IMP if either the class or one of its superclasses implements the method, otherwise it returns NULL.

If the method was not implemented at all, or if it is implemented by a superclass, then you need to add the method with class_addMethod. This is identical to overriding the method normally. If class_addMethod fails, you know the class directly implemented the method you are swizzling. You instead need to replace the old implementation with the new implementation using method_setImplementation.

When you're done, you return the original IMP, and it's your caller's problem to make use of it. You do that in a category on the target class, NSNotificationCenter, as shown in the following code.

NSNotificationCenter+RNSwizzle.h (MethodSwizzle)

```
@interface NSNotificationCenter (RNSwizzle)
+ (void)swizzleAddObserver;
@end
```

NSNotificationCenter+RNSwizzle.m (MethodSwizzle)

```
@implementation NSNotificationCenter (RNSwizzle)
static IMP sOrigAddObserver = NULL;

static void MYAddObserver(id self, SEL _cmd, id observer,
                          SEL selector,
                          NSString *name,
                          id sender) {
  NSLog(@"Adding observer: %@", observer);

  // Call the old implementation
```

```
  NSAssert(sOrigAddObserver,
          @"Original addObserver: method not found.");
  if (sOrigAddObserver) {
    sOrigAddObserver(self, _cmd, observer, selector, name,
                    sender);
  }
}

+ (void)swizzleAddObserver {
  NSAssert(!sOrigAddObserver,
          @"Only call swizzleAddObserver once.");
  SEL sel = @selector(addObserver:selector:name:object:);
  sOrigAddObserver = (void *)[self swizzleSelector:sel
                                withIMP:(IMP)MYAddObserver];
}
@end
```

You call `swizzleSelector:withIMP:`, passing a function pointer to your new implementation. Notice that this is a function, not a method, but as covered in "How Message Passing Really Works" earlier in this chapter, a method implementation is just a function that accepts an object pointer and a selector. You then save off the original implementation in a static variable, `sOrigAddObserver`. In the new implementation, you add the functionality you want, and then call the original function directly.

Finally, you need to actually perform the swizzle somewhere near the beginning of your program:

```
  [NSNotificationCenter swizzleAddObserver];
```

Some people suggest doing the swizzle in a `+load` method in the category. That makes it much more transparent, which is why I don't recommend it. Method swizzling can lead to very surprising behaviors. Using `+load` means that just linking the category implementation will cause it to be applied. I've personally encountered this when bringing old code into a new project. One of the debugging assistants from the old project had this kind of auto-load trick. It wasn't being compiled in the old project, it just happened to be in the sources directory. When I used "add folder" in Xcode, even though I didn't make any other changes to the project, the debug code started running. Suddenly the new project had massive debug files showing up on customer machines, and it was very difficult to figure out where they were coming from. So my experience is that using `+load` for this can be dangerous. On the other hand, it's very convenient and automatically ensures that it's only called once. Use your best judgment here.

Method swizzling is a very powerful technique and can lead to bugs that are very hard to track down. It allows you to modify the behaviors of Apple-provided frameworks, but that can make your code much more dependent on implementation details. It always makes the code more difficult to understand. I typically do not recommend it for production code except as a last resort, but it is extremely useful for debugging, performance profiling, and exploring Apple's frameworks.

There are several other method swizzling techniques. The most common is to use `method_exchange Implementations` to swap one implementation for another. That approach modifies the selector, which can sometimes break things. It also creates an awkward pseudo-recursive call in the source code that is very misleading to the reader. This is why I recommend using the function pointer approach detailed here. For more information on swizzling techniques, see the "Further Reading" section.

ISA Swizzling

As discussed in the "Understanding Classes and Objects" section earlier in this chapter, an object's ISA pointer defines its class. And, as discussed in "How Message Passing Really Works" (also earlier in this chapter), message dispatch is determined at runtime by consulting the list of methods defined on that class. So far, then, you've learned ways of modifying the list of methods, but it's also possible to modify an object's class (ISA swizzling). The next example demonstrates ISA swizzing to achieve the same NSNotificationCenter logging you did in the previous section, "Method Swizzling."

First, you create a normal subclass of NSNotificationCenter, which you will use to replace the default NSNotificationCenter.

MYNotificationCenter.h (ISASwizzle)

```
@interface MYNotificationCenter : NSNotificationCenter
// You MUST NOT define any ivars or synthesized properties here.
@end

@implementation MYNotificationCenter
- (void)addObserver:(id)observer selector:(SEL)aSelector
              name:(NSString *)aName object:(id)anObject
{
  NSLog(@"Adding observer: %@", observer);
  [super addObserver:observer selector:aSelector name:aName
          object:anObject];
}
@end
```

There's nothing really special about this subclass. You could +alloc it normally and use it, but you want to replace the default NSNotificationCenter with your class.

Next, you create a category on NSObject to simplify changing the class:

NSObject+SetClass.h (ISASwizzle)

```
@interface NSObject (SetClass)
- (void)setClass:(Class)aClass;
@end
```

NSObject+SetClass.m (ISASwizzle)

```
@implementation NSObject (SetClass)
- (void)setClass:(Class)aClass {
  NSAssert(
    class_getInstanceSize([self class]) ==
      class_getInstanceSize(aClass),
    @"Classes must be the same size to swizzle.");
  object_setClass(self, aClass);
}
@end
```

Now you can change the class of the default NSNotificationCenter:

```
id nc = [NSNotificationCenter defaultCenter];
[nc setClass:[MYNotificationCenter class]];
```

The most important thing to note here is that the size of MYNotificationCenter must be the same as the size of NSNotificationCenter. In other words, you can't declare any ivars or synthesized properties (synthesized properties are just ivars in disguise). Remember, the object you are swizzling has already been allocated. If you added ivars, then they would point to offsets beyond the end of that allocated memory. This has a pretty good chance of overwriting the isa pointer of some other object that just happens to be after this object in memory. In all likelihood, when you finally do crash, the other (innocent) object will appear to be the problem. This is an incredibly difficult bug to track down, which is why I take the trouble of building a category to wrap object_setClass. I believe it's worth it to include the NSAssert ensuring the two classes are the same size.

After you've performed the swizzle, the impacted object is identical to a normally created subclass. This means that it is very low-risk for classes that are designed to be subclassed. As discussed in Chapter 15, key-value observing (KVO) is implemented with ISA swizzling. This allows the system frameworks to inject notification code into your classes, just as you can inject code into the system frameworks.

Method Swizzling Versus ISA Swizzling

Both method and ISA swizzling are powerful techniques that can cause a lot of problems if used incorrectly. In my experience, ISA swizzling is a better technique and should be used when possible because it only impacts the specific objects you target, rather than all instances of the class. However, sometimes your goal is to impact every instance of the class, so method swizzling is the only option. The following list defines the differences between method swizzling and ISA swizzling:

- Method Swizzling
  - Impacts every instance of the class
  - Highly transparent. All objects retain their class.
  - Requires unusual implementations of override methods
- ISA Swizzling
  - Only impacts the targeted instance
  - Objects change class (though this can be hidden by overriding class)
  - Override methods are written with standard subclass techniques

Summary

The Objective-C runtime can be an incredibly powerful tool once you understand it. With it you can modify classes and instances at runtime, injecting new methods and even whole new classes. Used recklessly, these techniques can lead to incredibly difficult bugs, but used carefully and in isolation, the Objective-C runtime is an important part of advanced iOS development.

Further Reading

Apple Documentation

The following document is available in the iOS Developer Library at `developer.apple.com` or through the Xcode Documentation and API Reference.

Objective-C Runtime Programming Guide

Other Resources

Ash, Mike. *NSBlog*. A very insightful blog covering all kinds of low-level topics. `www.mikeash.com/pyblog`

- Friday Q&A 2009-03-20: Objective-C Messaging

- Friday Q&A 2010-01-29: Method Replacement for Fun and Profit – The method-swizzling approach in this chapter is a refinement of Mike Ash's approach.

bbum. *weblog-o-mat*. bbum is a prolific contributor to Stackoverflow, and his blog has some of my favorite low-level articles, particularly his four-part opcode-by-opcode analysis of `objc_msgSend`. `friday.com/bbum`

- Objective-C: Logging Messages to Nil

- objc_msgSend() Tour

CocoaDev, "MethodSwizzling." CocoaDev is an invaluable wiki of all-things-Cocoa. The MethodSwizzling page covers the major implementations out there. `www.cocoadev.com/index.pl?MethodSwizzling`

Parker, Greg. *Hamster Emporium*. While there aren't a lot of posts here, this blog provides incredibly useful insights into the Objective-C runtime. `www.sealiesoftware.com/blog/archive`

- [objc explain]: Classes and metaclasses

- [objc explain]: objc_msgSend_fpret

- [objc explain]: objc_msgSend_stret

- [objc explain]: So you crashed in objc_msgSend()

- [objc explain]: Non-fragile ivars

Index